BRITAIN *in the* WORLD

Highlights from the Yale Center for British Art

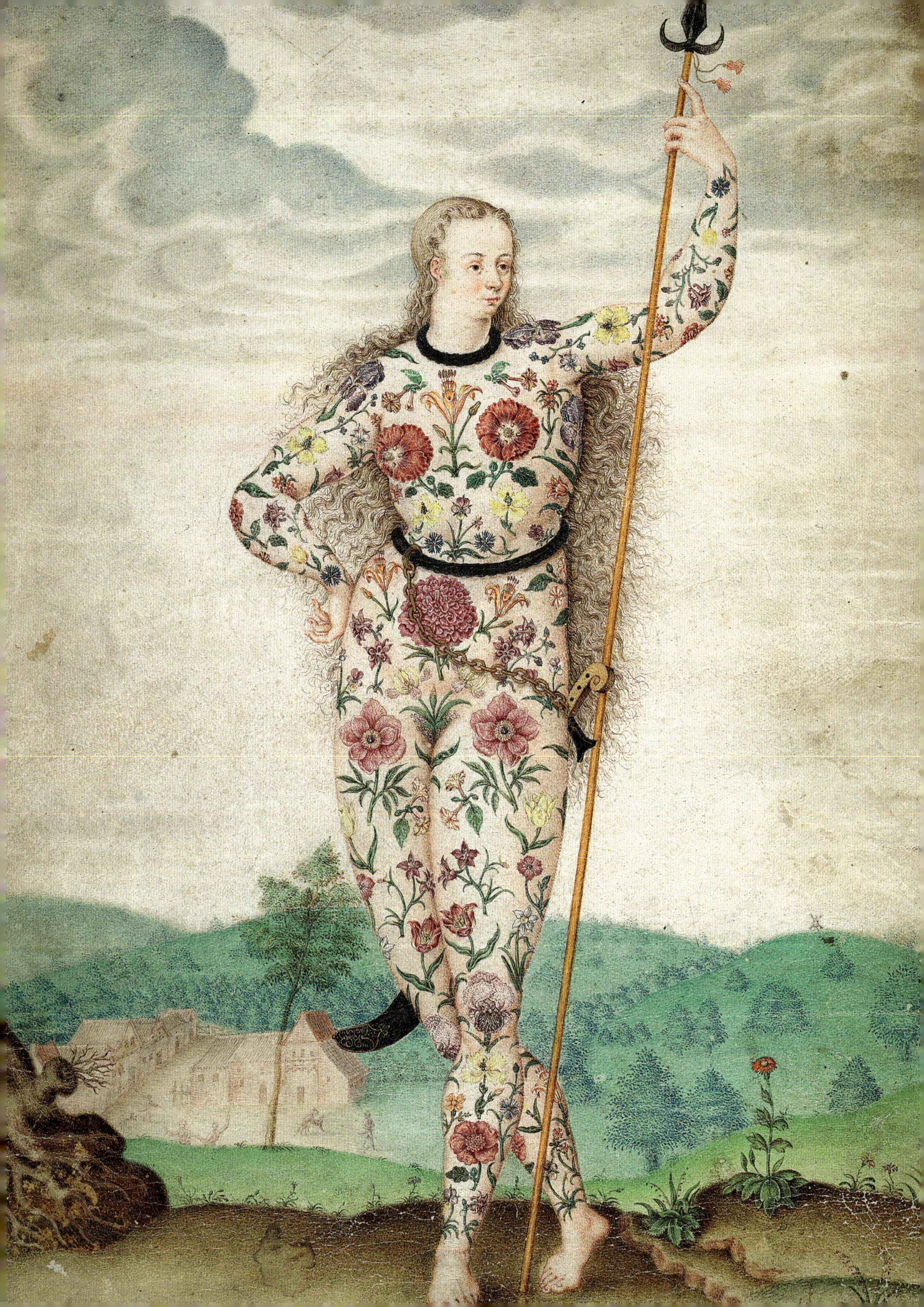

BRITAIN *in the* WORLD

Highlights from the Yale Center for British Art

In Honor of Amy Meyers

EDITED BY
Martina Droth, Nathan Flis,
and Michael Hatt

Yale Center for British Art, New Haven
Yale University Press, New Haven and London

CONTENTS

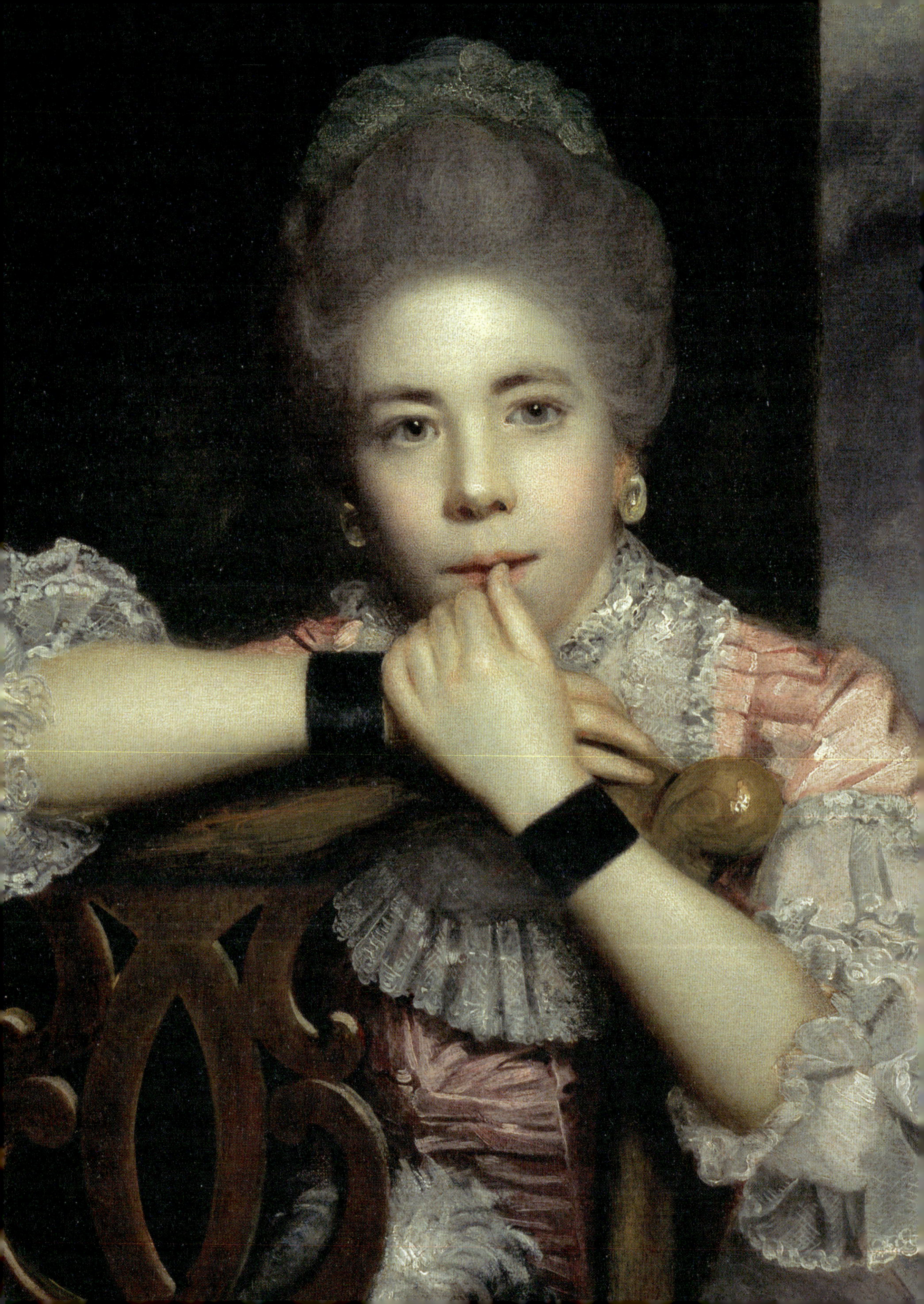

FOR AMY MEYERS

Hilton Als

While the relationship between a museum director and a curator is based, in part, on a series of negotiations—intellectual, logistical, and the like—what emerges quickly during any such exchange with Amy is her incredible heart and insight, especially when it comes to trying to marry your vision to the Center's purpose. Amy's ethos, based on trust and humor and imagination, supports the curator's belief that what he feels needs to be said should be said, even as he struggles to do it. It's rare to find someone who is as interested in *process* as Amy is. And even as you stumble, she's there cheering you on, not so much suggesting a new path, as you move blindly from one idea to another, as finding in your inchoate mess those bright spots that illuminate the ideas that interested her and you in the first place. Amy is her own brightness. She carries the kind of light that is borne by someone who is preternaturally hopeful and trusting. She approaches history as a scientist might. She does not ignore a set of given facts, certainly, but she is equally thrilled by the unexpected, the mystery unfolding right before her very eyes, and yours. What Amy protects and champions: all the ideas history gives us, inspires in us, and the ardor and poetry to be found in the long shot.

FOREWORD

Martina Droth, Nathan Flis,
and Michael Hatt

Those familiar with more typical surveys of British art, and those who know the Yale Center for British Art, may be surprised by the selection of works assembled here to introduce the collection. Alongside better-known objects, such as the great eighteenth-century landscapes and portraits by Reynolds, Turner, Constable, and other canonical artists, many of the objects selected have previously been overshadowed or overlooked. The resulting medley covers both a wide chronological range, from the Tudor period to the present, and a diversity of materials, including photographs, manuscripts, and mixed-media objects.

Such a selection offers a more accurate overview of the Center's vast and varied holdings. It also reveals the way in which the collection provides a significant perspective on British art and its history, for it emphasizes a vision of British art that is summed up in the book's title: *Britain in the World*. The objects chosen reveal that British art is a global phenomenon, shaped and characterized by cultural exchange, exploration, and scientific discovery, and, crucially, by the long, often violent history of colonialism and empire.

For much of its course, the history of art categorized paintings and sculpture into national schools, such as the Italian, Dutch, or British. The assumption was that each nation created art determined by and reflective of that nation's character and people, and it is no accident that this model of art history, divided up along the lines of national borders, emerged at the moment when the nation-state became the most powerful form of government and political power. Art was often used as a means of defining the nation and its people, to differentiate a country from its competitors and enemies, and to celebrate the achievements of that nation. This idea of a national school was for many decades the basis of surveys of British art and the display of British art in museums and galleries, and the "Britishness" of paintings and sculptures was understood to be exemplified by attributes such as the pastoral, urban, and rural traditions and a stable sense of national identity.

However, more recent scholarship has demonstrated that culture is defined not only by what happens within national borders but also by international and global networks. Cultures are not pure representations of a people or a national ethos but are hybrid, shaped by cultural encounters and exchanges, and the effects of such forces as migration, global trade, and colonization. Exploring the Center's collection, one sees other parts of the world wherever one looks. The selection in this book touches on South Africa, India, the West Indies, and Hong Kong; there are also works by artists from Venice, Rome, and Philadelphia; subjects include a pagoda, a zebra, and sea voyages; and the materials from which the works are made include elephant ivory and Dutch wax-printed cotton cloth produced for West African use. Viewed from this perspective, a richer and more plausible history emerges, one in which the "Britishness" of British art is less stable and more complex, changing across time and fractured by regional and ethnic differences, inclusion and exclusion, complicity and opposition. This exposes a history of British art inextricable from the history of Britain as a global power, a narrative running from the so-called First Empire (the colonization of America by Britain from the 1580s), through the largest of all empires spread around the globe from the eighteenth into the twentieth centuries, and into the contemporary postcolonial world.

For the past two decades, the examination of this history has been the focus of the Center's activities. This is visible in the display of the collection, which explores global connections at home and abroad, and this approach has also underpinned special exhibitions, publications, and research projects undertaken by the Center, its scholars, and its partners. The shift in the interpretation of the collection, from national school to global phenomenon, was instigated by Amy Meyers, the director of the Center from 2002 to 2019, to whom this book is dedicated. Meyers encouraged new scholarly approaches at the Center, looking beyond the coastline of Britain and its artistic institutions. Many of the themes that this book touches on—the visual culture of natural history, transatlantic networks, and the history of photography—have been hallmarks of Meyers's own scholarship. The channels opened by new approaches to British art history are not easy to navigate. While engaging with the quality and beauty of the objects in the Center's collection, we have to confront the often troubling histories in which they are embedded. Art does not stand apart from empire or slavery but is intimately entwined with them. While art may celebrate cultural exchange and progress, it has also been used to justify colonial violence and racial superiority.

Indeed, the understanding of British art in the world is in the very nature of the collection itself—in that many of the works here explicitly address these difficulties—and its creation. The Center houses the largest and most comprehensive collection of British art outside the United Kingdom, containing some 2,000 paintings, 50,000 prints and drawings, 35,000 rare books and manuscripts, and 250 sculptures. The core of this collection was given to Yale University in 1966 by Paul Mellon (Yale College, Class of 1929), along with the building that houses it, the last masterpiece by the great modernist architect Louis Kahn, which opened eleven years later, and which was conserved during Meyers's directorship following a three-phase plan (2008–16).

Mellon had begun collecting in earnest in 1959, and rather than just amassing a survey of the canonical artists, used to define the national school, he created an impressive interdisciplinary collection that included not only landscapes and portraits but also such genres as animal painting and the conversation piece (eighteenth-century informal group portraits), as well as a world-class collection of rare books, maps, and manuscripts. This meant that those works once seen as the epitome of an insular Britishness, untroubled by global currents and politics, were placed in dialogue with alternative strands of British art. George Stubbs's paintings of horses look very different when placed alongside his representation of a zebra; picturesque views of India take on a different resonance when juxtaposed with imperial maps. Thus, while Mellon acquired one of the great collections of canonical works, his bequest to Yale offers a more thoroughgoing picture of British visual culture and its legacies.

British art has always been about the world. Whether produced in a studio in Blackburn, Lancashire, or in Darjeeling with a view of the Himalayas; whether made by the president of the Royal Academy of Arts in London or by a colonial subject in Agra; whether a scientific illustration of a fruit bat or a contemporary mixed-media sculpture; artists and viewers have always been aware of its global context. This selection reveals some of the myriad ways in which visible and invisible global connections are present in the visual and material culture of Britain.

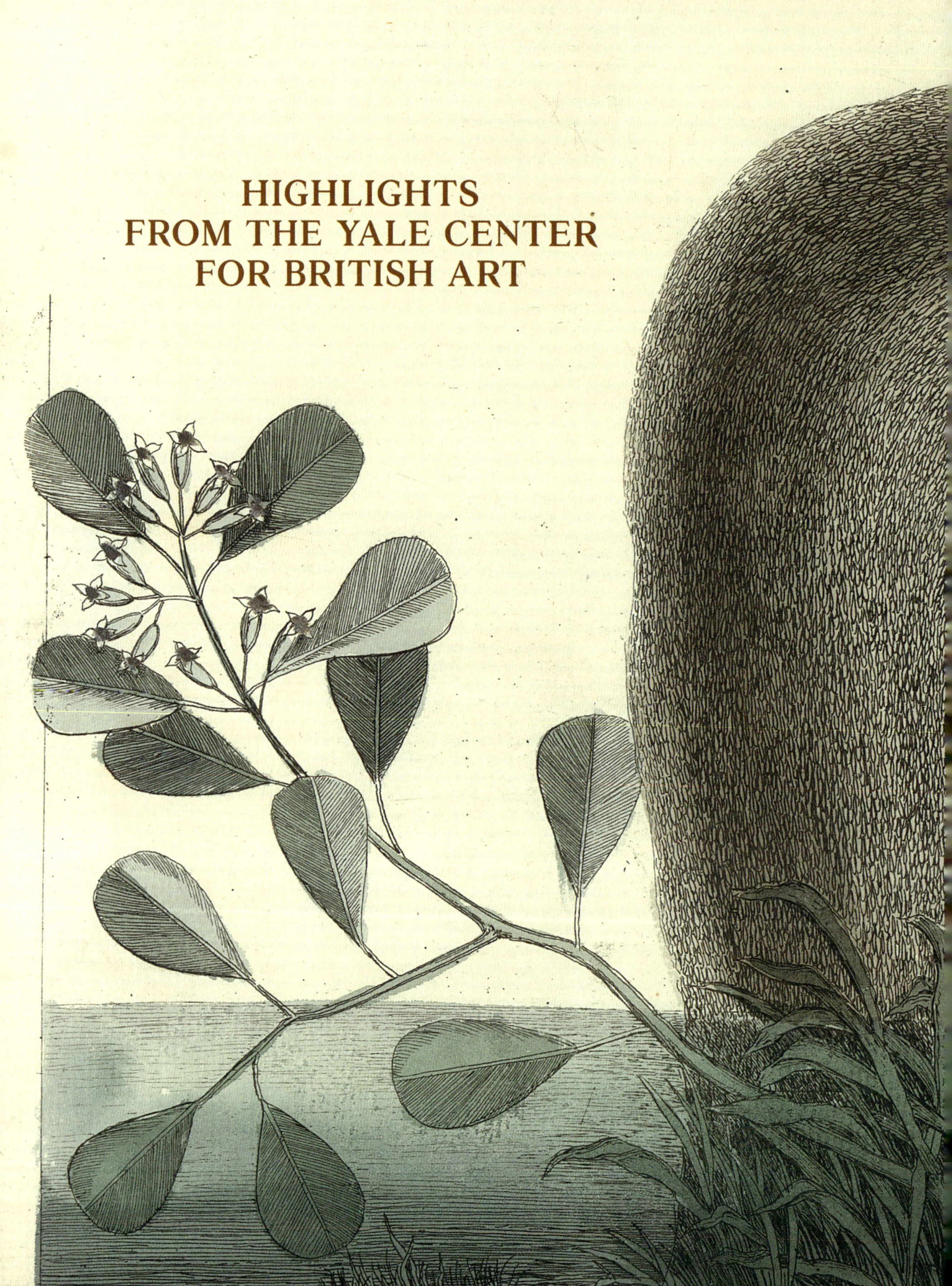
HIGHLIGHTS
FROM THE YALE CENTER
FOR BRITISH ART

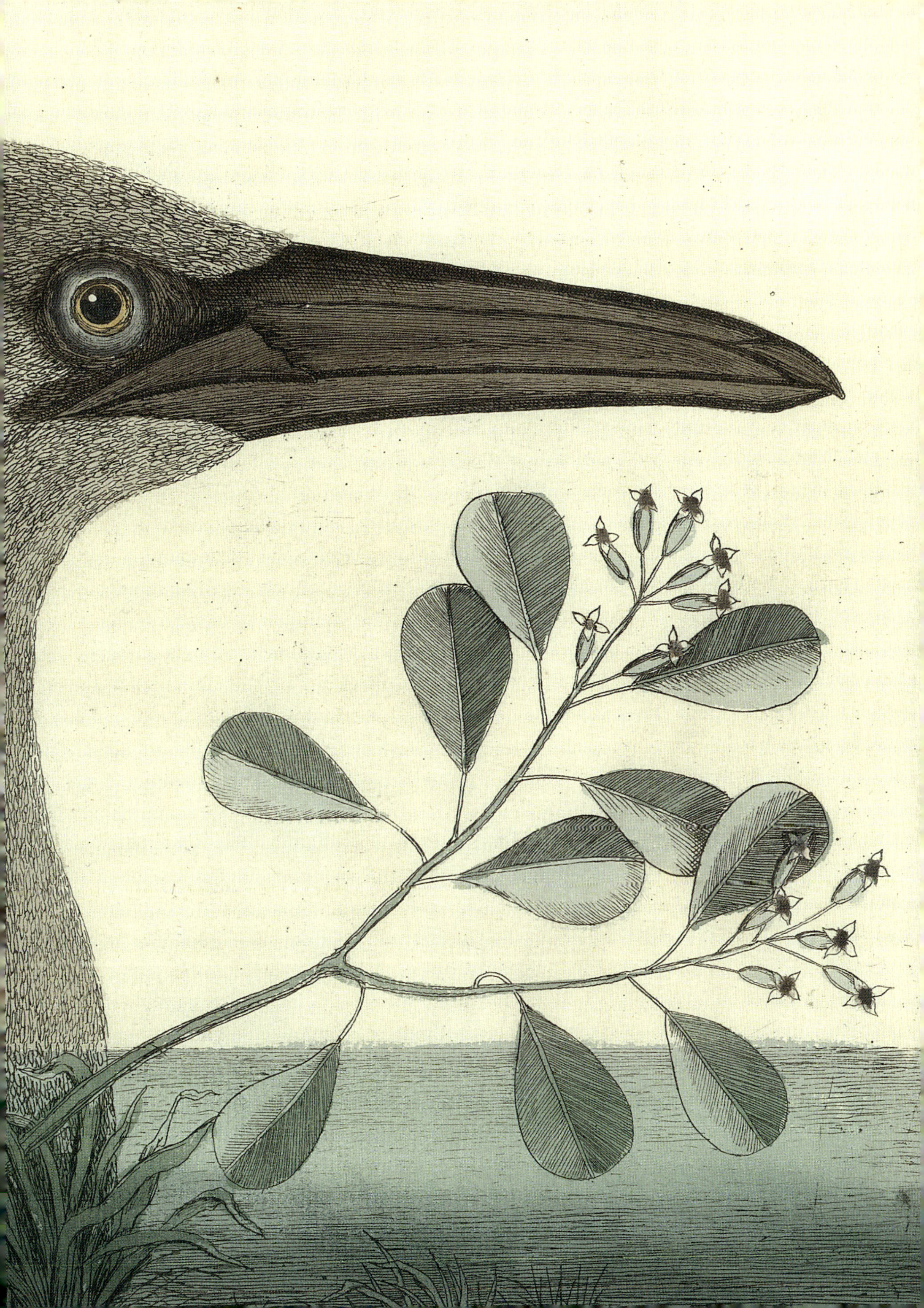

Unknown artist (English)
Helmingham Herbal and Bestiary, ca. 1500

Watercolor, gouache, and pen and ink on parchment

YALE CENTER FOR BRITISH ART, PAUL MELLON COLLECTION, FOLIO C.2014.4

Elisabeth R. Fairman

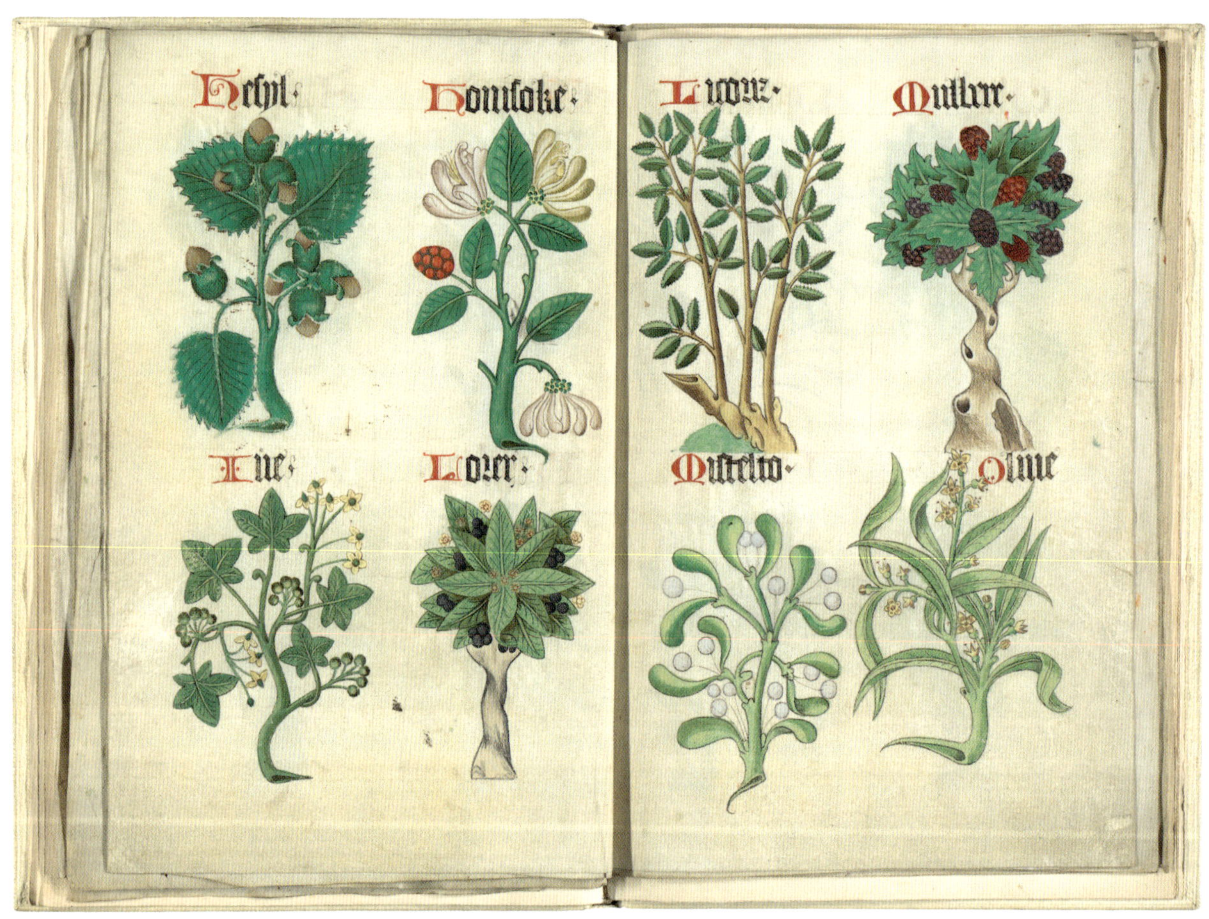

Fig. 1. *Helmingham Herbal and Bestiary*, leaves 11v–12r

Paul Mellon had been acquiring works of natural history from at least 1937, when he purchased the "double elephant" edition of John Audubon's *Birds of America* (London: 1828–39, printed on the largest paper then available); in 1939 and 1947 he acquired two of Pierre-Joseph Redouté's color plate books. Many of those early acquisitions remained with his wife, Rachel "Bunny" Lambert Mellon, as part of her remarkable Oak Spring Garden Library in Upperville, Virginia.[1] However, a number of Mellon's important works of natural history made their way to the Yale Center for British Art. The exquisitely drawn book of plants and animals known as the *Helmingham Herbal and Bestiary*, completed about 1500, was one of the great treasures in his collections now at the Center.

Mellon was a member of the exclusive Roxburghe Club, the oldest society of bibliophiles in the world (founded in 1832, its "membership is limited to 40, chosen from among those with distinguished libraries or collections, or with a scholarly interest in books"[2]). Each member "is expected to produce a book at his or her own expense for presentation to the other members," and Mellon selected the Helmingham manuscript to reproduce in facsimile. In the preface, he described the work as

> an aesthetically delightful rendering of what in fifteenth-century England was known about the inhabitants of her fields and woodlands, or what was imagined about the denizens of faraway lands. Whether it might often have been in the hands of children for study or entertainment, whether it guided the artisan in the limning of fabric or painted surfaces, and whether or not it was derived from earlier continental models, I see it simply as a charmingly natural and a thoroughly English work. I have also been impressed by the stark simplicity and directness of the drawing and colouring of the objects, as though there were a mysterious aesthetic kinship between these fifteenth-century artists or designers and our own twentieth-century artists.[3]

Acquired in 1961 at the Sotheby's sale of the library belonging to the Tollemache family of Helmingham Hall in Suffolk, England,[4] the manuscript, with its beautiful drawings of animals, birds, flowers, and trees, provides a remarkable picture of the depth of English knowledge of natural history in the Tudor period (1485–1603). The herbal portion of the work consists of ninety-five depictions of flowers and trees that are principally common species found in Britain, and the bestiary includes forty-nine illustrations of animals and birds, both real and imaginary.[5]

It is not known why these particular specimens were recorded, but scholars have speculated about the volume. It is most likely the drawings were meant to serve as patterns for decorative work, such as stained glass and panel or painted ceiling decorations or as designs for embroidery, needlework, or tapestries. The manuscript may also have been compiled simply as a primer for children or for some other educational purpose. Whatever its original intent, the work provides us with an extraordinary glimpse into a pre-Linnaean world order, where the organization of specimens was not standardized and a universal system of nomenclature had not yet been developed. Early herbals and bestiaries could be organized in different ways, where plants might be grouped by their medicinal qualities, and animals ranked according to their usefulness to man.[6] However, the overall principle of organization in the Helmingham manuscript is simply alphabetical: each specimen is identified by a common name.

Trees, shrubs, and vines are listed together in the herbal section. On the left-hand page in the opening shown here (fig. 1), for example, we see the hazelnut tree, honeysuckle, ivy, and laurel; and on the right, the licorice, mulberry, mistletoe, and a branch from an olive tree—the last not generally regarded as hardy in Britain, perhaps indicating that it is depicted here more for its symbolic significance. The animals and birds of the bestiary are a fascinating mix of the real and the fantastic. In the drawings here (overleaf), a dragon and a griffon (the legendary creature with the body, tail, and

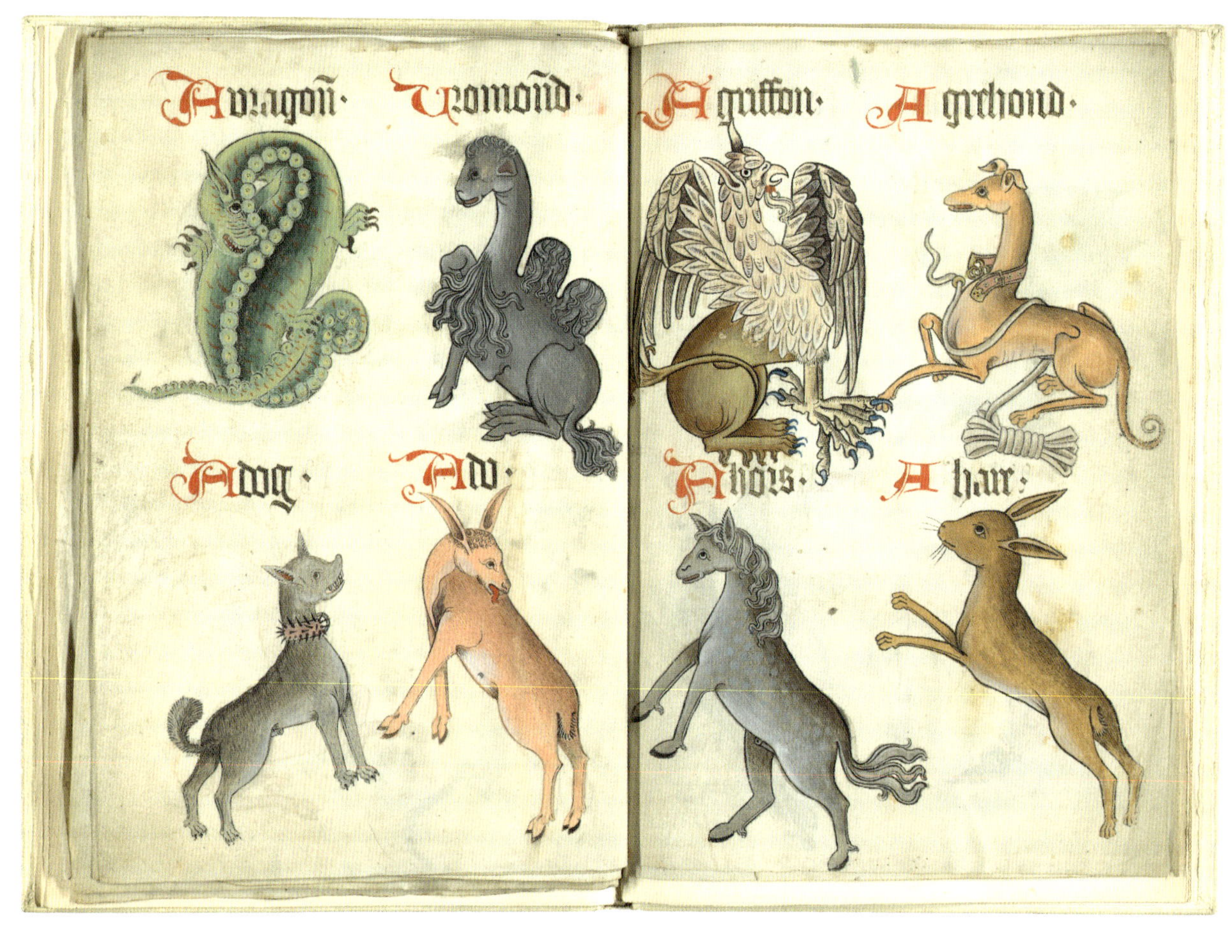

Fig. 2. *Helmingham Herbal and Bestiary*, leaves 17v–18r

back legs of a lion, the head, wings, and feet of an eagle) share the pages with a mastiff wearing a spiked collar (worn both to intimidate and to protect him from wolves and other wild animals), a double-humped camel, a female deer, a greyhound (drawn with a buckled leather collar and a leash), a horse, and a hare (fig. 2).

While the drawings of plants and real animals in the manuscript could have been based on direct observation, they likely reference earlier manuscript or printed sources. One candidate could be Konrad von Megenberg's encyclopedic *Buch der Natur*, compiled between 1349 and 1351. Considered the first text to include pictures of animals and plants, manuscript copies were in wide circulation in Europe through the fourteenth century.[7] It remained very popular after it was eventually printed in 1475; six editions were issued before 1500. Although the woodcuts of the plants and animals are clearly much cruder than the drawings in the Center's manuscript, there are certain similarities in the way the specimens are depicted that invite further investigation (fig. 3).

While we have not yet identified all the sources for the images nor conclusively established the manuscript's original intent, we can appreciate—as Paul Mellon suggests in his introduction to this intriguing work—how it demonstrates the continuity of past and present aesthetics, allowing us to acknowledge the ways in which artists in our own time continue to observe and record the natural world as they examine the intersections of art and science.

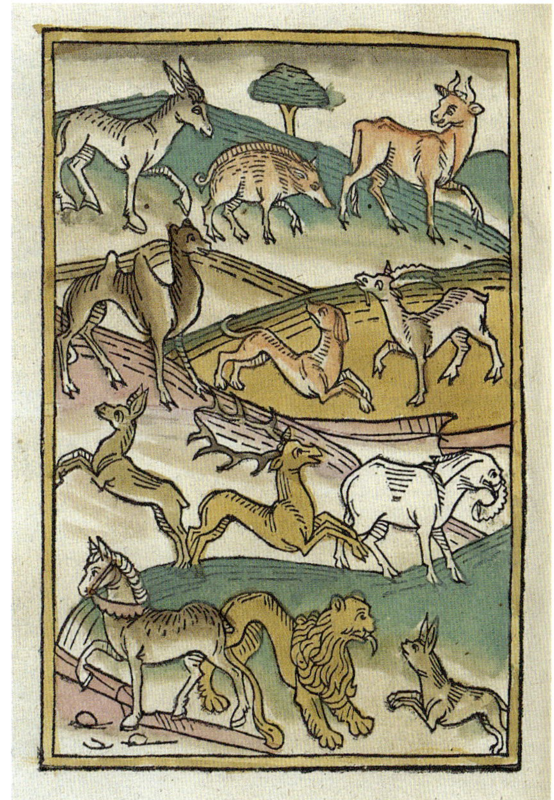

Fig. 3. Konrad von Megenberg, *Das Buch der Natur*, 1481, leaf 43v. Library of Congress, Lessing J. Rosenwald Collection

Notes

1. Rachel Mellon's library is now part of the Oak Spring Garden Foundation, whose mission is "to support and inspire fresh thinking and bold action on the history and future of plants, including the art and culture of plants, gardens and landscapes"; https://www.osgf.org/.
2. From https://www.roxburgheclub.org.uk/.
3. Nicolas Barker, ed., *Two East Anglian Picture Books: A Facsimile of the Helmingham Herbal and Bestiary and Bodleian Ms. Ashmole 1504* (London: Printed for presentation to the members of the Roxburghe Club, 1988), xiii. The text by Barker in this volume is the most useful source of information on the Center's manuscript, as well as the later copy held by the Bodleian Library, Oxford (MS. Ashmole 1504), known as *The Tudor Pattern Book*, and dated ca. 1520–30.
4. Sotheby & Co., *Catalogue of Highly Important Manuscripts & Printed Books from the Library at Helmingham Hall, Suffolk, the Property of the Rt. Hon. Lord Tollemache, June 6, 1961* (London: Sotheby & Co., 1961), lot 15.
5. A digitized version of the complete manuscript may be found in the Center's on-line catalogue, http://collections.britishart.yale.edu/vufind/Record/2038220.
6. See Robert McCracken Peck, "Natural Obsessions: From Specimens to Books," in *Of Green Leaf, Bird, and Flower: Artists' Books and the Natural World*, ed. Elisabeth R. Fairman (New Haven and London: Yale Univ. Press, 2014), 28.
7. One of the earliest and most complete Megenberg manuscripts, dating ca. 1350, belonged to Rachel Mellon and is now in the Oak Spring Garden Library. See Lucia Tongiorgi Tomasi and Tony Willis, *An Oak Spring Herbaria* (Upperville, VA: Oak Spring Garden Library, 2009), 3–9.

Jacques Le Moyne de Morgues
(French, ca. 1533–1588, active in England from ca. 1580)
A Young Daughter of the Picts, ca. 1585

Watercolor and gouache, touched with gold on parchment, 10¼ x 7⅜ in. (26 x 18.7 cm).
Inscribed in a later hand on the verso in graphite, lower right: "Georg Hüfnagel | 9822 | UBZZ."

YALE CENTER FOR BRITISH ART, PAUL MELLON COLLECTION, B1981.25.2646

Edward Town

The publication in 1590 of John White's drawings of the Algonquian peoples of coastal Carolina in Theodor de Bry's *A Briefe and True Report of the New Found Land of Virginia* can be cited as the first time the work of a British artist reached an international audience (fig. 4). Elizabethan England had, through the pursuit of colonial projects, established a role on the global stage, with talk of a "British Empire" justified upon a fantastical blend of Arthurian legend and Roman law.

Appended to the back of Thomas Harriot's account of his voyage to America were five engravings described by de Bry as "SOM PICTVRE OF THE PICTES WHICH IN THE OLDE tyme dyd habite one part of the great Bretainne." One of the five engravings shows the figure depicted in Jacques Le Moyne de Morgues's famous *Young Daughter of the Picts*, now in the collection of the Yale Center for British Art. Originally from France, Le Moyne (ca. 1533–1588) served as the artist and the cartographer on René Goulaine de Laudonnière's ill-fated expedition of 1564–65 to establish a Huguenot colony in Florida. Once domiciled in London, Le Moyne appears to have shared his recollections and records of these experiences with his fellow cartographer and near neighbor White, who copied drawings of the Floridian peoples and reciprocated by sharing what he had found "in a oolld English chronicle."[1] The intricate beauty of the tattooed flowers on *A Young Daughter of the Picts* speaks to

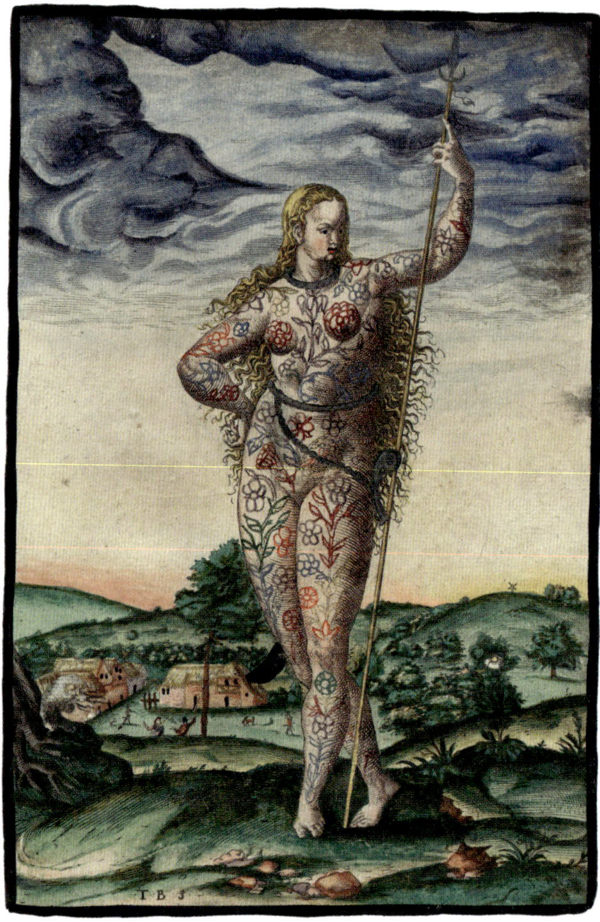

Fig. 4. Theodor de Bry after John White, *The trvve picture of a yonge dowgter of the Pictes III*, 1590, hand-colored engraving, 9½ x 6½ in. (24 x 16.5 cm). University of North Carolina at Chapel Hill, Louis Round Wilson Special Collections Library

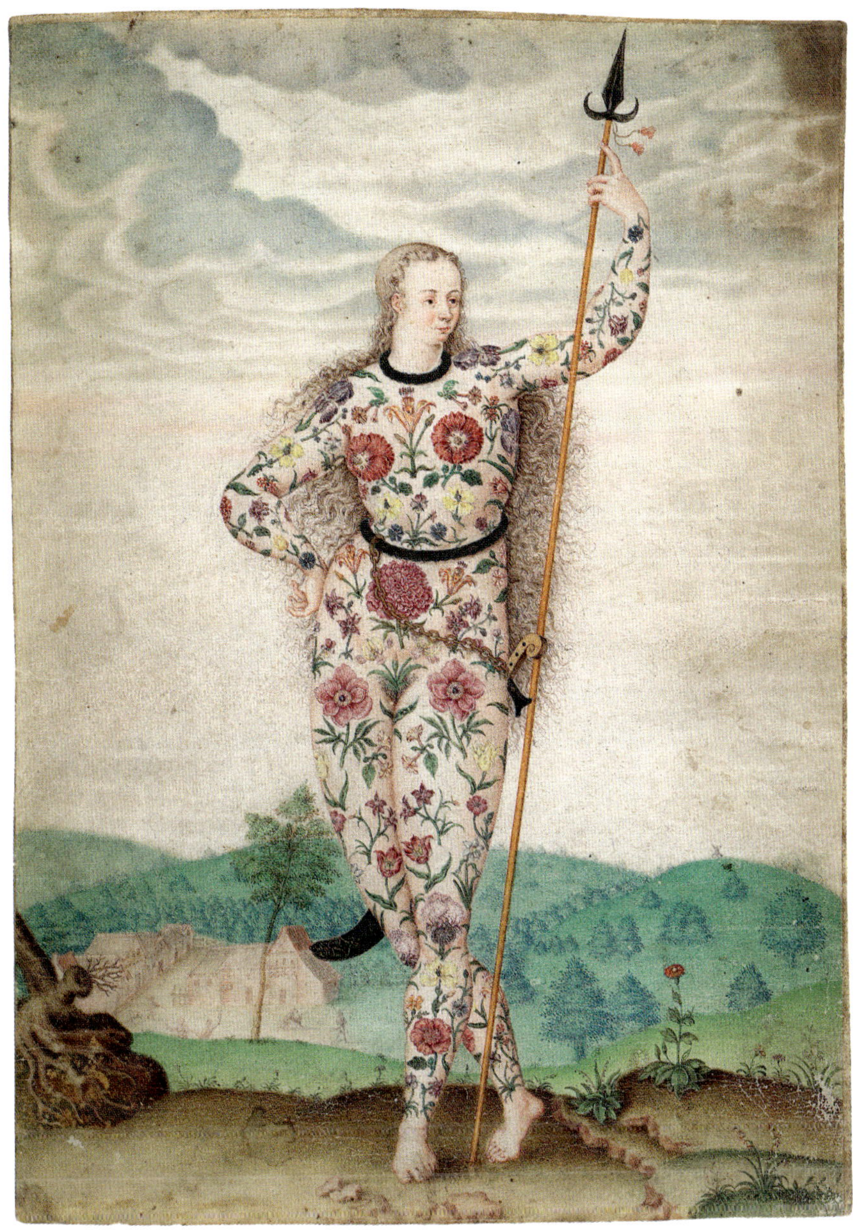

Le Moyne's talents as a botanical artist and his familiarity with the recent arrival from Asia Minor and America of the garden tulip (*Tulipa gesneriana* L.), the mourning iris (*Iris susiana* L.), and the marvel of Peru (*Mirabilis jalapa* L.).[2]

De Bry's description continued: "The painter of whom I have had the first of the Inhabitants of Virginia, gave me also these five figures following, found as he did assure me in an old English Chronicle, that I would do well to set at the end of these first Figures, for to show how that the inhabitants of the great Britain have been in times past as savage as those of Virginia." This painter, John White, who lived among the Algonquian peoples and considered some his friends, was alive to the fact that art and history could address complex issues regarding cultural difference and identity.[3] Yet while we know a good deal about many of the leading actors in this episode of global history, White remains frustratingly opaque. This short essay situates his career within the artisanal world of Elizabethan London and presents small pieces of evidence that shed light on his extraordinary life.

The coat of arms conferred upon White as Governor of Virginia in 1587 claimed descent from a Cornish family of Plymouth and Truro.[4] It is still not clear how White the painter was related to the main branch of this family, but his path to London followed that of a number of the provincial gentry who traveled to the capital to seek their fortune. The earliest record of White in London is his marriage on June 7, 1566, to Thomasine Cooper (d. 1591) at the parish of St Martin Ludgate. Thomasine was, in all likelihood, the daughter of the Painter-Stainer John Cooper (fl. 1558–1573), a well-established figure within his guild. By marrying the daughter of his master, White would have fulfilled a customary rite of passage, whereon completing his apprenticeship he gained his freedom and became a journeyman or householder, probably at around the age of twenty-five. For a short while, White remained in the parish: a son Thomas was baptized at St Martin's on April 27, 1567, and a daughter Eleanor on May 9, 1568.[5] However, after the burial of Thomas on December 26 that year, the records of White's activities fall silent for almost a decade. This begs the question as to why White chose to spurn the security of Cooper's household.

Part of the reason may have been that, despite being on good terms with a number of practicing members of his guild, John Cooper does not appear to have been active as a painter.[6] Instead, there is evidence of him fulfilling one of the most contemptible roles in Elizabethan society—that of the professional informer.[7] In the absence of any professionalized police force, the Crown was reliant upon private citizens to bring unlawfulness to their attention.[8] This was the litigious world into which White entered in the late 1560s, one of audits, surveys, and snitches, where instrumentation and accuracy began to take precedent over received wisdom and authority. It seems likely therefore that White gained his training as a painter outside of Cooper's household, working as one of the

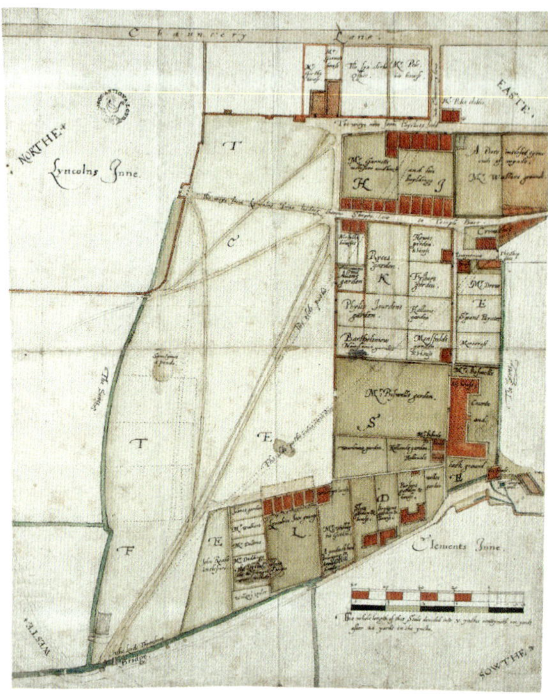

Fig. 5. John White, *Map of Ficketts Fields*, ca. 1583. The Society of Antiquaries of London

country's first professional surveyors, much like his near contemporary and fellow Painter-Stainer Ralph Treswell (fl. 1567; d. 1616 or 1617), and making surveys such as the map of Ficketts Fields now in the Library of the Society of Antiquaries (fig. 5).[9] It is also possible that White received instruction from another parishioner of St Martin Ludgate, William Boswell (fl. 1558; d. 1595), a painter with whom he worked on the "Masque of Amazons" presented at court on Twelfth Night of 1579. Unusually, a description of a complex satirical painting by Boswell juxtaposing historical and contemporary figures appears in William Bullein's publication *A Dialogue both Pleasant and Piety-full . . .* of 1564, which indicates that he was a painter of some small fame, and possibly also of ability.[10]

Hard by London's print market of St Paul's Churchyard and abutting the Blackfriars precinct—home to Jacques Le Moyne—St Martin Ludgate was, for a short while, a crucible of interaction between foreign and native-born painters, and White's early adulthood was spent during a period of unprecedented contact between these two groups.[11] It is unsurprising therefore to see the influence of the Flemish émigré painters Lucas de Heere (ca. 1534–1584), Marcus Gheeraerts the Elder (ca. 1520–in or before 1589), and Joris Hoefnagel (1542–1601) on White's work, which is most apparent in his depictions of the habits and costumes of various nations of the world.[12]

St Martin Ludgate's role as a conduit for cultural transmission was not to last. A decade on, the occupational geography of the city had changed, with many of the painters forced to the suburbs by the haberdashers and luxury retailers that had moved into the area. In 1581 John White took up a lease of a tenement on the north side of Arundel House on the Strand in the extramural parish of St Clement Danes, and this thrust White into the heart of the artisanal community that served the court.[13] His new neighbors included the Serjeant Painter George Gower (ca. 1540–1596), the instrument maker Bartholomew Newsam (d. 1593), and the painter, engraver, and mapmaker Richard Lyne (1542–1601), who was then in the employ of the architect of the anticipated "British Empire," John Dee (1527–1608 or 1609).[14]

On June 24, 1583, Ananias Dare, the father of the first English child baptized in America, married Eleanor White at St Clement Danes, a little over a month after her fifteenth birthday. Another small fact that has gone unnoticed is that on December 10, 1583, Ananias Dare was translated (i.e., transferred) from the Painter-Stainers' to the Tylers and Bricklayers' Company.[15] Remarkably, a silver spoon, customarily given in recognition of an apprentice fulfilling the terms of his indenture, inscribed "Ananias" and dated with a hallmark of 1582 is recorded in the silver store of the Painter-Stainers in the early twentieth century.[16] These two pieces of evidence suggest that Dare was John White's apprentice and that, like White before him, Dare married his master's daughter.

The next episode in their lives is known only too well. Dare would disappear with his wife and daughter when the Roanoke colony was lost. John White would attempt two transatlantic journeys to rejoin them, but after he left for England for supplies in 1587, he never saw them again.

Notes

1. See Sam Smiles, "John White and British Antiquity: Savage Origins in the Context of Tudor Historiography," in *European Visions: American Voices*, ed. Kim Sloan (London: British Museum Press, 2009), 106–12.
2. See Paul Hulton, *The Work of Jacques Le Moyne de Morgues*, 2 vols. (London: British Museum Publications in association with The Huguenot Society of London, 1977), 1:164.
3. For White, see Kim Sloan, *A New World: England's First View of America* (Chapel Hill: Univ. of North Carolina Press, 2007), 24–37; David B. Quinn, *The Roanoke Voyages, 1584–1590*, 2 vols. (London: Hakluyt Society, 1955), 1:40–49; Paul Hulton and David Quinn, eds., *The American Drawings of John White*, 2 vols. (London: British Museum; and Chapel Hill: Univ. of North Carolina Press, 1964), 1:12–13.
4. White of Truro: a chevron between three goats heads and razed sable. The other families cited were Kyllowe (of Lansallos) and Wyatt and Wymark of Truro, all of which appear in the pedigree of Cole of Cornwall. See John L. Vivian, *The Visitations of Cornwall* (London: W. Pollard, 1887), 90, 553.
5. London Metropolitan Archives (hereafter LMA) P69/MTN1/A/002/MS10213.
6. For Cooper, see Edward Town, "A Biographical Dictionary of London Painters, 1547–1625," *Walpole Society* 76 (2014): 57.
7. See The National Archives, Kew, London, TNA E159/356 10 Eliz.
8. See Ian Archer, Caroline Barron, Vanessa Harding, eds., *Hugh Alley's Caveat: The Markets of London in 1598, Folger Ms V. a. 318* (London: London Topographical Society, 1988).
9. For Treswell, see John Schofield, *The London Surveys of Ralph Treswell* (London: London Topographical Society, 1987).
10. For Boswell, see Town, "A Biographical Dictionary of London Painters," 40.
11. For the layout of the churchyard, and the booksellers and bookbinders within it, see Peter W. M. Blayney, "John Day and the Bookshop That Never Was," in *Material London, ca. 1600*, ed. Lena Cowen Orlin (Philadelphia: Univ. of Pennsylvania Press, 2000), 322–43.
12. For example, his *Tartar or Uzbek man* now in the collection of the British Museum (BM 10906,0509.1.33) and the *Greek or Turkish woman* (BM 10906,0509.1.35).
13. A survey made in April 1590 following the attainder of Philip Howard, twentieth Earl of Arundel, recorded that White had built this property himself. See Charles Lethbridge Kingsford, "Bath Inn or Arundel House," *Archaeologia* 72 (1922): 243–77, esp. 272.
14. For Newsam and other Elizabethan instrument makers, see Anthony Gerbino and Stephen Johnston, *Compass and Rule: Architecture as Mathematical Practice in England, 1500–1750* (New Haven and London: Yale Univ. Press, 2009), 60.
15. On Dare, see William S. Powell, "The Search for Ananias Dare," in *Searching for the Roanoke Colonies: An Interdisciplinary Collection*, eds. R. Thomson Shields and Charles R. Ewen (Raleigh: North Carolina Department of Cultural Resources, 2003), 62–66. For the translation, see LMA COL/AD/01/023 fol. 347r; COL/CA/01/01/023 fol. 11v.
16. Walter Hayward Pitman, *The Worshipful Company of Painters, otherwise Painter-Stainers: Its Hall, Pictures, and Plate* (London: W. H. Pitman, 1906), 50.

Unknown artist, after Lucas de Heere (Netherlandish, 1534–1584)
An Allegory of the Tudor Succession: The Family of Henry VIII, ca. 1590

Oil on panel, 45 x 71¾ in. (114.3 x 182.2 cm)

YALE CENTER FOR BRITISH ART, PAUL MELLON COLLECTION, B1974.3.7

Lisa L. Ford

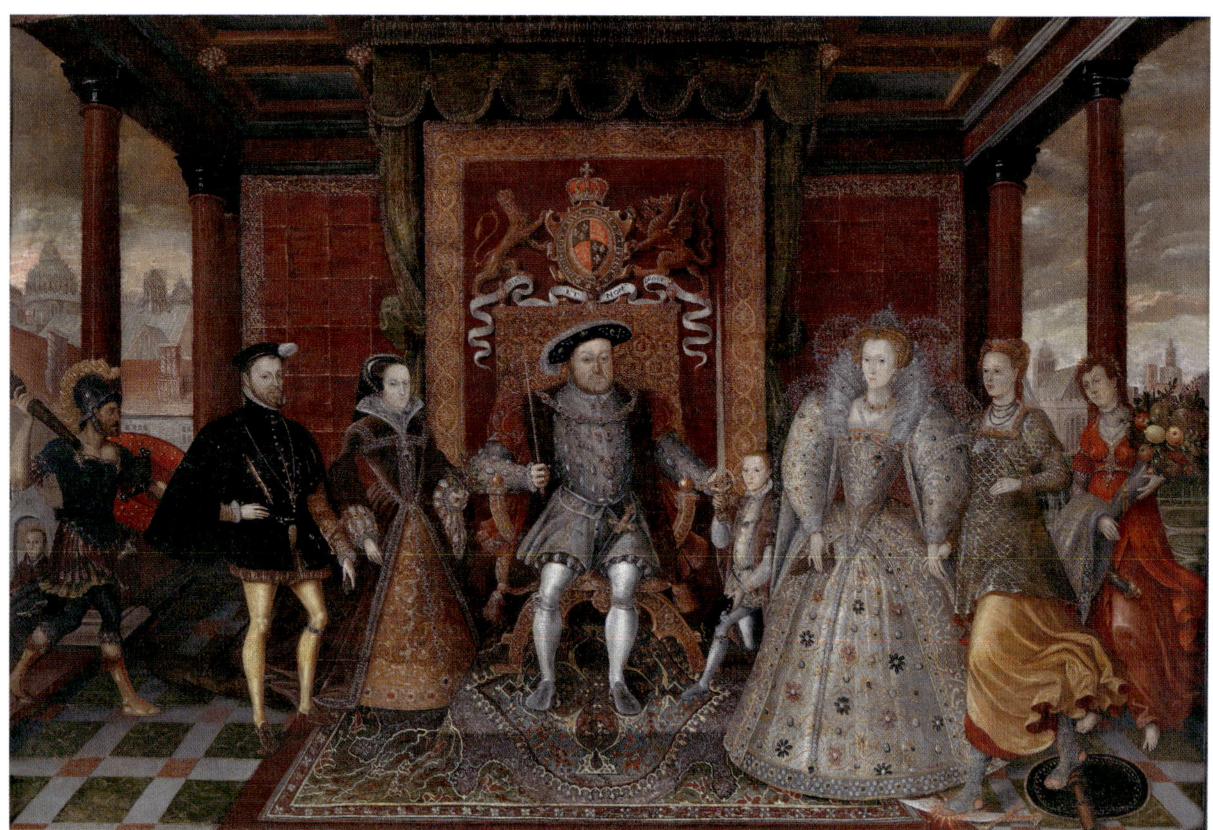

An Allegory of the Tudor Succession: The Family of Henry VIII can surely be counted as one of the great treasures of the Yale Center for British Art, and one of Paul Mellon's most important acquisitions. It is a historically impossible scene, as it shows the Tudor rulers from King Henry VIII to Queen Elizabeth I as they appeared during their reigns, but gathered together as if at a single moment in time. This group portrait seems to have been modeled on an earlier work from about 1572 (fig. 6) by the artist Lucas de Heere, given by Elizabeth I to Francis Walsingham, later one of her principal ministers, possibly in commemoration of the Treaty of Blois, which Walsingham negotiated as

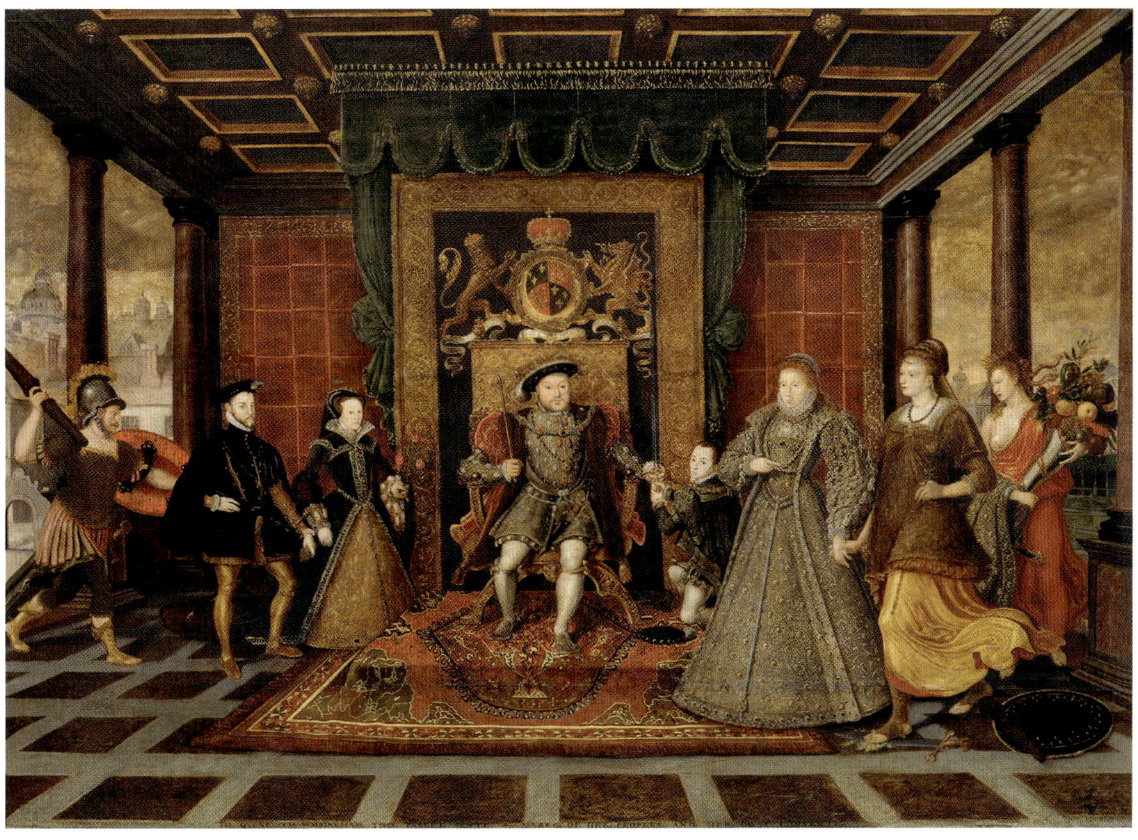

Fig. 6. Lucas de Heere, *The Family of Henry VIII: An Allegory of the Tudor Succession*, ca. 1570–75, oil on panel, 51⅝ x 72½ in. (131.2 x 184 cm). National Museum of Wales, Cardiff

ambassador to France and which established a mutual defense pact with the French against Spanish aggression.[1] In both the earlier painting and the Center's *Allegory*, Spain and Catholicism are visually presented as negative influences, linked to war through the figures of Mary I and her husband, King Philip II of Spain, while Henry VIII's Protestant heirs, Edward VI and Elizabeth I, are presented in a positive light as links to peace and prosperity.

The Center's painting is dated about 1590. The artist, as well as the commissioner of the work, remain unknown. An engraving of this same scene was produced by William Rogers around the same time, including verses that outline the virtues or failings of each of the rulers presented, and extol Elizabeth's restoration of peace and plenty to England. All the figures are based on recognizable pattern portraits, with the exception of Elizabeth I, whose figure closely resembles that in the so-called Ditchley portrait, which was painted around the same time as the Center's *Allegory* by the artist Marcus Gheeraerts the Younger for Sir Henry Lee.[2]

A 1984 exhibition at the Center dedicated to this work, *Painting in Focus: The Allegory of the Tudor Succession*, characterized it as being about "the virtues of an Elizabethan peace and a Protestant succession."[3] Henry VIII's position at the center represents his key role as head of church and state; he hands the sword of state, and thus the succession, on to his son, Edward VI, who ruled after his father and under whom Protestantism was advanced further. Next to Edward stands Elizabeth, during whose rule Protestantism as the state

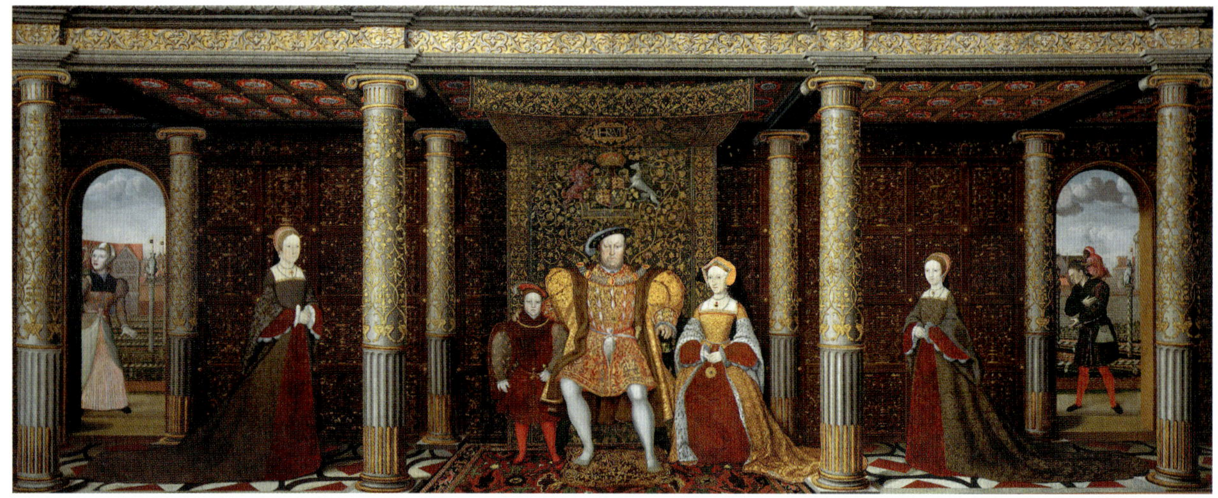

Fig. 7. British School, *The Family of Henry VIII*, ca. 1545, oil on canvas, 56⅞ x 140⅞ in. (144.5 x 355.9 cm). The Royal Collection Trust, London

religion was reaffirmed, displacing the Catholicism of Mary I's reign. Mary, rather than standing in the line of succession next to Edward, as was the case, is at the far side of the work, out of the line of Protestant Tudors, or standing "opposite to the Protestant successors."[4] The desirability of Protestantism is further augmented by the figures accompanying the two queens. Mary and her husband, Philip, lead in Mars, the god of war. On the other side, Elizabeth leads in the figures of Peace (stepping on a sword) and Plenty (carrying a cornucopia). The backgrounds glimpsed beyond the figures on each side of the picture are equally disparate: the left depicts a landscape of buildings, which include structures possibly meant to represent St Peter's and the Castel Sant'Angelo, implying the presence of Rome; the right shows a garden setting, which suggests the peace of Elizabeth's reign.[5] The left side thereby speaks of war and disruption, and the right of peace and abundance: following the line of Henry's arm, the turn of his head, and the handing on of the sword, the visual line of the painting, and the greater prominence of the figures of Henry, Edward, and Elizabeth, give the desirability of succession to Protestantism and to Elizabeth and Edward.

The Center's painting and the earlier Lucas de Heere version both relate to a still earlier portrait, *The Family of Henry VIII*, painted about 1545 by an unknown artist and now at Hampton Court (fig. 7). The painting depicts the King, his third wife, Jane Seymour, and his three children in a setting similar to that shown in the Center's painting, but with very different meaning. In the Hampton Court painting, Henry is again center stage with Edward and Jane Seymour immediately beside him, but Mary and Elizabeth are both set apart outside the central area beneath the canopy of state where the King, his male heir, and the wife who produced that heir are positioned. While this earlier painting simply presents the King and his heirs as a family group, Roy Strong comments that the subsequent 1572 *Allegory* divides the painting into "two opposing politico-religious sides," a tactic repeated in the Center's *Allegory*.[6]

A point of interest is the figure of a man peering through an archway in the lower left of the Center's picture. Though it has been conjectured that this may be a Catholic priest, no certain evidence has been found for this, and it is most commonly thought this is Will Somer or Sommers, who served as a court fool in the reigns of Henry VIII, Edward VI, and Mary I, and who is depicted in other paintings of Henry VIII and his family.[7] Somer's later reputation was that of an anti-Catholic figure, and it has been suggested his presence here is that of the wise fool, speaking truth to power as he offers a clear-eyed commentary on Catholicism.[8]

The *Allegory* serves as a representation of the political and religious debates that flourished through the sixteenth century as the break with Rome and the establishment of Protestantism as the state religion of England fluctuated significantly under the successive rules of the Tudor kings and queens. This group portrait may have been commissioned by a loyal Protestant subject seeking to promote the benefits of the Protestant succession and settlement of religion, or by a Catholic subject seeking to present an appearance of loyalty and conformity in the wake of the defeat of the Spanish Armada, and the continued concerns over Catholic aggression. But it offers the conclusion to the viewer that the Protestant succession and the firm establishment of that religion is the best for England, and that Elizabeth's rule has brought England lasting peace and prosperity.

Notes

1. Roy Strong, *Gloriana: The Portraits of Queen Elizabeth I* (London: Thames and Hudson, 1987), 74.
2. *Queen Elizabeth I* ("The Ditchley portrait"), by Marcus Gheeraerts the Younger, oil on canvas, ca. 1592, National Portrait Gallery, London, NPG 2561. Tabitha Barber, in her entry on the Sudeley *Allegory* in *Dynasties: Painting in Tudor and Jacobean England, 1530–1630*, ed. Karen Hearn (London: Tate Publishing, 1995), 81–82, comments that Elizabeth's dress in the YCBA *Allegory* resembles that in the Ditchley portrait, though the jeweled and patterned decoration is more like that in the Armada portrait.
3. Ellen Chirelstein and Nicola Shilliam, *Painting in Focus: The Allegory of the Tudor Succession*, exh. pamphlet (New Haven: Yale Center for British Art, 1984).
4. Chirelstein and Shilliam, *Painting in Focus*.
5. Chirelstein and Shilliam, *Painting in Focus*, proposes this possible identification of the buildings.
6. Strong, *Gloriana*, 76.
7. These include the *Family of Henry VIII* at Hampton Court and a painting at Boughton House, Northamptonshire, of Henry, his three children, and Somer. See http://www.boughtonhouse.co.uk/boughton-house/boughton-house-collection/the-great-hall/.
8. Chirelstein and Shilliam, *Painting in Focus*.

Right: detail of *The Family of Henry VIII*

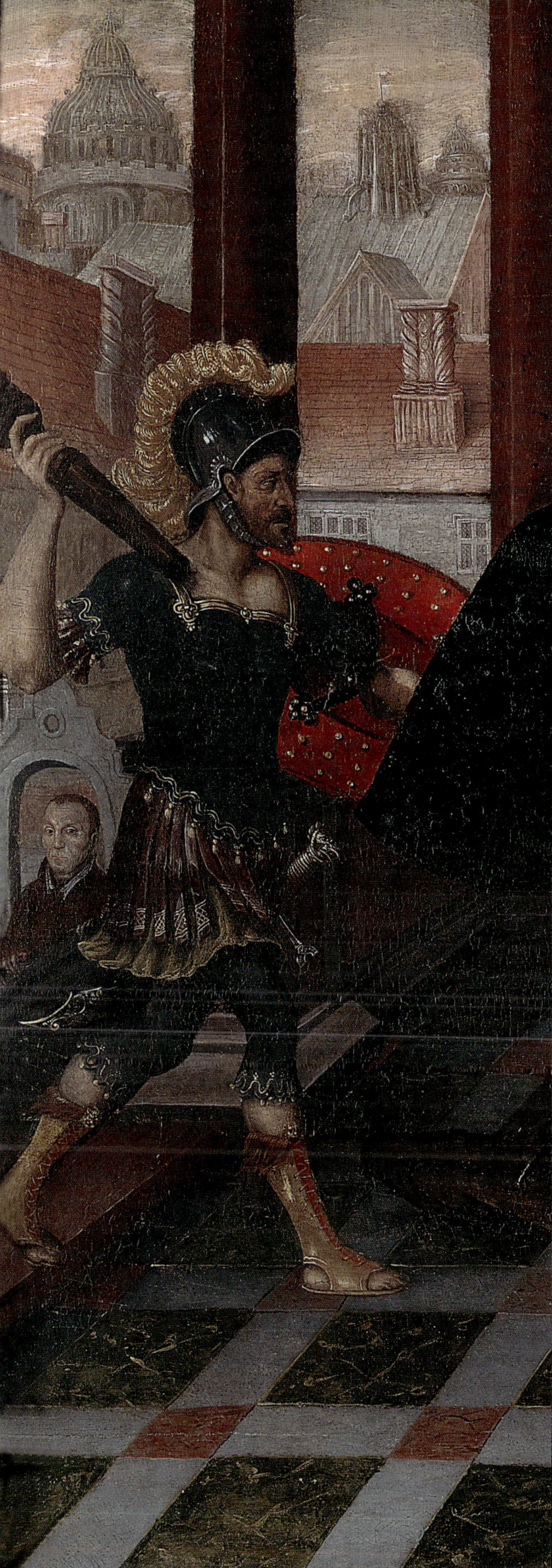

Attributed to Paul van Somer (Flemish, ca. 1576–1621; active in Britain from 1616) *A Lady, known as Elizabeth, Countess of Kellie*, ca. 1619

Oil on canvas, 81 x 48½ in. (205.7 x 123.2 cm)

YALE CENTER FOR BRITISH ART, PAUL MELLON COLLECTION, B1981.25.598

Pamela H. Smith

There is very little we know for certain about this painting: is it by Paul van Somer? Is it even a portrait of Elizabeth, Countess of Kellie?[1] We don't know precisely when Elizabeth Pierrepont was born—although an Elizabeth Pierrepont (ca. 1568–ca. 1621) certainly wed Thomas Erskine (1566–1639) in 1604, and Erskine became Earl of Kellie in 1619, hence Elizabeth's title, Countess of Kellie. The identity of the sitter turns out to be more obscure than her open gaze suggests. Such is the fate of most women of the past: they live and die without individual identity, subsumed in their fathers' and husbands' names and property, leaving few traces in the documentary record.

Elizabeth was the granddaughter of Elizabeth Hardwick (ca. 1527–1608), better known as Bess of Hardwick, a woman who did rise above the surface of this sea of erasure and invisibility. Bess was born into the gentry and succeeded at the most ambitious career open to a non-noble woman at this time: she married and was left a widow by four husbands, each wealthier than the last, making sure at each death that she got her portion—if not the whole—of the estates.[2] Bess's eldest child, Frances (1548–1632), gave birth to Elizabeth about 1568, the first of at least six children. According to one source, Bess of Hardwick called her granddaughter Bessie, and asked Mary, Queen of Scots, to serve as her godmother. When Bessie was seventeen (ca. 1585), her grandmother may have promoted a marriage for her with one of the Earl of Northumberland's sons, but apparently nothing came of it.[3] We may never know what in this account is true. Can the portrait give us any insight? Does it celebrate a marriage? There is only a suggestion of a gold band on the woman's middle finger, but it was not subsequently worked up by the artist.[4] The ornate gloves, often a part of marriage ceremonies, might also suggest a wedding portrait.[5]

While we may be certain about the identity of neither the artist nor the sitter, no such doubt exists about the intention of this over-life-size portrait: to convey wealth, status, and power. The putative Countess of Kellie is framed by luxury on every side, from the looping weave of the Turkey carpet, up the gilded legs of the green velvet chair to the naturalistically detailed depiction of tassels and loops formed by twisted threads of gold, to the gold finials of the chair, to the crimson book cover embroidered with silver threads, up to the green velvet drapery edged with gold embroidery, across to the substantial stone column, and, everywhere, the gold artfully counterfeited with varieties of gold-colored pigments and diverse techniques of application. As the viewer's eye is drawn to the extraordinary textiles—first, the elaborate yellow lace that sets off the woman's face, bodice, and hands, then the burgundy damask dress, shot through with patterns embroidered in gold and silver threads, and finally the slashed sleeves and matching train—it becomes clear that there is actually very little woman here; the shining eyes,

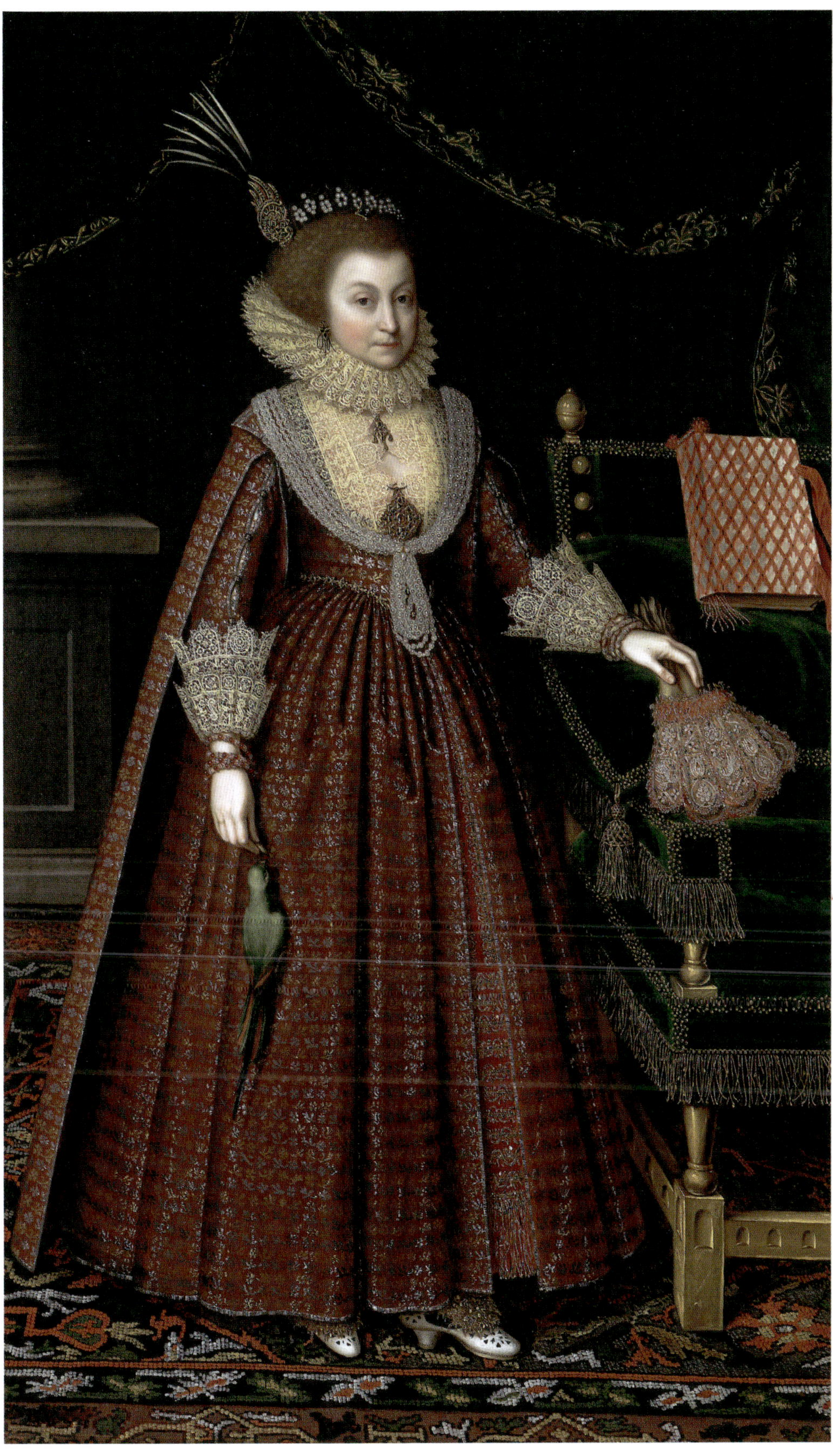

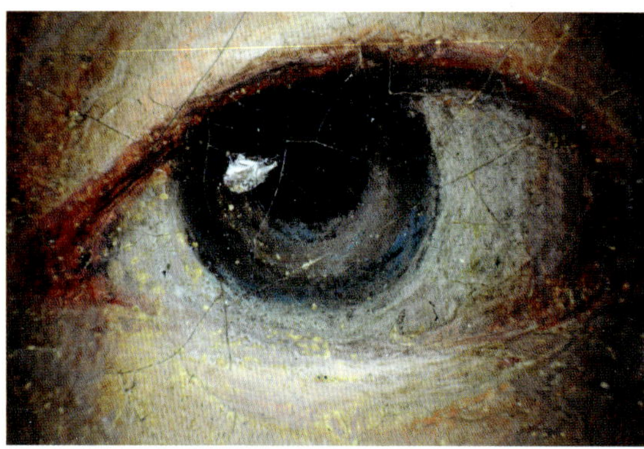

Fig. 8. Detail of *A Lady*: microphotograph of the right eye

the beautifully blended flesh tones, and carefully rendered hands merely set off with greater effect the possessions.

The naturalism of the painting belies a generic woman's portrait. Far more individual than the sitter's features are the gold hairpiece of her silver-and-pearl tiara, from which spreads a spray of stylish feathers; the remarkable earring and the gold broach studded with rubies and black-backed diamonds[6] and set off by a ruff and bodice of rare yellow lace, the height of fashion during the later years of James I's reign; the six enormous ropes of pearls looping over her shoulders and gathered together to drape down below her waist, where her farthingale pushes out her damask skirt.[7] Her right hand, encircled by a long, twisted string of red and silver beads, holds an almond, toward which an exotic and expensive parrot clinging to her dress strains; while her left hand, resting on the stunning gloves, is wrapped in yet another beaded string.

Dwelling on these details exposes the second certainty of this portrait: the consummate skill of the artist in rendering the rich surfaces of precious objects in paint. He made only the loosest sketch beneath the hands and a few lines under the face and costume, making very few changes as he painted. Microphotography and the close observation of conservator Jessica David eloquently reveal how the artist worked up wet-in-wet all parts to a high finish, afterward applying the final details "sequentially, dry over wet, starting from the background and moving forward onto the figure," creating subtle differences in texture and volume.

The shining right eye (fig. 8) was built up thinly, with the cream-colored ground showing through at the edges; "each sclera was painted in with a cool blue color, a mixture of lead white, black and azurite(?), applied with quick semi-circular brushstrokes around the gray irises, which were simply a darker mixture of the same pigments." Then, to achieve the illusion of depth, "a few loose strokes of azurite were added to each sclera and iris. The pupils and outer edges of the irises were reinforced with a solid black pigment. Finally, dabs of pure lead white were added to the upper-left corner of each iris."

The hand (fig. 9) was constructed by first laying down a very thin underpainting in a warm earth brown on the cream-colored ground, imparting "a cool 'turbid' effect" when the flesh pigments were subsequently thinly applied. The painter composed his "carnation," or flesh tone, from lead white, yellow ocher, black, and a fine red, laying it thinly across her face and hands. Then he added rosy hues with a mixture of lead white and the same fine red by brushing "linear strokes of this pink paint on the folds of the eyes, the inner eyelids, the nostrils, and fingernail beds, often overlapping and (perhaps intentionally) softening the transitions between the light flesh paint and the darker brown underpainting," and blending it on knuckles "to a thin veil of color over the cooler flesh." Transparent brown paint was applied over the flesh hues to reinforce the shadows and sharpest contours, and finally, "highlights, composed of the same base flesh tone plus more lead white, were added to highpoints along the left side of the face and hands," and blended "to eliminate brushwork except for . . . crisper highlights on her nails that capture their hard, smooth surface."

Last of all, once the paint had dried on the rest of the portrait, the yellow lace (fig. 10) was created. The painter subtly varied his mixture of lead tin

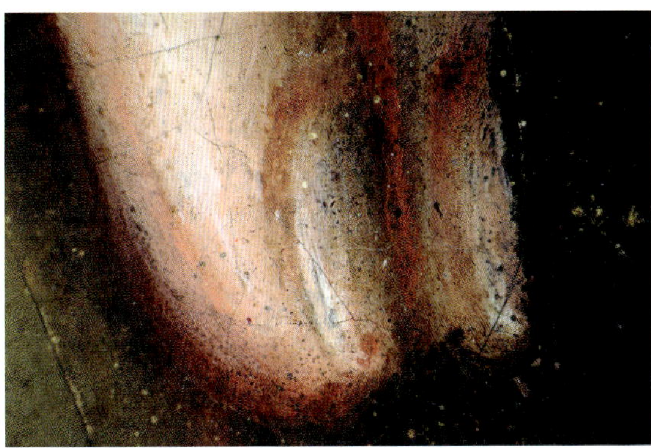

Fig. 9. Detail of *A Lady*: microphotograph of the forefingers of the right hand

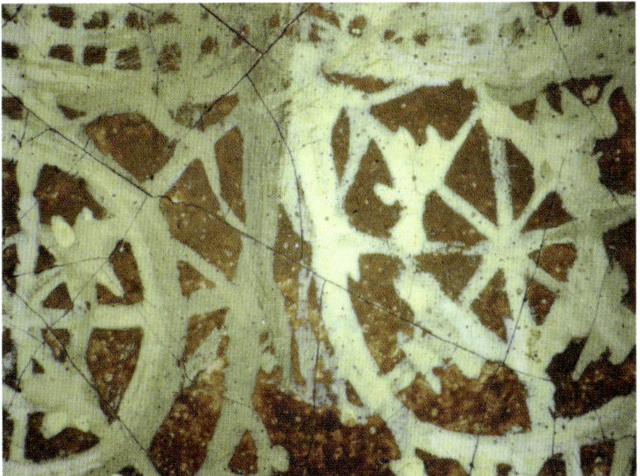

Fig. 10. Detail of *A Lady*: microphotograph of the lace of the chin ruff

yellow, brown earth, and black, making it slightly darker in areas of shadow, then adding on top a second layer of lead tin yellow and white, "picking out fine detail across the lace pattern with more impasto strokes." Because the lighter color was added while the darker was still wet, the artist's brush dragged and blended the colors.

This brief exercise in close looking reveals the convergence of wills to represent: the sitter's determination to project affluence and status, and the tremendously sure capacity of the artist to blend and layer pigments to give substance to the artifice of that representation.

Notes

1. "The Rt Honorbly / Countess of Kelly" is painted in ocher-colored paint and later overpainted with black, both apparently later additions; Yale Center for British Art, Painting Conservation Examination Report (2013). Sincere thanks to Jessica David, Associate Conservator of Paintings, for sharing the report. The painting was examined as part of the "Reformation to Restoration" project, an in-depth technical and historical study of the Center's Tudor and early Stuart portraits, conducted by David and by Edward Town, Head of Collections Information Access and Assistant Curator of Early Modern Art, in partnership with Yale's Institute for the Preservation of Cultural Heritage and the National Portrait Gallery, London.

2. See Bess of Hardwick's Letters: The Complete Correspondence, c. 1550–1608, http://www.bessofhardwick.org, edited by Alison Wiggins, Alan Bryson, Daniel Starza Smith, Anke Timmermann, and Graham Williams, University of Glasgow; web development by Katherine Rogers, University of Sheffield Humanities Research Institute (April 2013).

3. Mary S. Lovell, *Bess of Hardwick: Empire Builder* (New York: W. W. Norton, 2005), 319–20.

4. YCBA, Painting Conservation Examination Report.

5. Andrew Morrall and Melinda Watt, eds., *English Embroidery from The Metropolitan Museum of Art, 1580–1700: 'Twixt Art and Nature* (New York: The Bard Graduate Center for Studies in the Decorative Arts, Design, and Culture, and The Metropolitan Museum of Art; New Haven: Yale Univ. Press, 2008), 182.

6. See Joanna Whalley, "Faded Glory: Gemstone Simulants and Enhancements," *Studies in Conservation* 57 (2012), 313–21.

7. See Julia Marciari-Alexander, *This Other Eden: Paintings from the Yale Center for British Art* (New Haven: Yale Univ. Press), 26.

Benedetto Gennari (Italian, 1633–1715; active in Britain, 1674–1689)
Cleopatra, ca. 1674

Oil on canvas, 49 x 41½ in. (124.5 x 105.4 cm)

YALE CENTER FOR BRITISH ART, PAUL MELLON FUND, B2004.1

Julia Marciari-Alexander

The Restoration in 1660 of Charles II both reseated the English monarchy and established at the court a diverse and cosmopolitan artistic culture. By the 1670s artists such as Benedetto Gennari, an Italian who had thrived in the studio of the internationally renowned Bolognese painter Guercino (1591–1666), made their names traveling through the courts of Europe. In late 1674 Gennari left Versailles, where he had worked successfully for Louis XIV from 1672, to seek fortune at the Restoration court. Although the reasons for his choice of the English court remain obscure, his move to London would certainly not have been hindered and may even have been prompted by the rising fortunes of Louise de Kéroualle, a French noblewoman—and a Catholic—who had been made Duchess of Portsmouth by Charles II in 1672 after she bore him a son. In fact, the first paintings Gennari made in England included portraits of the Duchess of Portsmouth and her son (by the King).[1]

The ascension to power of the King's French mistress, who quickly eclipsed his longtime companions Barbara Villiers, Duchess of Cleveland, and the popular actress and commoner Nell Gwyn, was considered just one of many signs of a rising tide of Catholicism at court. Attempts to stem this perceived "Roman" or Catholic infiltration—and continental European influence—led to the passage of regulations such as the Test Act by Parliament in 1673, which required all those holding civil and military office to disavow the tenets and practices of Roman Catholicism and to receive the Eucharist under the laws of the Church of England. In some ways, then, the arrival at the English court in September 1674 of Gennari, best known for his religious paintings and subject pictures, not only reflected the increasingly visible leanings of the court but also further aligned the ostensibly Protestant king Charles II with his Catholic counterparts.

On his arrival Gennari presented the King with a subject painting, *Diana and Endymion*, painted in France for the duc de Richelieu but never delivered (probably for nonpayment). Shortly thereafter, he painted *Cleopatra* for the monarch. The artist described the work in his notebook:

> A painting of a half-length figure of Cleopatra lying on a bed in the act of throwing herself towards death by a serpent and this done for the King [who had it put in the room which already held my other painting of Endymion, which I had presented to him when I arrived in England].[2]

The fourth picture painted after his arrival at court, Gennari's *Cleopatra* holds a key position in the oeuvre he created in England. It stands at the beginning of a long and fruitful career at the Stuart court, for which he was allotted (if only occasionally paid) a yearly stipend of £500. During the years prior to Charles II's death in 1685, the painter produced 102 works for a variety of patrons, and he stayed on to produce another 35 works for James II

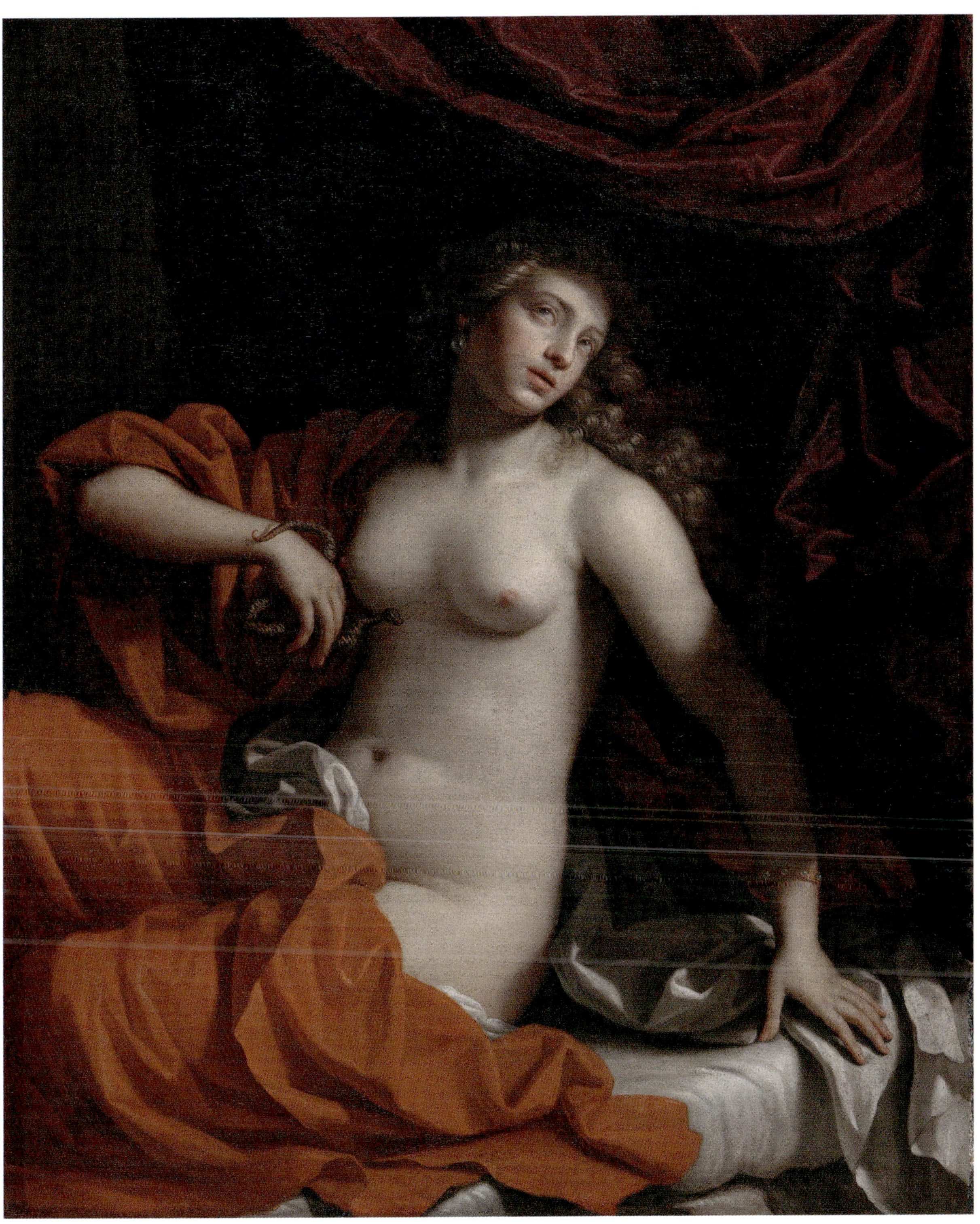

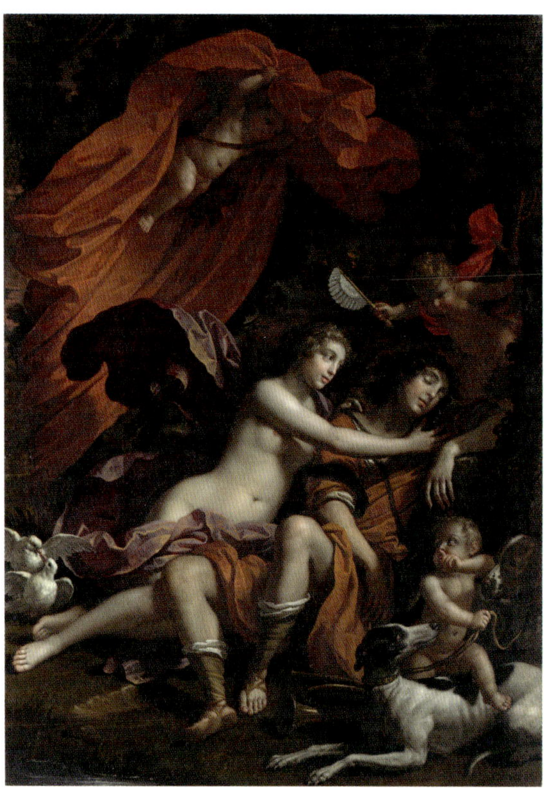

Fig. 11. Benedetto Gennari, *Venus and the Sleeping Adonis*, ca. 1677–78, oil on canvas, 89 x 64½ in. (226.1 x 163.7 cm). The Royal Collection Trust, London

and Mary of Modena, whom he followed into exile at St. Germain-en-Laye in 1689; there he produced another 30 paintings before returning to Italy in 1692.[3]

It is revelatory to consider Gennari's *Cleopatra* within the context of the ambitious redecoration of Windsor Castle, which began shortly after the conclusion of the Third Anglo-Dutch War in 1674.[4] Windsor was a place of relatively private function, and Charles II sought to have the languishing medieval property renovated by the most fashionable artists, including René Cousin, Grinling Gibbons, and Antonio Verrio. As part of this renovation, Gennari's *Cleopatra*, which the artist tells us the King hung "in his rooms," was quickly joined by a group of mythological paintings by the artist that were acquired and/or commissioned by the King, among them *Danae Receiving the Shower of Gold* (ca. 1672–74) and *Sleeping Venus with Cupids* (ca. 1675–85). Shortly thereafter, another set of large pictures by Gennari joined paintings by Titian and Tintoretto in adorning the King's more public Dining Room;[5] all painted around 1676, Gennari's works depicted four scenes from Ovid's *Metamorphoses: Venus and the Sleeping Adonis* (fig. 11); *The Triumph of Galatea*; *Hercules and Omphale*; and *Cephalus and the Dying Procris*, all of which remain in the Royal Collection. When considered together within the context of the private and sumptuous decorative program of the King's rooms at Windsor, then, Gennari's individual paintings and the monumental set in the Dining Room anchored what amounted to a totalizing environment celebrating the triumphs and tragedies of love.

Like the tales from Ovid, episodes from the life of the Egyptian queen Cleopatra were familiar to late seventeenth-century viewers.[6] Among the moments in her story that held particular fascination for artists and patrons was her choice to commit suicide by the bite of an asp rather than be captured as a prize by the Romans. Gennari's painting depicts this scene, but rather than memorializing the sanguine moment after the fatal snakebite, the painter cannily chose the moment just prior, providing viewers with an unfettered, bloodless view of Cleopatra's naked body, writhing among luxuriant bedding. As in the other scenes in the group of paintings for the King, Gennari exploits his "historical" subject primarily as a visual prompt for erotic pleasure.

While it has been suggested that the present picture may be a *portrait historié* (which casts the sitter "in the guise of" a mythical, literary, or biblical figure), there is no evidence to connect the model with a specific woman at the Restoration court. The nonroyal provenance of a later, similar painting of Cleopatra by Gennari (fig. 12) now in the Victoria Art Gallery, Bath, and the fact that the model in the present picture is blond, has led to some casual speculation that the King's version depicts Nell Gwyn.[7] In both paintings the model's features are stylized, and her pose eschews the conventions of *portraits historiés* in that the model does not gaze directly at the viewer. Although it is unlikely that Gennari's *Cleopatra* was meant to be a disguised portrait of one of Charles's notorious mistresses, the painting's eroticism, especially when considered within the larger group of paintings in the King's private rooms, would have been no subtle reminder of his well-known penchant for, and public practice of, pleasure.

Purchased by the Yale Center for British Art in 2004, Gennari's *Cleopatra* is among a small number of history paintings in the collection that date to the seventeenth century, a period represented at the Center by an exceptional group of portraits, still lifes, and marine paintings. With its subject matter and royal provenance, this painting by one of the leading, if under-studied, artists working at the Restoration court significantly bolsters the Center's holdings and provides through its presence a richer, more accurate picture of the visual—and political—culture at Charles II's complex and creative court.

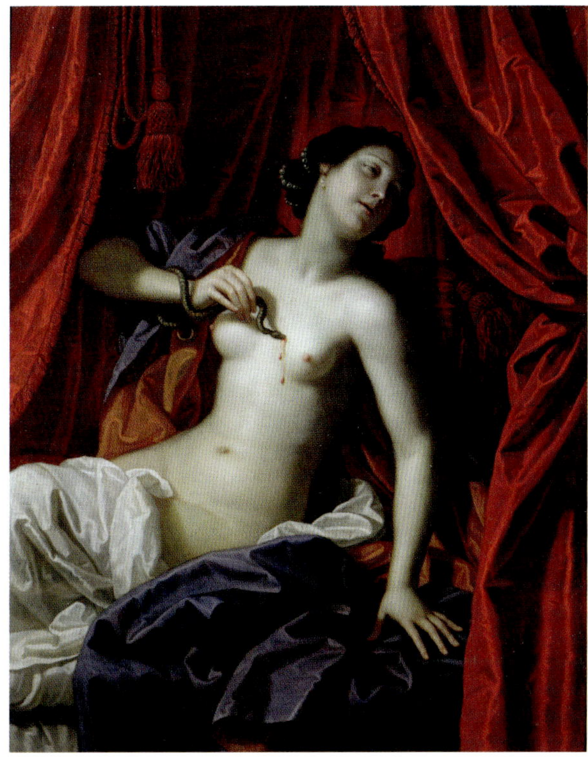

Fig. 12. Benedetto Gennari, *The Death of Cleopatra*, 1686, oil on canvas, 51 x 39⅞ in. (129.5 x 101.2 cm). Victoria Art Gallery, Bath and North East Somerset Council

Notes

1. The paintings are recorded in Gennari's diary, Benedetto Gennari, *Raccolta di memorie di Benedetto Gennari*, Biblioteca Comunale, Bologna, MSB.344, transcribed in Prisco Bagni, *Benedetto Gennari e la bottega del Guercino* (Bologna: Nuova Alfa, 1986), 147.
2. Author's translation. The brackets were added by Gennari himself to a later autograph copy of his diary. See Gennari, *Raccolta*, 147.
3. Little attention has been paid to Gennari's work in England. The most in-depth discussions include: Dwight C. Miller, "Benedetto Gennari's Career at the Courts of Charles II and James II and a Newly Discovered Portrait of James II," *Apollo* 117, no. 251 (January 1983), 24–29; Susan Steer, "The Early History of Benedetto Gennari's 'Death of Cleopatra' at the Victoria Art Gallery, Bath," *Burlington Magazine* 149, no. 1252 (July 2007), 485–87; and relevant passages and entries in the recent publication accompanying an exhibition of the same name, *Charles II: Art & Power*, eds. Rufus Bird and Martin Clayton (London: Royal Collection Trust, 2017). See also Brett Dolman, *Beauty, Sex and Power: A Story of Debauchery and Decadent Art at the Late Stuart Court, 1660–1714* (London: Scala/Historic Royal Palaces, 2012), 50, 51.
4. Bird and Clayton, *Charles II*, 186.
5. Bird and Clayton, *Charles II*, 186.
6. Made popular earlier in the century by Shakespeare, the story of Cleopatra would become the subject of a number of theatrical works later in the 1670s. For an in-depth analysis of Cleopatra as a subject in Restoration portraits, see Susan Shifrin, "'Subdued by a Famous Roman Dame': Picturing Foreignness, Notoriety, and Prerogative in the Portraits of Hortense Mancini, Duchess Mazarin," in *Politics, Transgression, and Representation at the Court of Charles II*, Catharine MacLeod and Julia Marciari Alexander, eds. (New Haven and London: Yale Center for British Art/Paul Mellon Centre for Studies in British Art, 2007), 141–74.
7. The painting now in Bath was once in the collection of the Rt. Hon. Francis Gwyn, MP, who held various governmental and court posts between 1679 and 1714. For an in-depth discussion of the Bath painting and the tenuous yet alluring relationship of its patron to Nell Gwyn, see Steer, "The Early History of Benedetto Gennari's 'Death of Cleopatra.'"

Bartholomew Dandridge (British, baptized 1691, died in or after 1754)
A Young Girl with an Enslaved Servant and a Dog, ca. 1725

Oil on canvas, 48 x 48 in. (121.9 x 121.9 cm). Signed lower right: "B. Dandridge Pinx[...]."

YALE CENTER FOR BRITISH ART, PAUL MELLON COLLECTION, B1981.25.205

Mark Aronson and Jessica David

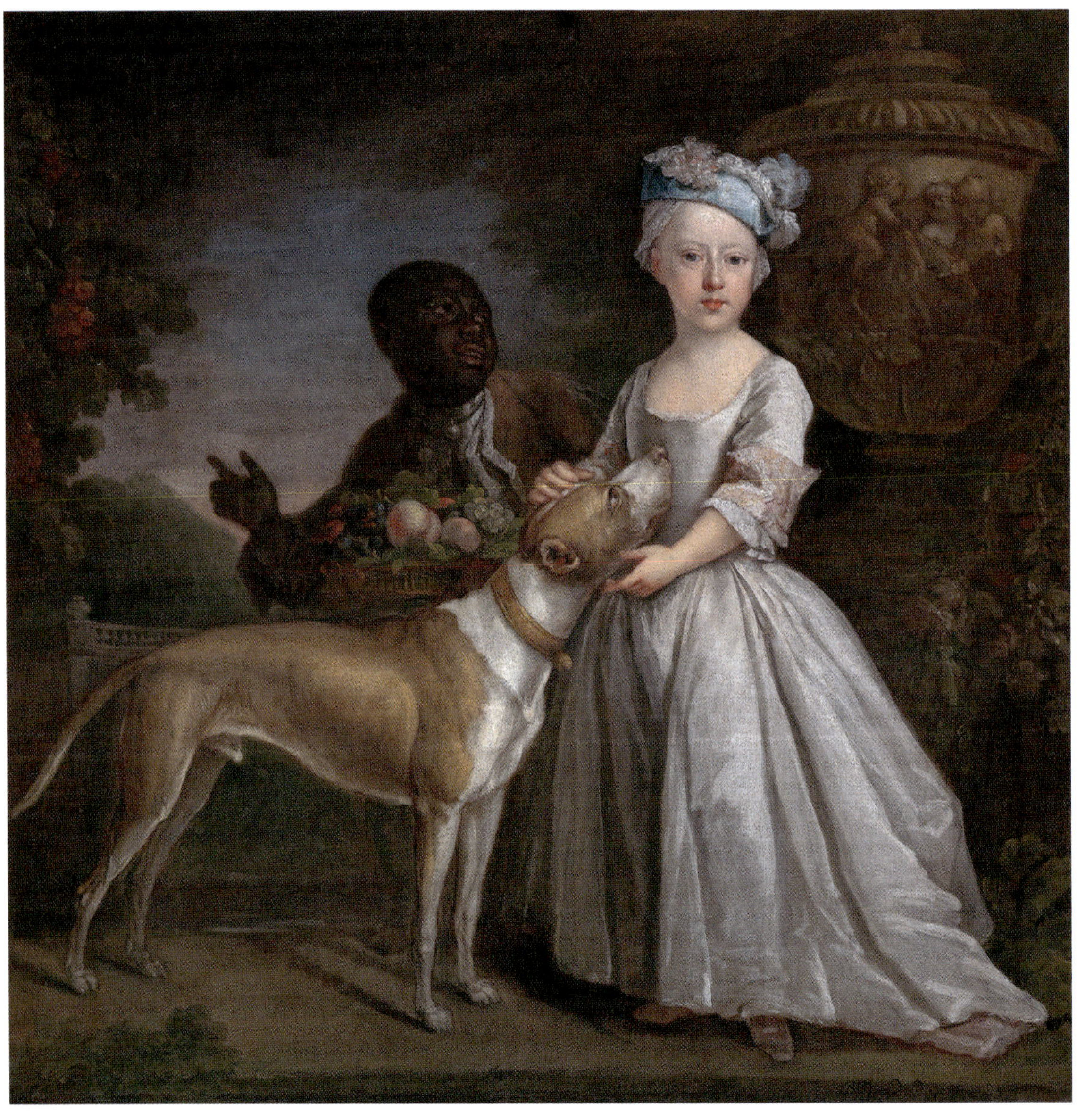

Few paintings in the Paul Mellon Collection are as damaged as Bartholomew Dandridge's *A Young Girl with an Enslaved Servant and a Dog* (fig. 13). Long consigned to storage with a thick, yellowed varnish and expanses of discolored overpaint, the murky conversation piece was rarely seen in the galleries. Previous restoration had obscured and misinterpreted Dandridge's painting, both in terms of the composition and the significance of the subject. When the curators of *Figures of Empire: Slavery and Portraiture in Eighteenth-Century Atlantic Britain* proposed that the painting be included in the exhibition, there was a collective gasp from the conservation department.[1] However, the exhibition permitted a full, collaborative restoration of the work, which in turn offered an opportunity to connect painting conservation with scholarship on the depiction of race in Western painting, demonstrating the ways in which the two kinds of art-historical analysis can benefit each other. Moreover, the technical analysis exploring the picture's paint structure and degradation provided valuable insights into Dandridge's understudied painting practice.[2]

Shown is an intimate classical garden landscape dominated by a young child in a pale gray dress with blue head covering, accompanied by a large dog and a partially hidden, enslaved black male. Most scholars identify the child as female, but the gender is uncertain, and the figure could equally be a young boy not yet breeched. Both dog and slave have metal collars locked around their necks, signaling that they are owned and subservient to the child. The painting serves as a depiction of not just progeny but property.

The condition of the painting made it very difficult to read. The extent of paint loss across the canvas obscured many details, especially on the child's face and dress. The now illegible name on the dog's collar presumably referred to the owner of the dog, of the young slave, and of the painting itself. The spatial relationship between the white child, the attending enslaved black male, and the dog suggests a social hierarchy, yet their proximity, their relative flesh tones, and expressions were concealed by the painting's poor state. Similarly, the layers of old varnish warmed the color temperature of the sitters' skin and skewed the reading of the black slave, making him appear as a generic figure rather than a life likeness. The space of the

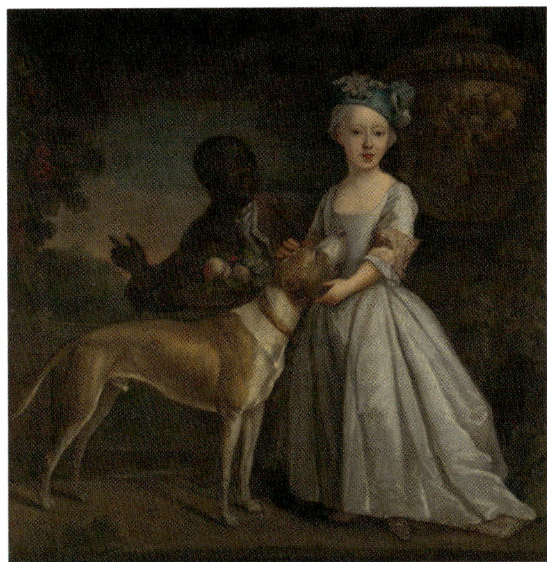

Fig. 13. Painting before treatment

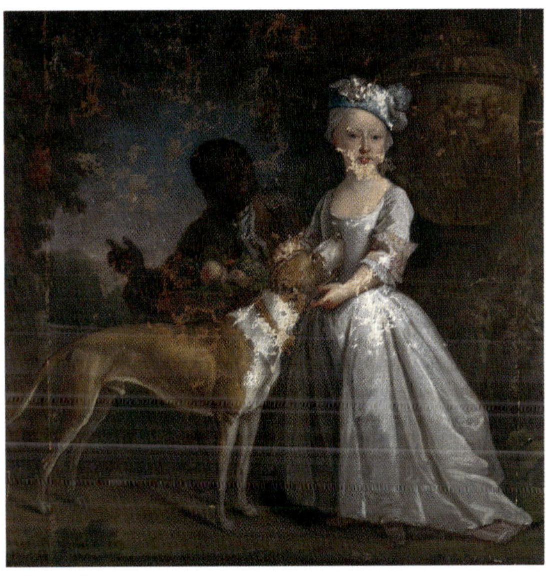

Fig. 14. Painting during treatment, after removal of the degraded varnish and extensive, old restorations

painting, and thus the distance between the owner and the owned, was compressed by a coating that darkened highlights and lightened the darks. It was clear that cleaning the painting would permit a truer view of its original content and intended social dynamic.[3]

As anticipated, the removal of varnish and overpaint uncovered large losses in the paint, revealing a number of erroneous changes made by a previous restorer (fig. 14). Dandridge's style, sometimes described as "English Rococo," was underpinned by the technical traditions of Godfrey Kneller and the St Martin's Lane Academy. The energetic swishes and feathery brushstrokes, a painterly shorthand that left many details ambiguous and contours fluid (the young man's torso and legs, the child's costume, and the landscape), had been replaced with stagnating, thick overpaint. The reconstruction of the child's face, for example, had adjusted its slight angle to a straightforward, gaunter gaze; the lips were thinned and crevices around the mouth suppressed, depriving it of the fleshy, cherubic shape typical of Dandridge's portraits.

The young man's face did not suffer the same degree of paint loss as the child's but was equally obscured by age and restoration (fig. 15). Paint cross section and ultraviolet examination showed that his flesh was covered with a thicker buildup of varnish than any other passage analyzed. This was possibly related to the sensitivity of the pigments used to paint him (which past restorers avoided by leaving the varnish layer intact) or, perhaps, to the historical prioritization of the light-skinned figure in the foreground; in other words, it is possible that a past restorer was more concerned with the figure of the young white girl, while Dandridge had taken more care with the figure of the young man.[4] As a result, the male figure's flesh was better preserved than much of the painting and still showcases Dandridge's swift, sensitive handling of expression and complexion.

While clearly subservient, half-kneeling, holding a basket of fruit, and wearing a collar similar to the dog's, the young man is infused with

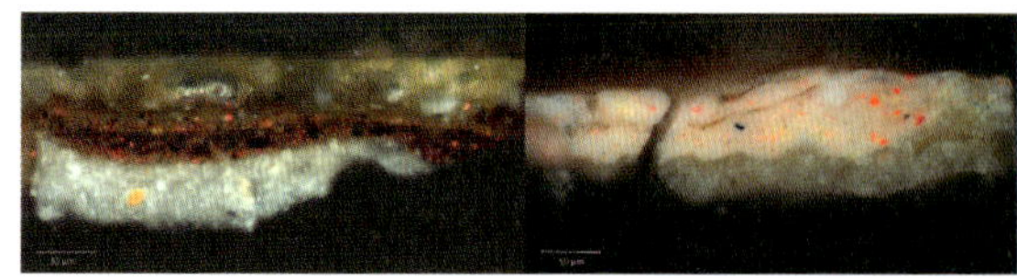

Fig. 15. Paint cross sections taken from areas of loss on the shadow (right) sides of the foreheads of the young man and child: The young man's flesh comprises more layers of thinly applied paint and much more varnish (seen as the soft yellow haze above the paint layers) than the child's flesh.

an energy absent from the child; his lips parted, head turned, and hand raised as if to draw attention. Dandridge clearly referenced a tradition of representing young black "genre" figures, some obviously enslaved, in fancy dress or livery and presenting luxury items, a practice exemplified in the work of such artists as Anthony van Dyck and Peter Lely. Arguably, Dandridge's ability to capture the young man's complexion and character matches and even rivals the skill of his predecessors, showing that he drew not only from their motifs but, like them, combined a prescribed method of mixing flesh tones with life study. This practice could well have been transmitted to Dandridge from Lely through Kneller, his one-time mentor; it had also crept into contemporary manuals on flesh painting, such as Thomas Page's *The Art of Painting* (1720), in which, for the first time in English, Page offers descriptions on how to paint different shades of skin including "fair," "brown sanguine," "tawney," and "black."[5]

Examination of the paint layer with microscopy, infrared imaging, and x-radiography shows that the composition was planned, the figures and dog initially placed with loose strokes of reddish brown oil paint. The figures were worked up (or painted in several layers) at about the same time and the landscape was completed around them, except for final touches to their faces and costumes, which overlap dry background paint. Paint cross sections taken from the forehead of each figure provided further information about Dandridge's palette and process. The young man's face, for instance, comprises numerous thin layers of paint, more than are used for the child. The delicate layer structure of his face implies that Dandridge was more careful with the tonality and transparency of his paint there than on the child's solid, opaque visage.

This differentiation is also evident in the initial blocking in or "dead coloring" of the skin tones. The young man was initially defined with a vibrant, warm paint mixture containing much red earth and vermilion pigment, whereas the child was assigned a light peach color made of the same reds plus a great deal of lead white and sparse Prussian blue particles. The child's rosy complexion was added on top of this paint after it had dried, while the warmth of the young man's skin emanates from the reddish hue beneath the paint surface, explaining why Dandridge added paint sparingly above that warmer underlayer.

Dandridge's system for painting flesh vaguely follows Page's directions for "black" and "fair" complexions. Page, for example, does not recommend using much, if any, vermilion for darker skin tones, specifically not in the upper (shadow and highlight) layers. Dandridge used very little vermilion for the young man, apparently only in the first, very warm, blocking-in layer, above which are mainly earth pigments and a small amount of lead white. Brushwork on the young man's face is also looser or more open than on the child's, perhaps to render him slightly out of focus and thereby more distant, but Dandridge's idiosyncratic method of moving paint is evident on both. He turns and angles the brush, exploiting its shape to make different marks on the canvas—impasto flecks for strong highlights on the eyes, soft daubs of red on the lips, and feathery touches of reflected light, like the bluish haze across the young man's cheek.

The conservation treatment lasted almost a year, much of it devoted to careful reconstruction of lost paint passages. Like any three-hundred-year-old painting, *A Young Girl* has undergone irreversible change, but the tonal balance of the composition was improved and the vigor of Dandridge's brushwork revived. The status of the young black man as a slave, placed behind and lower than the other figures, is as clear as it was before conservation, but the recovery of his animated features and the nuanced play of light and color across his skin change his status from genre figure to individual. His individuality, which draws attention from the staid expression of the child, suggests that Dandridge captured him from life and with greater consideration than the young sitter—his typical subject—making him the focal point of an otherwise stark presentation of society. This conservation project highlighted the rich dialogue that results when restorations are taken beyond routine maintenance and into the realm of scholarly research.

Notes

1. The exhibition *Figures of Empire: Slavery and Portraiture in Eighteenth-Century Atlantic Britain* took place October 2–December 14, 2014, at the Yale Center for British Art. It was organized by the Center and curated by Esther Chadwick (PhD Yale University, 2016) and Meredith Gamer (PhD Yale University, 2015), then PhD candidates in the Department of the History of Art at Yale, and Cyra Levenson, then Associate Curator of Education at the Yale Center for British Art.
2. Cleaning was done by Kristin Bradley Egan, then a fourth-year intern from the training program at The Conservation Center of the Institute of Fine Arts, New York University. Reconstruction was carried out by YCBA conservation staff Jessica David and Mark Aronson, and Yale student Jaena Kwon (MFA Yale School of Art, 2014).
3. For a good discussion of the spatial change wrought by discolored varnish, see Gerry Hedley, "Long Lost Relations and New Found Relativities: Issues in the Cleaning of Paintings," in *Appearance, Opinion, Change: Evaluating the Look of Paintings* (London: United Kingdom Institute for Conservation, 1990), 8–13.
4. When certain pigments are mixed with drying oil, such as those containing lead, they form a more durable paint film than other colorants, including iron oxide pigments (siennas and umbers), lake pigments, and lamp black, the primary constituents of the young slave's flesh paint. A paint film comprising these darker, finer pigments is particularly sensitive to cleaning agents and surface abrasion. This may explain why past restorers favored cleaning the lighter, lead-containing paint passages over the darker ones. Specific pigments in *A Young Girl with an Enslaved Servant and a Dog* were analyzed from paint cross sections by Dr. Richard Hark, Assistant Conservation Scientist, Institute for the Preservation of Cultural Heritage, Yale University. See the unpublished analytical report (YCBA_1937.1484_Dandridge).
5. Thomas Page Jr., *The Art of Painting* (Norwich: W. Chase, 1720), 66–68. See also Anonymous, *The Strasbourg Manuscript: A Medieval Painters' Handbook, 1400–1570* (London: Alec Tiranti, 1966), 54–58; and Ann-Sophie Lehmann, "Fleshing Out the Body: The 'Colours of the Naked' in Dutch Art Theory and Workshop Practice, 1400–1600," in *Body and Embodiment in Netherlandish Art*, eds., Ann-Sophie Lehmann and Herman Roodenburg (Zwolle, Netherlands: Waanders, 2008), 86–109.

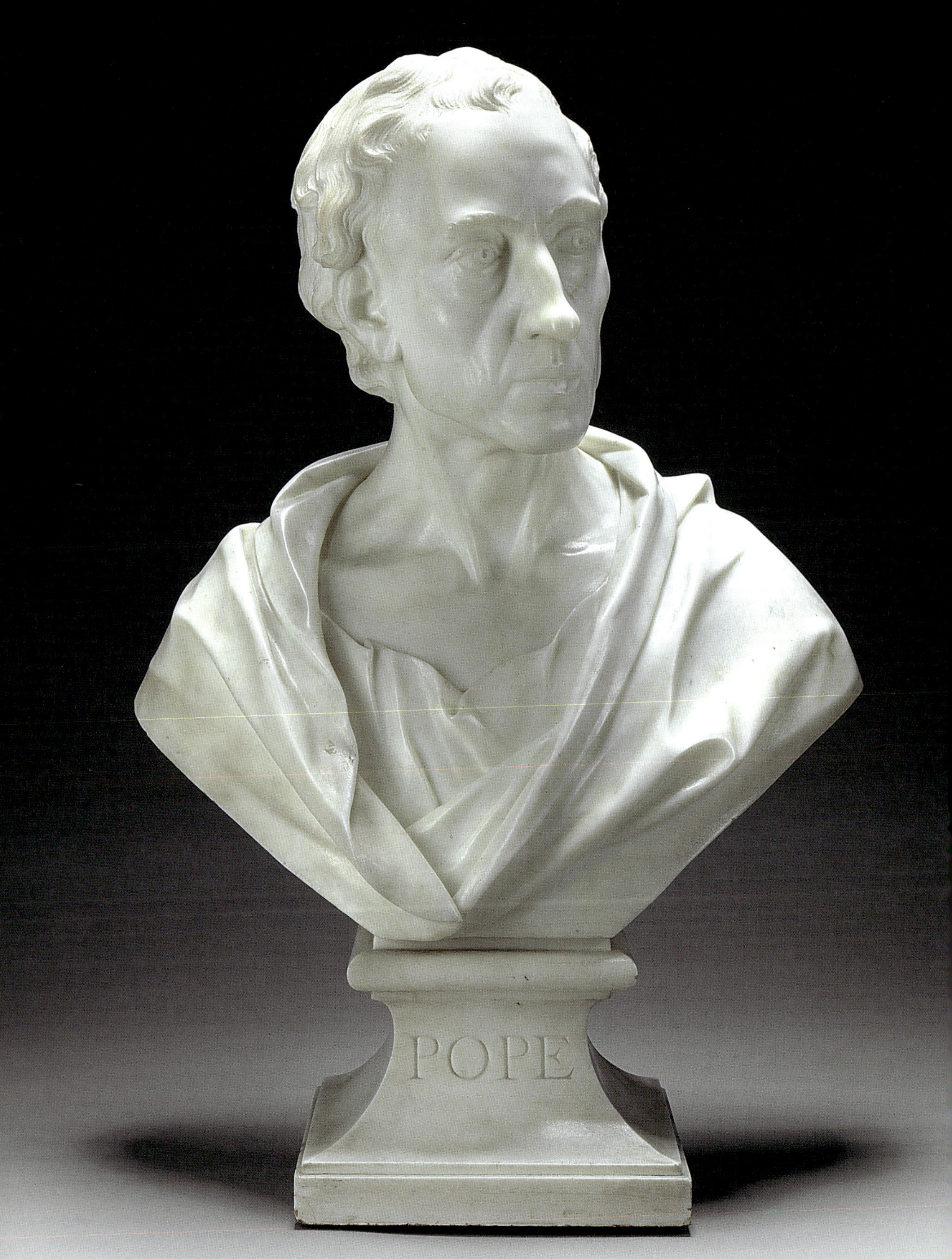
POPE

Louis François Roubiliac
(French, 1702–1762; active in Britain from 1730)
Alexander Pope, 1741

Marble, overall: 24 ¾ x 17 x 9 in. (62.9 x 43.2 x 22.9 cm). Chiseled on front of socle: "POPE," and under sitter's shoulder, left: "ALEX. POPE. Nats. LONDINI, | die 80. junii anno MDCLXXXVIII. | Obiit in vico Twickenham prope | Urbem, die 80. maii MDCCXLIV,"

YALE CENTER FOR BRITISH ART, PAUL MELLON COLLECTION, GIFT OF PAUL MELLON IN MEMORY OF THE BRITISH ART HISTORIAN BASIL TAYLOR (1922–1975), B1993.27

Malcolm Baker

As one of the definitive representations of the most important English poet of the eighteenth century by the outstanding sculptor of the period, Louis François Roubiliac's marble bust of Alexander Pope (1688–1744) registers both the centrality of sculptural portraiture at this period and the new importance of images of authors within British eighteenth-century culture. Already in 1733 Voltaire had commented on the ubiquity of Pope's image, writing that "The Picture of the Prime Minister hangs above the chimney of his own Closet, but I have seen that of Mr. Pope in twenty of noblemen's houses."[1] As much as any painted portrait, however, Roubiliac's bust has been seen as one of the most evocative and powerful images of the poet. With its virtuoso, subtle carving of the surfaces of head and face, this marble suggests both an intense thoughtfulness and a physical fragility, in accord with Sir Joshua Reynolds's comment that Pope "had an extraordinary face, not an everyday countenance—a pallid studious look; not merely a sharp, keen countenance, but something grand like Cicero's."[2] Here Roubiliac employs a classicizing form of drapery already employed for sculptures of other British sitters but especially appropriate for a writer whose verse constantly refers to and adapts the conventions used by classical poets, whose images he himself collected and displayed in his villa at Twickenham.

Before its acquisition by the Yale Center for British Art in 1993, Roubiliac's bust had a distinguished provenance, beginning in 1791 when it was recorded as being "in possession of Mr. Bindley, Commissioner of Stamps."[3] It was next purchased by the collector George Watson Taylor, a patron of the sculptors Sir Francis Chantrey and John Gibson. Subsequently bought by the former prime minister, Sir Robert Peel, in whose collection portraits of writers figured prominently, it was acquired in 1900 by the fifth Earl of Rosebery, from whose descendants it was bought by the Center. A Yale connection had, however, already been established in the mid-1960s, when it was shown on the cover of the magisterial study of Pope's portraits by William K. Wimsatt, Frederick Clifford Ford Professor of English. Along with the Pope biographer Maynard Mack, Wimsatt was one of a group of literary scholars who made Yale the leading center for the study of eighteenth-century literature.

While celebrated as one of the sculptor's outstanding portraits, the Yale marble is not alone. It has an enhanced significance through being one of no less than eight versions, which can be confidently described as autograph works from Roubiliac's studio. Six of the busts had indeed been assembled by Wimsatt in 1961 for an exhibition of Pope's portraits at the National Portrait Gallery, London

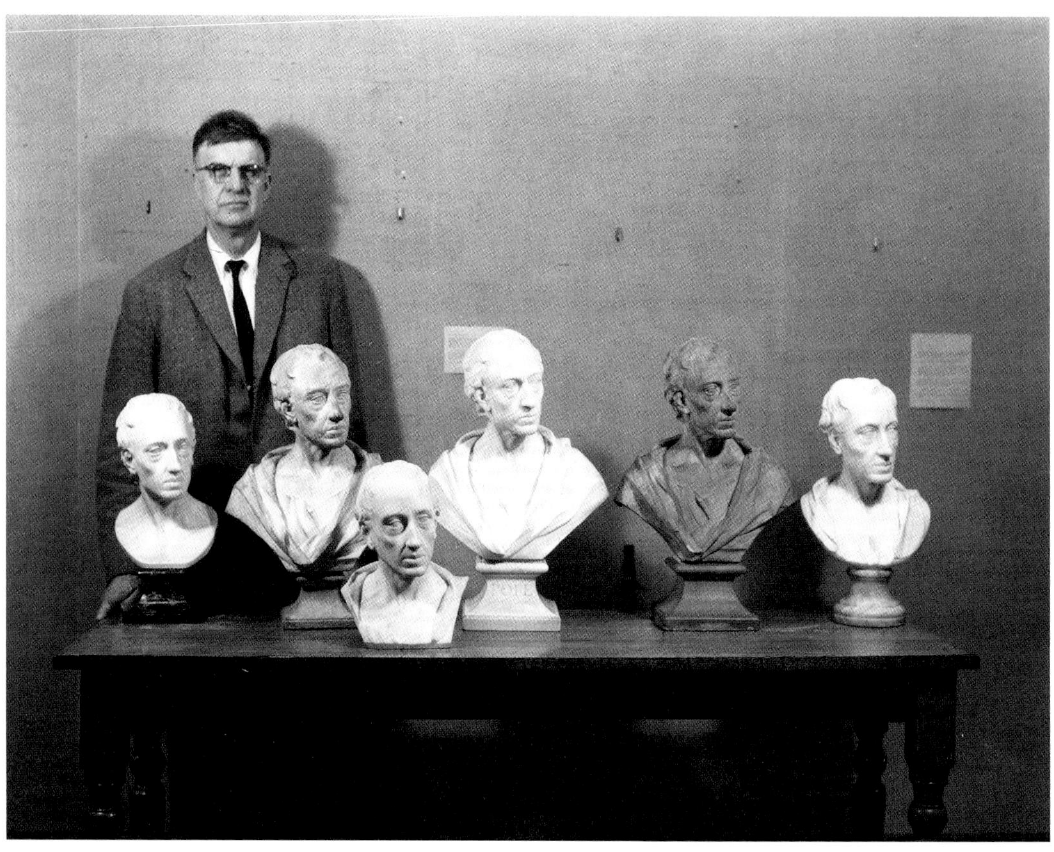

Fig. 16. Anonymous photographer, *William K. Wimsatt*, ca. 1961. Beinecke Rare Book & Manuscript Library, Yale University, The James Marshall and Marie-Louise Osborn Collection

(fig. 16). The eight busts constitute the largest known group of multiples to have been produced in a single sculptor's workshop in the first half of the eighteenth century, but their relationship is complex.[4] Three marbles (dated 1738, 1740, and 1741) represent (in different ways) the head and shoulders rather than the complete bust shown in both the Yale marble and a superb terracotta, now in the collection of Birmingham University's Barber Institute. This last may have been the model seen by George Vertue in June 1741, when he described it as "more like than any other Sculptor has done."[5] A further marble and a plaster (purchased at the sculptor's sale by the British Museum in 1761) were probably made shortly before Roubiliac's death. The juxtaposition of these various versions was made possible by the Center's 2014 exhibition *Fame and Friendship: Pope, Roubiliac, and the Portrait Bust in Eighteenth-Century Britain*. The exhibition was complemented by a technical study and three-dimensional scanning project carried out at Yale's West Campus, allowing the relationship between the busts to be more fully understood.[6] Despite the probability that the terracotta precedes all the marble versions, the smaller busts show considerable variation in details of the hair and even the position of the ears, and only in 1741 in the Yale bust is the model fully and accurately followed.

None of the autograph busts appears to have belonged to Pope himself. The 1740 marble was carved for Pope's friend, the lawyer William Murray, later Earl of Mansfield (fig. 17), and the 1741 marble was acquired by the actor David Garrick, probably in the year when Pope attended one of the actor's performances of *Richard III*.[7] But the early ownership of the Yale bust is uncertain. One confusing feature of this marble is an additional inscription, which not only states that it was made from the life in 1741 but also records both the date of the poet's birth and his death date in 1744, suggesting that it had remained in the workshop until then. In fact, both dates are given wrongly, suggesting it may have been made for (or at least purchased by) an admirer of the poet, rather than a close friend in his circle.

Unlike this larger work, the more intimate scale of the three smaller busts could suggest that these were made for Pope's friends. All three are finished at the back in seemingly arbitrary ways and have idiosyncratic lettering untypical of Roubiliac's later busts. By contrast, the Yale bust is inscribed very regularly, and its back is finished in a manner that from 1741 onward became standard for Roubiliac's marble portraits. It is likely that the Yale bust was produced at a point when Roubiliac's workshop was expanding and he had taken on someone with specialist skills in carving inscriptions. Even if the terracotta of the full bust had been modeled by Roubiliac in 1738, its execution in marble seems not to have happened until 1741, the earlier of the two dates on the Yale bust. It was around this date that the sculptor's practice became more organized and ambitious. The Yale bust thus marks a turning point in Roubiliac's workshop procedures. Around the same time, the replication of busts of popular subjects in a variety of materials, including terracotta and plaster, seems to have become a staple part of Roubiliac's business as a sculptor. The image of Pope offered opportunities. The Yale bust may be seen as a more public image than the earlier smaller busts. It is also a bust in which Roubiliac could show off to the fullest extent his virtuoso qualities as a carver as well as his capacity to use subtle gradations in the handling of the marble surfaces to engage the viewer in a sustained contemplation of the subject represented.

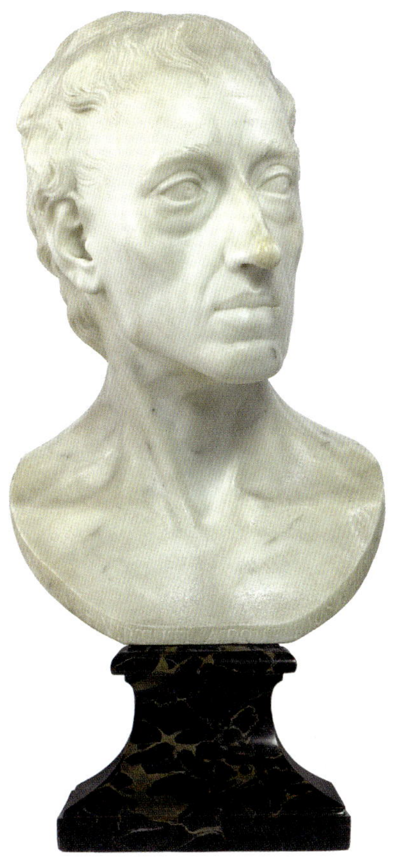

Fig. 17. Louis François Roubiliac, *Alexander Pope*, 1740, marble. Private collection

Notes

1. Voltaire, *Letters Concerning the English Nation*, ed. Nicholas Cronk (Oxford: Oxford Univ. Press, 1994), 113.
2. See William K. Wimsatt, *The Portraits of Alexander Pope* (New Haven and London: Yale Univ. Press, 1965), 223–66.
3. James Prior, *Life of Edmund Malone* (London: Smith, Elder & Co., 1860), 428–29, cited by Wimsatt, *The Portraits of Alexander Pope*, 244.
4. See Malcolm Baker, *The Marble Index: Roubiliac and Sculptural Portraiture in Eighteenth-Century Britain* (New Haven and London: Yale Univ. Press, 2014), 167–73, 261–75; Malcolm Baker, *Fame and Friendship: Pope, Roubiliac, and the Portrait Bust* (Waddesdon Manor: Rothschild Foundation, 2014).
5. See Alexander J. Finberg, ed., *Vertue Note Books*, vol. 3 (Oxford: Printed for the Walpole Society at the University Press, 1934), 105.
6. See *Fame and Friendship: Pope, Roubiliac, and the Portrait Bust in Eighteenth-Century Britain*, exh. cat. (New Haven: Yale Center for British Art, 2014). An interpretation of the relationship of the various versions, based on a detailed comparison of the three-dimensional scans, will be published in an article, currently in preparation, by Malcolm Baker and Chelsea Graham.
7. Malcolm Baker, "Busts and Friendship: The Identity and Context of William Murray's Version of Roubiliac's Bust of Alexander Pope," *Sculpture Journal* 22, no. 2 (2013): 65–76.

Mark Catesby (British, 1682–1749)
"An Thymelaea foliis obtusis; Anseri Bassano &c: The Great Booby," plate 86 from *The Natural History of Carolina, Florida and the Bahama Islands*, vol. 1, second edition (London: C. Marsh, 1754)

Etching and engraving with original hand coloring on medium, moderately textured, cream laid paper, 14⅜ x 20½ in. (36.5 x 52.1 cm)

YALE CENTER FOR BRITISH ART, GIFT OF JOHN D. VIENER, YALE AB 1961, B2011.20.1

Henrietta McBurney

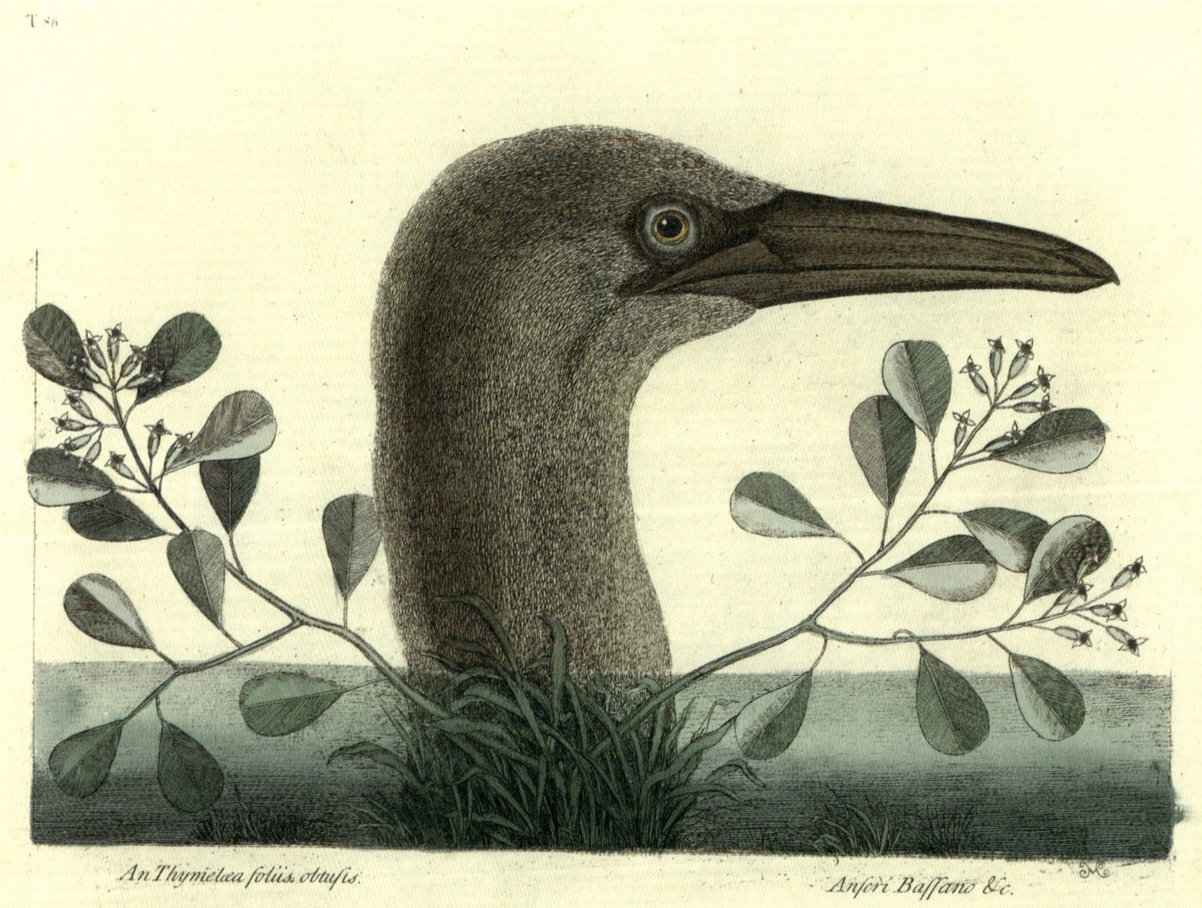

On August 15, 1724, Mark Catesby handed over a consignment of animal and plant specimens to Captain Martin, commanding officer of the *Blandford*, a twenty-gun man-of-war, which was docked at Charleston, South Carolina.[1] The consignment was destined for Catesby's patron in London, the collector and botanist Sir Hans Sloane. In a letter to Sloane packed into one of the cases, Catesby wrote:

> Honourable Sir,
>
> . . . I send now the first half of the Summers collection which I hope will afford you many new plants for many of them are ye same of those distroyed by the Pyrates. The Bird's head in a Box has a Body as big as a goose and web footed. I call it the fisher from it's preying on fish, which it does after the manner of the Kingfisher precipitating it self from on high into the water with great violence and there remaining about a Minute. They are never seen but at Sea Bays and the mouths of large Rivers.[2]

Before preserving and packing up the bird's head, Catesby had made a life-size drawing of it (fig. 18). He had probably found the bird dead or wounded on a river or sea shore in Georgia, recording that he had "several times found [these birds] disabled, and sometimes dead," surmising that they had met "with Sharks, and other large voracious Fishes, that maim and sometimes devour them."[3] Fortunately, this time, the frigate was not attacked by pirates during its long passage back across the Atlantic, and Catesby's consignment reached Sloane some three months later in November 1724. Sloane straightaway entered the new addition in the catalogue of his already spectacular collection of natural and man-made curiosities: "The head of a bird from Mr. Catesby from Carolina called by him the Fisher."[4]

Several years after Catesby's return to London from his four-year collecting expedition to South Carolina and the Bahama Islands, he used his drawing as the model for a plate in his book *The Natural History of Carolina, Florida and the Bahama Islands* (1731–43). This large folio in two volumes, containing two hundred twenty hand-colored etched plates with supporting text, a preface, map, and "An Account of Carolina and the Bahama Islands" took him twenty years to complete. Issued by subscription in eleven parts with twenty plates each, its publication was the culmination of his life's work.

A self-trained artist and naturalist, Catesby was described in 1721 by Dr. William Sherard, another of his patrons, as "A gentleman who designs and paints in watercolours to perfection."[5] From an early age, Catesby had shown a passionate interest in "Plants, and other productions in nature," had sat at the feet of the great naturalist John Ray, and learned about plant collecting from Ray's friend, the apothecary Samuel Dale. During a seven-year stay in Virginia between 1712 and 1719, when he collected and painted plants and birds, he came to the belief that "a clearer Idea may be conceiv'd from the Figures of Animals and Plants in their proper colours, than from the most exact Description without them."[6] On his return to England, his plant collections and paintings came to the notice of Sherard and a group of other naturalists and collectors centered around the Royal Society of London. Sponsored by them, Catesby returned to America, this time to collect and paint the lesser-known natural history of South Carolina and the Bahama Islands.

Short of funds on his return from America, and unable to employ professional engravers to make the plates for his book, he sought help from a leading London printmaker, Joseph Goupy, so that he could learn to etch his drawings himself. Arranging the hundreds of pen-and-ink sketches and watercolors to make up the finished compositions for the copperplates was an exacting process. For the image of the "Great Booby," he first experimented with adding a pen-and-ink outline of a plant to his watercolor; splitting the specimen he had gathered at its base, he drew the two parts of it so that they framed the bird's head. When he came to etch his design, he made the plant appear as if it were growing from the shore by adding a section of seawater and "sedge" leaves along the lower edge of the print.[7] By altering the composition in this way, Catesby ingeniously created the illusion that the viewer is looking between two branches of the shrub at the bird as it surfaces from the water.

The bird can be identified as a juvenile northern gannet, *Morus bassanus*. Catesby decided to name it "The Great Booby" as "it so resembles the Booby [brown booby, *Sula leucogaster*] . . . that I thought the name of Great Booby best agreed with it." Fascinated by the sight of the young birds plunging into rivers and sea inlets after fish, "in the like manner as the Booby does at Sea, continuing under water a considerable time," it seems he never saw the spectacular adult bird, with its mainly white plumage, black face stripe, and black wing tips.[8] Rescuing a dead or injured immature bird, he examined closely its markings and colors:

> These Birds were of a dark brown colour, elegantly spotted with white on their heads, the spots are thick and small, on the neck and breast they are thicker and broader, and on the back thinnest and broadest . . . The feet are black and are shaped like those of a Cormorant.

The plant is identifiable as the white mangrove, *Laguncularia racemosa*. Catesby gathered the specimen from a shrub he found growing "on the rocky shores amongst Sedge" in the Bahama Islands; he gave it the Latin epithet *An Thymelaea foliis obtusis* ("possibly the 'Thymelaea' with blunt leaves").[9]

Catesby is remembered as one of the first naturalist artists to show animals in their native habitats. Although he recorded seeing the "Great Booby" in mainland America, it is possible he also saw it in the Caribbean, where he later found the "Thymelaea." In combining the bird and plant in this plate, Catesby vividly conveys the rich natural environment he experienced in the New World; through balancing science and art, he creates a monumental quality to his image.

Notes

I would like to thank the following people for their advice: Mark Carine, Stephen Harris, Charlie Jarvis, Shepard Krech III, Arthur MacGregor, Serena Marner, Xander Ryan, and Gillian Sutherland.

1. The *Blandford* had been employed in escorting merchant convoys between Charleston and the West Indies since her arrival in Charleston in 1719/20. Captain William Martin (ca. 1696–1756) served as her captain and commanding officer between 1724 and 1726/7.
2. British Library, Sloane MS 4047, ff. 212–13.
3. Mark Catesby, *The Natural History of Carolina, Florida, and the Bahama Islands*, 2 vols., second edition (London: C. Marsh, 1754), 1:86. While Catesby noted that the birds "frequent the Rivers and Sea Coast of Florida," the area he explored was later to become the northeastern corner of Georgia. Regarding the production of the second edition of *The Natural History*, "seen through the press" rather than "revised by" George Edwards, see: Leslie K. Overstreet, "The publication of Mark Catesby's *The natural history of Carolina, Florida and the Bahama islands*," in *The Curious Mister Catesby: A "Truly Ingenious" Naturalist Explores New Worlds*, eds., E. Charles Nelson and David J. Elliott (Athens: Univ. of Georgia Press, 2015), 166.
4. Natural History Museum, London, Sloane's MS catalogue, "Fossils V: Fishes, Birds, Quadrupeds," f. 193, no. 575.
5. Sherard to the botanist Richard Richardson, *Extracts from the Literary and Scientific Correspondence of Richard Richardson*, ed. Dawson Turner (Yarmouth: Charles Sloman, 1835), 157–58.
6. Catesby, *Natural History*, preface, vi-vii.
7. Catesby's inspiration for the "sedge" was derived from Francis Barlow's clumps of bulrushes found in several of his etched illustrations to *Aesop's Fables* (1703), a book of which Catesby owned a copy.
8. Juvenile birds can wander from the breeding stacks at least as far, if not in some cases farther, than the adults (Shepard Krech III, pers. comm.).
9. Hundreds of the plant specimens, which Catesby preserved and sent back to his patrons, survive to this day in the herbaria of Sloane and Sherard. See http://folio.furman.edu/projects/botanicacarolini-ana/Parallels.html and https://herbaria.plants.ox.ac.uk/bol/Catesby; this plant, however, does not appear to be among them.

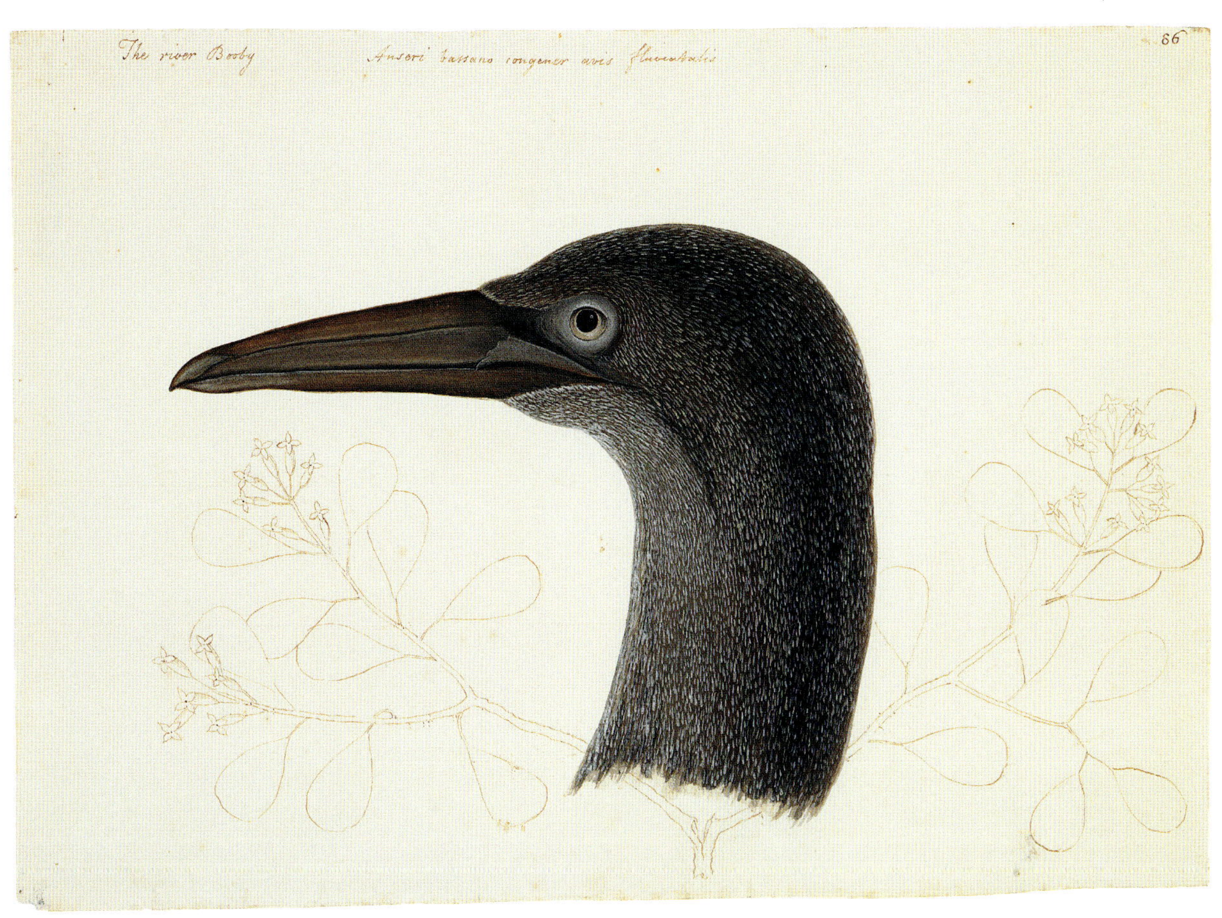

Fig. 18. Mark Catesby, *The Great Booby and An Thymeleoea foliis obtusis*, watercolor and bodycolor with outline of white mangrove plant in pen and ink. The Royal Collection Trust, London

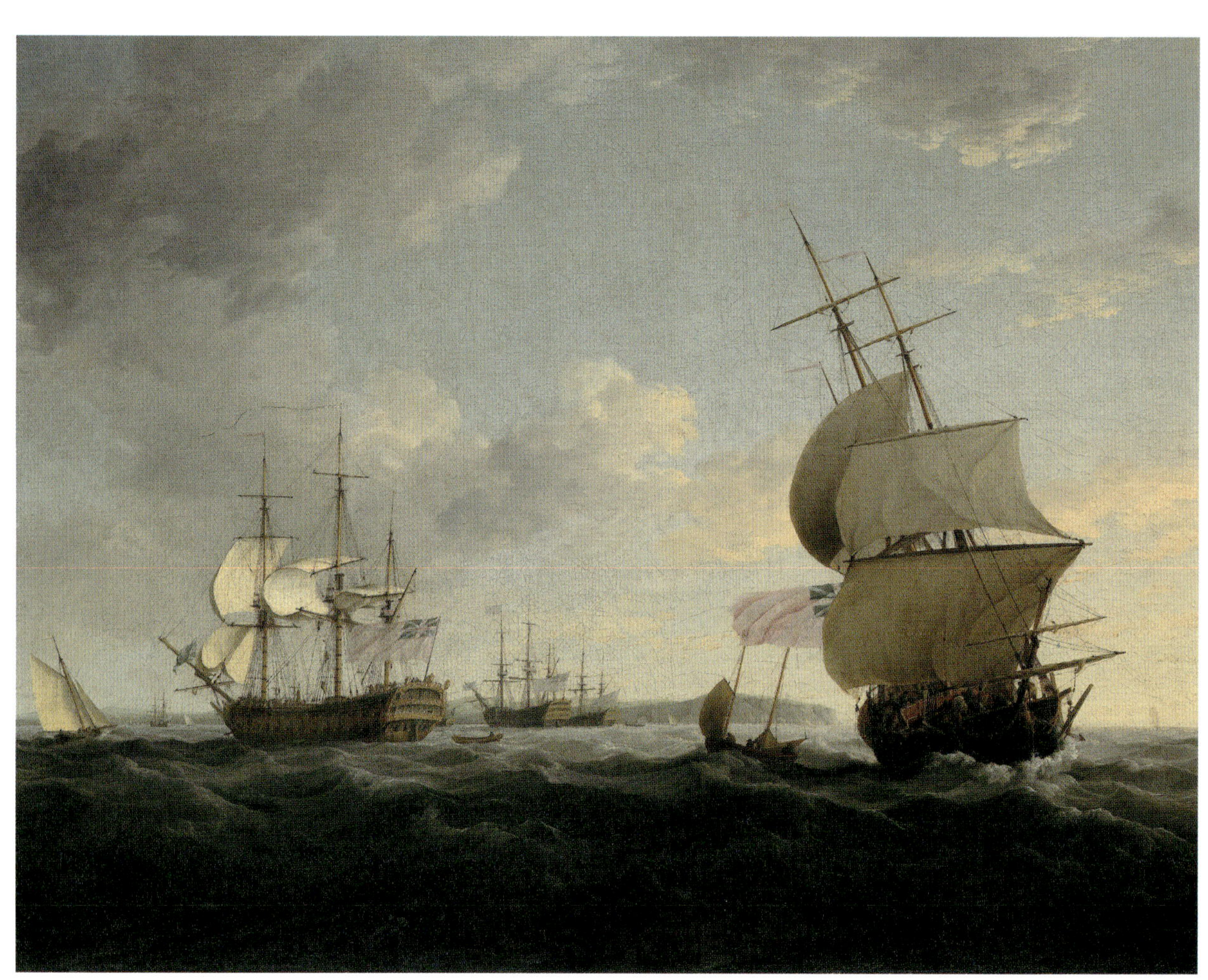

Charles Brooking (British, 1723–1759)
Shipping in the English Channel, ca. 1755

Oil on canvas, 35½ x 46⅜ in. (90.2 x 117.8 cm). Signed lower left: "C. Brooking."

YALE CENTER FOR BRITISH ART, PAUL MELLON COLLECTION. B1981.25.65

Eleanor Hughes

There can be few more confident or optimistic images of Britain's place in the mid-eighteenth-century world than Charles Brooking's painting known as *Shipping in the English Channel*. Dominating the foreground, a ship of the Royal Navy plunges toward the viewer as it leaves its anchorage on the southeast coast of England, an emblem of the maritime sinews of power that acquired, policed, and maintained the overseas territories of empire. The painting demonstrates, too, the extraordinary abilities of an artist about whom little is known but who was clearly at the height of his own powers when this work was created.

Brooking is assumed to be the son of Charles Brooking, a painter-decorator who worked at Greenwich Hospital between 1729 and 1736, from whom the younger Brooking could have learned technical aspects of painting.[1] His contemporary Edward Edwards stated that Brooking "was bred in some department of the dockyard at Deptford," and Joseph Farington wrote that he "had been much at sea."[2] Until the early 1750s Brooking seems primarily to have painted on spec for a picture dealer, and on at least one occasion worked as an illustrator. In his introduction to *An Essay towards a Natural History of the Corallines, and Other Marine Productions of the Like Kind, Commonly Found on the Coasts of Great Britain and Ireland* . . . , the botanist and zoologist John Ellis wrote: "In August 1752, I went to the Island of Sheppey on the coast of Kent; and took with me Mr. Brooking, a celebrated Painter of sea-pieces, to make the proper Drawings for me."[3] The expedition aimed at a study of corallines, then understood to be plant-like animals that grow on the shells of mollusks. Brooking and Ellis were assisted in their study by "a very Commodious Microscope of Mr Cuff's, the optician in Fleet Street"—presumably John Cuff, sitter in a portrait by Johan Zoffany now in the Royal Collection.[4] Brooking's illustrations for Ellis, his earliest known commission, gesture to the array of activities undertaken by marine painters in the competitive eighteenth-century art market; the skills of observation and delineation that defined marine painting were well suited in service to natural history.[5]

Aged twenty-nine at the time of the expedition, Brooking was then by no means "celebrated"; however, by the time Ellis's book was published in 1755, he had been rescued from obscurity by Taylor White, treasurer of the Foundling Hospital, the institution established by Thomas Coram (an ex-merchant sea captain) for the protection of abandoned children. White is said to have spotted the marine painter's work in the window of an unscrupulous picture dealer who, on receipt of Brooking's paintings, obliterated the artist's signature to preserve his own role as middleman. White, "being struck with the merits of some sea-pieces, desired to know [the artist's] name; but . . . was only told that if he pleased they would procure any that he might require from the same painter." On an occasion when the dealer was away, the dealer's wife received a painting from Brooking and put it

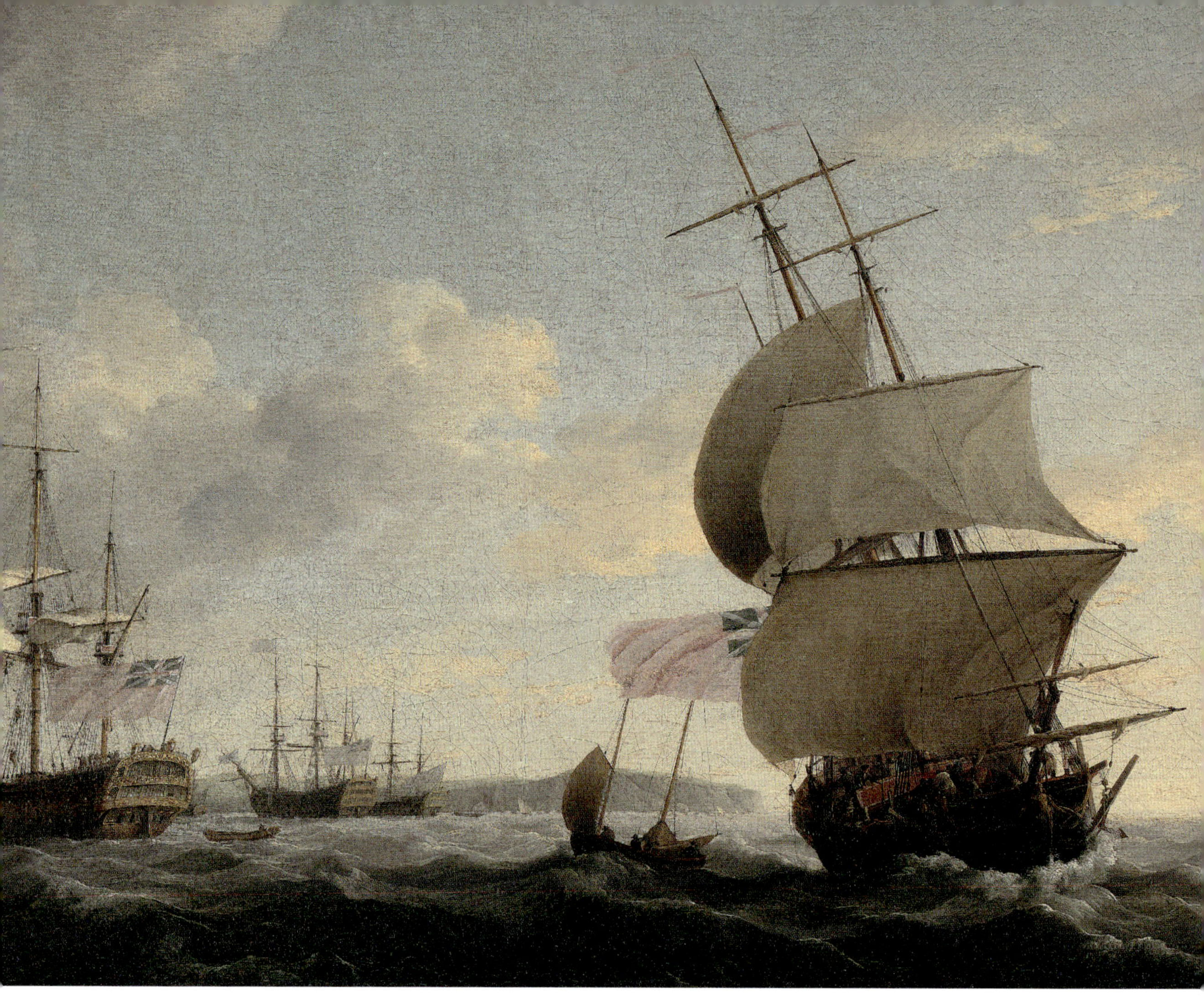

Detail of *Shipping in the English Channel*

in the window without removing the signature. White saw it, "advertised for the artist to meet him," and "from that time became his friend and patron."[6]

The majority of the works Brooking produced until this point were presumably small, cabinet-scale pictures, of which there are eleven in the Center's collections. They include one of eight known versions of a composition that Brooking adapted in 1754 to create, at White's behest, a painting for the Foundling Hospital, part of a scheme initiated in the 1740s by William Hogarth to promote native artists and to attract potential supporters to the hospital.[7] The marine painters Peter Monamy and Samuel Scott were among the first artists to agree to contribute works, along with Thomas Gainsborough, Allan Ramsay, Francis Hayman, Sir Joshua Reynolds, and Richard Wilson; each was in turn elected a governor and guardian of the hospital. Brooking's enormous and magnificent canvas, conceived as a pendant to Monamy's contribution, is the only one of the eighteenth-century marine paintings to remain at the Foundling Museum.[8] Although a smaller picture, *Shipping in the English Channel* is no less monumental in its depiction of British naval power.

Along with Monamy and Scott, Brooking was one of a generation of marine painters who sought to forge new ways of representing British maritime subjects in the wake of the prolific and influential Willem van de Veldes (father and son), Dutch marine painters who had settled in London in the 1670s. Their works circulated among British artists in the eighteenth century, providing models of composition, accurate draftsmanship, and painterly technique. Compared to his contemporaries, Brooking made few images of identifiable vessels or actions; the majority of his works are "generic" seascapes that tend toward more intense explorations of mood and atmosphere. Dating from 1754 or later, *Shipping in the English Channel* expresses a mood of optimism that may be reflective of the artist's shift in fortunes.

The setting of the picture can be identified as the Downs, a safe anchorage for shipping, sheltered to the north and west by the English coast, and to the east by the ten-mile-long sandbank known as the Goodwin Sands. The ship at right has just safely navigated the hazardous, shifting shoals with the assistance of a knowledgeable pilot, who has been dropped off in the boat to the left of the ship. A two-decker on the left may be about to undertake the same operation in reverse, picking up a pilot from the vessel entering the frame on the left in order to proceed to the anchorage. This narrative is conveyed through a wealth of detail. On the deck of the foreground ship, sailors work to hoist its sails, which are filling with the breeze just as the bow wave begins to froth with the ship's forward motion. On board the two-decker at left, sailors in the rigging work to take in sails. In the next instant, the ships will have pulled apart, one returning to its home base, the other departing for some destination within British imperial interests—the Mediterranean? North America? The Caribbean? As in many of Brooking's paintings, vessels are deployed in a tightly formulated rhythmic arrangement across the picture plane, the composition creating, in tension with its unfolding narrative, what the art historian Basil Taylor called "a most precarious equipoise, as if a film, arrested at the point of a well-designed frame, is about to dissolve into the fluidity of motion." The whole is illuminated by Brooking's evocation of early-morning sunlight, "at once scrupulous and lyrical," that both reveals ships and shoreline in all their accurate delineation and, shining through sea haze and spray, reduces far-off vessels to shadows on the horizon.[9] The quality of light lends a sense of golden possibility to the enterprise undertaken by the foreground ship as it sets out to sea, and a sense of singularity—even majesty—to an otherwise unremarkable scene of arrival and departure that would have been endlessly repeated through the activities of the eighteenth-century navy.

Notes

1. See David Cordingly, "Charles Brooking (1723–1759)," *Oxford Dictionary of National Biography*, Oxford Univ. Press, 2004: http://dx.doi.org/10.1093/ref:odnb/3562 (accessed April 27, 2012); Basil Taylor, *Charles Brooking, 1723–1759: Paintings, Drawings and Engravings*, exh. cat., Aldeburgh Festival, Bristol City Art Gallery (London: Westerham Press, 1966), 6; Edward H. H. Archibald, *Dictionary of Sea Painters* (Woodbridge, UK: Antique Collectors' Club, 1980), 73.
2. Edward Edwards, *Anecdotes of Painters*. . . (London: Leigh and Sotheby, 1808), 5; Joseph Farington, *The Diary of Joseph Farington*, eds. Kenneth Garlick and Angus Macintyre, 16 vols. (New Haven and London: Yale Univ. Press, 1978 onward), 3:766.
3. John Ellis, *An Essay towards a Natural History of the Corallines, and Other Marine Productions of the Like Kind, Commonly Found on the Coasts of Great Britain and Ireland*. . . (London: Printed for the author and sold by A. Millar, 1755), vii.
4. Ellis, *Natural History of the Corallines*, viii. See Martin Postle, ed., *Johan Zoffany RA: Society Observed*, exh. cat. (New Haven: Yale Center for British Art; London: Royal Academy of Arts, in association with Yale Univ. Press, 2011), 227–28.
5. See Eleanor Hughes, "Nicholas Pocock: Accuracy and Agency," in Hughes, ed., *Spreading Canvas: Eighteenth-Century British Marine Painting* (New Haven and London: Yale Univ. Press, 2016), 63–87.
6. Edwards, *Anecdotes of Painters*, 5–6.
7. *An English Flagship under Easy Sail in a Moderate Breeze*, ca. 1750, oil on canvas, 14½ x 22½ in. (36.8 x 57.2 cm), Yale Center for British Art, Paul Mellon Collection, B1981.25.66. Other versions of this composition are now at Tate, the National Maritime Museum, and in private collections.
8. *A Flagship before the Wind under Easy Sail*, 1754, oil on canvas, 70 x 123 in. (177.8 x 312.4 cm); see Hughes, *Spreading Canvas*, cat. 40.
9. Taylor, *Charles Brooking*, 4.

Studio of Francis Harwood (British, 1726/7–1783; active in Italy)
Bust of a Man, ca. 1758

Black limestone on a yellow marble socle, overall: 28 x 20 x 10½ in. (71.1 x 50.8 x 26.7 cm)

YALE CENTER FOR BRITISH ART, PAUL MELLON COLLECTION, B2006.14.11

Cyra Levenson

Boxer, king, warrior, noble savage, lover, blackamoor, bust of a man, bust of a black man, boyfriend. Brave, majestic, sensuous, gruesome. In the two hundred sixty years since Francis Harwood created this work, it has been called many things. Two versions of this bust are known: as well as the work at the Yale Center for British Art, a second bust is in the collection of the J. Paul Getty Museum. While Harwood has not been ranked as a major figure in the history of British art, these two busts have received considerable attention, particularly since 2011 when the Center's version appeared on the cover of a volume in the groundbreaking series *The Image of the Black in Western Art: From the "Age of Discovery" to the Age of Abolition.*[1] In the same year, artist Ken Gonzales-Day published *Profiled*, a book whose cover featured a photograph of the Getty version, and then reproduced this image on a billboard over a freeway in Los Angeles.[2] In 2015, the Center mounted the exhibition *Figures of Empire: Slavery and Portraiture in Eighteenth-Century Atlantic Britain*, which prominently featured the Harwood bust within the exhibition space. Why was so much attention paid to these two busts all at once after years of relative obscurity? What is it that not only scholars and artists but also the general viewing public want, and perhaps even need, from these two objects today?

Speaking in 1861, Frederick Douglass, the great African American reformer and abolitionist, argued that a photographic portrait can produce a revenant, or one who returns from the dead. As Laura Wexler describes,

> The *Revenant* is an effect of "liveness" produced over time. It requires images that repeat, or return, and to which *we* may also return multiple times to try to comprehend the intentions of their makers and what has happened to the fulfillment of their aims. The *Revenant* belongs as much to the future as to the past, as we project persistence of the liveliness that it inserts into the historical record. And thus it is in part a political concept . . . to serve the ends of freedom.[3]

We might say that Harwood's busts have become revenants. Facts, such as names, dates, and life stories, cannot be recuperated for those who were systematically made invisible by the transatlantic slave trade, flattened in the archive into statistics. While we will likely never know whether the living model who posed for Harwood was enslaved or free, the busts allow contemporary viewers an affective encounter with a three-dimensional life-size embodiment of an eighteenth-century black man who has returned, and who allows them to dream a life story. Marcia Pointon has argued that the power of portraiture lies in its ability to show an "absence made present."[4] For Douglass, the absence or death is not just an individual death but the social death of slavery, and the busts must still be read within the context of the slave trade. They were created by

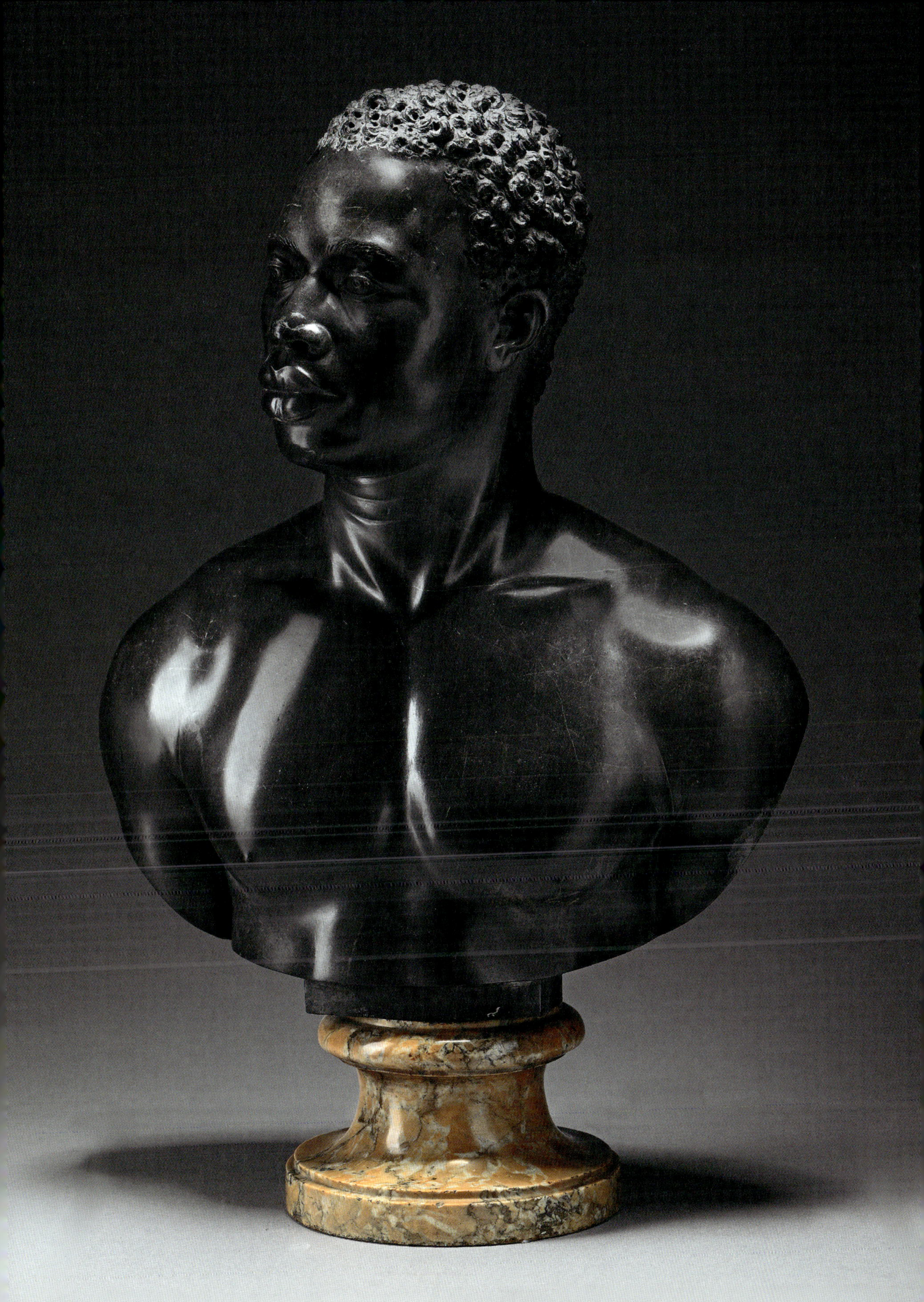

a British artist working on commission from British grand tourists at a moment when the culture and economy of that nation was inextricably bound to the transatlantic slave trade. Harwood's busts seem to have the power to reanimate today.

As Gonzales-Day describes it, encountering the Harwood bust at the Getty for the first time was like experiencing a kind of social death. Placed near a passageway in a room of primarily classical white marble sculptures, the bust was the only depiction of a person of color in the space. As a Getty fellow, Gonzales-Day watched visitors walk by the bust routinely without stopping to look on their way to a nearby garden with a grand view. His photograph and subsequent billboard depicts the Harwood bust in profile, eye to eye with a blackened bronze bust of a classicized Greek male figure, also in profile. They face off across a blank white space that effectively reanimates them. Harwood's bust returns from the dead, larger than life, revealing the "scope of human similarity across difference."[5] The photograph turns the bust from object into subject, returning a life force to it in the process. As Gonzales-Day describes,

> I wanted the image to remind us that each work was the result of physical acts, created in different moments, which when brought together, might add up to more than a literal description of light on stone in a still evolving narrative that is very much tied to the present: tied to what is visible, and what can never be visible.[6]

How do we challenge ourselves to see the unnamed black figures painted and sculpted during the eighteenth century as individuals with histories despite their anonymity?

The *Figures of Empire* exhibition attempted to tackle this question by examining the ways in which Britons negotiated their relationship with slavery through portraiture. The Harwood bust was placed centrally in the gallery among approximately sixty paintings, sculptures, prints, drawings, and decorative objects drawn primarily from the Center's collections. Most of the black figures in the exhibition were portrayed in paintings alongside white sitters, often as anonymous subjects. In portraiture, qualities that eighteenth-century Britons valued—freedom, whiteness, and refinement—were imagined in opposition to the bondage and blackness of those who arrived in Britain from Africa or the Caribbean as slaves. The physical centrality of the Harwood bust provided a different frame of reference for viewing the other objects in the exhibition space, creating new dialogues between visitors and works of art. Motivated by the idea that a portrait might be defined less in terms of likeness, or even a particularized representation, and more as an encounter between sitter and artist—and image and viewer—the exhibition challenged its visitors to consider all the figures depicted as subjects with histories, and as people whose lives were shaped by Britain's imperial world.

At the center of the exhibition, the Harwood bust asked viewers to imagine a life story for the figure while respecting the limits of what we can know with respect to the lives of those who were enslaved.[7] Viewers were invited to engage with the bust. The combination of both violence and resistance (as embodied in the scar on the forehead), the resolutely square shoulders, and the dignity of facial expression, the pose, scale, and overall gravitas of the figure seem to draw viewers and scholars alike to it today. Somehow, in that space, it became an object one could look at, live with, and even pose next to without feeling implicated in the dehumanizing past of Atlantic slavery. The life-size scale and solid, weighty presence of the marble bust create a different kind of human encounter, an implied personhood registered by our human senses as such. The bust also became the catalyst for a series of revelatory connections made by viewers linking our racial present and our slavery past.[8]

Douglass argued that "rightly viewed, the whole soul of man is a sort of picture gallery," and that photography—and, perhaps, all forms of portraiture—could bring these "thought pictures"

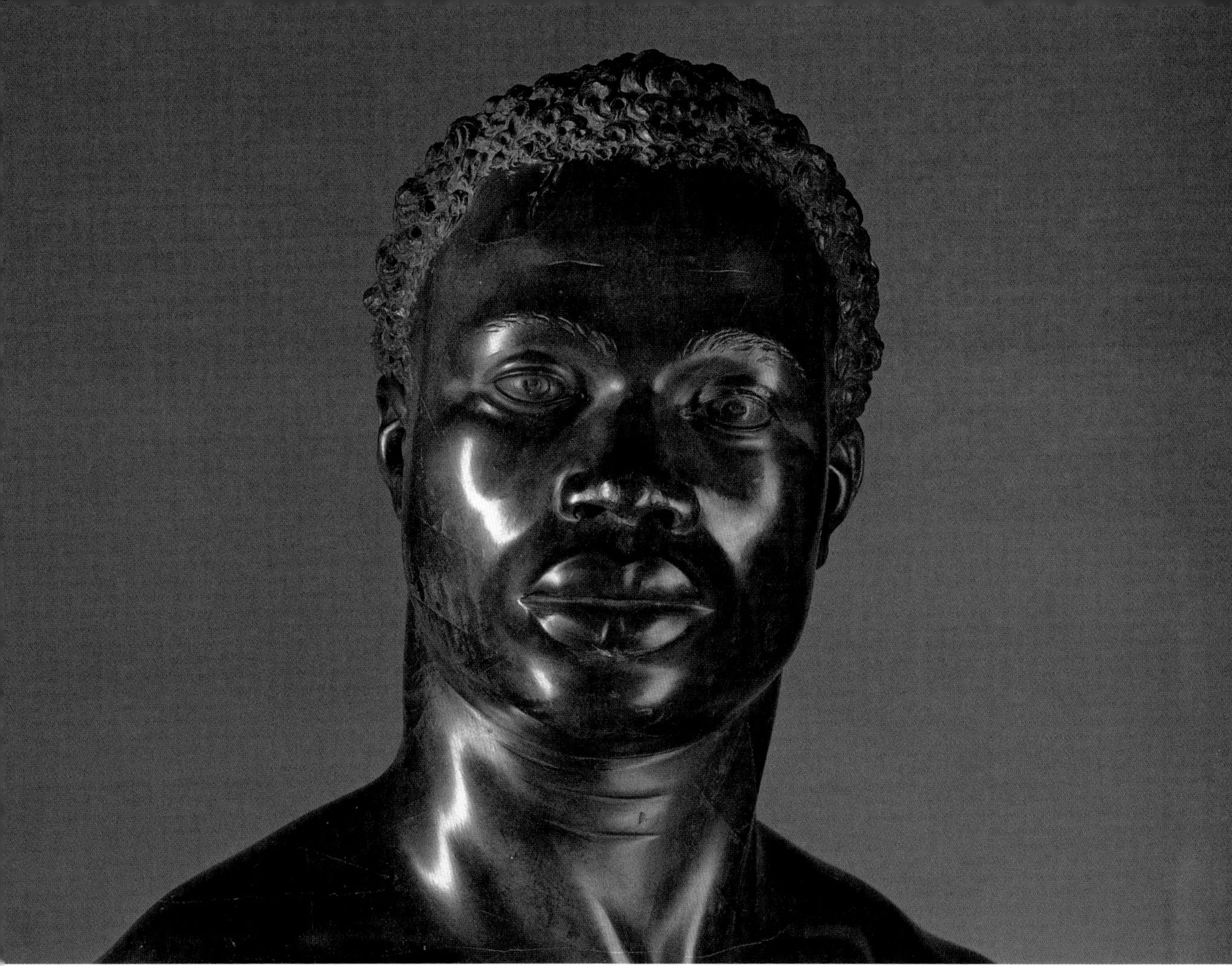

to light, while also allowing more people to fashion their self-image so as to broaden the objectivity with which we can see and understand each other. Representations of enslaved individuals in eighteenth-century portraiture, be it sculpture, painting, or photography, ultimately fail to dehumanize their subjects and instead allow us to see individuals in relationship to others and in negotiation with power. Harwood's bust and model have returned to view, *revenir*, like a ghost or a dream, participating now in a twenty-first-century conversation about race. A continued interrogation of the way we see those negotiations with power is critical if we are to accomplish Douglass's task set forth over one hundred and fifty years ago.

Notes

1. David Bindman and Henry Louis Gates Jr., eds., *The Image of the Black in Western Art, Vol. III: From the "Age of Discovery" to the Age of Abolition; Part 3: The Eighteenth Century* (Cambridge, MA: Harvard Univ. Press, 2011).
2. Ken Gonzales-Day, *Profiled* (Los Angeles: Wallis Annenberg Photography Department, Los Angeles County Museum of Art, 2011).
3. Laura Wexler, "A More Perfect Likeness," in *Pictures and Progress: Early Photography and the Making of African American Identity*, eds. Maurice O. Williams and Shawn Michelle Smith (Durham, NC: Duke Univ. Press, 2012), 33.
4. Marcia Pointon, *Portrayal and the Search for Identity* (London: Reaktion Books, 2013).
5. Chi-ming Yang, Cyra Levenson, and Ken Gonzales-Day, "Haptic Blackness: The Double Life of an 18th-century Bust," *British Art Studies*, no. 1 (November 2015), https://doi.org/10.17658/issn.2058-5462/issue-01/harwood/000.
6. Yang et al., "Haptic Blackness."
7. See Saidiya V. Hartman, "Venus in Two Acts," *Small Axe* 12, no. 2 (June 2008): 1–14.
8. See Cyra Levenson, Slavery and Portraiture in Eighteenth-Century Atlantic Britain, interactive.britishart.yale.edu/slavery-and-portraiture/timeline.

Richard Wilson RA (British, 1712/13–1782; active in Italy, 1750–1756)
Kew Gardens: The Pagoda and Palladian Bridge, 1762

Oil on canvas, 18¾ x 28¾ in. (47.6 x 73 cm)

YALE CENTER FOR BRITISH ART, PAUL MELLON COLLECTION, B1976.7.172

Joanna Marschner

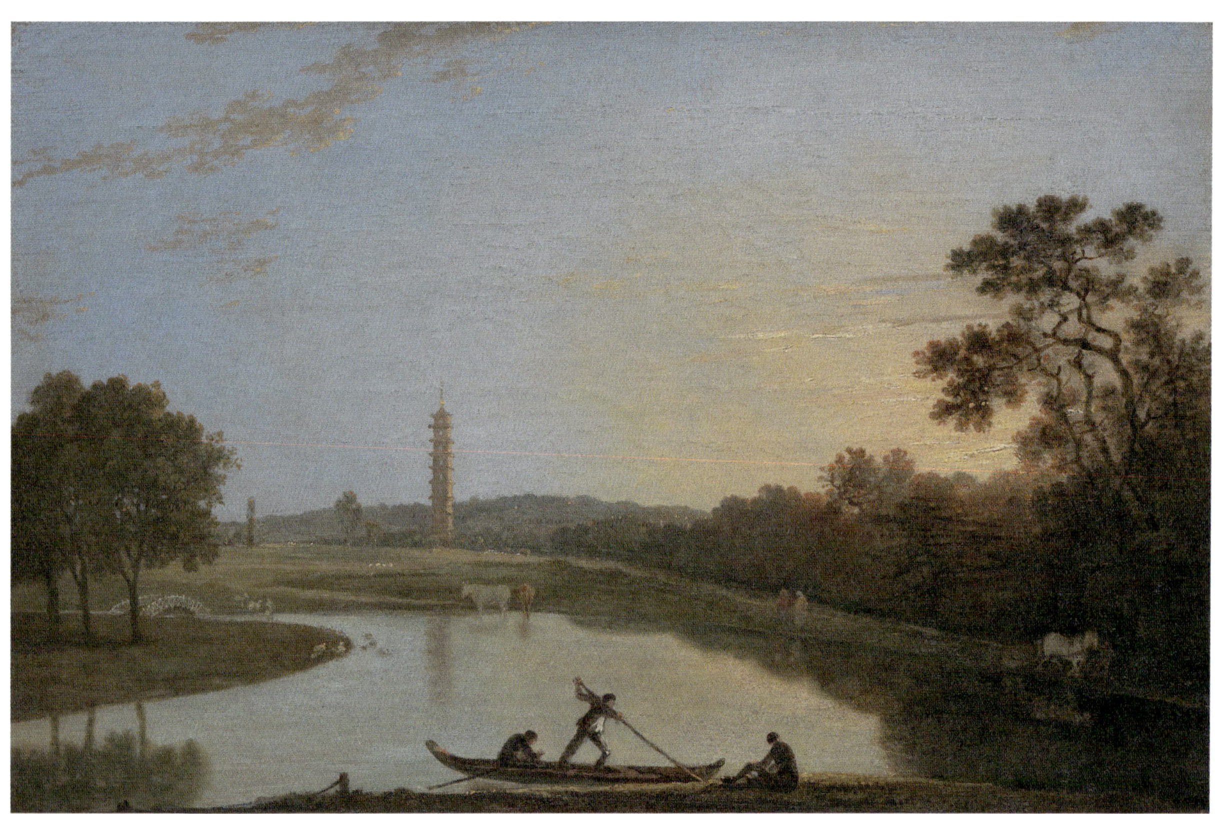

According to Benjamin Booth, a leading collector of Richard Wilson's work in the late eighteenth century, *Kew Gardens: The Pagoda and Palladian Bridge*, and its companion work *The Ruined Arch in Kew Gardens*, were painted with the ambition to secure the young King George III as patron.[1] This was not Wilson's first attempt to attract a royal client. However, none of his early works in which he prominently depicted Frederick, Prince of Wales, George's father, or the attractive small-scale version of his portrait of Francis Ayscough, a royal tutor, with Frederick's sons Prince George and Prince Edward—possibly produced with a royal purchaser in mind—proved appealing.[2] Nonetheless, by 1760, with a growing circle of influential friends and a building reputation after the recent sale of *The Destruction of the Children of Niobe* to Frederick's brother, Prince William Augustus, Duke of Cumberland, he took new confidence.[3] He selected a subject likely to be alluring: views across the gardens of the White House at Kew, the favorite home of Princess Augusta of Saxe-Gotha, Frederick's widow and mother of the new King.

Frederick had taken on the lease of the estate at Kew in 1730. Located on the banks of the Thames, a short distance from Richmond Lodge, the summer residence of his parents, King George II and Queen Caroline, his choice may have been led by a desire to ease tensions in his fractured family. His efforts were spectacularly unsuccessful, and aware that visual and experiential aspects of court life could carry political messages, he started to embellish and extend house and garden to become a gathering place for the politically disenfranchised and socially aspirant young generation. After Frederick's death in 1751, Augusta recast the design for the garden. In this she was encouraged by John Stuart, third Earl of Bute, her late husband's Lord of the Bedchamber, whom, in 1755, she had asked to serve as tutor to her eldest son, Prince George. The project was facilitated by Swedish-born architect William Chambers, who with Bute's encouragement was appointed, in 1757, to teach the Prince architecture.

By 1763, when Chambers published *Plans, Elevations, Sections, and Perspective Views of the Gardens and Buildings at Kew in Surry* (fig. 19), a new infrastructure was set, and "what was once a desert is now an Eden."[4] Behind the house, lawns extended south to a lake cut with irregular contour to give the impression of greater size. Beyond the lake there were views over more lawns to a wilderness, thickly planted with trees. A belt of shrubs and trees, cut through with meandering paths, was planted around the perimeter of the estate, disguising the boundary. Preexisting stands of trees were cleverly incorporated to suggest that the new garden was more established than it actually was.

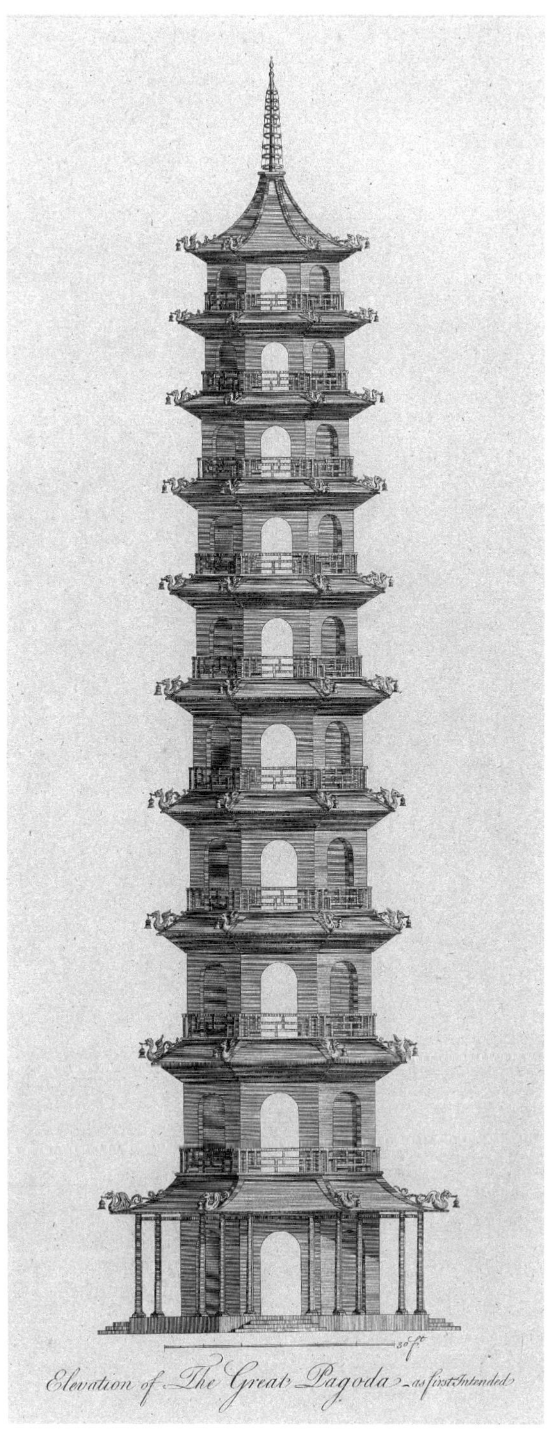

Fig. 19. William Chambers, "Great Pagoda as first intended," plate 23 from *Plans, Elevations, Sections, and Perspective Views of the Gardens and Buildings at Kew in Surry* (London: J. Haberkorn, 1763). Yale Center for British Art, Paul Mellon Collection

Set within the encircling belt of trees were many little buildings, often of theatrical, flimsy construction, in styles symbolic of British imperial ambition, as well as a botanic garden, aviary, and menagerie, into which the living appropriations from that territorial expansion were drawn. For Prince George, the garden also served as an extension of the schoolroom in which his academic exercises in architecture could be practically realized. Wilson, a friend of Chambers after their meeting in Rome, depicts the Palladian Bridge, remarkable for being constructed over one night, "by torchlight," as a surprise present for Augusta, and the pagoda, set in the wilderness at the farthest reach of the garden.[5] Knots of laborers and cattle provide foreground interest, and the whole scene is bathed in rosy evening light, in the manner of Claude Lorrain—the style favored by many of the artists with whom Wilson had studied in Rome.[6] Despite its beauty, the painting did not find a royal buyer (it was, however, copied as an engraving in 1789 by William Russell Birch, thus reaching a broad viewership; see pp. 92–95).

Booth suggests that had a royal client wanted a landscape painting in the Italian Grand Manner, there were more-established artists to consider.[7] As topographical record, the painting fell short too: after the model of fellow Rome-based artists, Wilson had manipulated the scene to draw the bridge and pagoda artificially into the same view. The pagoda, which may still have been under construction as the painting was made, was depicted with straight sides and proportions following models illustrated in the travel literature of China then available.[8] Had the ambition at Kew been grounded simply in the contemporary fashion for Chinese exoticism in the garden, this simplified image might have served. However, it did not capture the actual beauty and ingenuity of the pagoda, nor its truth to Chinese examples. Chambers, though undoubtedly influenced by travel writing, and by the works of British garden theorists that touched upon Chinese landscape philosophy, had as a young man, in 1733–34 and 1748–49, traveled to Canton in the service of the Swedish East India Company, and later, in 1757, he published *Designs of Chinese Buildings, Furniture, Dresses, Machines, and Utensils*, which included engravings drawn more immediately from Chinese originals.[9] Chambers's pagoda, 163 feet tall, had 10 stories of diminishing diameter, incorporating many technological innovations; the roofs were covered with iron plates enameled and varnished by Roterman and Bolton, on the corners of which perched carved dragons enameled with iridescent finish.[10]

Most importantly, perhaps, Wilson's serene Italianate vision for Kew did not equate with the vision of its creators. Chambers, in his essay "On the Art of Laying out Gardens among the Chinese," speaks of the visitor experiencing a garden as a series of episodes, variously "pleasing, horrid and enchanted."[11] The poet Henry Jones uses the dramaturgy of travel writing as he describes Kew's paths "stretching forward in fairy maze."[12] The five paintings Augusta commissioned in 1760 from Johann Jakob Schalch to record her garden (see fig. 20) reveal a far more picturesque, romantic, and emotional intention behind its making.[13] However, Wilson's painting has a place in the development of his pioneering landscape style. In the mature artist, the influence of his Roman experience would give way to a new delight in the depiction of the landscape of his homeland, drawing meaning directly from its individuality and particularities.

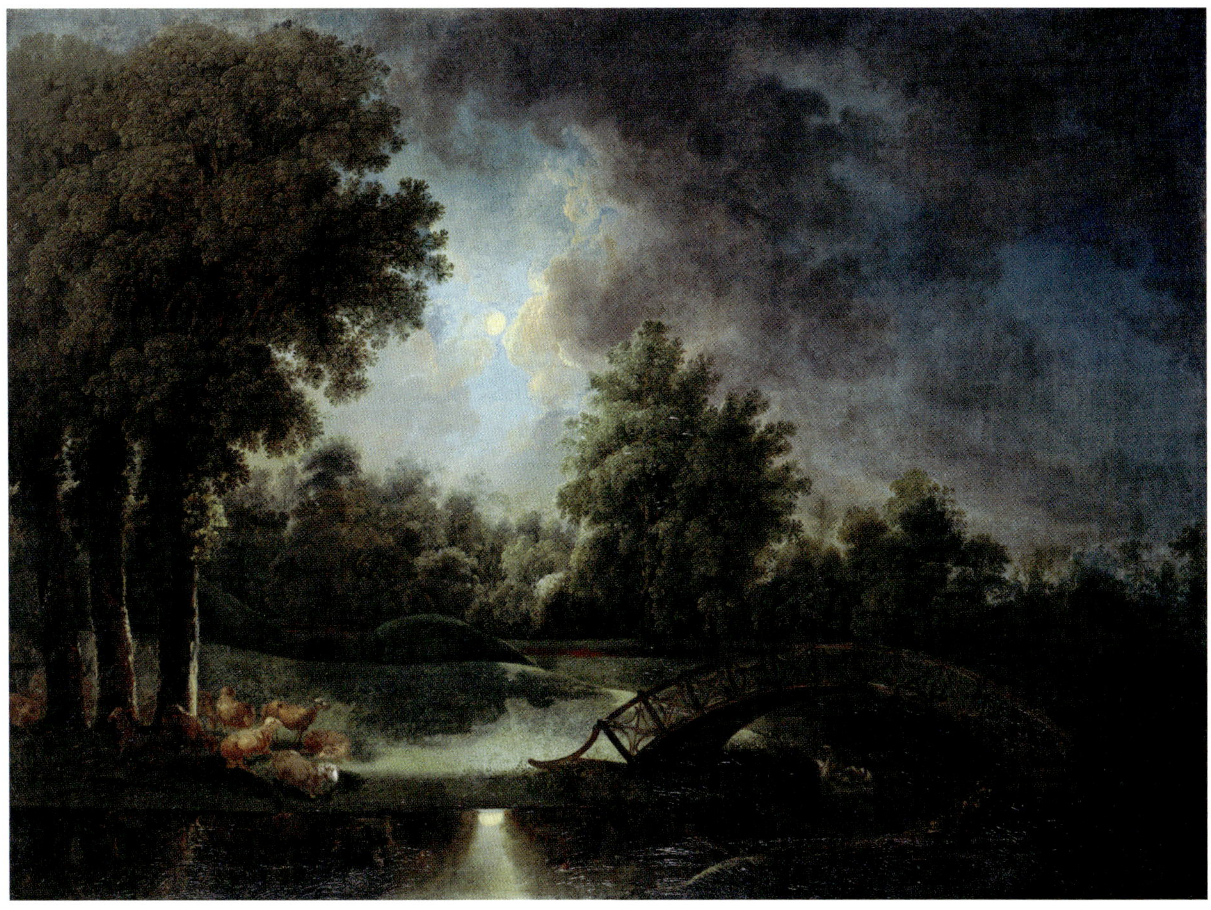

Fig. 20. Johann Jakob Schalch, *The Gardens at Kew by Moonlight*, 1760, oil on canvas, 30 x 41 in. (76.1 x 104.2 cm). The Royal Collection Trust, London

Notes

1. Benjamin Booth, manuscript notes, document 4, Brinsley Ford Collection. Richard Wilson, *The Ruined Arch in Kew Gardens*, ca. 1761–62, Brinsley Ford Collection, London, BB18.
2. Attributed to Richard Wilson, *View of Carlton House, with a Royal Party in the Grounds*, ca. 1732–36, Tate Britain, N05560; Richard Wilson, *The Hall of the Inner Temple after the Fire of 4th January 1737*, ca. 1737, Tate Britain, N02984; Richard Wilson, *Francis Ayscough with the Prince of Wales (later King George III) and Edward Augustus, Duke of York and Albany*, ca. 1749, National Portrait Gallery, NPG 1165; small version: Yale Center for British Art, Paul Mellon Collection, B1981.25.689.
3. Yale Center for British Art, Paul Mellon Collection, B1977.14.81.
4. William Chambers, *Plans, Elevations, Sections, and Perspective Views of the Gardens and Buildings at Kew in Surry* (London: J. Haberkorn, 1763), 2.
5. Chambers, *Plans, Elevations, Sections*, 6.
6. Compare: Claude Lorrain, *Pastoral Landscape with the Flight into Egypt*, 1663, Museo Nacional Thyssen-Bornemisza, Madrid, 226 (1966.3).
7. Booth, manuscript notes.
8. See Johannes Nieuhof et al., *An Embassy from the East-India Company of the United Provinces, to the Grand Tartar Cham, Emperour of China . . .*, trans. John Ogilby (London: John Macock, 1669), illustration of Canton opposite p. 38.
9. William Temple, *Upon the Gardens of Epicurus . . .*, 1685, ed. Albert Forbes Sieveking (London: Chatto and Windus, 1908), 53; Joseph Addison, *Spectator*, no. 414 (June 25, 1712): 550; William Chambers, *Designs of Chinese Buildings, Furniture, Dresses, Machines, and Utensils* (London: 1757), 2.
10. Royal Academy of Arts, London, Add. MS. 55507.
11. Chambers, *Designs of Chinese Buildings*, 15.
12. Henry Jones, *Kew Gardens: a poem* (London: J. Browne, 1767), 43.
13. Royal Academy of Arts, London, Add. MS. 55465. The five paintings are held by the Royal Collection Trust, London: RCIN 403514, 403515, 403516, 403517, 503419.

George Stubbs (British, 1724–1806)
Zebra, 1763 (exhibited)

Oil on canvas, 40½ x 50¼ in. (102.9 x 127.6 cm)

YALE CENTER FOR BRITISH ART, PAUL MELLON COLLECTION, B1981.25.617

Samuel Shaw

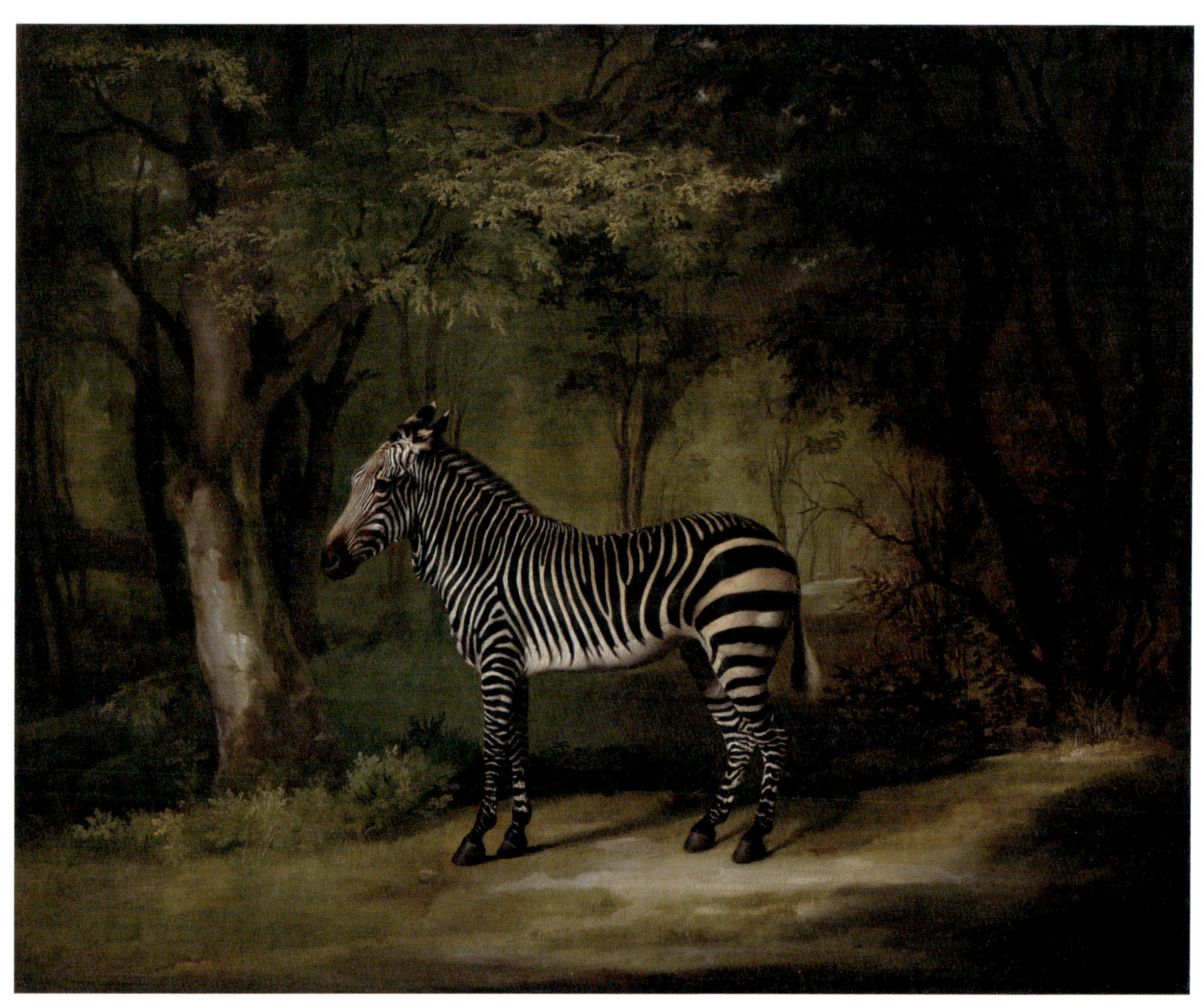

The female Cape mountain zebra (*Equus zebra zebra*) that appears in this painting is often described as the "first zebra seen in England."[1] This is not quite accurate. In 1751 naturalist and artist George Edwards included a representation (fig. 21) of what he called a "female zebra" in volume 1 of his *Gleanings of Natural History, Exhibiting Figures of Quadrupeds, Birds, Insects, Plants, &c.*[2] This animal lived, according to Edwards, "several years at a house of his Royal Highness the Prince of Wales, at Kew."[3] This, then, was the first zebra—although it was, in fact, what came to be known as a quagga (*Equus quagga quagga*), supposed for centuries to be an entirely separate species but recently revealed to be a subspecies of the plains zebra (*Equus quagga*).[4] So, while Edwards was wrong in supposing that the partially striped, largely orange animal at Kew was the female version of the familiar black-and-white-striped creature, he was right in identifying it as a true zebra.

This correction is not offered to diminish the standing of the animal that appears in Stubbs's painting of 1763. In fact, comparison of Edwards's rather crude hand-painted etching and Stubbs's meticulous painting only highlights the uniqueness of the latter, in both its subject and its treatment. While it may not represent the first zebra to reach British shores, Stubbs's zebra was certainly the most famous, most documented, and most controversial zebra ever to live in the country. Presented to Queen Charlotte in 1762 by Sir Thomas Adams, who had captured a pair of zebras in the Cape of Good Hope (the male died in transit), the zebra was subsequently exhibited at Buckingham House in London to a large and enthusiastic public.[5] Not only was the zebra itself a lively specimen, rumored to have a nasty kick, it also engendered a lively subculture. Long after the animal had died, been stuffed, toured, and superseded by a second zebra, its legend lived on—in the memorable bawdy words of the poem "The Queen's Ass, a new humorous allegorical song," for instance, or in the many political cartoons that followed in which connections were often made between the Queen's flamboyant son (later George IV) and her exotic zebra (see fig. 22). The zebra was not only valued for its

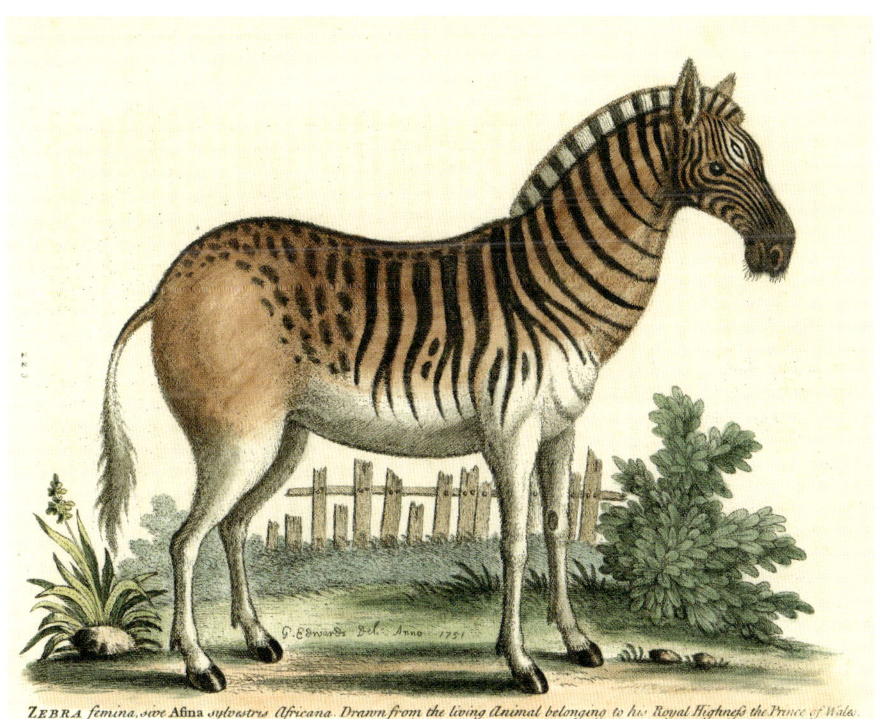

Fig. 21. George Edwards, *The female zebra*, 1751, hand-colored etching, 11¼ x 8⅝ in. (28.6 x 22 cm). The Royal Society, London

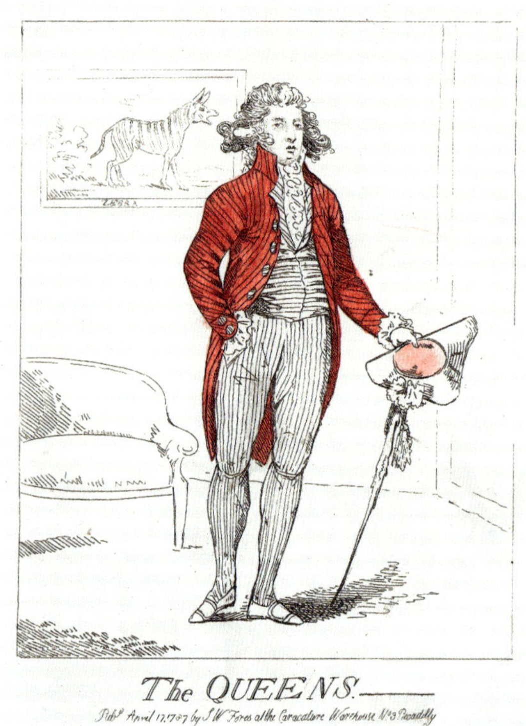

Fig. 22. Henry Kingsbury, *The Queen's* ____, 1787, hand-colored etching. Lewis Walpole Library, Yale University

own attributes but also used—as animals regularly are—as a conduit for, or symbol of, wider political and social frustrations.

We do not know what George Stubbs thought of the carnivalesque atmosphere that surrounded this particular zebra following its arrival in Britain, but we do know that he chose not to allude to it in his celebrated portrait. In essence, though working on a much larger scale and in the medium of oil, he opted for a similar approach to that of George Edwards, in which the animal is represented from the side, centered in the image, well lighted, and situated within a nonspecific landscape. Stubbs's image comfortably functions as a scientific tool, with its typical dedication to the finer details of the animal in question. As friend of the anatomists John and William Hunter—by whom some of his animal paintings were commissioned—Stubbs was no stranger to animal dissection.[6] He was never concerned with the mere appearance of the animals he painted; he wanted to know how their bodies worked.[7] More than two hundred years later, there is no mistaking the species of this zebra, or doubting that Stubbs observed it carefully (more so, one suspects, than Edwards observed the quagga at Kew).[8] However, Stubbs's zebra is much more than a representative specimen. Not only does this feel like the portrait of an individual, but there are other oddities, not least the landscape in which the zebra stands. This is not recognizable as southern Africa, where the zebra was born, nor does it represent the paddock outside Buckingham House where the zebra was exhibited.[9] It is a stock background of English woodland, in which this zebra (as far as we know) never had the opportunity to live.

In this sense, as in others, the painting is a fantasy. The slight laying-back of the ears we see here would probably be interpreted by zoologists today as a sign of hostility or wariness. Overall, however, we are presented with an uncharacteristically docile and melancholy animal, waiting patiently in a verdant open landscape, far from the enclosed paddock in which it resided, surrounded by prying eyes. Could Stubbs be imagining a better life for this particular zebra, or perhaps a future for its species as a whole? Ever since European visitors had encountered zebras in the wild, they had been convinced of their fitness for domestication.[10] It may be possible that Stubbs is envisaging just such a scenario: the African zebra, famed for its skittish behavior, standing tame in an English glade. Again, there are similarities with Edwards's image in which the zebra is pictured standing in front of a wooden fence, like a domesticated horse in a field. This is a fantasy of imperialism in which the exotic animal is introduced to, seemingly becalmed by, and ultimately made "useful" within a civilized European landscape.[11]

However, the way Stubbs presents his zebra is subtly different. There is, after all, a significant amount of space surrounding his animal, space that exaggerates the loneliness of the zebra and makes the juxtaposition of the black-and-white equid and rich green foliage all the more startling and surreal. Zebras are herd animals, usually found in family groups of six or seven, which form parts of larger herds that may number a hundred or more. The single zebra, so common in European art, is therefore a natural anomaly. Though we can only speculate as to Stubbs's knowledge of the natural history of the zebra—and must take care when reading subsequent learning into the image—Stubbs appears to sense this issue, highlighting as best he can the incongruity of the scene, one in which both the wonders and the costs of the Enlightenment are made clear. As an artist with a passion for the natural sciences, he could not have resisted the thrill of seeing an exotic animal; at the same time, he seems to appreciate that this is a false situation, with potentially sad consequences for the animal in question. The double nature of Stubbs's engagement with the zebra—in which general scientific curiosity collides with the encounter with an individual animal—was in this sense typical, anticipating the simultaneous respect for and desire to destroy nature that we find, for instance, in cultures of hunting. Stubbs's portrait displays genuine veneration of its intriguing subject; however, the artist's access to the animal relied on processes that would lead to the downfall of the species. Less than a hundred years after Stubbs painted the mountain zebra, numbers in southern Africa were already visibly declining.[12] The quagga, subject of Edwards's etching, would be extinct by 1883.

Projecting such ideas onto Stubbs's painting may seem presumptuous. The fate of the zebra as a species, let alone the ecological impacts of imperialism, may not have crossed the artist's mind. While he may have considered the effects of removing an animal from its natural habitat, it is highly unlikely that he would have imagined the extinction of an entire subspecies. Nevertheless, the complex and intriguing afterlife of this painting—an image which continues to inspire contemporary artists—points toward key attributes that do lend themselves to challenging readings.[13] The ambiguity of the image, I would go so far as to argue, is deliberate and suggestive. This is a meditation on human-animal relationships as much as it is an attempt to accurately render a mountain zebra. It is for this reason, and not just because of the painting's outstanding beauty and rich social history, that Stubbs's zebra still speaks to us more than two hundred and fifty years later.

Notes

1. John Baskett et al., *Paul Mellon's Legacy: A Passion for British Art* (New Haven: Yale Center for British Art, 2007), 252. The origins of this statement remain unclear. "The First Zebra Seen in England" is listed as an alternative title and may well relate to claims made when the zebra itself was publicly exhibited. For more on the painting, see Judy Egerton, *George Stubbs, Painter* (New Haven and London: Yale Univ. Press, 2007), 50–51, 180–81.

2. George Edwards, *Gleanings of Natural History, Exhibiting Figures of Quadrupeds, Birds, Insects, Plants, &c.*, 3 vols. (London: Royal College of Physicians, 1751), 1:28–30.

3. Edwards, *Gleanings of Natural History*, 1:28–30.

4. See Colin Groves and Catherine Bell, "New Investigations on the Taxonomy of the Zebras genus *Equus*, subgenus *Hippotigris*," *Mammalian Biology* 69, no. 3 (2004): 182–96.

5. For a detailed description of the zebra's life (and afterlife), see Christopher Plumb, "'The Queen's Ass': The Cultural Life of Queen Charlotte's Zebra in Georgian Britain," in *The Afterlives of Animals: A Museum Menagerie*, ed. Samuel Alberti (Charlottesville: Univ. of Virginia Press, 2011), 17–36.

6. For more on the relationship between Stubbs and the Hunters, see Helen McCormack, *William Hunter and His Eighteenth-Century Cultural Worlds: The Anatomist and the Fine Arts* (London: Routledge, 2017), chap. 5; and Mungo Campbell and Nathan Flis, with the assistance of María Dolores Sánchez-Jáuregui (New Haven: Yale Center for British Art, 2018), 360–65.

7. This is shown most clearly in the series of anatomical engravings and drawings Stubbs made after horses, fowl, tigers, and humans, examples of which can be found in the Yale Center for British Art's collection.

8. Mountain zebras are distinct from the plains and Grévy's zebras on account of their smaller size, markings, and conspicuous dewlap (flap of skin hanging from the neck). They were also the species that European visitors were most likely to encounter first at the Cape in the late eighteenth century.

9. Admittedly, eighteenth- and nineteenth-century imaginings of Africa were often rather fanciful: see, for example, Ramsay Reinagle's painting *Landscape with Animals (An African Scene)*, 1828, Doncaster Museum and Art Gallery.

10. For more on this topic, see Christopher Plumb and Samuel Shaw, *Zebra* (London: Reaktion, 2018).

11. A criticism made of zebras in 1781, shortly after Stubbs painted the zebra, was that they were "useless" and "untameable," comments that did not dissuade European colonists from trying to domesticate them. See Thomas Pennant, *History of Quadrupeds*, 2 vols. (London: B. White, 1781), 1:14.

12. The Cape mountain zebra, the subspecies depicted here, is still listed as vulnerable despite conservation efforts.

13. For contemporary artists' responses to Stubbs's painting, see Plumb and Shaw, *Zebra*, 131–33.

James Bolton (British, 1735–1799)
"House Wren (*Troglodytes aedon*) or Winter Wren (previously *T. troglodytes*, now *T. hiemalis*) and eggs with specimen from the rose family (*Rosaceae*), peacock butterflies (*Nymphalis io*), both closed and open, a butterfly chrysalis, larva caterpillar, daddy longlegs spider (*Phalangida*) with egg case, and snout beetle, all from the natural history cabinet of Anna Blackburne," ca. 1768

Watercolor and gouache over graphite on parchment, 9 x 7½ in. (23 x 19 cm)

YALE CENTER FOR BRITISH ART, PAUL MELLON FUND, IN HONOR OF JANE AND RICHARD C. LEVIN, PRESIDENT OF YALE UNIVERSITY (1993–2013), FOLIO A.2016.25, NO. 8

Mark Laird

Of the twenty watercolors by the naturalist and artist James Bolton from the natural history cabinet of Anna Blackburne (1726–1793), two are of a wren. As with much else in the history of these drawings, the twin wrens are intriguing. Here is an attempt, then, to puzzle out a private natural history moment of about 1768 and to piece together a later history: how the Eurasian wren and its nest came to public recognition in Bolton's *Harmonia ruralis* of 1796.

Anna Blackburne lived at Orford Hall, near Warrington, Lancashire, where her father, John Blackburne (1694–1786), had built a collection of living plants that gardener Adam Neal catalogued in 1779.[1] John Blackburne was related, through his wife, Catherine, to Sir Ashton Lever, famed for his private natural history museum in London. Anna, following the early death of her mother, assumed domestic and scientific roles at Orford Hall, and, while remaining unmarried, was known as Mrs. Blackburne. Her own natural history collection was well established by 1771, when she initiated correspondence with Linnaeus, who responded to the "lady of celestial mind," praising her as "a true naturalist whose esteem I covet."[2]

In his study of Bolton, John Edmondson wrote: "He is known to have botanised in the Warrington area, and to have visited Orford Hall."[3] It is reasonable to believe, then, that Anna Blackburne commissioned drawings during his field trips of 1768–69. While Bolton's significant publications came later, the importance of the early drawings should not be underestimated.

Bolton stated that his earliest botanical illustrations were of 1761; his earliest signed flower portraits date from about 1782.[4] While Bolton might have met the great botanical artist Georg Dionysius Ehret (1708–1770) at Bulstrode, the home of his later patron Margaret Bentinck, Duchess of Portland (1715–1785), direct tutelage by the master appears unlikely. Copying Ehret's works, instead, Bolton was largely self-taught.

A comparison with Ehret's sublime art suggests that Bolton's drawings are "flat" and "lifeless";[5] but he should be deemed a "talented amateur."[6] While he might have followed the style of such naturalist-artists as Mark Catesby and Maria Sibylla Merian,[7] he was not drawing birds and insects observed in natural settings. Instead, Blackburne had Bolton make her cabinet appear

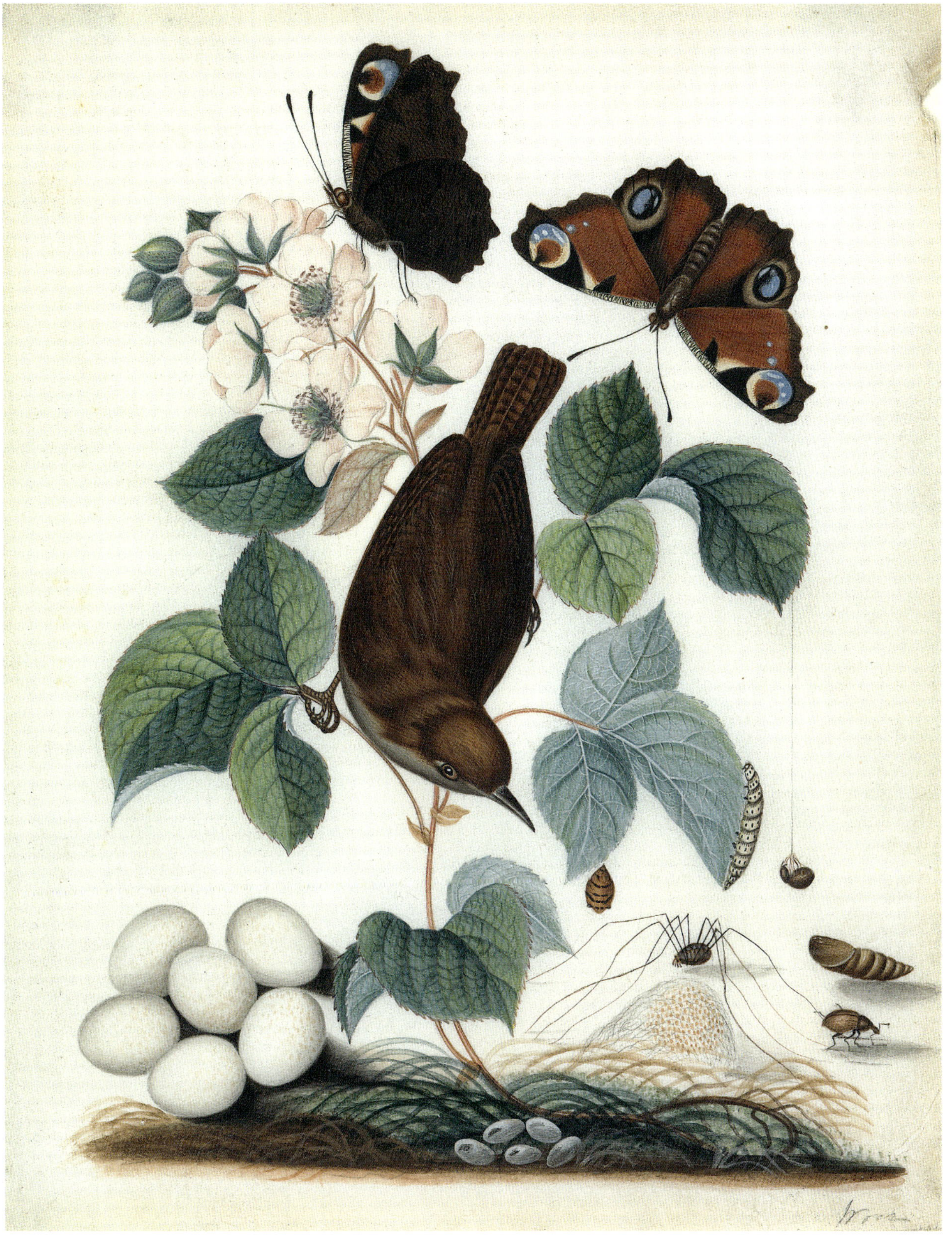

naturalistic; a striking characteristic of nine out of twenty drawings is Bolton's fondness for depicting fruit-bearing plants.

The earlier of the two wren portraits is presented against a fruiting raspberry (*Rubus idaeus*; fig. 23), the later portrait against a flowering plant in the rose family (*Rosaceae*)—perhaps a bramble with leaves closely white-felted beneath. In the later image, the curve of the wren is echoed by the curve of the blooms. Above them, an open peacock butterfly (*Nymphalis io*) patterns the page, while its closed companion alights on the flowers. The caterpillar and chrysalis to the lower right suggest something of a life cycle after Merian. Yet this is no metamorphosis of the peacock, whose larva is typically found on nettles.

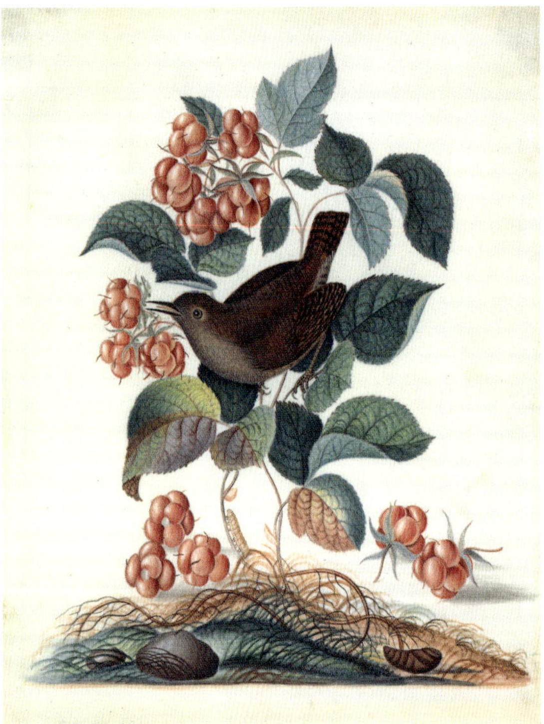

Fig. 23. James Bolton, "Eurasian wren (*Troglodytes troglodytes*), with raspberry (*Rubus idaeus L.*), and wood lice (*?Isopoda*), and pupa (*Lepidoptera ?Saturniidae*) from the natural history cabinet of Anna Blackburne," ca. 1768, watercolor and gouache over graphite on parchment. Yale Center for British Art, Paul Mellon Fund, in honor of Jane and Richard C. Levin, President of Yale University

The six white eggs at lower left, with pale reddish brown spots at the larger end of the egg, match the clutch and egg descriptions of the wren. That these birds eat beetles and spiders may explain a snout beetle and daddy longlegs spider with egg case, both depicted as lowly life forms. A bramble scrub, with insects at ground level, matches the habitat of the wren—an undergrowth dweller.

Bolton shows the wren's tail as truly stubby in this portrait. In the earlier wren portrait with raspberry, the tail is cocked and the bill is open for the amazingly loud song this small bird pours forth. Downward and upward poses are presented as Bolton's male and female wrens (*Troglodytes troglodytes*) in *Harmonia ruralis*:

> The Honourable Daines Barrington allows it a considerable place in his Balance of Singing Birds; ascribing to it, twelve degrees of sprightly notes, four degrees of composition, and four degrees of execution.[8]

Harmonia ruralis (1794–96), with forty copperplates, was a natural history of British songbirds, dedicated to "The British Ladies, to Naturalists, and to all such as admire the beauty or melody of the Feathered Warblers" (see fig. 24). By contrast, Blackburne had Bolton feature what looks like an Asian white-cheeked starling, a red avadavat of the Indian subcontinent, a beautiful nuthatch of the Far East, and a Central American hummingbird amid English songsters—goldfinch, robin, and nuthatch.

Bolton might have painted the Eurasian wren (*Troglodytes troglodytes*) from a live English wren, while the other—uncertainly a house wren (*Troglodytes aedon*) or a winter wren (previously *T. troglodytes*, now *T. hiemalis*)—was likely from a specimen sent to Blackburne by her brother, Ashton. He was collecting near New York by 1771 and probably some years beforehand. This led Blackburne to offer Linnaeus birds and insects out of Ashton's annual enrichments of her "Cabinet."

Though poorly documented as a "rather mysterious fellow,"[9] Ashton Blackburne had a substantial

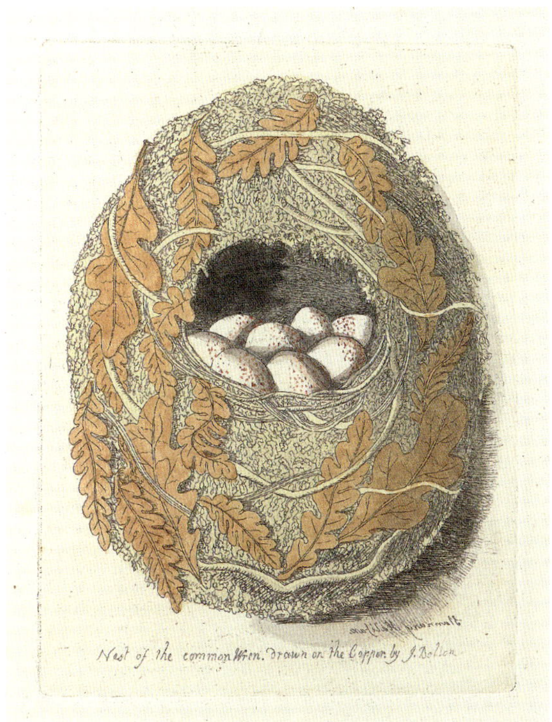

Fig. 24. James Bolton, "Nest of the common Wren drawn on the Copper by J. Bolton," plate LXVIII from *Harmonia ruralis, or, An essay towards a natural history of British song birds* (Manchester: 1794–96). Beinecke Rare Book & Manuscript Library, Yale University

impact on the ornithology of North America. Thomas Pennant, who had indirect contact with Orford Hall by 1768, named that most handsome of warblers—the Blackburnian warbler—after Ashton and Anna. However, despite many scientific names still being recognized by authorities as Pennant's descriptions of Ashton's specimens, the Blackburnian warbler's scientific names, *Setophaga fusca* and *Dendroica fusca* (Müller, 1776), are not his own.

Today, among Bolton's birds, the beautiful nuthatch (*Sitta formosa*) is listed as "vulnerable" on the International Union for Conservation of Nature's (IUCN) Red List of species considered to be "vulnerable, endangered . . . extinct in the wild, extinct."[10] While the "House Wren" and "Winter Wren" of the Americas and the "Northern Wren" of Eurasia have the IUCN status of "least concern," the endangered word "wren" appears to need its defender. In Robert Macfarlane's book *The Lost Words*, "wren" and "bramble" appear in his cultural Red List: vulnerable, fading way, gone, "all of them gone!"[11]

Back in 1796 James Bolton was vehemently defending nature by cultural comparison, arguing that the "strange" derogatory thoughts of another ornithologist on the "utter darkness" of the wren's habitation required a riposte. This remarkable man, at once illuminating and enlightening, should command the final word:

> I believe I ought not to have said a strange thought, but a strange want of thought. Any one who thinks about it, and compares the dimensions of the window, with the dimensions of the house within, will instantly perceive, that a Wren's nest is more strongly lighted than any gentleman's palace in the kingdom.[12]

Notes

I am grateful to John Edmondson and Jeff Harrison for their help throughout.

1. See entries by Ann B. Shteir, "Blackburne, Anna," and by John R. Edmondson, "Blackburne, John," in *Oxford Dictionary of National Biography*, http//www.oxforddnb.com/view/article/ (accessed 14 July 2018).
2. See V. P. Wystrach, "Anna Blackburne (1726–1793)—A Neglected Patroness of Natural History," *Journal of the Society for the Bibliography of Natural History* 8, no. 2 (1977): 148–68, esp. 155.
3. John R. Edmondson, *James Bolton of Halifax* (Liverpool: National Museums and Galleries on Merseyside, 1995), 9.
4. See E. Charles Nelson, "James Bolton's Botanical Paintings and Illustrations, and His Association with Georg Ehret," *Naturalist*, no. 106 (1981): 141–47.
5. See Nelson, "James Bolton's Botanical Paintings and Illustrations," 145, for assessment of Bolton's work.
6. Wilfrid Blunt, *The Art of Botanical Illustration* [1950], ed. William T. Stearn (Woodbridge, Suffolk: Antique Collectors' Club, 1994), 167.
7. See Lisa L. Ford, "James Bolton, Self-Taught Naturalist," in *Of Green Leaf, Bird, and Flower: Artists' Books and the Natural World*, ed. Elisabeth R. Fairman (New Haven and London: Yale Univ. Press, 2014), 150–51.
8. James Bolton, *Harmonia ruralis, or, An essay towards a natural history of British song birds* . . ., 2 vols. (Manchester: 1794–96), 2:67.
9. Wystrach, "Anna Blackburne," 160.
10. See https://www.iucnredlist.org/species/22711231/94285206.
11. Robert Macfarlane and Jackie Morris, *The Lost Words* (London: Hamish Hamilton, 2017), under "Bramble" and "Wren."
12. Bolton, *Harmonia ruralis*, 2:68.

Joseph Wilton RA (British, 1722–1803)

Thomas Dawson, first Baron Dartrey (Later first Viscount Cremorne), ca. 1771

Carrara marble on an original socle, without the socle: 21½ x 16½ x 9½ in. (54.6 x 41.9 x 24.1 cm). Chiseled on the front of the socle: "THOMAS LORD DARTREY," and on the reverse above the socle, right: "J. Wilton Sculpt."

YALE CENTER FOR BRITISH ART, PAUL MELLON COLLECTION, B1977.14.33

Matthew Hargraves

On February 13, 1769, Lady Mary Coke visited Lady Charlotte Finch, intimate friend of Queen Charlotte and governess to the royal children. "I found her in low spirits," she confided to her journal. "She thinks her Sister, Lady Anne Dorson [*sic*] in a dangerous state of health."[1] That same day Anne Dawson wrote her last letter to another sister, Lady Louisa Clayton, as she lay dying of tuberculosis far away in County Monaghan, Ireland: "I have, my dearest, been declining the whole winter and now believe I am not very far from being removed out of this world."[2] Anne reassured Louisa that "I trust in the mercies of my gracious God, thro' the mediation of my dear Redeemer, to everlasting happiness with him."[3] She died on March 1, 1769. When contemplating Anne's death that summer, her friend Elizabeth Carter wrote to fellow bluestocking Elizabeth Vesey, Anne's cousin by marriage: "what a delightfully painful conversation could we hold on the subject of dear Lady Anne Dawson . . . Can it be possible, my dear Mrs. Vesey, that with so noble an enthusiasm for the excellence of dear Lady Anne's character, you should not feel the evidence of those divine principles which raised her to so exalted a pitch of virtue?"[4]

That domestic tragedy in Ireland in March 1769 would before long bring forth one of Joseph Wilton's finest achievements in portrait sculpture, his bust of Thomas Dawson, Anne's widowed husband. In this bust, Dawson is represented informally wearing a thin shirt covered by a loose banyan meeting in the front. His own hair falls in disheveled curls at his temples and over his ears, while his face turns upward. The incised pupils of his eyes imply that he is focused on something specific beyond himself rather than surveying the world before him. The parted lips and furrowed brow give the entire bust an extraordinary degree of animation quite distinct from the impassively polite and urbane faces of the previous generation. This portrait at Yale is in fact a replica household bust, taken from Dawson's effigy in a monument erected to his late wife.[5] Indeed, the first connection between Dawson and Wilton came on July 23, 1771, when the sculptor was commissioned to make that funerary monument to commemorate Anne. Wilton was contracted to "execute . . . according to the best of his Abilities in the Art of Sculpture one Monument consisting of three Figures, with an Urn Ornamented," which was shipped from his London workshop to Dublin in the summer of 1774 before making its final journey to Dawson Grove.[6] The inscription, composed by Anne's loving friend Elizabeth Carter, proclaimed that Dawson had raised the memorial "in a grateful and affectionate Sense of the Blessings he enjoyed in such a Wife." The three figures were Dawson himself; Richard, his son and heir; and an angel hovering in front of Anne's urn, gesturing up to heaven. The entire

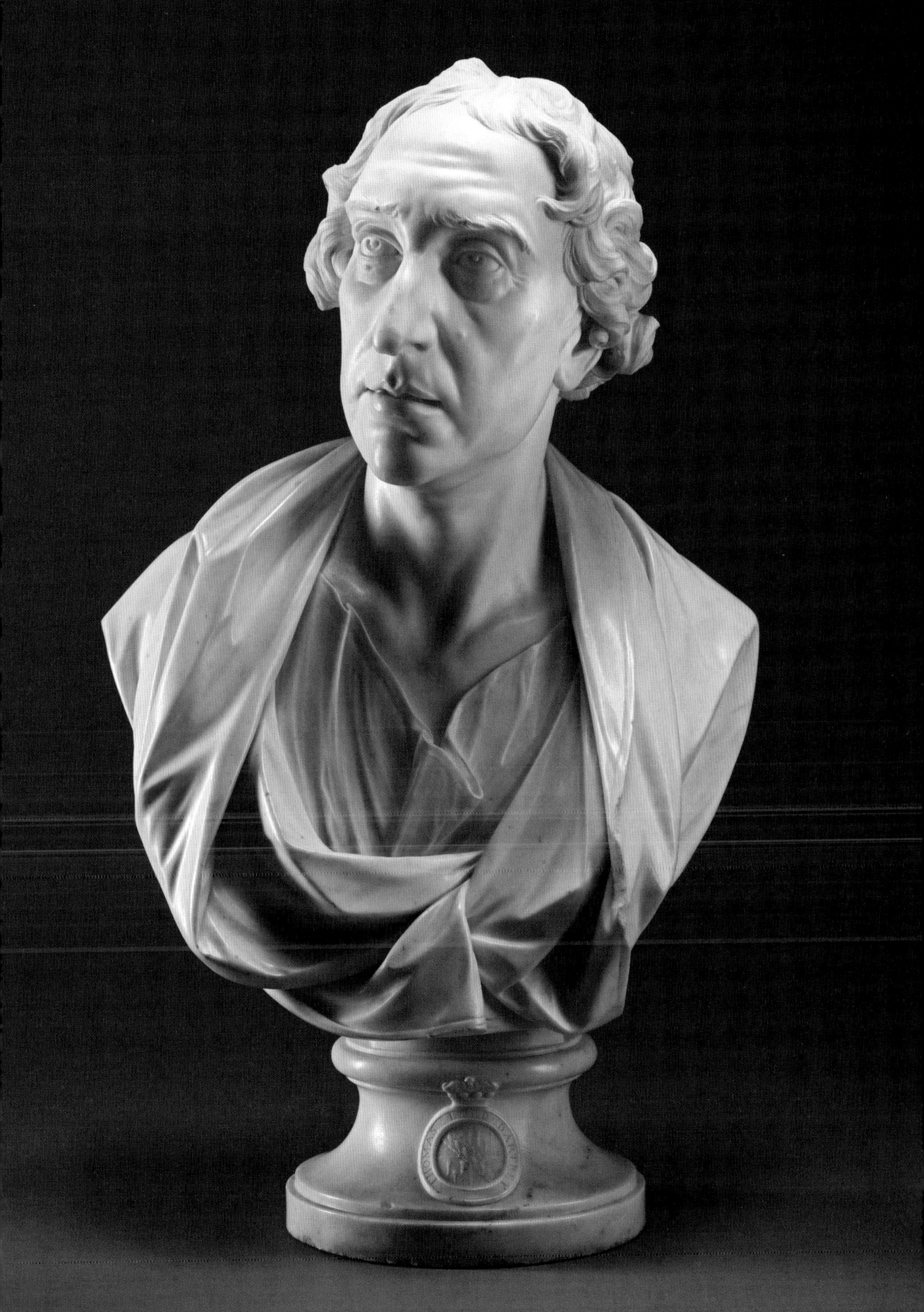

design was adapted from Wilton's monument for the Countess of Mountrath in Westminster Abbey of 1771, designed in collaboration with William Chambers. This was, as Matthew Craske argues, "the point of departure for an entire movement in British monumental sculpture that fostered comforting fantasies of death as a communion with the angels."[7] Unlike the Mountrath monument, or others of its type, Anne's did not represent her directly. Instead it was Dawson himself who was memorialized in effigy as the grief-stricken husband to whom his motherless son clings for comfort.

Detached from the narrative of death and resurrection, the bust becomes a testament to Dawson's own exquisite sensibility. The lack of affectation and adornment, the spontaneity of the turn of the head and parted lips, the sense of direct connection between vision and the feeling heart, with its associated moral sentiments, all shift the portrait away from a conventional image of politeness and define Dawson instead as a man of feeling. It is no surprise to find that Dawson was formed within the most advanced intellectual circles at the court of George III, where Jean-Jacques Rousseau's exhilarating ideas were eagerly devoured and where Rousseau was offered a pension during his English exile in the 1760s. After all, "the Pre-revolutionary cult of Rousseau was not political but aesthetic. What it saw Rousseau promulgating was not so much liberty, equality, and fraternity as the feeling heart, the simple life, and the familial bond."[8] And, as Clarissa Campbell Orr has noted, Thomas Dawson was exactly the kind of decent, discrete man of blameless domestic character that the royal couple liked to have around them, especially at those times of year when the court was reduced to a minimum and the King could shed the less-honorable figures that necessity required him to have with him.[9]

But it is also possible the bust was once integrated into a narrative of its own, made up of sculpted or painted objects; perhaps it gazed fixedly at a portrait of Anne, either at Dawson Grove or at one of Dawson's London homes, Cremorne House in Chelsea or his town house on Stanhope Street.[10] The bust in this context would have been a votive object keeping permanent vigil before Anne's image, testifying to his abiding love and regard for his lost wife. A related object, which Dawson perhaps knew, was Pompeo Batoni's full-length portrait of the Irishman and fellow loyal courtier Wills Hill, Earl of Hillsborough (oil on canvas, private collection), commissioned in Rome in 1766 in the first rush of grief after his wife Margaretta died on the Grand Tour. There, the bereaved husband gazes forlornly at a fictive oval portrait of his wife resting on a sarcophagus, held up by Death extinguishing his torch.

These new uxorious images mark the emergence of the sentimental man, something underscored by the intimacy of Dawson's undress and the sense of emotional transparency in the bust, those very qualities that were rooted in a deep-seated sense of renewed Christian virtue. Wilton's portrait becomes a heightened representation of a man of feeling whose moral sentiments are based on a devout heart. Wilton's own tastes were always Baroque, a preference underscored during his residence in Rome between 1747 and 1751. That Wilton's bust self-consciously evokes the saints' heads in contemporary Roman sculpture, or those painted by Guido Reni and his followers, so popular with British collectors, is no coincidence, for in all these examples the upturned eyes are implicitly associated with a longing for God.[11] The death of Anne that so afflicted court circles in 1769 allowed Wilton to effect a transformation in portrait sculpture, one based on the new cult of feeling, the refined man of sensibility, and the place accorded to the influence of women in reshaping court and society.

Notes

I am grateful to Dr. Courtney Skipton Long for her assistance in the writing of this essay.

1. James Archibald Home, ed., *The Letters and Journals of Lady Mary Coke, Volume Third, 1769–1771* (Bath: Kingsmead Reprints, 1970), 23–24.
2. Lady Anne Dawson to Lady Louisa Clayton, February 13, 1769, in *The Field Day Anthology of Irish Writing*, 5 vols., eds. Angela Bourke et al. (Cork: Cork Univ. Press, 2002), 4:505.

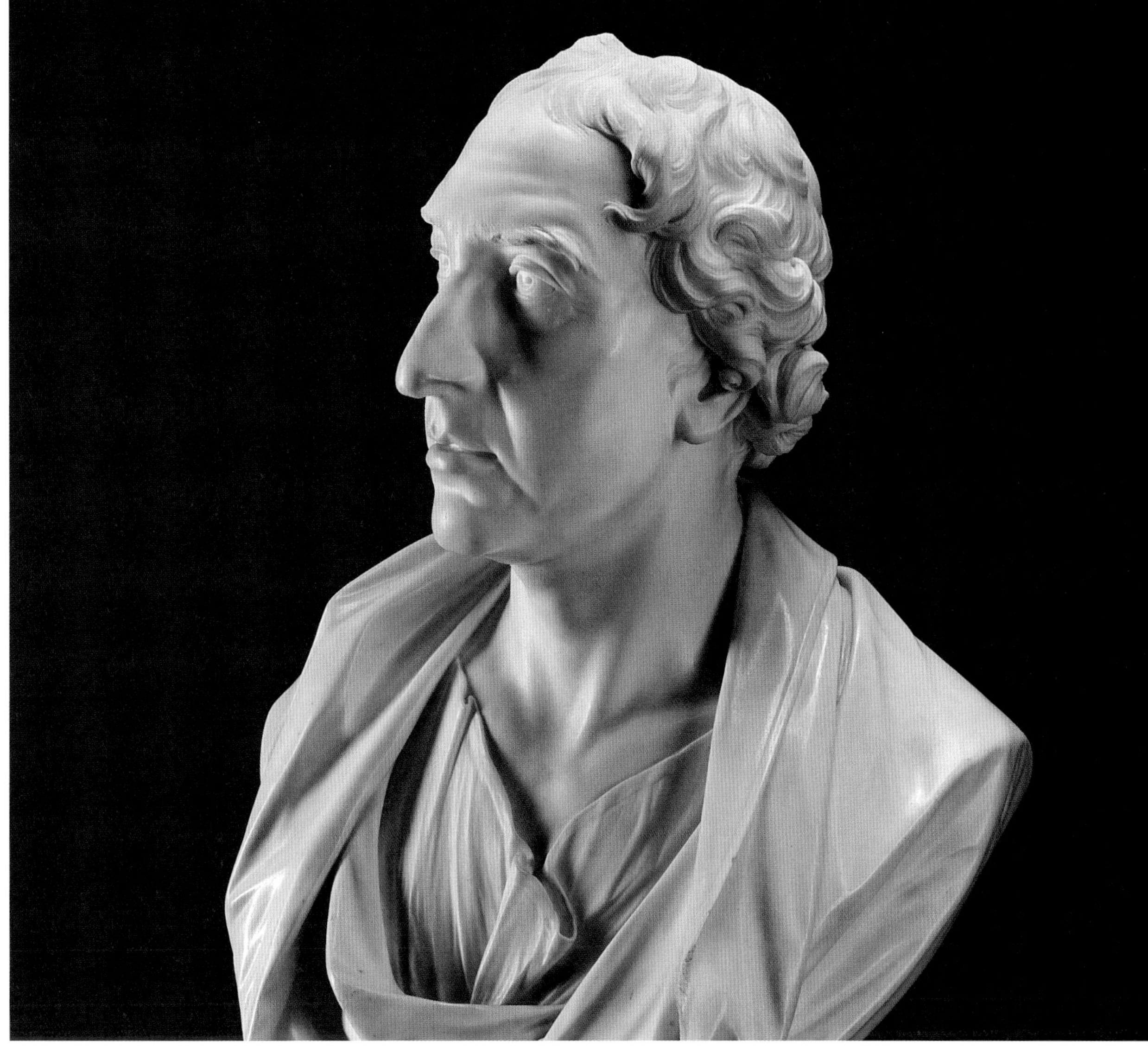

3. Bourke et al., *The Field Day Anthology of Irish Writing*, 4:505.
4. Elizabeth Carter to Elizabeth Vesey, July 28, 1769, in Elizabeth Carter, *A Series of Letters between Mrs. Elizabeth Carter and Miss Catherine Talbot, from the Year 1741 to 1770: To Which are Added Letters from Mrs. Carter to Mrs. [Elizabeth] Vesey between the Years 1767 and 1787*, 4 vols. (London: F. C. & J. Rivington, 1809), 3:366–68.
5. No mention of a bust was made in the contract Dawson signed with Wilton, so he must have commissioned the portrait after seeing either Wilton's clay model for his effigy or the finished monument itself.
6. Agreement for a monument to Lady Anne Dawson, July 23, 1771, Royal Academy of Arts, London 785/6.
7. Matthew Craske, *The Silent Rhetoric of the Body: A History of Monumental Sculpture and Commemorative Art in England, 1720–1770* (New Haven and London: Yale Univ. Press, 2008), 185. It is conceivable that Dawson was inspired to commission his monument after seeing the Mountrath monument unveiled in 1771.
8. Edward Duffy, *Rousseau in England: The Context for Shelley's Critique of the Enlightenment* (Berkeley: Univ. of California Press, 1979), 29.
9. I am grateful to Clarissa Campbell Orr for informative conversations on the Dawson and Finch families and their connections to the court as well as the impact of Rousseau on this circle.
10. I am indebted to Malcolm Baker for this suggestion, made during a workshop on the portrait bust at the Yale Center for British Art, November 5, 2010. We know from Dawson's will of 1813 that he kept a portrait of Anne close by to the end, since it describes an unspecified portrait still hanging "in my room in Stanhope Street in Testimony of my regard and tender affection [for] my dearest Lady Anne Dawson." National Archive, London PROB 11/1542/521.
11. As Sir Nicholas Penny notes, this was also the inspiration for Joseph Nollekens's slightly later bust of Maria Howard (ca. 1803; Oxford, Ashmolean Museum), itself taken from an effigy in the Brocklesby Mausoleum in Lincolnshire. Nicholas Penny, *Catalogue of European Sculpture in the Ashmolean Museum: 1540 to the Present Day*, 3 vols. (Oxford: Clarendon Press, 1992), 3:140.

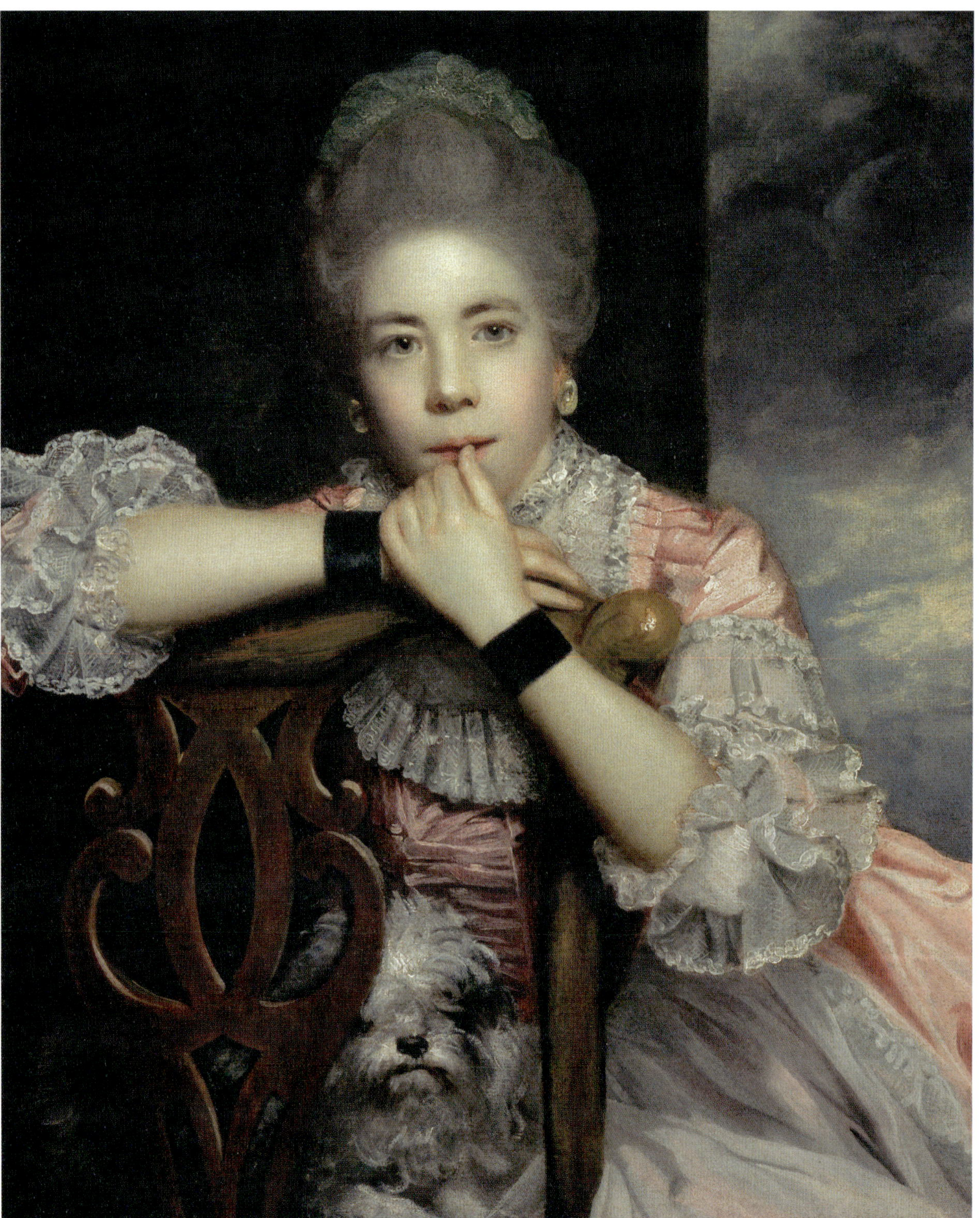

Sir Joshua Reynolds RA (British, 1723–1792)
Mrs. Abington as Miss Prue in "Love for Love" by William Congreve, 1771–73

Oil on canvas, 30¼ x 25⅛ in. (76.8 x 63.8 cm)

YALE CENTER FOR BRITISH ART, PAUL MELLON COLLECTION, B1977.14.67

Martin Postle

Joshua Reynolds first came to know Frances Abington in the summer of 1764, when she was likely introduced to him by David Garrick, the great actor-manager. Over the next few years Reynolds and Mrs. Abington became close friends. But while Garrick had a fraught relationship with Abington, who was by nature a strong-willed, independent woman, Reynolds relished her company and was avid in his attendance at her stage performances and benefit nights. The mutual rewards they derived from their friendship were expressed through a series of four portraits that he painted of her.[1] The first of these, made during the mid-1760s, was a full-length depiction of Mrs. Abington as Thalia, the comic muse, a picture she may have commissioned but which passed during her lifetime to another of Reynolds's friends, Frederick, third Duke of Dorset.

Reynolds exhibited a second portrait of Mrs Abington at the Royal Academy of Arts in 1771. Until recently, it had been assumed that this was *Mrs. Abington as Miss Prue in "Love for Love" by William Congreve*. However, Mark Hallett has revealed that the portrait in question actually depicted Mrs. Abington swathed in a white satin cardinal cloak (fig. 25).[2] *Mrs. Abington as Miss Prue* was probably painted around the same time, or shortly after, in 1772–73.[3] Unlike the exhibited portrait, which was engraved in 1772, no print was made of *Mrs. Abington as Miss Prue* during Reynolds's lifetime, and few people beyond the artist's immediate circle would have been familiar with it.[4] In order to understand better the intimate nature of the present painting and the associated issue of private ownership, we need to explore further the connection between Mrs. Abington and Miss Prue as visualized by Reynolds in his most sensual of female portraits.

David Garrick revived *Love for Love*, William Congreve's bawdy Restoration farce, at Drury Lane in 1769, where it ran until November 1771.

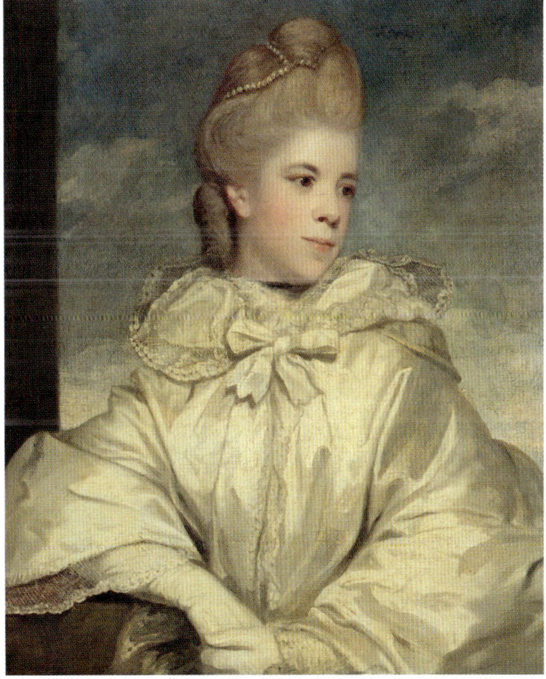

Fig. 25. Sir Joshua Reynolds, *Mrs. Abington*, ca. 1771–1773, oil on canvas, 29⅛ x 25¼ in. (74 x 64 cm). Private collection

Although Reynolds clearly intended the portrait to relate to Mrs. Abington's role as Miss Prue, the precise nature of the connection is open to question.[5] In the late nineteenth century the art critic Frederic George Stephens asserted that Reynolds was alluding specifically to an exchange between Miss Prue and the boorish character Ben Legend, who, in his inept attempt to court her, offers to "haul a chair" for her to sit on next to him (Act III, Scene VII, line 1).[6] Stephens presumed that the presence of the chair in the portrait must have a direct link to the plot. Reynolds, however, was making a more subtle statement concerning the visual exchange between an object of desire and the male viewer. It is suggested here, in the context of Congreve's play, that Reynolds is exploring how Mrs. Abington and the character of Miss Prue look upon a would-be lover, and how he in turn regards her. In this respect, the relationship in the play that springs to mind is between the "half-witted beau," Tattle, and Miss Prue, "a silly awkward country-girl," and which can be compared to the virtual relationship that existed in real life between a host of male admirers and Mrs. Abington.

Turning to the play, we learn that Tattle, who has a high regard for his prowess as a lover, owns a very particular collection of portraits consisting of previous conquests: his so-called closet of beauties. These pictures are, he says, "sacred to love and contemplation. No man but the painter and myself was ever blessed with the sight." Upon being asked by Miss Prue's aunt whether a woman might view them, Tattle retorts: "Nor woman, till she consented to have her picture there too—for then she's obliged to keep the secret" (Act I, Scene XIV, lines 27–30). Armed with this knowledge, the viewer observes Tattle's subsequent attempt to seduce Miss Prue. Should Tattle succeed, he would, we may assume, add Miss Prue's portrait to his "closet of beauties." In the seduction scene with Miss Prue, Tattle explains that she must play hard to get: "If I ask you to kiss me, you must be angry, but you must not refuse me. If I ask you for more, you must be more angry, but more complying" (Act II, Scene XI, lines 19–20). The female object of male desire must therefore feign resistance while encouraging her lover. In Reynolds's portrait, the alluring Miss Prue, her thumb poised provocatively at her slightly parted lips, leans over the back of a chair, which at once enhances the sense of sexual frisson and forms a physical impediment to further intimacy. Mrs. Abington is, of course, also an object of desire in her own right—a woman who engages with the male viewer through her sensual body language, hand gesture, and unwavering gaze, and who yet remains elusive. In Reynolds's portrait, Mrs. Abington and her fictive character are linked inextricably, and yet coexist physically and in the mind's eye.

An early owner of *Mrs. Abington as Miss Prue* was Reynolds's old friend and patron John Parker.[7] An earthy country squire with a penchant for blood sports and gambling, Parker was characterized by the Duchess of Devonshire on a visit to his home, Saltram House in Devon, "as dirty, as comical, and talking as bad English as ever."[8] Parker, a widower following the death of his wife in 1775, had plenty of money to devote to his pleasures. They included the refurbishment of the interiors at Saltram by Robert Adam and stocking it with paintings by Reynolds, including the sensuous portrait of Mrs. Abington and that of the celebrated courtesan Kitty Fisher in the character of Cleopatra (fig. 26).[9] *Mrs. Abington as Miss Prue* remained in the library at Saltram, beyond the public gaze, for much of the nineteenth century, accessible only through a modest mezzotint engraving made probably at some point in the 1820s.[10] The portrait itself was displayed briefly at the Reynolds retrospective exhibition mounted by the British Institution at their Pall Mall gallery in 1813. It did not reemerge until 1867, when it was shown at the South Kensington Museum's massive survey exhibition of "National Portraits." There, the Pre-Raphaelite writer and critic William Michael Rossetti referred to it in passing as "Reynolds's *Mrs Abington* in some hoydenish stage-part."[11]

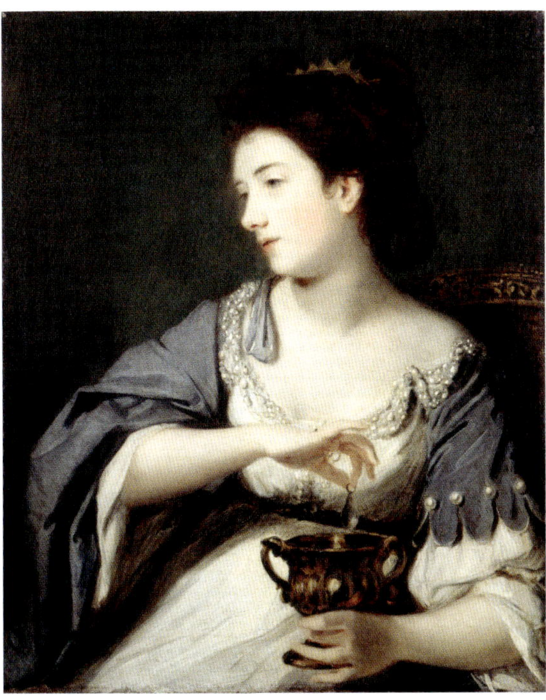

Fig. 26. Sir Joshua Reynolds, *Kitty Fisher as Cleopatra*, ca. 1759, oil on canvas, 29⅞ x 24¾ in. (76 x 63 cm). The Iveagh Bequest, Kenwood, London

The big break came in 1883 at the major Reynolds exhibition mounted by Sir Coutts Lindsay at London's Grosvenor Gallery, when *Mrs. Abington as Miss Prue*—now owned by Sir Charles Mills—was awarded a fulsome catalogue entry by Frederic George Stephens and a prominent position in the display. From then on, and into the twentieth century, *Mrs. Abington as Miss Prue* was a must-have for any self-respecting exhibition dedicated to Reynolds. In 1986 its status was underlined by its selection as the poster image and cover for the catalogue accompanying the Royal Academy's blockbuster Reynolds exhibition. *Mrs. Abington as Miss Prue*, by now in the collection of the Yale Center for British Art, was thus confirmed as a very notable public work of art.

Notes

1. David Mannings and Martin Postle, *Sir Joshua Reynolds: A Complete Catalogue of His Paintings*, 2 vols. (New Haven and London: Yale Univ. Press, 2000), 1:55–56, nos. 28, 29, 31, 32. The fourth portrait, not discussed here, is of Mrs. Abington as Roxalana in *The Sultan*, by Isaac Bickerstaff, exhibited at the Royal Academy in 1784.
2. Mark Hallett, "Experiments in Serial Portraiture: Reynolds and Mrs Abington," in *Joshua Reynolds: Experiments in Paint*, eds. Lucy Davis and Mark Hallett (London: Paul Holberton, 2015), 75–77.
3. Mrs. Abington had sittings with Reynolds in December 1771, and on several occasions in 1772 and 1773. Reynolds's pocket books for 1774–76 are missing. See Mannings and Postle, *Sir Joshua Reynolds*, 1:56.
4. The mezzotint engraving by Elizabeth Judkins of the exhibited portrait was published by her brother-in-law, James Watson, on May 20, 1772.
5. In 1819, when the portrait hung in the library at Saltram, Devon, it was described as "Mrs Abington, as Miss Prue, in Love for Love." See *Catalogue of the Pictures, Casts, and Busts, belonging to the Earl of Morley at Saltram* (Plymouth: P. Nettleton and Son, 1819), no. 127.
6. F. G. Stephens, *Exhibition of the Works of Sir Joshua Reynolds, P.R.A. with Historical Notes* (London: Chiswick Press, 1883), 11–12. The edition of the play referred to in the present essay is the Project Gutenberg e-book transcribed from the 1895 Methuen edition, *Comedies of William Congreve*, vol. 2; http://www.gutenberg.org/files/1244/1244-h/1244-h.htm.
7. The portrait is first noted in the collection of Parker's son, the Earl of Morley, in 1813 when it was exhibited at the British Institution. There can be little doubt that he had inherited the picture from his father, not least because he had no interest himself in the acquisition of works of art.
8. Earl of Bessborough, ed., *Georgiana: Extracts from the Correspondence of Georgiana, Duchess of Devonshire* (London: John Murray, 1955), 55.
9. Mannings and Postle, *Sir Joshua Reynolds*, 1:188, no. 612. *Kitty Fisher as Cleopatra* was painted for or sold to Sir Charles Bingham, from whom it evidently passed to John Parker, who may by that time have also owned *Mrs. Abington as Miss Prue*.
10. More than three hundred fifty engravings, made by Samuel William Reynolds after Sir Joshua Reynolds (no relation), were published in four volumes between 1821 and 1836.
11. William Michael Rossetti, *Rossetti Papers, 1862 to 1870* (New York: Charles Scribner's Sons, 1903), 239.

Thomas Gainsborough RA (British, 1727–1788)
Mountain Valley with Figures and Distant Village, 1773–77

Oil on canvas, 48 x 58 ¾ in. (121.9 x 149.2 cm)

YALE CENTER FOR BRITISH ART, PAUL MELLON COLLECTION, B1981.25.295

Alexander Nemerov

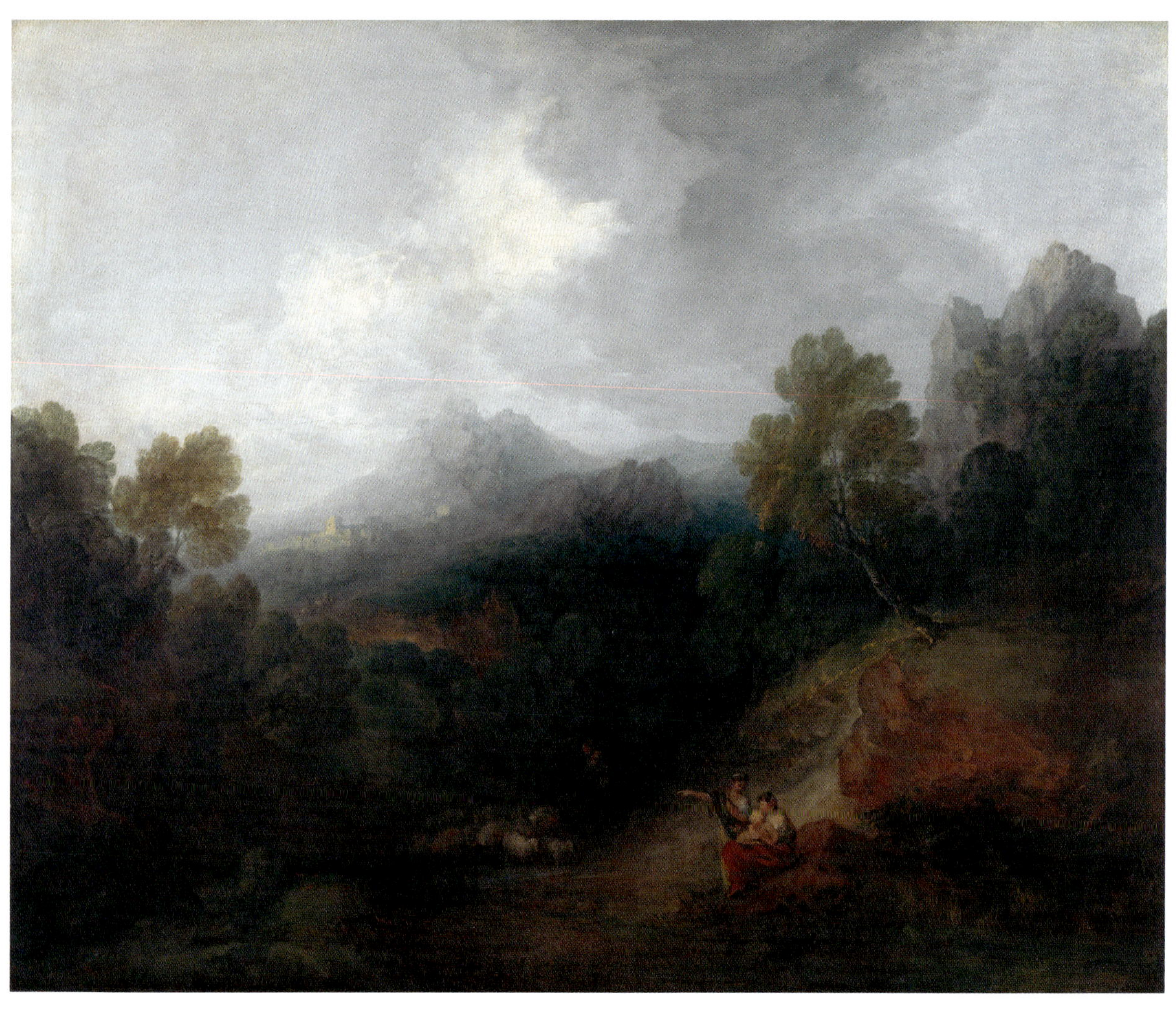

The scene is a fantasy. One of Gainsborough's later landscapes, it is a far cry from the precise style of his early pictures, back in the 1740s, when he catalogued a squire's possessions, the wife in comely milkmaid's costume, the fields swept of grain and labor. Now, more than thirty years later, the artist relied on imagination. Possibly the painting owes to the little models Gainsborough made in those years—a mirror for a lake, lumps of coal for rocks, broccoli for trees. At most, he took a single episode from nature—a chance sight of country people, the feather of a tree against the sky—and started from there, leaving all else to make-believe. Relying on Claude Lorrain for the template, he was free to invent his dream.

There were no politics to the fantasy. Unlike his fellow landscape painter Richard Wilson, who painted a "landscape of reaction" in those years (in the phrase of David Solkin),[1] Gainsborough had no political purpose in mind. For a land-owning class, Wilson asserted the timelessness of a feudal order in the midst of economic change, but Gainsborough painted no one's land, no one's point of view, not even his own, exactly. His only faith was an aristocratic one—which he as the son of a wool merchant appropriated—that held that political argumentation is in poor taste, that art might be free of the muck and ruckus of contestation. Gainsborough's art was irresponsible, or the opposite.

The painting is its own world. The faraway village lit by the last of the sun will never come nearer—never become an object of knowledge. The figures on horseback who ride toward it do so on a winding road like the ones that turn in Leonardo's *Mona Lisa*—their path is a mystery. The blue-gray three-summited mountain above the sunlit village is like Leonardo's, too—the soft granitic atmosphere of another world. The cryptic Italian master and misanthrope is proof against the idea that paintings must fit the maladroit powers of argumentation, attitude, and fact.

Instead there is only a murk, the thick, clouded forestation of the midground, for instance, that keeps us lost. The trees crowd into a declivity,

Fig. 27. Detail showing shepherd

pouring themselves into the greater darkness of the valley. Like everything else in the painting, the trees lack hardness, thickness; they mix their leaves in the evening's softness. It is impossible to feel that their downward energy is heavy or hurried. The world falls with barely a whisper.

A man lurks at the base of those trees—a shepherd, walking to the left, minding his flock (fig. 27). He is barely visible, leagued with the verdant darkness; he might be the trees' sylvan offspring, their pantheist keeper. His half-perceived walk through the valley attunes to the trees, as though they could not spill downward without his presence, or else (for this is possible, too) they could not rise out of that valley if he did not appear in it. Like some English Johnny Appleseed, like some sower of Millet, he plants the world. But he does so in darkness, a mysterious man of whom no dendrochronology will announce the age.

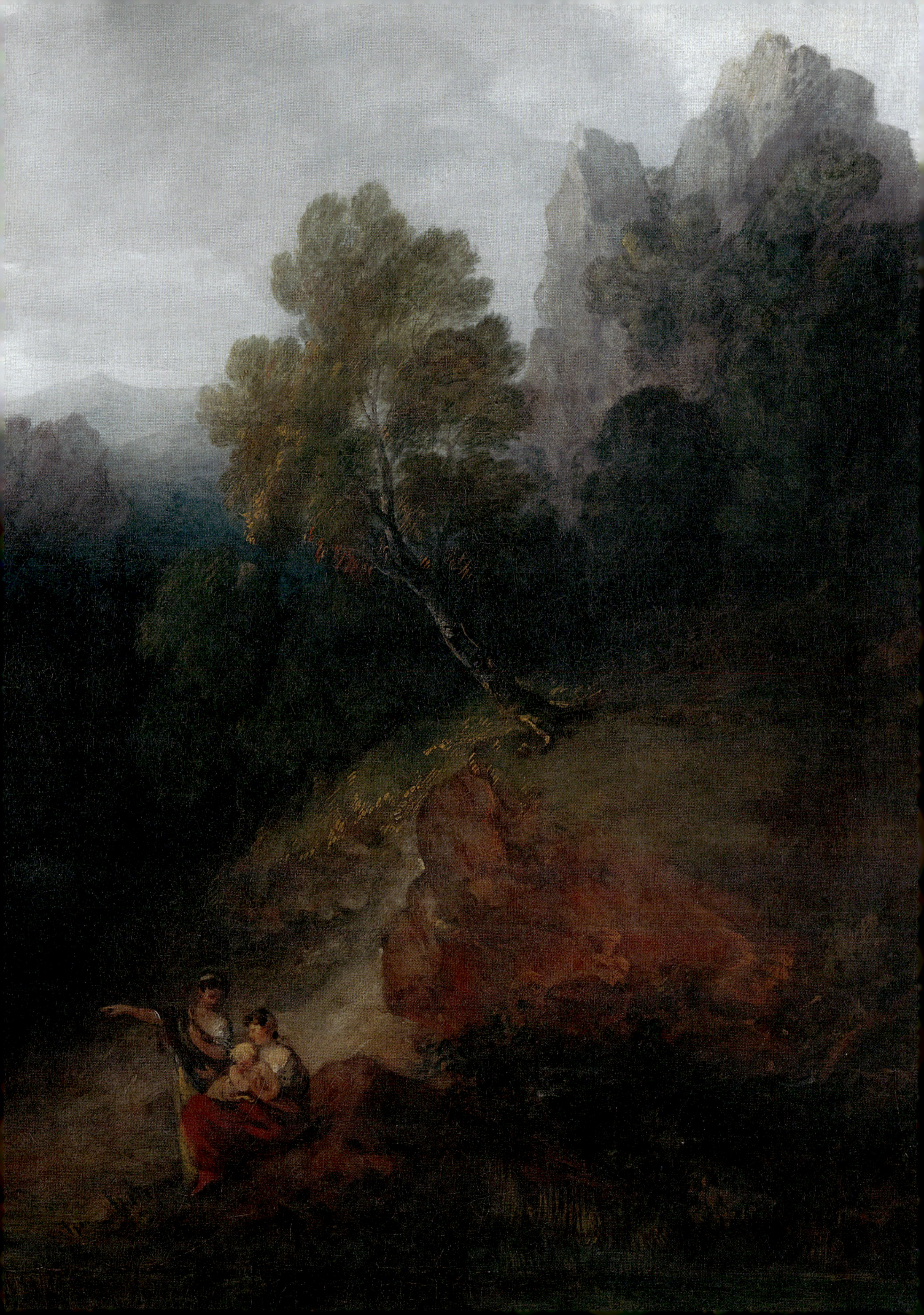

So we look to the foreground figures, saving them for last, since they are our best hope, our likeliest witnesses (fig. 28). A dark-haired mother sits at the base of a rock, holding a blond baby on her lap. A young girl, part of the family group, points to the left, gesturing with the authority of Caravaggio's Jesus or Michelangelo's God. Her finger dips slightly down. Does she point to the sheep? Or to the shepherd (the father of the family)? Or is she pointing to the visible darkness in which the man walks?

Whatever the girl does, she instructs. She looks down at the squirming baby, who turns in rough accord with her gesture. It is a first lesson, an early attempt to name the things of the world, to turn darkness into a little light, the Rousseau innocence of the light-haired child. A path runs down from a lone tree to the family, a simple sweep of dirt connecting tree and girl in echoes of natural eloquence. But the girl's pose of knowledge is muted and small, a locality in the universe, nothing to the seductive silver-gray clouds.

The humble world is Gainsborough's interest. He does not focus on the town but on what happens in the countryside. Out there, the shepherd and his family—if that is what they are—must barely feel the centripetal pull of the chimneys and roofs. The market day, such as it is, may draw them down the road. And the little girl's gesture, sunlit like the town, owes something to the seesaw balance of dependents and villages—the little family at lower right, the stone place at upper left. But the family's world is so replete in that valley, so beyond earshot of anything that might happen elsewhere, that Gainsborough imagines modest gestures exalted on their own, without reference to town.

They are dignified, these gestures, because they drown. Folkways continue the practice and lore of generations. Memory contributes its share. But Gainsborough portrays all that vanishes. He envisions the ephemeral moment, barely lit and barely to be remembered. He wants to show it as it disappears, tiding to gentle invisibility. There is no mordancy or melancholy in this. It is a factual matter—how to show the fading of the world, its ongoing, day-to-day, second-to-second evaporation from one moment to the next. This change happens without town, it happens without sound. It is part of the flux that makes the world—that Leonardo, for instance, knew so well: how water flows, how clouds transform, how night falls.

Note

1. David Solkin, *Richard Wilson: The Landscape of Reaction* (London: Tate Publishing, 1982).

Opposite: Fig. 28. Detail showing foreground figures

James Forbes (British, 1749–1819) "A View of the Ocean, Between the Tropics, As it is Generally Animated, by a Variety of Fish and Birds," folio 257 from *A Voyage from England to Bombay with Descriptions in Asia, Africa, and South America (1765–1800)*, vol. 9, 1776

Watercolor on paper, pasted into album, 8¼ x 11 in. (21 x 28 cm)

YALE CENTER FOR BRITISH ART, PAUL MELLON COLLECTION, SAVE 2511

Jennifer Tucker

This watercolor drawing of a variety of fish leaping out of the sea was made by James Forbes in 1776 for volume 9 of his thirteen-volume folio series, *A Voyage from England to Bombay with Descriptions in Asia, Africa, and South America* .[1] Forbes, the son of a London merchant, was an author, amateur artist, and traveler. He began his career in Bombay in 1765 as a sixteen-year-old writer for the East India Company and worked for nearly twenty years before returning to England in 1784.[2] In Bombay he rose quickly through the Company ranks. A largely self-taught artist, he devoted many hours to sketching and painting, including richly illustrated descriptive letters that were later to form the basis of several volumes describing the flora, fauna, manners, religion, and archaeology of the west coast of India, which he published at his own expense. By the time he left India, he had filled almost one hundred fifty notebooks describing the nature and people he encountered, including views of buildings and forts of interest to the colonial administration, and drawings and paintings of the islands' flora and fauna.

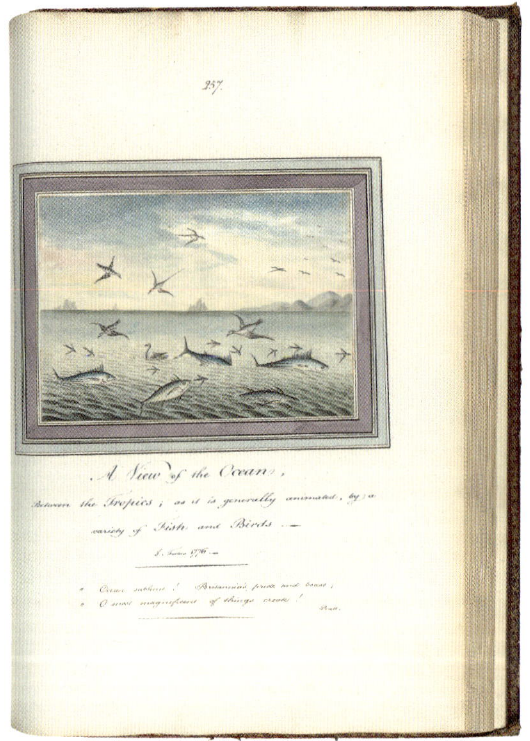

At the time that he compiled the drawings for this volume, Forbes was returning to England, afflicted by illness, though he was back in Bombay by 1777. Most of the drawings in his albums are from the Cape of Good Hope and other parts of Africa.[3] The fish drawings and watercolors are mainly from along the coast of Guinea: for example, the "Medusa" (fig. 29) and "Cuttle fish."[4] Fish might seem an inglorious subject for British art. Yet drawings and watercolors of fish tell us an immense amount about the nexus of art, natural history, and empire. Few topics fascinated people in Britain

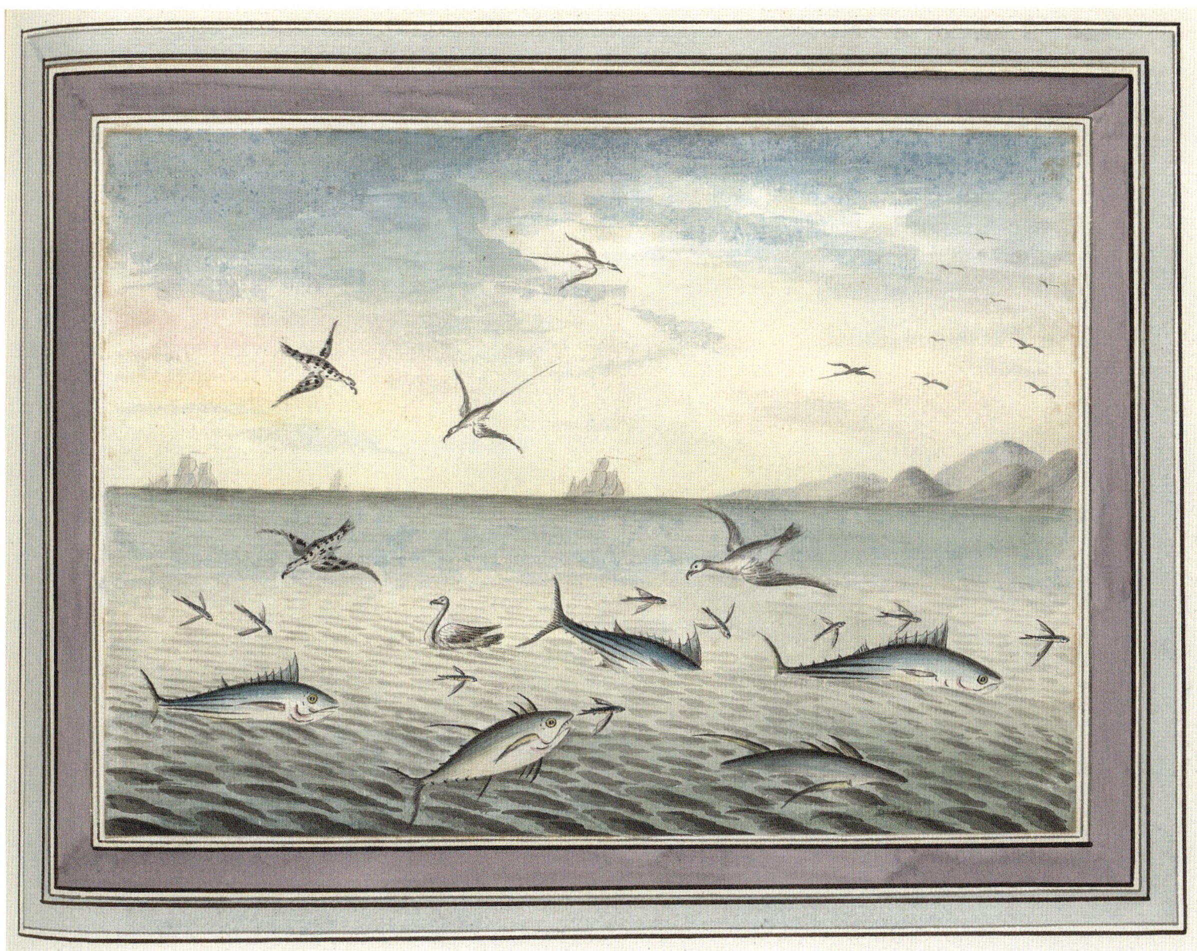

during the eighteenth and nineteenth centuries more than the sea. Britons from a variety of classes and backgrounds had intimate, practical acquaintance with life at sea. Even those who stayed on land were intrigued by its possibilities and dangers. Britain was, of course, a naval power, and battles at sea, merchant shipping, and the slave trade all became central to the creation and maintenance of the British Empire. But the ocean fascinated audiences in Britain for other reasons as well. In an age when natural philosophers had encyclopedic ambitions to command and classify knowledge of the world, the ocean remained stubbornly full of secrets. Drawings of fish seen during oceanic voyages expressed the plenitude of nature and the potential of the empirical sciences to reveal the mysteries beneath the ocean's surface.

Painting fish posed many practical difficulties. Unlike other natural specimens, fish were not easily preserved. Often fish flew on board. Naturalists then secured and drew them while the colors were still bright. Usually, for this reason, fish had to be drawn "on the spot" to assure that the colors were faithful. Drawings of fish provided visual documentation of new species and marked progress in zoology, particularly in the Linnaean period (1750–1850). Although Forbes was not a trained naturalist, his artworks express the wider fascination of the time in both the sheer abundance of oceanic life and the specificity of individual physical descriptions and nomenclature. There is an especially ecological aspect to Forbes's *View of the Ocean*, capturing as it does, and in a very striking way, the relationship of the fish, flying out of the

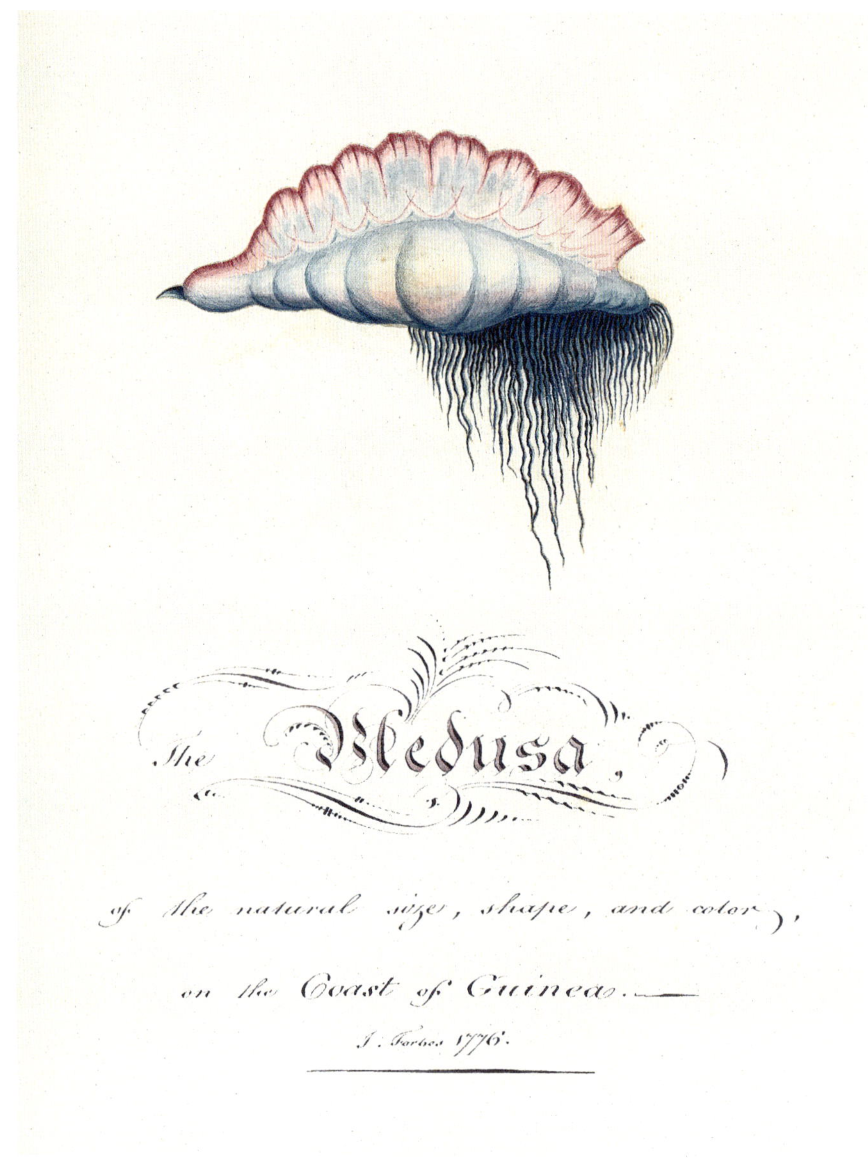

Fig. 29. James Forbes, "Medusa," fol. 237 from *A Voyage from England to Bombay with Descriptions in Asia, Africa, and South America*, vol. 9, 1776, watercolor. Yale Center for British Art, Paul Mellon Collection

sea, to the birds, flying through the air. The composition seems to emphasize the animation from beneath the surface, to the surface itself (the seabird on the water), and then into the sky—and movement across the boundary of the ocean's surface. In other words, the illustration is not only about individual species but also about their interaction.

Forbes accentuated the beauty, natural size, and colors of fish in his drawings. Of the Medusa jellyfish, found off the coast of Guinea, he wrote that "It seems like a large bubble, or transparent inflated bladder, in general two or three inches long, and of an oval shape; at each end is a protuberance, something like a bird's head and beak" (see fig. 29).[5] His drawings and illustrations exemplify the concern for color as both a scientific and aesthetic interest. Fish of the surface waters, like the mackerel and herring, often are blue and green; so are the floats of the Portuguese men-of-war and the azure-tinted wings of the swimming snails. Although the color of fish was particularly hard to record because it recedes after they are captured and lifted from the water, eighteenth-century travelers were generally aware that the color of marine animals varies according to their oceanic zones. Beneath the surface waters, where the water becomes more deeply blue, many creatures, such as glassworms and jellies, are crystal clear. At a thousand feet and down, silvery fish are common, while at depths greater than fifteen-hundred feet most fishes are black, deep violet, or brown. Intent upon capturing exactly the "natural size and colours" of the fish that he encountered during his ocean travels, Forbes was also meticulous in depicting as precisely as he could the appearance of eyes, scales, and feelers.

Travel across the ocean could be mind-numbingly boring, but painting fish was both a way of passing the time and an empirical pursuit with the potential to share the knowledge of oceanic experiences with others after the voyage. Some sense of why Forbes was interested in fish comes from his letters, in which he writes of the tedium of ocean travel. Even calm days, he said, "present nothing to amuse a distant correspondent, or to employ the descriptive pen . . . only sky and water, soon grows tedious."[6] He repeated in one of the first volumes of his album a paraphrase of Samuel Johnson: "The Traveller has a mind replete with images, which he can vary and combine with pleasure." Thus he made a connection between ocean travel, natural history, and the new technologies of visual entertainment—a theme that resonated equally through the worlds of eighteenth-century recreation and the serious study of the natural world. At the same time, however, Forbes's observations of marine life often pointed to sinister political realities; for example, he commented negatively on slavery in connection with sightings of sharks that followed slave ships to America and the West Indies "to eat the bodies of the poor Negroes who are so fortunate as to die on the voyage, and escape from Christian bondage."[7]

The transformation of fish into art was a product of the emergence of European empires. In their beauty and utility, drawings and paintings of fish like these belong to the family of works signified by the theme of "Art of the British Empire," extending our understanding both of how art recast nature, and of how nature animated art.

Notes

1. James Forbes, *A View of the Ocean, Between the Tropics, As it is Generally Animated, by a Variety of Fish and Birds*, in Forbes, *A Voyage from England to Bombay with Descriptions in Asia, Africa, and South America (1765–1800)*, 13 vols. (1776), 9:fol. 257: hereafter, *Voyages and Travels*. In addition to descriptive letters, volume 9 includes approximately 520 watercolor drawings, a number of colored and uncolored engravings, and engraved and manuscript maps. The manuscript was finished in 1800, although most of the drawings seem to have been done at the time of the voyage, ca. 1765–76.
2. See Pauline Rohatgi, "Early Impressions of the Islands: James Forbes and James Wales in Bombay, 1766–95," in *Bombay to Mumbai: Changing Perspectives*, eds. Pauline Rohatgi and Pheroza Godrej (Mumbai: Marg Foundation, 2007).
3. In addition to watercolors of fish, other watercolors by Forbes contained in volume 9 include drawings from the Cape of Good Hope and other parts of Africa. These reflect his wider interest in the natural history of India and Africa. They include, for example, representations of the camel-leopard, a rhino, a hippo, an ostrich egg ("natural size") sold as a cage for small birds, and watercolors of plants of Africa admired by European botanists.
4. James Forbes, "The Medusa, of the natural size, shape, and color, on the Coast of Guinea," *Voyages and Travels* (1776), 9:fol. 237.
5. Forbes, *Voyages and Travels* (1776), 9:216–18; quote on 216.
6. Ibid., 9:125.
7. Ibid., 9: 218. He followed the description with a poem, which described "the terror of the seas" where "dwells the direful Shark – Lur'd by the scent / Of steaming crowds, of rank disease, and deaths."

Agostino Brunias (Italian, 1728–1796; active in Britain, 1758–1770, 1777–1780s)
Linen Market, Dominica, ca. 1780

Oil on canvas, 19⅝ x 27 in. (49.8 x 68.6 cm). YALE CENTER FOR BRITISH ART, PAUL MELLON COLLECTION, B1981.25.76

Agostino Brunias (Italian, 1728–1796; active in Britain, 1758–1770, 1777–1780s)
A Leeward Islands Carib Family outside a Hut, ca. 1780

Oil on canvas, 12⅛ x 9¾ in. (30.8 x 24.8 cm). YALE CENTER FOR BRITISH ART, PAUL MELLON COLLECTION, B1981.25.78

Joseph Roach

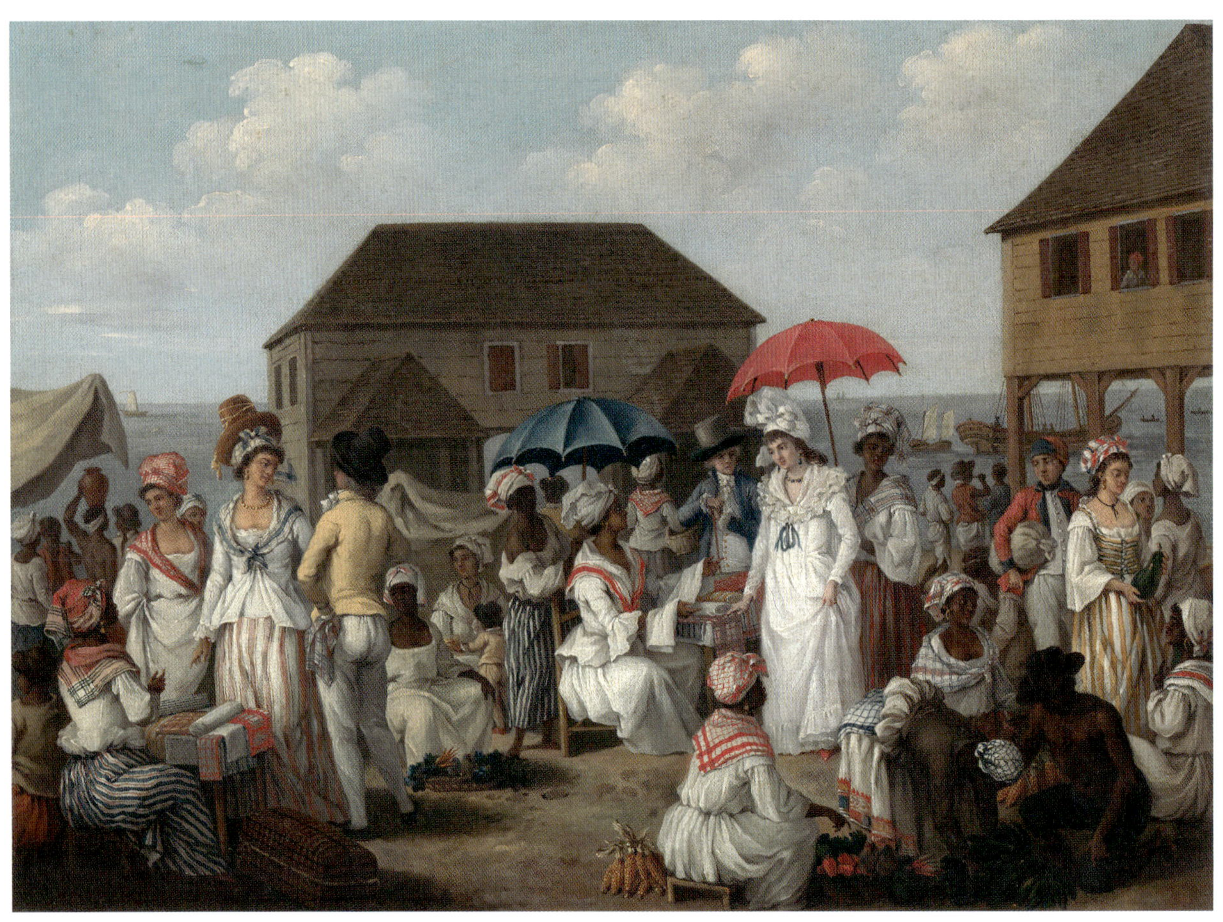

Color tells. Among the many large, blue pictures, long-established and apparently serene in their preeminence, there suddenly appeared a burst of small, pink prints. Like rude pictorial telegrams arriving on the natural Belgian linen walls of the Yale Center for British Art, they startled the eye by contrast, for size also matters. Featured in the exhibition and prize-winning catalogue *Art and Emancipation in Jamaica: Isaac Mendes Belisario and His Worlds* (2007), they changed more worlds than Belisario's (see fig. 30). Taken from the artist's *Sketches of Character, In Illustration of the Habits, Occupation, and Costume of the Negro Population of the Island of Jamaica* (1837–38), they refocused the gaze of their many beholders, enlarging the visual field of metropolitan Britain's dominant culture to include the flourishing but long underrepresented intercultures of colonial empire and subsequent postcolonial relations. This eye-opening change of focus highlighted, among other things, different strengths of the Center's existing collections. Few among them rival for vividness of detail the West Indian scenes of Agostino Brunias, the Italian painter and draftsman who followed Sir William Young after he took up his post as Commissioner and Receiver for sale of lands in the islands of Dominica, St. Vincent, and Tobago in 1764.

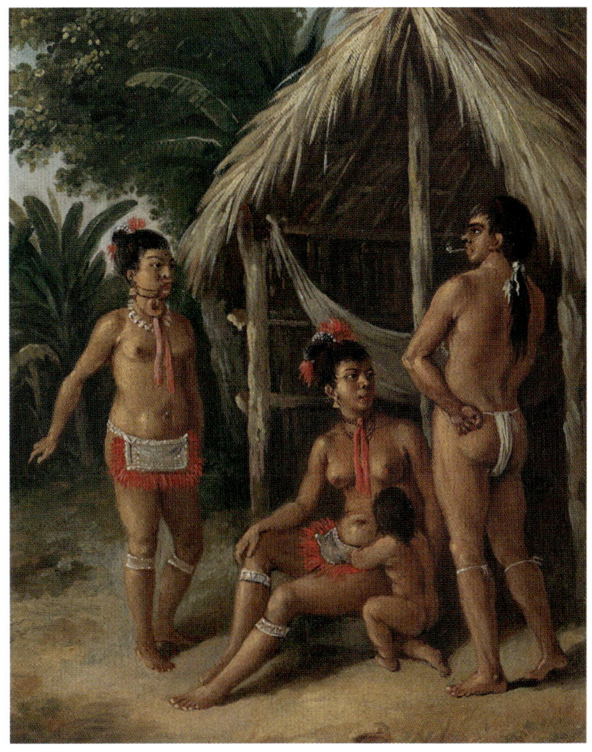

Like Belisario on Jamaica sixty years later, Brunias employed warm hues and varied tints to produce small pictures that illustrate the habits, occupations, and costumes of the multiracial populations, enslaved and free, of the Caribbean archipelago. He documents nodal points in a cultural network that has captured the sustained attention of historians of British art only relatively recently. To Kay Dian Kriz, the keyword is *refinement*, which refers to processing not only sugar but also people.[1] To David Bindman, it is *fluidity*, which refers to movement, not only of people but also of commodities and practices, over water.[2] Both are apposite, but the one I want to foreground, following Mia L. Bagneris, is *colour*.[3]

Agostino Brunias's masterpiece in the Center is titled *Linen Market, Dominica* (ca. 1780). Overcrowded with flesh and cloth, it is a scene of prosperity unfolding against a backdrop of peace—blue sky, calm sea, happy natives. Also of note by way of complement is Brunias's Edenic *A Leeward Islands Carib Family outside a Hut* (ca. 1780), which is a scene of pastoral tranquility staged in front of a palm-frond hut—naked flesh, lush foliage, happy natives. In *Linen Market*, linen-draped women, their white dresses as dreamy as the distant clouds, mingle in the marketplace, shopping for more linen. The lightest-skinned shopper among them is shaded by a red parasol, carried behind her by a dark-skinned slave. All the women, even those wearing hats, cover their hair with the *chignon* (in Louisiana, *tignon*). By custom and later by law in the Francophone Caribbean, this special headdress was required of all females among the *gens de couleur*, enslaved or free, especially after generations of race-mixing had made it difficult to distinguish between lighter-skinned "black" women and darker-skinned "white" women. Such small differences in color made some of them but not others available for purchase as slaves or for appropriation as mistresses under the system of sanctioned concubinage known as *plaçage*.

After France ceded the islands to Britain by terms of the Treaty of Paris (1763), Commissioner Young was charged with the difficult task of attracting more tradesmen, small farmers, and professionals to populate the islands with English-speaking settlers, loyal to king and country. Whatever else may have motivated Brunias to paint scenes such as the one depicted in the *Linen Market*, which advertised corporeal superabundance in a prosperous commercial setting, or in the *Carib Family*, which reassured doubters about the docility of the natives, his patron must have hoped that such images would at least catch the eye of potential colonists. Brunias eventually exhibited at the Royal Academy of Arts in London, and his works circulated as prints, while Young wrote earnest pamphlets, acknowledging with disarming candor the difficulties of persuading Britons to make the risky move to a colony, while nevertheless encouraging them to consider it. Brunias ultimately set an example by settling in Dominica himself.

In fact, Young and Brunias were working within a familiar, if precarious, genre of colonial promotion. Young was wise to approach it with caution, because it had proven its appeal with disastrous effect four decades earlier. François-Gérard Jollain's colorful image of an imaginary New Orleans, engraved on a hand-colored copperplate and produced between 1719 and 1721, depicts the dream colony that the Scottish financier John Law promoted in France under the aegis of his royally chartered Mississippi Company (fig. 31). New Orleans was then an island, the northernmost of the Caribbean archipelago, reliably accessible only by ship or boat until the nineteenth century. Law named it after the prince regent, Philippe, duc d'Orléans, and sold shares backed by paper notes, precipitating the wild run of speculative investment known as the "Mississippi Bubble," which was shortly succeeded by the "South Sea Bubble" in Britain. In 1720, when the Mississippi Bubble burst, shares in Law's company became all but worthless overnight, faith in the value of paper money evaporated, and the most vulnerable investors of all, the colonists lured to New Orleans by Law's scheme, were left stranded and starving in a storm-lashed puddle of wretched huts. Jollain's background, showing the picturesque mountains in which the spired and crenellated city of New Orleans nestles, is an especially mendacious flourish, for Law spread word that Louisiana was rich in gold. Identifying the Native Americans with Mexico, as Jollain's come-on does, further insinuates that trade with

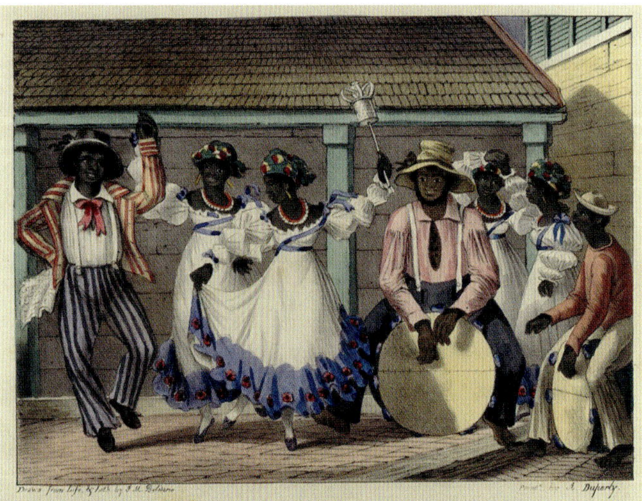

Fig. 30. Isaac Mendes Belisario, "French Set-Girls," from *Sketches of Character, In Illustration of Habits, Occupation, and Costume of the Negro Population in the Island of Jamaica*, 1837–38, lithograph with watercolor, 7⅛ x 9¾ in. (18.1 x 24.8 cm). Yale Center for British Art, Paul Mellon Collection

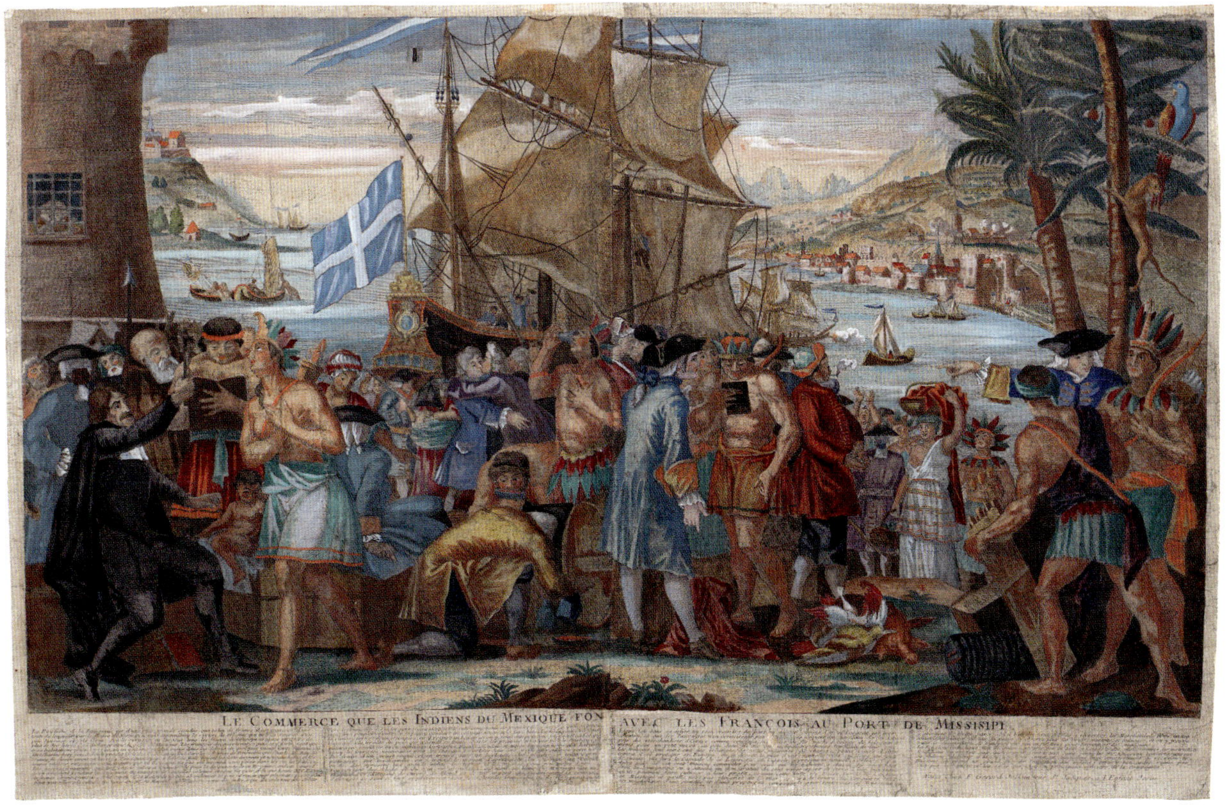

Fig. 31. François-Gérard Jollain, *Le commerce que les Indiens du Mexique font avec les François au Port de Missisipi*, 1719–21, engraving with watercolor, 18 3/16 x 32 3/4 in. (46.2 x 83.2 cm). The Historic New Orleans Collection

the bullion-rich Spanish colonies likewise beckons from just around the corner. Identifying the so-called Indians with heaps of produce, game, and pelts signifies sources of natural abundance and also a potentially captive labor force. Identifying the Indians as grateful converts suggests easy pacification, while the first consignment of enslaved Africans arrived punctually in 1719.[4] Ruthlessly managed, exploited labor is worth more than gold.[5] The not wholly dissimilar world depicted by Brunias in the second half of the eighteenth century—a predominantly Francophone colony of many colors whose ultimate fate was to be assimilated by an English-speaking regime—suggests that somewhere within the promotional hyperbole and racist presuppositions of the *Linen Market* and the *Carib Family* may linger the wispy vision, shimmering at the uttermost perimeter of the future where horizon becomes mirage, of a truly postracial society the like of which the world has not yet seen

Notes

1. Kay Dian Kriz, *Slavery, Sugar, and the Culture of Refinement: Picturing the British West Indies, 1700–1840* (New Haven and London: Yale Univ. Press, 2008), 3–5.
2. David Bindman, "Representing Race in the Eighteenth-Century Caribbean: Brunias in Dominica and St Vincent," *Eighteenth-Century Studies* 51, no. 1 (2017): 14–15.
3. Mia L. Bagneris, *Colouring the Caribbean: Race and the Art of Agostino Brunias* (Manchester: Manchester Univ. Press, 2018), 23.
4. Erin M. Greenwald, ed., *New Orleans, the Founding Era*, (New Orleans: Historic New Orleans Collection, 2018), 110–11.
5. Sarah Thomas, "Envisaging a Future for Slavery: Agostino Brunias and the Imperial Politics of Labor and Reproduction," *Eighteenth-Century Studies* 52, no. 1 (2018): 115–33.

James Forbes (British, 1749–1819)
"The Large Indian Bat," folio 197 from *A Voyage from England to Bombay with Descriptions in Asia, Africa, and South America (1765–1800)*, vol. 12, 1782

Ink and watercolor on paper, opened: 21¼ x 30¼ in. (54 x 76.8 cm)

YALE CENTER FOR BRITISH ART, PAUL MELLON COLLECTION, SAVE 2511

Holly Shaffer

In 1782 the East India Company official James Forbes drew "The Large Indian Bat"—*Vespertilio magnus*—stretched a foot and a half across the page of one of thirteen red-leather-bound albums that he would present to his twelve-year-old daughter Elizabeth Forbes in 1800, after his return from India.[1] The bat on the page is a mere portion of the animal's actual wingspan of "upwards of six Feet"; it is displayed to convey that breadth from below with a furry body and veined wings. Its clawed feet curve inward, and its five bony fingers extend from its winged arms, including the thumb to hook onto the branch of a tree.

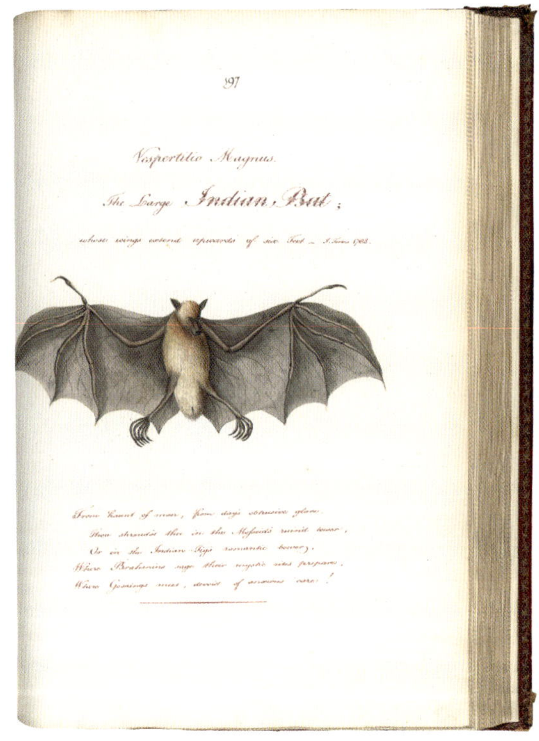

Forbes limned the bat as if both bird and beast. In a related disquisition, he stressed its dual classification: "As the monkey seems to unite the brute with the human species, in the great chain of creation, so the bats form the link between the birds and beasts."[2] He called on ancient and modern naturalists to determine to "which class they belong." "Pliny and the ancients," he wrote, "place them among the former; but the moderns seem more properly to fix them with quadrupeds—like a bird, they have wings, and the power of flying; but on the contrary they bring forth their young alive, and suckle them."[3]

Forbes wrote in the preface to his albums that his letters were "chiefly intended to elucidate the drawings, which accompanied them."[4] But they also added layers of association. If Forbes leaned toward a scientific assessment in part of his description, he turned to poetry for the fearsome and romantic. The sensitively drawn sly eye, pert ears, and upturned mouth of the bat paralleled his judgment that "these of their size, are a kind of monster, extremely disagreeable, both in their smell and appearance." The bat leaves the realm of classification to enter that of horror in Forbes's

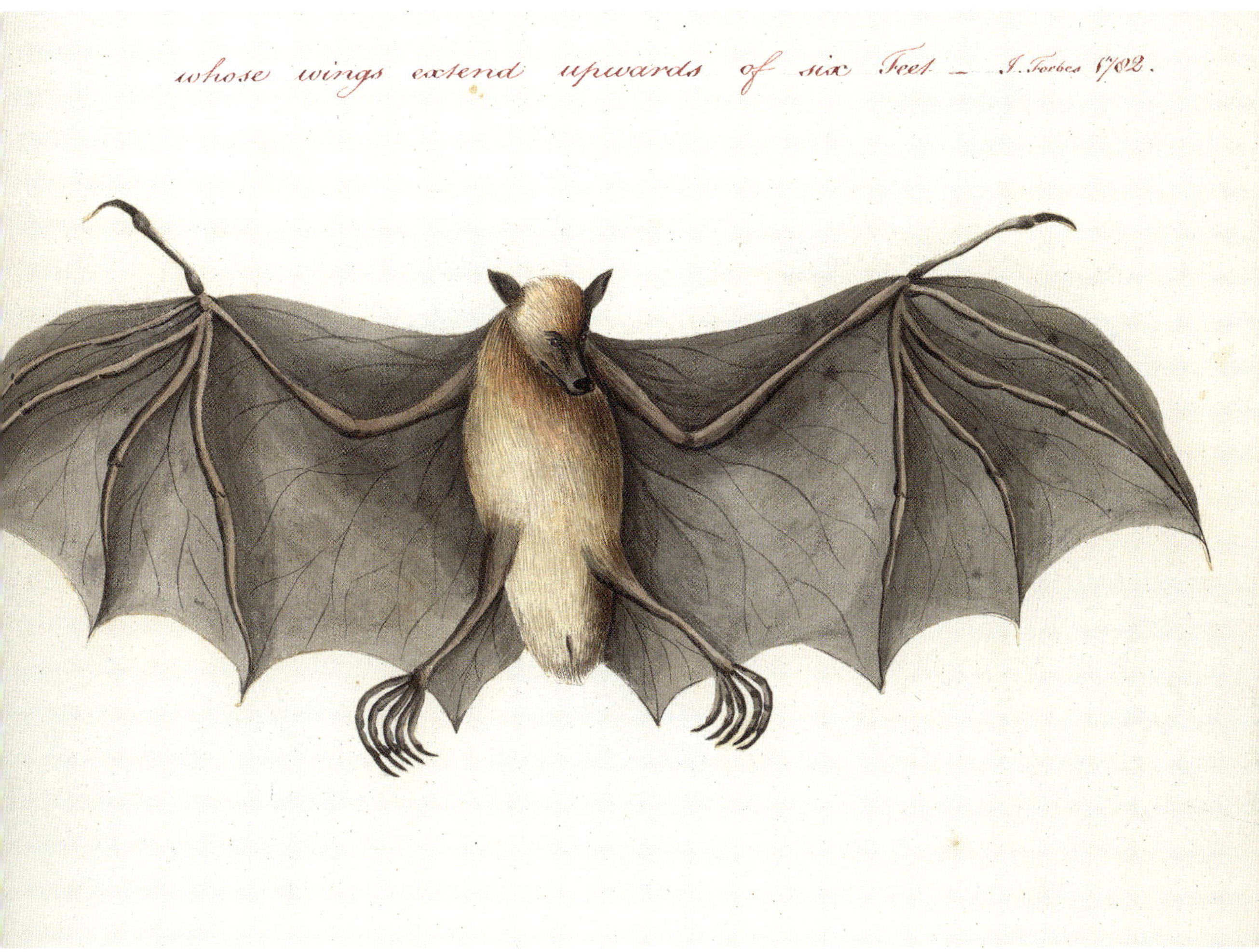

evaluation, resembling a fright well-known in the West, "most probably the Harpies, so often mentioned by Virgil."[5]

Yet Forbes drew the bat because he witnessed it in western India. He went to great lengths to "delineate the different subjects in natural history" in his written and visual accounts. He sought to "record the occurrences of the day" before he retired to rest, "from the imperial elephant to the smallest insect; with almost every bird, fish, fruit, plant, and flower" that he "met with in his travels." Indeed, Forbes made his observations while traveling in his palanquin "or reposing under the friendly shade of the Banian tree" with "the scene" before his eyes.[6]

His encounter with bats hanging from the many-branched banyan tree by the banks of the Narmada River in Gujarat made up one "scene." These bats inspired the one drawn splayed on the page. In an adjacent letter, Forbes wrote that

> the Bats at Cabbee-Buri are of an enormous size, frequently exceeding six feet from the tip of one wing to the other; they are . . . termed flying foxes, from their resemblance to that animal . . . These bats, when they repose or eat, suspend themselves by their claws, with their head downwards, and hang by thousands on the lofty branches of this tree.[7]

In the drawing and letter in his album, Forbes wove together his memory of the tree and the bats, crowded in its knotted branches, with cultural and

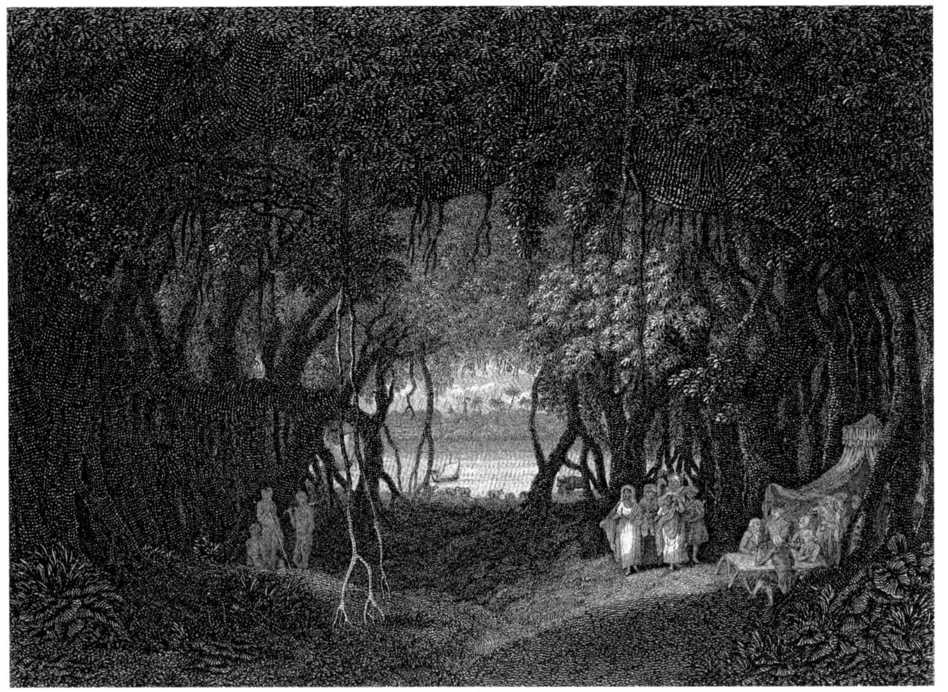

Fig. 32. James Forbes, "View of Cubbeer Burr, the celebrated Banian Tree on the Banks of the Nerbudda," plate 4 from *Oriental Memoirs*, vol. 1 (London : Printed for the author by T. Bensley, Bolt Court; published by White, Cochrane, and Co. Horace's Head, Fleet-Street, 1813), engraving on paper. Yale Center for British Art, Paul Mellon Collection

literary associations. In a poem copied in neat cursive beneath the watercolor, he added characters, a set, and lighting:

> From haunt of man, from day's obtrusive glare,
> Thou shroud'st thee in the Mosseid's ruin'd tower,
> Or in the Indian-Fig's romantic bower,
> Where Brahmins sage their mystic rites prepare,
> Where Gosaings meet, devoid of anxious care![8]

The depiction of the bat's wingspan above encases the gloomy picture described in the lines below. It draws into the mind the ruins of a mosque's tower and the sacred space of a temple along with priests and yogis who invoke, and add to, the tree's awesome aura. Forbes was haunted by the activity within this bower. For the first volume of his book *Oriental Memoirs* (1813), he had the banyan's branches engraved in deep velvety lines that seem to echo the span of the bat's stooping scalloped wings, which would have been folded tightly, suspended in the tree's depths (fig. 32).

Forbes's writings claim verity. He had learned to draw as a schoolboy and Company cadet, but he was essentially, and proud to be, an innocent. "In my youthful days I never was desirous of any extraneous embellishment," Forbes wrote. "I sought for truth and novelty; but I wished the former to be the only foundation for the superstructure of the latter."[9] Yet the variety of text that he accrued around the drawing wraps it in an encroaching aesthetic of the gothic that motivated so many Company officials, artists, and travelers in this period.[10]

Forbes was not the only artist in thrall of the large Indian bat, nor was he alone in melding his observations with romance. Indian artists infused their depictions of the great bat with a sublime and particular animation. While working for Sir Elijah Impey, the Chief Justice of Bengal, the Mughal-trained artist Bhawani Das, and others in his circle, painted bats (see fig. 33). Here also, the bat is not simply a bat. From this artist's hand, the bat's dark pupils stare gleaming at the viewer, its muscles flexed to extend one wing and fold the other, to make knowing contact.

The bat as "monster" had a literary genealogy that extended to Indian antiquity as it did in the

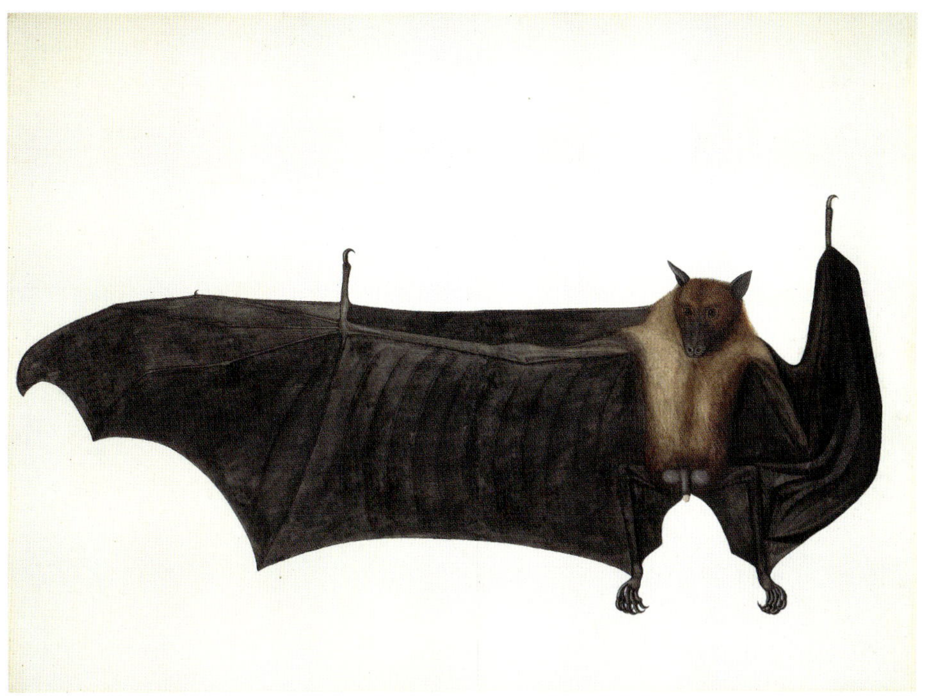

Fig. 33. Bhawani Das, *Great Indian Fruit Bat*, ca. 1777-82, pencil, ink, and opaque watercolor on paper, 23½ x 32¾ in. (59.7 x 83.2 cm). The Metropolitan Museum of Art, New York

West to Roman antiquity. A series of Sanskrit texts strung together as the *Baital Pacisi* tell the story of King Vikrama and his encounter with one of his "brothers," a corpse-eating ascetic who hangs upside-down from a tree like a bat.[11] The orientalist Richard Burton published a translation of these tales in 1870 as *Vikram and the Vampire*, but the popularity of a part zombie-yogi, part vampire-bat has deeper origins. In fact, the *Baital Pacisi* and other tales, as David Gordon White has discussed, were chosen by British colonial educators to teach Indic languages to new Company recruits at Fort William College in Calcutta.[12] Deemed lucid and informative examples of colloquial "Hindostani," the undoubtedly compelling texts introduced the Indian bat, the vampire, and the yogi to a British audience already attuned to such knowledge.

The large Indian bat thus spoke in languages familiar to many audiences, not only English, Latin, Sanskrit, and "Hindostani" but also in natural and literary history, in tales and reminiscences, and thin watercolor washes of veins, hairs, and finger claws that goaded gothic imaginings.

Notes

1. See Elisabeth Fairman, "Catalogue 130: James Forbes, A Voyage from England to Bombay, with Descriptions in Asia, Africa, and South America, 1766–1784," in John Baskett et al., *Paul Mellon's Legacy: A Passion for British Art* (New Haven: Yale Center for British Art, 2007), 273–74.
2. James Forbes, *A Voyage from England to Bombay with Descriptions in Asia, Africa, and South America (1765–1800)*, 13 vols., 12:174.
3. Ibid.
4. Ibid., 1:7–9.
5. Ibid., 12:174.
6. Ibid., 1:7–9.
7. Ibid., 12:174.
8. Ibid., 12:197.
9. Ibid., 1:7 9.
10. See Romita Ray, *Under the Banyan Tree: Relocating the Picturesque in British India* (New Haven and London: Yale Univ. Press, 2013), 110–18; and Hermione de Almeida and George H. Gilpin, *Indian Renaissance: British Romantic Art and the Prospect of India* (Aldershot, UK: Ashgate, 2005), 41–42.
11. David Gordon White, *Sinister Yogis* (Chicago: Univ. of Chicago Press, 2009), 6–7, 21–23.
12. White, *Sinister Yogis*, 238.

Reverend John Lightfoot (British, 1735–1788)
A Catalogue of the Portland Museum: Lately the Property of the Duchess Dowager of Portland, Deceased (London: Mr. Skinner and Co., 1786)

Printed book: 11 x 17 in. (27.9 x 43.2 cm), opened

Jane Wildgoose

Following a direction in the Duchess of Portland's (1715–1785) will stating that "I desire all my China Japan Shells and Prints may be sold," her "Grand Museum, in which she expended so much of her fortune" was put up for auction at her London residence in Whitehall during the spring and early summer of 1786.[1] Originally assembled at Bulstrode—the Duchess's country house in Buckinghamshire where she maintained extensive gardens, a well-stocked menagerie, and an aviary containing peacocks and other exotic birds—her collection of natural history and fine and decorative arts became known as the Portland Museum and was the focus of a "Hive" of scientific and artistic activity.[2] The Duchess's friend Mary Delany, who made regular extended visits to Bulstrode over many years, regarded the house and all it contained as a "Philosophic Cabinet" and a "*noble school*" in which to study nature.[3] Delany's correspondence offers an intimate picture of life at Bulstrode: where learned natural history specialists, artists, and other visitors, including members of the Royal Family, were attracted as much by the Duchess's seemingly limitless passion for celebrating, documenting, and ordering nature as by the multitude of specimens and artifacts that she accumulated.

The "Articles of *Virtu*" in the sale of the Portland Museum included "curious snuff boxes" and "exceeding curious articles," as well as porcelain, prints, coins and medals, drawings, miniatures and other pictures, "*Chinese* and *Indian* Artificial Curiosities," jewels, and "matchless Antiquities." The most valuable artifact of all was lot 4155: "*the most celebrated antique* VASE, *or* SEPULCHRAL URN, *from the* Barberini *cabinet, at* Rome"—afterwards known as the Portland Vase, and now in the British Museum in London.[4] But the majority of the 4,156 (mostly compound) lots consisted of natural history specimens representing "the Three Kingdoms of Nature, the *Animal*, *Vegetable*, and *Fossil*."[5] Of these, the Duchess's shell collection, which included rare specimens from Captain James Cook's voyages—as well as from her own and her friends' explorations of the coast of England, with purchases from fellow enthusiasts, sailors, fishermen, and specialist dealers—was unequaled "in Number and Variety" by any other in Europe.

Together with great quantities of corals and minerals, shells took up business on twenty-nine of the thirty-eight days on which the auction took place.[6] Writing in the preface to the *Catalogue of the Portland Museum: Lately the Property of the Duchess Dowager of Portland, Deceased* (1786), its compiler, the naturalist Reverend John Lightfoot,[7] explains that "the celebrated" taxonomist "*Linnæus*, who had studied the Subject, and methodized the Materials of it, has not described One Fourth Part of the Objects contained in the Museum now offered to the Public." The Duchess, Lightfoot adds, aimed "to have had *every unknown* Species" of shell "described and published to the World," and employed one of Carl Linnaeus's favorite pupils,

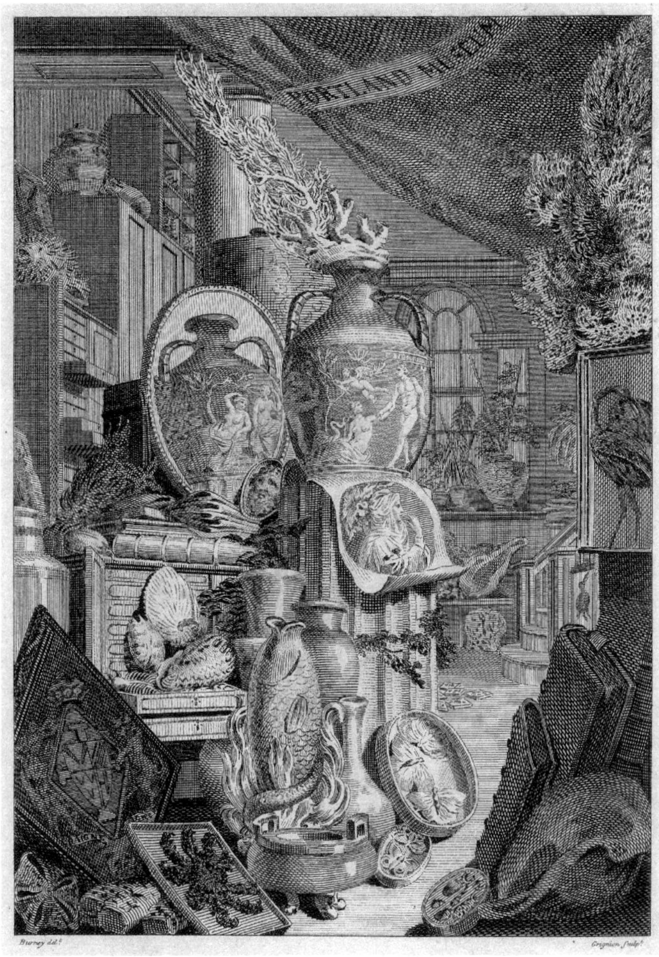

Daniel Solander, to catalogue them. However, her ambitious project was prematurely curtailed: first by Solander's death in 1782 and then, "to the great and irreparable loss of Science, by her *own* also."[8]

Had the Duchess of Portland lived longer, Lightfoot mused, all the shells itemized in the *Catalogue* would have been described and named using the Linnaean system. But in the end, that immense task would fall to Lightfoot, who drew on Solander's unfinished work and did the best he could in the time available between the Duchess's death in July 1785 and the sale, which took place a little under a year later. Lamenting the "Promiscuous Assemblage of the various subjects" presented for auction, Lightfoot regretted that the natural history specimens had to be grouped thematically, rather than in scientific order, which would have necessitated sorting them either into large groups of the same species, or as single items, or in pairs: making them less attractive as lots to buyers who liked variety, and extending the sale by many weeks.

I first encountered the *Catalogue* of the sale of the Portland Museum in the Yale Center for British Art's Rare Books and Manuscripts Department in 2007, when I was commissioned to devise an artist installation containing a cabinet celebrating the friendship between the Duchess of Portland and Mary Delany, to accompany the Center's exhibition *Mrs. Delany & Her Circle* (September 24, 2009–July 18, 2010). The *Catalogue* became a constant reference as I went about planning and configuring a "memory theater" of specially made new artifacts, presented with hundreds of objects selected from the natural history, decorative arts, and rare books and manuscripts collections at Yale, which together illustrated the *promiscuous assemblage* of the auction lamented by Lightfoot. At the same time, this display evoked the Duchess and Mrs. Delany's *friendship*, founded on a shared enthusiasm for the scientific and decorative ordering of nature within their respective domestic environments, and *the order of things*: the evolution of the taxonomical method introduced by Linnaeus (of which both women were knowledgeable at the time of its inception), foundational to the organization of natural history collections in museums today (fig. 34).

Lightfoot, who "was scientifically inclined . . . toward botany and conchology," was a Fellow of the Royal Society from 1781 and a founding member of the Linnaean Society of London.[9] He served in the Duchess's household for eighteen years as her librarian and chaplain, from 1767 until her death in 1785, and was well placed to propose that the *Catalogue* would "in a great Measure demonstrate" the diligence of the Duchess of Portland's "Enquiries into Natural Knowledge and the Polite Arts," as well as the success of "her endeavours to encrease the Stores of them."[10]

How has Lightfoot's prediction stood the test of time? Writing almost two hundred years later, Harald A. Rehder (a curator in the Division of Mollusks at the Smithsonian Institution's National Museum of Natural History) noted that the Portland *Catalogue* has been "used as a reference source of scientific names almost since its publication" and continued to be well-known among mollusk specialists "as a document of nomenclatural significance," with many of the names first assigned in it still in use in the 1960s.[11] Ilya Temkin suggests that according to the most recent nomenclatural standards, "111 molluscan specific and 2 generic names were validly proposed" in the *Catalogue*, "of which 62 are available names and are attributed to Lightfoot" today.[12]

In the fields of art history and the history of collecting, at the turn of the twenty-first century the *Catalogue's* capacity to stand as testament to the Duchess of Portland's "Enquiries into Natural Knowledge and the Polite Arts" seemed to have stood the test of time less well. With one commentator dismissing the Duchess as one of a number of "wealthy collectors . . . with varying degrees of interest in the science" for whom "amassing a high-quality collection was enough in itself," the Duchess's obscurity was attributed to the dispersal of her collection after her death by another.[13] Beth Fowkes Tobin (whose research on the Duchess's shell collecting is comprehensive and compelling) observes that she was "long overlooked within the fields of history of science, women's history, cultural history, and museum studies."[14]

But in 2006 the exhibition *Duchess of Curiosities: The Life of Margaret, Duchess of Portland*, at the Harley Gallery at Welbeck, in Nottinghamshire, vividly resurrected the richness and diversity of the Duchess's museum. Writing in the accompanying booklet, Rebecca Stott succinctly defined the way in which the Duchess's home at Bulstrode "was not just an elaborate display case of rare and curious things" but also "a working environment," where collecting encompassed "classifying and labeling" in collaboration with "her entourage of botanists, illustrators, and naturalists."[15] More recently, Madeleine Pelling is investigating the Duchess of Portland's collecting from the perspective of her female friendships with fellow bluestockings, including Mary Delany, Mary Hamilton, and Elizabeth Montagu, and the pursuit of a range of domestic crafts, such as decorative shellwork, spinning, lacquerwork, and turning intricate items in ivory and amber on a lathe at Bulstrode—where Delany also produced the greater part of her renowned "paper mosaicks": almost one thousand botanically accurate illustrations of flowers made from cut, colored paper, many of the subjects of which had been cultivated in the Duchess's botanical gardens and hothouse.[16]

The Duchess of Portland's reputation as a collector is clearly in good hands today. But should future generations lapse into any doubt about the significance of her collecting, or the seriousness of her scientific aspirations concerning it, the *Catalogue*

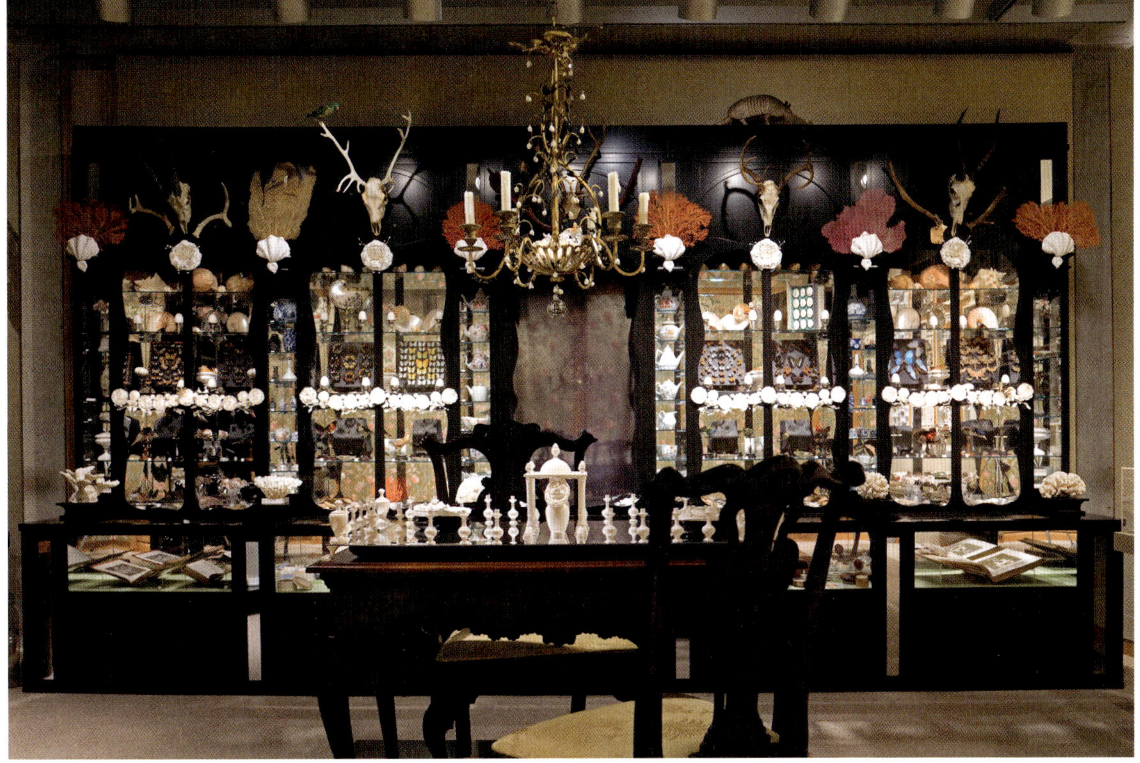

Fig. 34. Installation view of the south-wall cabinet from Jane Wildgoose's *Promiscuous Assemblage, Friendship, & The Order of Things*, Yale Center for British Art, September 24, 2009–July 18, 2010

(with Lightfoot's illuminating preface) continues to offer a "primary reference for her achievements and a vivid"—and enduring—"mnemonic of the remains of the Portland Museum."[17]

Notes

1. *Times* (London), July 20, 1785: 3; Rev. John Lightfoot, *A Catalogue of the Portland Museum, Lately the Property of the Duchess Dowager of Portland, Deceased* (London: Mr. Skinner and Co., 1786), i.
2. Mary Delany, *The Autobiography and Correspondence of Mary Granville, Mrs. Delany: With interesting reminiscences of King George the Third and Queen Charlotte*, 3 vols. (London: Richard Bentley, 1861), 3:345.
3. Delany, *Autobiography and Correspondence*, 2:282, 1:173.
4. Lightfoot, *Catalogue*, vii–viii, 194.
5. Lightfoot, *Catalogue*, iii.
6. Lightfoot, *Catalogue*, vii–viii, 178, 190.
7. S. P. Dance, "The authorship of the *Portland Catalogue* (1786)," *Journal of the Society for the Bibliography of Natural History* 4, no. 1 (1962): 30–34.
8. Lightfoot, *Catalogue*, iv.
9. Harald A. Rehder, "Valid Zoological Names of the Portland Catalogue," *Proceedings of the United States National Museum* 121, no. 3579 (1967): 1–2; Alexandra Cook, "Botanical Exchanges: Jean-Jacques Rousseau and the Duchess of Portland," *History of European Ideas* 33, no. 2 (June 2007): 145.
10. Rehder, "Valid Zoological Names," 2; Lightfoot, *Catalogue*, 3.
11. Rehder, "Valid Zoological Names," 2; E. Alison Kay, "The Reverend John Lightfoot, Daniel Solander, and the Portland Catalogue," *Nautilus* 79, no. 1 (July 1965): 10.
12. Ilya Temkin, "Linnaeus, Solander and Conchology," in *Linnaeus: Life and Sciences* (Uppsala University, 2006), 7.
13. Robert Huxley, "Natural History Collectors and Their Collections: 'Simpling Macaronis' and Instruments of Empire," in *Enlightenment: Discovering the World in the Eighteenth Century*, ed. Kim Sloan (London: British Museum Press, 2003), 87; Cook, "Botanical Exchanges," 144.
14. Beth Fowkes Tobin, "The Duchess's Shells: Natural History Collecting, Gender, and Scientific Practice," in *Material Women, 1750–1950: Consuming Desires and Collecting Practices*, eds. Maureen Daly Goggin and Beth Fowkes Tobin (London and New York: Routledge, 2009), 260. Also see Beth Fowkes Tobin, *The Duchess's Shells: Natural History Collecting in the Age of Cook's Voyages* (New Haven and London: Yale Univ. Press, 2014).
15. Rebecca Stott, *Duchess of Curiosities: The Life of Margaret, Duchess of Portland* (Welbeck: Pineapple Press, 2006), 4–5.
16. Mary Delany's *A Catalogue of Plants copyed from Nature in Paper Mosaick, finished in the year 1778, and disposed in alphabetical order according to the Generic and Specific names of Linnæus* is in the Department of Prints and Drawings at the British Museum.
17. Jane Wildgoose, *Promiscuous Assemblage, Friendship, & the Order of Things: An Installation by Jane Wildgoose in Celebration of the Friendship between Mrs. Mary Delany & the Duchess Dowager of Portland*, exh. booklet (New Haven: Yale Center for British Art, 2009), x.

William Russell Birch (British, 1755–1834; active in the United States, 1794–1834) after Richard Wilson RA (British, 1712/13–1782; active in Italy, 1750–1756)
A View in Kew Gardens, 1789

Stipple engraving and etching on medium, slightly textured, cream wove paper, 6⅞ x 7½ in. (17.5 x 19.1 cm). YALE CENTER FOR BRITISH ART, PAUL MELLON COLLECTION. B1977.14.17350

Therese O'Malley

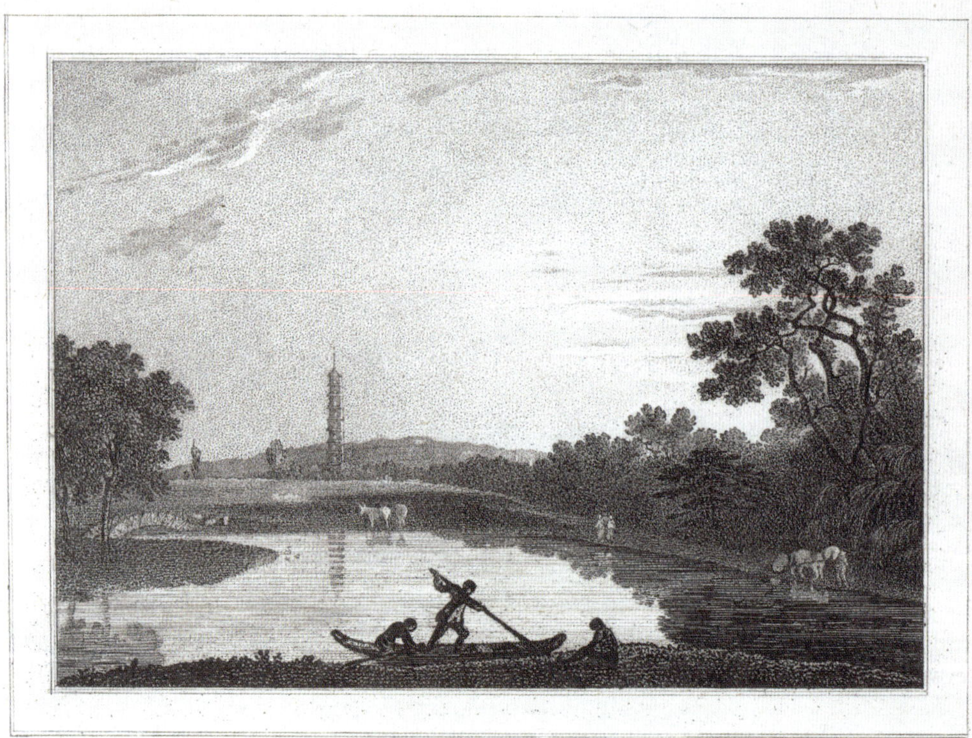

A View in Kew Gardens (1789) is an engraving by William Russell Birch after Richard Wilson's oil painting *Kew Gardens: The Pagoda and Palladian Bridge* (1762) (see pp. 52–55). In 1791 Birch published this print in his commercially successful book of engravings, *Delices de la Grande Bretagne*, which included copies after landscape paintings of notable seats and sites of interests in England.[1] Within a few years, under pressure for his perceived political sympathies, Birch would emigrate to Philadelphia, the temporary capital of the United States and the center of arts and sciences in the new nation.[2] Birch evolved from a copyist and minor arts figure in England to one of the most important artists of the early federal period.[3] His engraving of the gardens at Kew, an institution built upon the international exchange of plants and cross-cultural exploration, offers some curious parallels to the transplanted artist's work in America.

The image depicts Kew Gardens around the time John Stuart, third Earl of Bute, a botanist and plantsman, was helping Princess Augusta of Saxe-Gotha establish the exotic collections. Kew featured a variety of American plants, many if not most of which came from Philadelphia, the heart of the transatlantic plant trade.[4] Landscape historian Mark Laird points out that the shrubbery seen on the right, bounding the west perimeter walk, contained "the Americans," exotic plants displayed in a theatrical arrangement.[5]

Dominating the landscape view is the Great Pagoda (1762), designed by architect William Chambers, whose ornamental buildings at Kew complemented Bute's effort to gather exotic plants from around the world.[6] Chambers visited China in 1744 and 1748 with the Swedish East India Company, making him one of the most prominent interlocutors on the aesthetic culture of the Chinese, and his designs and publications profoundly influenced European and, consequently, American taste.[7] Although many publications on Chinese design were available on both sides of the Atlantic, Chambers's claim to authenticity and eyewitness accounts accentuated his authority.[8]

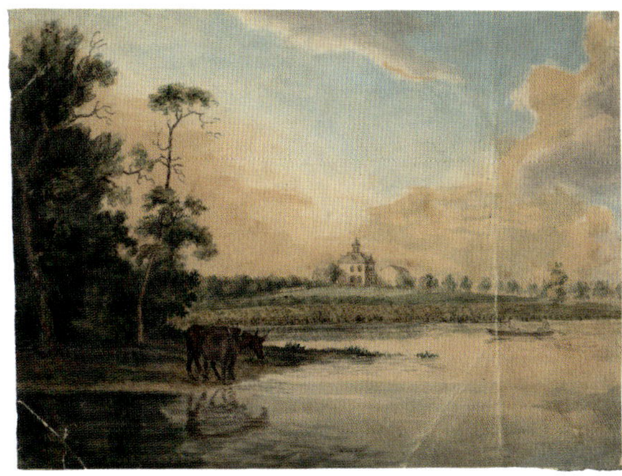

Fig. 35. William Russell Birch, *Van Brant's [sic] place on the Delaware River; View of China Retreat*, 1798–1808, watercolor on paper, 5.5 x 7.5 in. (15 x 20 cm). The Library Company of Philadelphia

In eighteenth-century America, European landscape theory and practice were conveyed through imported images and texts and the influence of a handful of individuals, such as Birch, who had transatlantic experience of both the English and American scenes. Chambers, Birch, and other authors of illustrated books on architecture and gardens understood that reproductive prints, whether single sheets or bound, were potent because they made visible that which was only seen by private owners and their guests. Whether they were images of gardens, architecture, or works of art, prints expanded the knowledge of their histories and status exponentially. Birch's prints after English landscape paintings made their way to America prior to his own immigration in 1794. After a few years in the new capital, he issued the first American view book, *The City of Philadelphia in the State of Pennsylvania North America; as it appeared in the Year 1800*, produced with his son, Thomas Birch.[9]

In addition to continuing his career producing prints, enamels, and miniatures, Birch struggled to establish a landscape-design practice, using his property at Springland, Pennsylvania, as a display garden, in order "to propagate taste . . . as a sample to serve the country."[10] Following the success of the

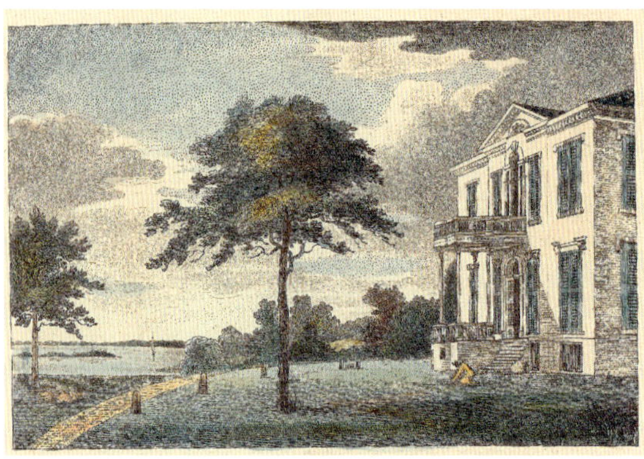

Fig. 36. William Russell Birch, "China Retreat," plate 6 from *The Country Seats of the United States of North America: With Some Scenes Connected with Them* (Springland near Bristol, Penn., 1808), etching and mixed media. Beinecke Rare Book & Manuscript Library, Yale University

City views, he undertook, again with his son, the first color-plate book on American scenery, *The Country Seats of the United States of North America.* Published in 1808, it consists of twenty views of eighteen stately homes, following the English model of picturesque views.[11] Although he traveled the East Coast visiting estates, Birch included primarily those situated on the scenic Schuylkill and Delaware Rivers in Philadelphia, his adopted home.

One estate featured in *Country Seats*, called China Retreat, was visible from Birch's own home and studio at Springland.[12] It bears comparison to Birch's English work, specifically, the view after Wilson's *Kew Gardens*. China Retreat belonged to Andreas van Braam Houckgeest, with whom, Birch tells us in his autobiography, "he spent much time."[13] Birch made portraits in enamel of van Braam, a colorful figure who had spent many years in China. A watercolor by Birch shows the picturesque setting of van Braam's house, which, although being in the fashionable Adamesque style, was surmounted, remarkably, by a Chinese pagoda visible in the center of the image (fig. 35). Contemporaneous accounts described the pagoda as ornamented with silver bells and "golden serpents in the Chinese manner."[14]

Like Chambers, van Braam also lived in China. Initially, from 1758 to 1777, he worked for the Dutch East India Company and subsequently he was a diplomat, from 1794 to 1795. Also, like Chambers, he produced an epic book, *Voyage de l'Ambassade de la Compagnie des Indes Orientales Hollandaises, vers l'Empereur de la Chine*. Written while he lived in Philadelphia, which had emerged as the center of America-China trade, it chronicled his trip from Guangzhou (Canton) to Peking to meet the emperor.[15] This book, like Chambers's, was praised for "the truthfulness of [its] narrative" and for its "corroborative evidence," meaning the book's illustrations, which were made by Chinese artists with whom van Braam traveled.[16] The two-volume work was first published in Philadelphia in 1797–98 in French, with editions in English, German, and Dutch following within the decade.[17] Van Braam's vast collection of Chinese paintings and porcelain was exhibited at China Retreat in 1796, the first public display of Chinese art in the United States. Unlike Chambers's life and work, however, van Braam's, although worthy of study, had received little attention for two hundred years until the recent discovery of much of the collection, once thought to have been lost at sea.[18]

Birch's engraving of China Retreat in *Country Seats* (fig. 36) is strikingly different from the watercolor. The house is close to the picture plane, the pedimented facade tilted at a sharp angle. Only the lawn portion of the grounds is depicted, dotted with young trees in protective frames. Most obvious is that Birch excluded the signature pagoda from view. Instead, the Chinese presence, which reportedly suffused van Braam's home and lifestyle, is only subtly suggested in the yellow-draped kneeling figure, perhaps one of his many Chinese servants, gardening in front.

For his print of China Retreat, Birch seems to have returned to the conventional perspective he used in the *Delices*. In fact, the whole composition closely resembles the plate of the Robert Adam–designed house Kenwood, the home of Birch's beloved British patron, William Murray, first Earl of Mansfield (fig. 37). Coincidently, as with China Retreat and Springland, Birch's cottage on Hampstead Heath

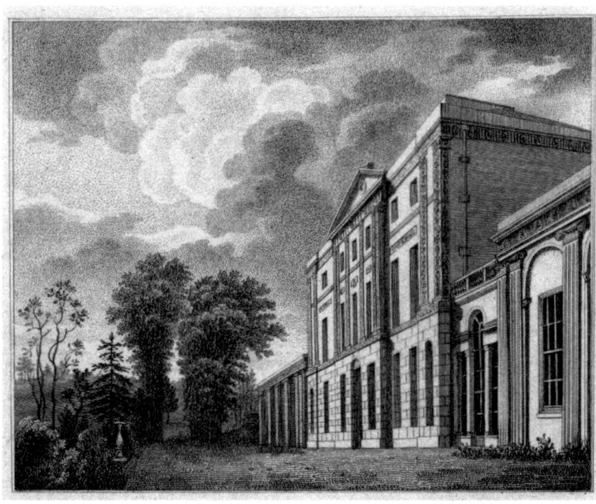

Fig. 37. William Russell Birch, *The Garden Front at Kenwood*, 1789, engraving and etching on medium, slightly textured, cream wove paper. Yale Center for British Art, Paul Mellon Collection

neighbored Kenwood, and he recalls in his autobiography the many hours he spent there with Lord Mansfield before he left for America.[19] Unlike most of the views in *Delices*, which are copies after other artists' paintings, the view of Kenwood is Birch's original work. He depicts Mansfield's garden on the left, which one writer described as "a sweet shrubbery immediately before the front." It was also described as an "American" garden by John Claudius Loudon in 1822.[20] Shrubberies of exotics had been established at Kenwood by the previous owner, none other than the third Earl of Bute. Within a decade, Lord Bute would sell Kenwood to Lord Mansfield and go on to help create the Royal Gardens at Kew, which brings our story full circle.

Notes

1. *Delices de la Grande Bretagne* (London: Engraved and Published by William Birch; sold by Edwards, Pall-Mall; and Dilly, in the Poultry, 1791).
2. For an in-depth study of this topic, see Amy R. W. Meyers, ed., *Knowing Nature: Art and Science in Philadelphia, 1740–1840* (New Haven and London: Yale Univ. Press, 2011).
3. Emily T. Cooperman is the leading scholar on William Birch. Her doctoral dissertation is "William Russell Birch (1755–1834) and the Beginnings of the American Picturesque" (PhD diss., University of Pennsylvania, 1999). See also Emily T. Cooperman and Lea Carson Sherk, *William Birch: Picturing the American Scene* (Philadelphia: Univ. of Pennsylvania Press, 2011).
4. Mark Laird, "This Other Eden," in Meyers, *Knowing Nature*, 96–127.
5. Mark Laird, *A Natural History of English Gardening: 1650–1800* (New Haven and London: Yale Univ. Press, 2015), 254–58.
6. Laird, *A Natural History*, 233–35.
7. David Porter, "Beyond the Bounds of Truth: Cultural Translation and William Chambers's Chinese Garden," *Mosaic* 37, no. 2 (June 2004): 55–56.
8. Judy Bullington, "The Chinese Manner in Early American Gardens," in *Global Trade and Visual Arts in Federal New England*, eds. Patricia Johnston and Caroline Frank (Lebanon: Univ. of New Hampshire Press, 2014), 165.
9. Cooperman and Sherk, *William Birch*, 81. *The City of Philadelphia in the State of Pennsylvania North America; as it appeared in the Year 1800* (Philadelphia: W. Birch, 1800) contained twenty-seven engravings of buildings and street life in Philadelphia and enjoyed commercial success.
10. See Therese O'Malley, "'Models in this Art': Tracing the Brownian Landscape Tradition in America," *Garden History* 44, suppl. 1 (Autumn 2016): 78–79.
11. William Russell Birch, *The Country Seats of the United States*, ed. Emily T. Cooperman (Philadelphia: Univ. of Pennsylvania Press, 2009).
12. Julian Ursyn Niemcewicz, *Under Their Vine and Fig Tree: Travels Through America in 1797–1799, 1805, with Some Further Account of Life in New Jersey*, trans. and ed. Metchie J. E. Budka (Elizabeth, NJ: Grassmann, 1965), 62–64.
13. Cooperman and Sherk, *William Birch*, 202. In between two long trips to China, van Braam moved to Charleston, South Carolina, as Dutch counsel in 1783, but became an American citizen in 1784. He settled in Philadelphia following the second trip.
14. Niemcewicz, *Under Their Vine and Fig Tree*, 62–63. Edward R. Barnsley, "History of China's Retreat," *Bristol Courier* (May 9–11, 1933): 11.
15. See Janice Neri, "Cultivating Interiors: Philadelphia, China, and the Natural World," in Meyers, *Knowing Nature*, 195.
16. Henry W. Kent, "Van Braam Houckgeest, An Early American Collector," *Proceedings of the American Antiquarian Society* 40, no. 2 (October 1930): 161.
17. André Everard van Braam Houckgeest, *Voyage de l'Ambassade de la Compagnie des Indes Orientales Hollandaises, vers l'Empereur de la Chine, dans les années 1794 et 1795* (Philadelphia: Moreau de Saint-Méry, 1797–98). See Joseph G. Rosengarten, "Moreau de Saint Mery and His French Friends in the American Philosophical Society," *Proceedings of the American Philosophical Society* 50, no. 199 (May–August 1911): 168–78. Van Braam dedicated the two-volume work to U.S. President George Washington.
18. See Bruce MacLaren, "The Guangdong Commission—van Braam's Albums of China, 1790–1795," http://independent.academia.edu/maclarenbruce (accessed Sept. 24, 2018). The Peabody Essex Museum, in Salem, Massachusetts, has 249 drawings from van Braam's collection. These were only attributed after 2001.
19. Cooperman and Sherk, *William Birch*, 159, 178–79. Cooperman points out that the inscriptions for Kenwood and China Retreat are similar in that they both praise the intellectual achievements of the owner.
20. See Mark Laird, "Approaches to Planting in the Late Eighteenth Century: Some Imperfect Ideas on the Origins of the American Garden," *Journal of Garden History* 11, no. 3 (1991): 154–72. In 1804 the book *Select Views of London and its Environs* described the house and gardens using the name Caen. Cited in Walter Thornberry, *Old and New London: A Narrative of Its History, Its People, and Its Places* (London: Cassell, 1892), 441–43. J. C. Loudon, *An encyclopaedia of gardening; comprising the theory and practice of horticulture, floriculture, arboriculture, and landscape-gardening, including all the latest improvements* (London: Longman, Hurst, Rees, Orme, Brown, and Green, 1822), 1226.

Attributed to Gangaram Chintaman Tambat (Anglo-Indian)
Utensils, ca. 1790s

Gray wash and graphite with pen and black ink and pen and brown ink on medium, slightly textured, cream laid paper, 8⅝ x 11½ in. (21.9 x 29.2 cm)

YALE CENTER FOR BRITISH ART, PAUL MELLON COLLECTION, B1977.14.22311

Edward S. Cooke, Jr.

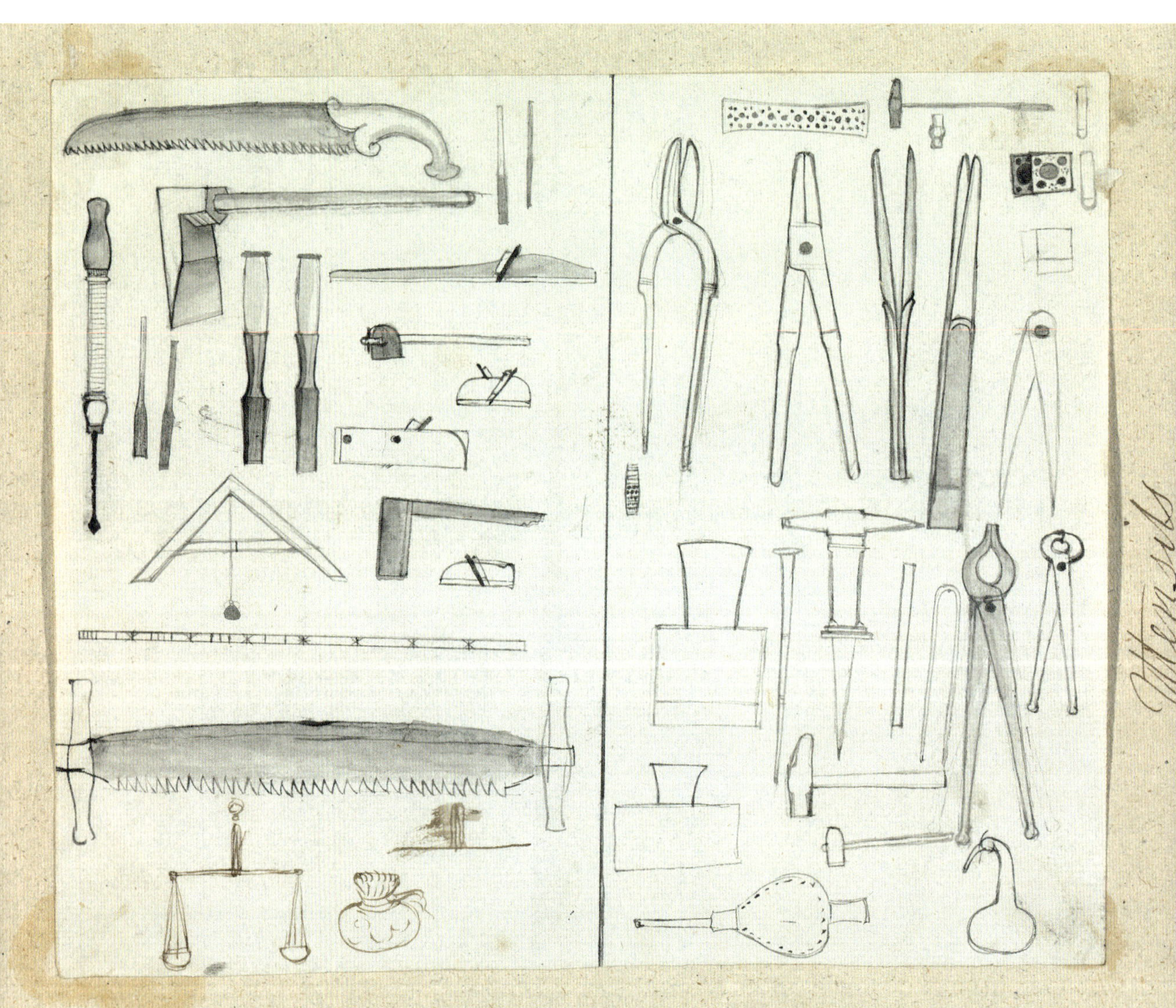

Among the drawings and manuscripts in the archive assembled by Sir Charles Warre Malet, the East India Company's Resident in Pune from 1785 to 1798, is a sheet marked on its mount "Utensils" in a brown ink script. It is one of several such sheets in the Malet collection, but its title is rather vague, suggesting that whoever assigned it did not fully understand the sorts of items that were depicted.[1] What utensils might these be? And who might have made this drawing?

The drawing is one of several related examples in the Malet archive. The format of these drawings is recognizable to scholars familiar with the *arts et métiers* illustration genre of the late seventeenth and eighteenth centuries. The taxonomical project of laying out the tools of a specific craft as an organized graphic composition was linked to the European Enlightenment practice of natural history illustration: to observe, draw, flatten, and organize comprised a method of gaining, displaying, and contributing to knowledge. To understand the work and *techne* of different trades—the mastery of the "art, trade, and mystery" of a craft—necessitated breaking down a process to its constituent tools and, oddly enough, given their use, abstracting them and denying their very tangible nature. In this way, a gentleman might believe he could fully comprehend and analyze the mechanical arts.[2]

This particular sheet depicts woodworking tools on the left and metalworking tools on the right. The upper three quarters of the former features (roughly top to bottom) a tenon saw, adze, drill brace and bits, chisels, joining plane, measuring gauge, molding plane, plow plane, square, level, rule, and whip saw. The layout and the head-on viewpoint, which offers little sense of depth or perspective, are remarkably similar to the arrangement of the joiner's tools in plate 4 of Joseph Moxon's *Mechanick exercises: or The doctrine of handy-works*, a late seventeenth-century serial publication by one of England's prominent natural philosophers and member of the Royal Society (fig. 38).[3] The most notable differences from the English plate are the lack of workbenches and holdfasts (suggesting work was not undertaken while standing), the inclusion of a bow-driven drill brace, and the club-like shape of the long joining plane. These subtle differences suggest that the artist was not constrained or burdened by the need to copy but rather adapted the genre to individual experience.

Along the bottom of the left side, the artist added in brown ink two items more commonly associated with metalworking: a set of scales, likely to weigh the raw material before melting, and a pouncing bag used to lay out designs from a paper pattern. The right side of the sheet includes more metalworking tools such as (top to bottom) a board

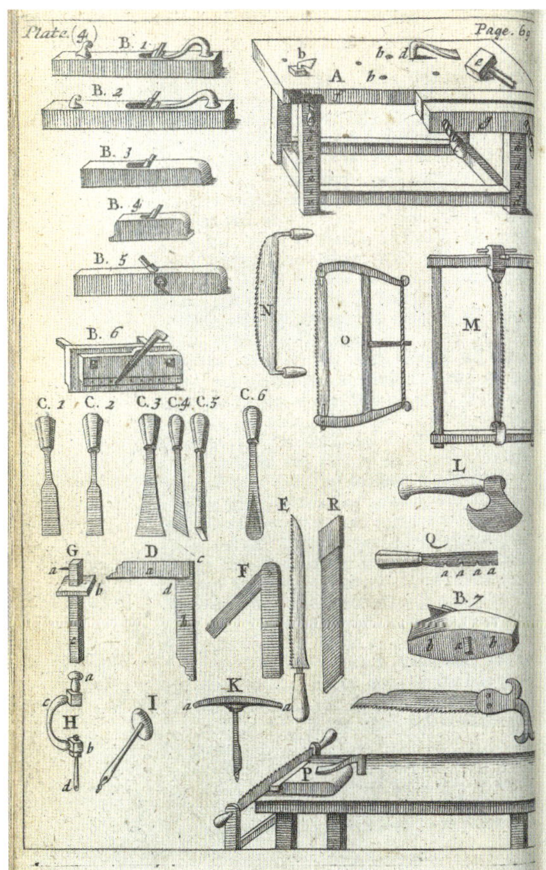

Fig. 38. Joseph Moxon, plate 4 from *Mechanick exercises, or, The doctrine of handy-works: applied to the arts of smithing, joinery, carpentry, turning, bricklayery: to which is added Mechanick dyalling: shewing how to draw a true sun-dyal on any given plane*, 3rd edition (London: 1703). Yale Center for British Art, Paul Mellon Collection

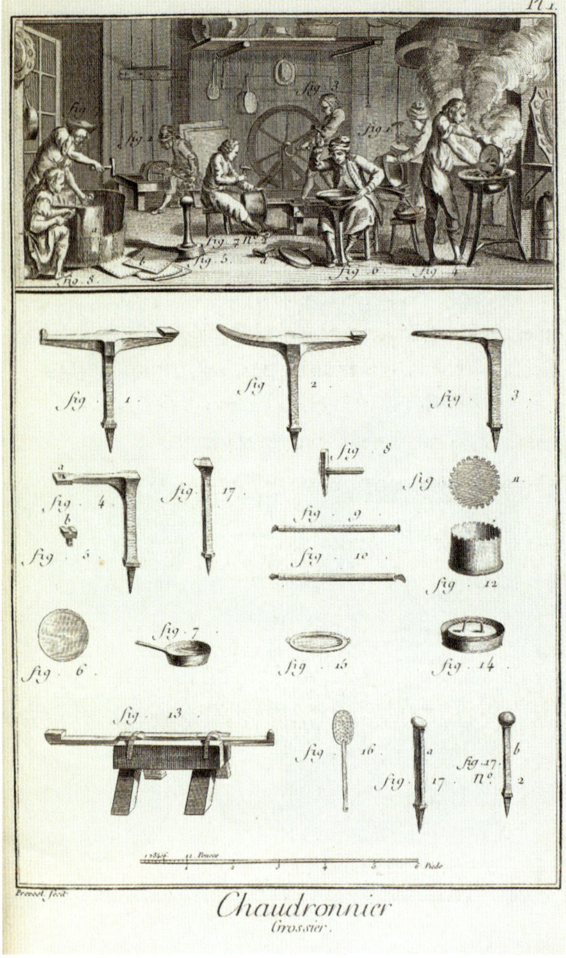

Fig. 39. Denis Diderot, "Chaudronnier," from *Encyclopédie; ou Dictionnaire raisonné des sciences, des arts et des métiers* (Paris: 1751–72). Lewis Walpole Library, Yale University

or box filled with chasing tools for embossing metal (seen from the tips), long-handled chasing hammer, tongs for holding hot work when pulled from the forge, steel swage to form hemispheres or globes, measuring calipers, cylindrical anvils set on blocks of wood for flattening ingots into sheets, stakes to drive into the ground or a wood block for raising or shaping metal, pincers for cutting, heavier hammers for raising and shaping, bellows, and a snarling stake to get inside a vessel and push the metal outwards.[4] But the specific details of the metalworking tools in the drawing do not resemble the blacksmith's tools shown in Moxon's plate 1. Rather, the drawing looks like an amalgam of the plates for a coppersmith (fig. 39) and a gunsmith from Denis Diderot's *Encylopédie*, but without the accompanying images of the interior of a shop or even workbenches.[5] The tools are once again depicted primarily in head-on profile rather than given dimension with shading.

The impact of the *Encylopédie* makes sense because Malet owned "a voluminous dictionary of arts and sciences," likely a resource for the various artists and artisans he employed in Pune to gather and record visually the geography, architecture, people, customs, and culture of the Marathas.[6] Among the team were the British artist James Wales, the British soldier and draftsman Robert Mabon, and the Pune artisan Gangaram Chintaman Tambat. Gangaram, as the art historian Holly Shaffer has revealed, played a particularly important role in this endeavor.[7] But his background also suggests that he was the person who made these drawings. Gangaram belonged to the occupational caste of the coppersmiths. *Tamba* is the Marathi word for copper, and *tambat* for coppersmith. In the late fifteenth century Peshwa rulers had recruited a *tambat* community from the Pavagadhi region of Gujarat to move to Maharashtra in order to fabricate copper household items (betel-nut boxes; *kalshi*, *lota*, and other vessels; and *bumba*, or large boilers to heat water) as well as weapons, musical instruments, architectural finials, and jewelry.[8] They were skilled with hammers, raising complex shapes from sheet copper and using chasing tools to emboss designs. Given Gangaram's familiarity with tools and the likely access he had to Malet's *Encylopédie*, we can attribute this drawing to him, as well as those related drawings of the musical instruments, domestic utensils, and weapons, all the products of the *tambat*. However, the handwriting of the titles on the drawings' mounts and the vagueness of the titles suggest that someone other than Gangaram gathered the sheets, mounted them, and labeled them. A more accurate title for the right side of this drawing would be "Tools of the *Tambat*."

The drawing indicates how a skilled South Asian craftsman could internalize European graphic principles from printed sources and European techniques of light watercolor wash on laid paper, while inserting a detailed specificity developed out of deep knowledge and familiarity from his own close perspective as a chaser (for a later, mid-nineteenth-century example from Kashmir, see fig. 40). The same blending can be observed in the drawings Gangaram made for Malet of architectural and sculptural monuments. Gangaram's incorporation of local visual traditions with British ones made him an indispensable member of Malet's artistic team. While the drawing was misunderstood by the British person who labeled the mounted version, Gangaram fully understood that he had organized his familiar tools in a European manner. This is not an example of an image made by a metropole artist seeking to organize and represent artifactual curiosities from a distant exotic place but, rather, a visually aware indigenous artisan adapting parts of a foreign system of representation.

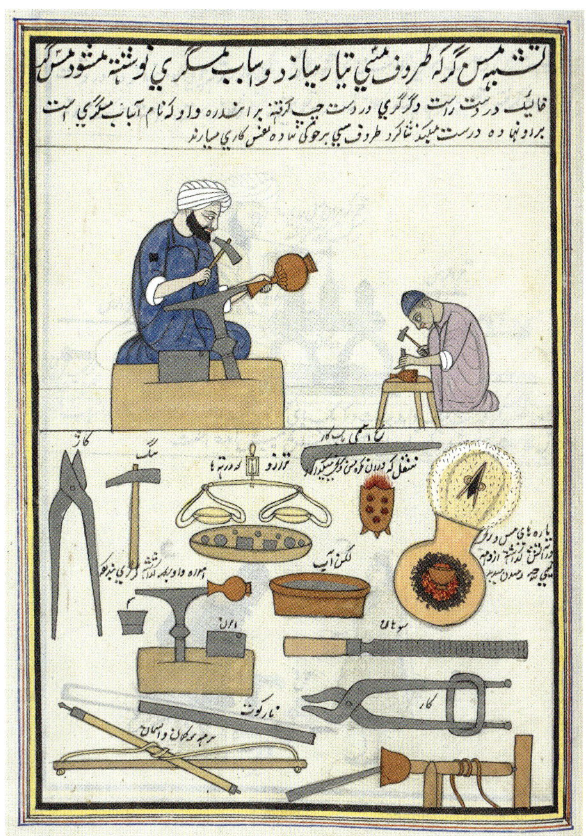

Fig. 40. Coppersmiths, from *Album of Kashmiri Trades*, 1850–60. British Library, London

Notes

1. The other sheets are identified more specifically as "Musical Instruments" (B1977.14.22312), "Military Weapons," "Female Ornaments," and "Utensils for Culinary + Religious Purposes" (B1977.14.22313).
2. For a recent study of the *arts et métiers* genre, see Paola Bertucci, *Artisanal Enlightenment: Science and the Mechanical Arts in Old Regime France* (New Haven and London: Yale Univ. Press, 2017).
3. Joseph Moxon, *Mechanick Exercises: or The Doctrine of Handy-Works*, 1678 (New York: Praeger Publishers, 1970, reprint edition).
4. For the accurate identification of these tools, I am grateful for conversations with the master Pune coppersmith Bhalchandra Kadu and the design historian Prasad Boradkar, September 2015.
5. Denis Diderot, *Encyclopédie, ou Dictionnaire raisonné des sciences, des arts et des métiers* (Paris, 1751–72), plates for the *chaudronnier* and the *arquebusier*.
6. Holly Shaffer, "'Of men and gods, and things': The Making of Maratha Art in India and Britain, 1700–1900," (PhD dissertation, Yale University, 2015), 157.
7. Shaffer, "'Of men and gods, and things'"; and Holly Shaffer, *Adapting the Eye: An Archive of the British in India, 1770–1830* (New Haven: Yale Center for British Art, 2011).
8. On the history of the tambats in Maharashtra, see Priyansi Nimish Tambat and Ketaki Chandrakant Joshi, "Promoting Craft Entrepreneurship by Rejuvenating *Tambat* Craft in Old *Tambat Ali*, Nashik," *Journal of Heritage Management* 2, no. 1 (2017): 53–75; and Pranjali Bhonde Pethe, "All that Glitters is Copper: Artisans in Tambat Ali Follow a Decade-Old Tradition of Making Copper Vessels," *Hindu*, June 2, 2018.

Paul Sandby RA (British, 1731–1809)
A View of Vinters at Boxley, Kent, with Mr. Whatman's Turkey Paper Mills, 1794

Gouache, watercolor, and graphite on Whatman wove paper, laid down on canvas, 27 5/16 x 40 3/16 in. (69.3 x 102 cm). Signed and dated, lower left: "P. Sandby | 1794."

YALE CENTER FOR BRITISH ART, PAUL MELLON FUND, B2002.29

Scott Wilcox

On April 17, 1794, James Whatman II (1741–1798), the most successful papermaker in Britain, paid the artist Paul Sandby for a portrait of his estate showing his newly remodeled manor house, Vinters, and the largest of his three paper mills, indeed the largest paper mill in England at the time, the Turkey Mill.[1] One might have expected a scene of bustling industry, yet Sandby's painting, done in opaque watercolors on a double elephant sheet of paper produced in that very mill, is a vision of autumnal tranquility.[2]

A few delicate wisps of smoke rise from the chimneys of the complex of mill buildings at the center of the scene. Two miniscule figures, one on horseback and one pushing a wheelbarrow, move around the mill. Otherwise, nothing breaks the stillness. Horses gambol in a field. A milkmaid drives three cows along a lane. A mounted traveler, who has just passed her, rides toward a crossroads to which a stagecoach is approaching on its way to nearby Maidstone. The hop harvest, which would have shortly before made this countryside a scene of purposeful activity, is now over; the conical stacks of the hop poles quietly dot the landscape. It is a scene of resolute peacefulness, which belies, and was at least in some ways consciously intended to belie, transitions and tensions in Whatman's life, in the papermaking industry, and in the country.

Whatman had inherited the mill from his father, James Whatman I, who had acquired it by marriage and then gained preeminence in papermaking, introducing wove paper in the 1750s. With its absence of the chain lines and laid lines of traditional handmade papers, Whatman wove paper, originally developed for the printing of fine volumes, would become the paper of choice for printmakers, cartographers, architects, and the artists of the revolution in watercolor painting, of whom Paul Sandy was an early leader. The younger Whatman carried on the traditions of innovation and excellence established by his father. In 1783 he purchased the adjacent Vinters estate, which gave him another paper mill, and allowed the removal of the family residence from the Turkey Mill complex to the manor house, which he renovated, on the hill above the mill. In 1790 Whatman suffered a stroke; he recovered, but continuing health issues, together with indications of labor unrest in the papermaking industry, and the political and commercial uncertainties introduced by the French Revolution, led Whatman to sell off his papermaking operations in the autumn of 1794. Under the new owners, papers with the "Whatman" and "Whatman Turkey Mill" watermarks would enjoy a reputation as high-quality artist papers through the twentieth century.[3]

Sandby's painting of Vinters and the Turkey Mill, with its adoption of a standard country-house portrait format, but with the house displaced from its expected central position by the industrial buildings of the mill, was thus intended by Whatman to commemorate his business at the very moment that he was relinquishing it. In retirement, he had plans to develop the Vinters estate, commissioning the landscape designer Humphry Repton to produce one of his celebrated Red Books, surveying the estate and outlining proposed improvements.[4] But this was a troubled time for Whatman, and his suicide two years later meant that Repton's recommendations were never implemented.

A View of Vinters at Boxley, Kent, with Mr. Whatman's Turkey Paper Mills was one of three works that Sandby showed at the Royal Academy of Arts in the annual exhibition of 1794. A year into what would turn out to be a twenty-two-year-long conflict with France, Sandby presents an image of the Kentish countryside, "the garden of England," unruffled by war, quietly drawing attention to the noted features of the local economy: hop growing and papermaking.[5] Sandby had been one of the founding Academicians in 1768, and he was still highly respected in the Academy and the profession, but by 1794 his brand of topographical picture-making had begun to seem outdated. His works were failing to sell and, like Whatman, he had health problems. If Sandby hoped that at a moment of national crisis his painting of Kent for Mr. Whatman would sound a reassuringly patriotic note with a broader audience, we have no indication that his intentions were recognized.

Notes

1. The painting was the focus of an exhibition at the Yale Center for British Art, February 22–June 4, 2006. Most of the information in the present essay is drawn from the catalogue of that exhibition: Theresa Fairbanks Harris and Scott Wilcox, *Papermaking and the Art of Watercolor in Eighteenth-Century Britain: Paul Sandby and the Whatman Paper Mill* (New Haven and London: Yale Univ. Press, 2006). The page from the Whatman Account Book showing payment for the painting (Centre for Kentish Studies) is reproduced by Stephen Daniels, "A Prospect for the Nation," in Fairbanks Harris and Wilcox, *Papermaking and the Art of Watercolor*, 31.

2. Technical information on the painting is given by Theresa Fairbanks Harris, "Paul Sandby's Creation of the Watercolor *A View of Vinters at Boxley, Kent, with Mr. Whatman's Turkey Paper Mills*," in Fairbanks Harris and Wilcox, *Papermaking and the Art of Watercolor*, 121–31.

3. For the Whatmans as papermakers and the development of wove paper, see John Balston, *The Whatmans and Wove Paper, Its Invention and Development in the West: Research into the Origins of Wove Paper and of Genuine Loom-Woven Wire-Cloth* (West Farleigh, UK: J. Balston, 1998); and Theresa Fairbanks Harris, Michael Fuller, and Maureen Green, "Papermaking and the Whatmans," in Fairbanks Harris and Wilcox, *Papermaking and the Art of Watercolor*, 61–119. Scientific laboratory filtration papers continue to be produced under the Whatman brand.

4. Like Sandby's painting of Vinters and the Turkey Mill, Repton's Red Book for Whatman, *Vinters in Kent, A Seat of James Whatman, Esq.*, was acquired from descendants of the Whatman family by the Yale Center for British Art (Rare Books and Manuscripts, Folio A.2011.13). The introduction, signed by Repton, notes: "First visit on the spot March 1797; Plans sent . . . May 15, 1797." The Whatman Account Book notes payment to Repton on May 24, 1797 (Centre for Kentish Studies), reproduced by Daniels, "A Prospect for the Nation," in Fairbanks Harris and Wilcox, *Papermaking and the Art of Watercolor*, 50. For a general account of Repton's practice, see Stephen Daniels, *Humphry Repton: Landscape Gardening and the Geography of Georgian England* (New Haven and London: Yale Univ. Press, 1999).

5. For the significance of Sandby's imagery of Kent and the place of the Vinters/Turkey Mill painting in Sandby's work, see Daniels, "A Prospect for the Nation," in Fairbanks Harris and Wilcox, *Papermaking and the Art of Watercolor*, 23–59. For a more general consideration of Sandby's art and career, see John Bonehill and Stephen Daniels, eds., *Paul Sandby: Picturing Britain*, exh. cat. (London: Royal Academy of Arts, 2009).

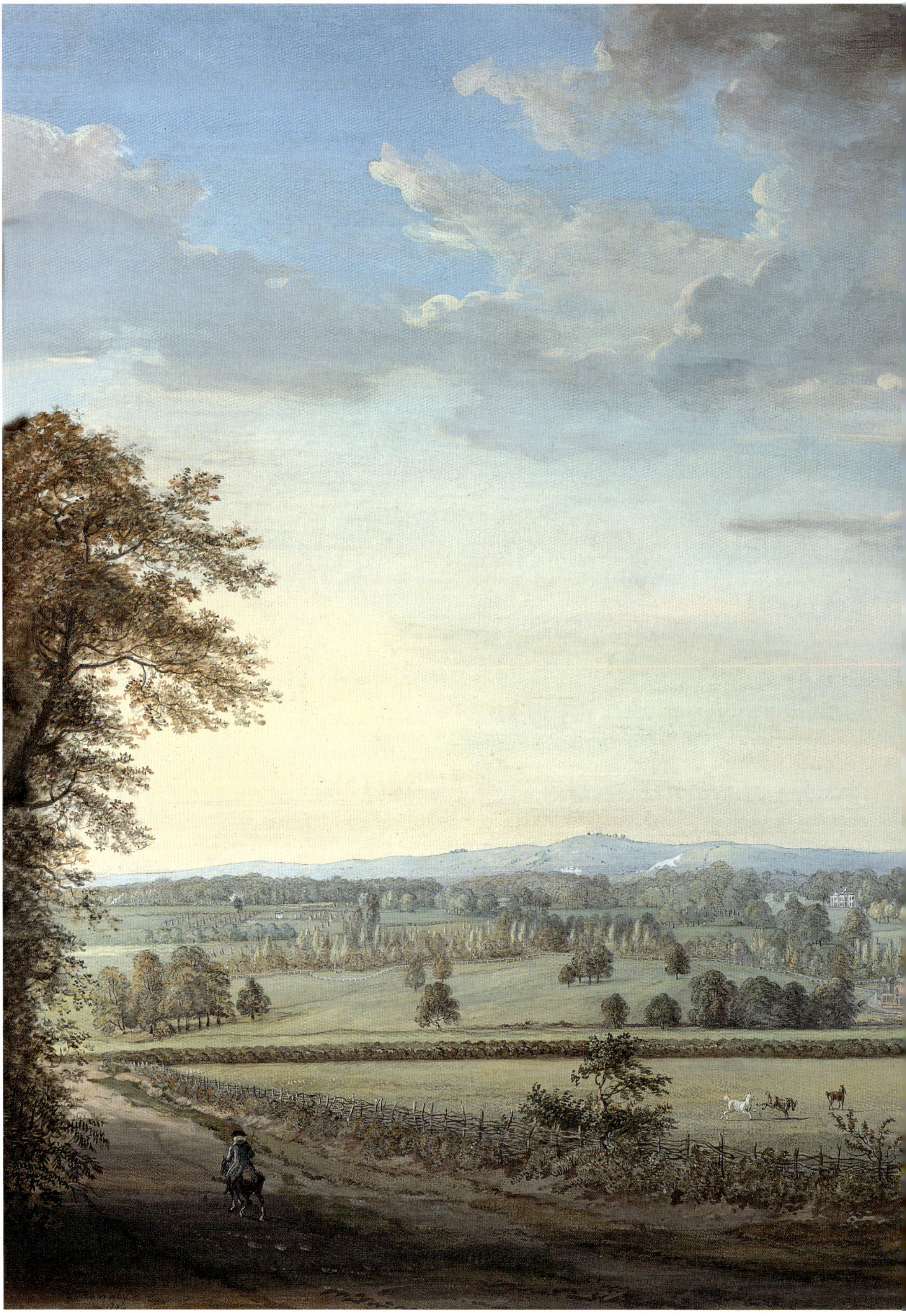

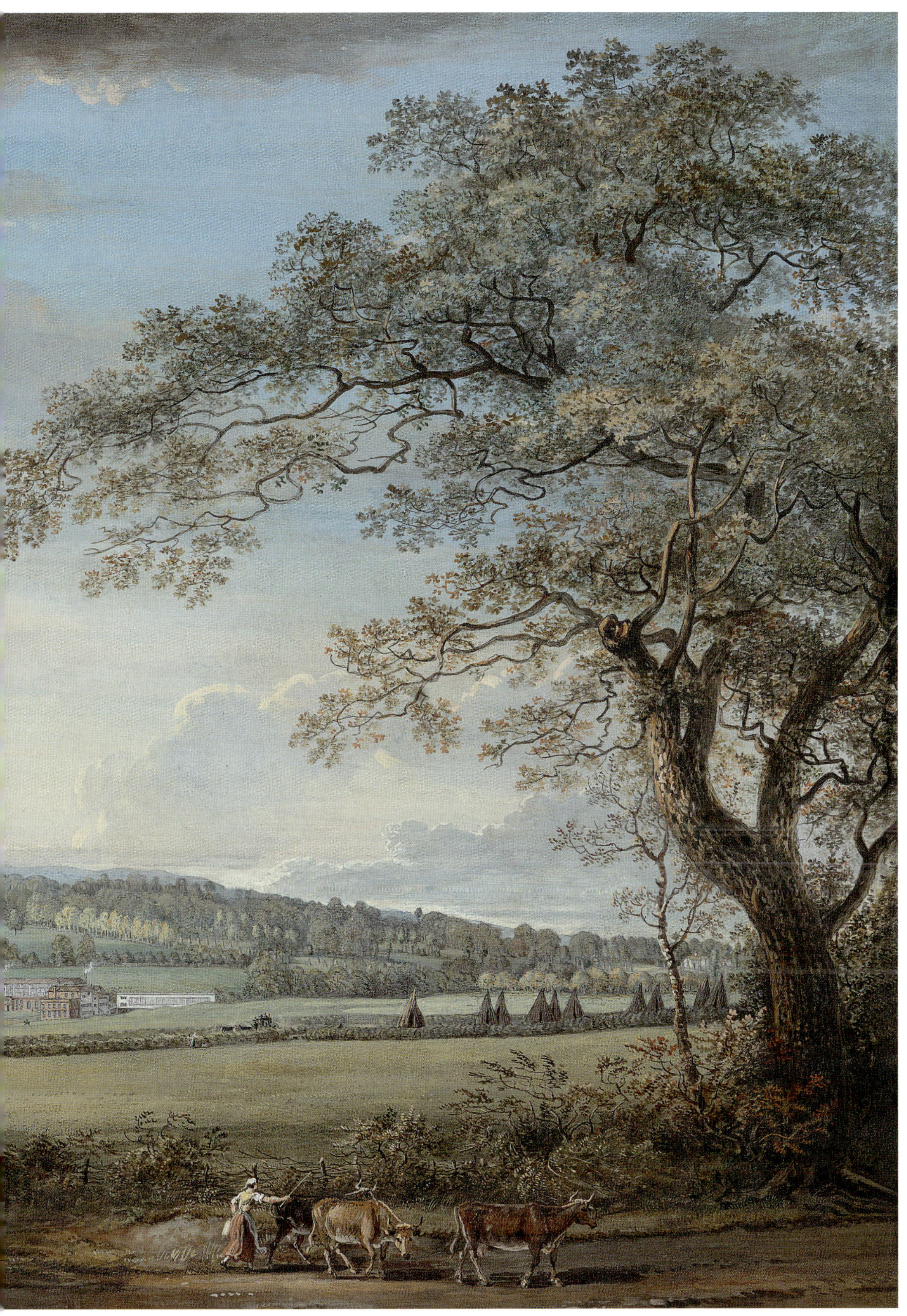

Joseph Mallord William Turner RA (British, 1775–1851)
Dort or Dordrecht: The Dort Packet-Boat from Rotterdam Becalmed, 1818 (exhibited at the Royal Academy of Arts)

Oil on canvas, 62 x 92 in. (157.5 x 233.7 cm). Inscribed, lower right: "Dort"; signed and dated, lower right: "JMW Turner RA 1818."

YALE CENTER FOR BRITISH ART, PAUL MELLON COLLECTION, B1977.14.77

Gillian Forrester

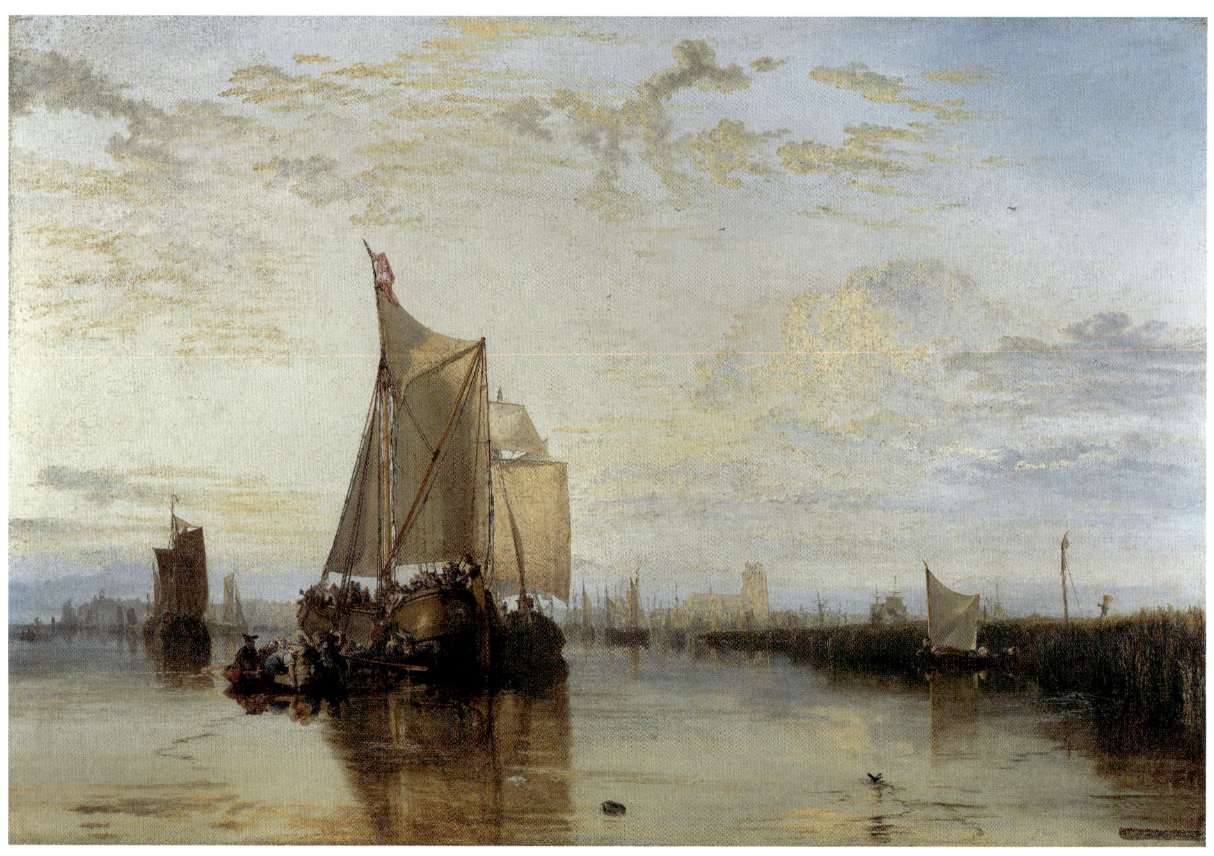

One of Joseph Mallord William Turner's lifelong objectives was the formation of a British school of landscape painting, but, while he assiduously cultivated his identity as a deeply patriotic artist who espoused conservative politics, the artist's outlook was emphatically transnational. Protracted wars between the outbreak of the French Revolution and the defeat of Napoleon at Waterloo in 1815 drastically restricted European travel, but Turner made at least twenty-two trips to the

Continent, and the resulting works constitute a penetrating chronicle of the social, economical, political, technological, and physical landscape of contemporary Europe.

In 1817 Turner visited the Netherlands and Rhineland for the first time. Although he spent just a day and a half in Dordrecht (known locally as Dort), Turner made numerous graphite drawings, and the visit evidently made a profound impression, since he exhibited a painting of the city, viewed from the north, at the Royal Academy of Arts in 1818. Entitled *Dort or Dordrecht: The Dort Packet-Boat from Rotterdam Becalmed*, this luminous painting depicts the ferry *Zwaan* temporarily marooned near the confluence of the rivers Noord and Merwede.[1] *Dort* attracted considerable critical attention. The *Morning Chronicle* reviewer deemed it as "one of the most magnificent pictures ever exhibited," but the painting was not universally lauded and generated intense debates regarding Turner's controversial artistic and exhibitionary practices. His patron, Walter Fawkes, appears to have admired *Dort* unreservedly, however, since he acquired the painting from the exhibition, likely on the day of the Private View, and hung it in the Drawing Room at Farnley Hall, his Yorkshire home. The price was 500 guineas, a huge sum, though Turner probably was never paid. The painting remained with the Fawkes family until 1966, when Paul Mellon bought it, and it has hung almost continuously at the Center since it opened in 1977.

Turner did not visit the Netherlands until he was over forty, but he was already familiar with many of the Dutch Old Master paintings that proliferated in British collections. *Dort* was a direct response to a painting by one of his most formative Dutch influences, Aelbert Cuyp; the motif of the "packet-boat" (mail boat) is directly borrowed from Cuyp's *Maas at Dordrecht*, which was included in a high-profile exhibition of Flemish and Netherlandish paintings from British collections at the British Institution in 1815 (fig. 41).[2] The British Institution had generated controversy from its foundation in 1805 because of the patrician nature of its self-

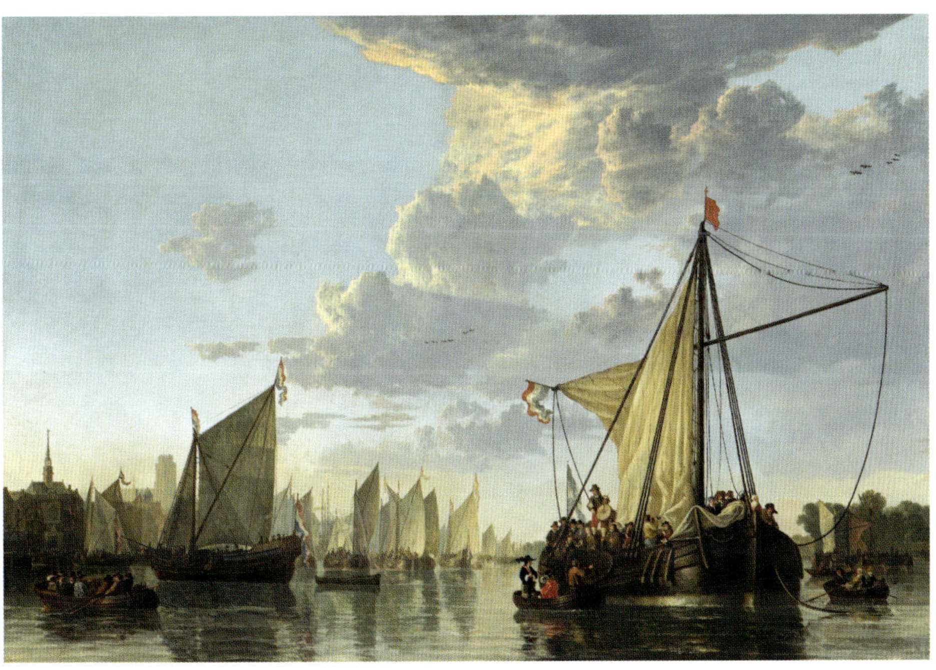

Fig. 41. Aelbert Cuyp, *The Maas at Dordrecht*, ca. 1650, oil on canvas, 45¼ x 67 in. (114.9 x 170.2 cm). National Gallery of Art, Washington, DC, Andrew W. Mellon Collection

appointed group of Directors and the conservative agenda that privileged Old Masters over living painters. Turner participated in these debates, and he may have intended *Dort* as a riposte to the 1815 exhibition that was organized in order to "excite in the British artist the ardour of emulation" yet castigated by its target audience, who resented its prescriptive agenda; the majority of Royal Academicians declined the invitation to attend a special evening opening, and the Directors were excoriated in an anonymous satirical publication. The connoisseur Sir George Beaumont, who was a founding Director of the British Institution and a major driving force of its activities, was an outspoken critic of Turner's work. Beaumont, whose preference was for darkly hued Old Master paintings, designated Turner and several of his (predominantly working-class) contemporaries as "white painters," a pejorative term he coined as a critique of Augustus Wall Callcott's strikingly muted palette.[3] With its nuanced juxtaposition of cool and warm colors, *Dort* may have been intended by Turner both as a subtle rebuke to Beaumont and a gesture of solidarity to Callcott, his close friend and fellow "white painter."

Turner's decision to embark on *Dort* was almost certainly stimulated by *The Pool of London* (fig. 42), Callcott's own luminous tribute to *The Maas at Dordrecht*, which he exhibited to acclaim at the Royal Academy in 1816, and which Turner had declared to be worth a thousand guineas.[4] Callcott, who was on the Academy's 1818 Hanging Committee, graciously agreed to Turner's request to move Callcott's own painting, *Mouth of the Tyne*, from its original placement in order that the *Dort* might be hung prominently on the wall at the end of the Great Room.[5] Turner exhibited two other canvases at the Royal Academy in 1818, *Raby Castle, the Seat of the Earl of Darlington* and *The Field of Waterloo*, the latter, like *Dort*, an outcome of Turner's 1817 tour.[6] Exhibited with verses from *Childe Harold's Pilgrimage* by Byron, *The Field of Waterloo* was unequivocally antiheroic; Turner focused on the aftermath of battle rather than the actual event, depicting the relatives of the fallen common soldiers searching for their loved ones after night has fallen, and stressing the human cost of the military triumph. Turner may have intended the paintings as companion works that articulate the dialectic of war and peace and tacitly advocate for peace. *Dort* also seems to have been a direct precursor to the radiant paintings of the port cities of Cologne and Dieppe that Turner exhibited in 1825 and 1826. The triad represents the German Confederation, France, and the United Kingdom of the Netherlands, three key entities of post-Napoleonic Europe.[7]

Dort was a personal manifesto rather than merely an homage to the Dutch Old Master, a point Turner underscored by the emphatic inscription of his name on the floating log in the foreground. As John Gage noted, the bright chromatic scale remarked upon by contemporary viewers (the painter Henry Thomson told the diarist Joseph Farington that the brilliance of the painting "almost puts your eyes out") marks a watershed in Turner's practice.[8] Some literal-minded critics objected to the unnaturalistic representation of light, which cannot be traced to a single source and floods the entire canvas with its sensuous glow, and Turner's increasing reliance on yellow pigments, including the recently introduced chrome yellow, was also critiqued. Turner's unconventional handling of

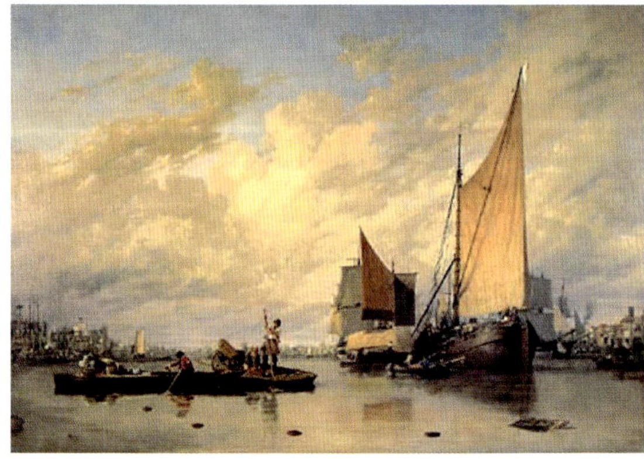

Fig. 42. Augustus Wall Callcott, *The Pool of London*, exhibited 1816, oil on canvas, 60¼ x 87 in. (153 x 221 cm). Trustees of the Bowood Estate, Wiltshire, England

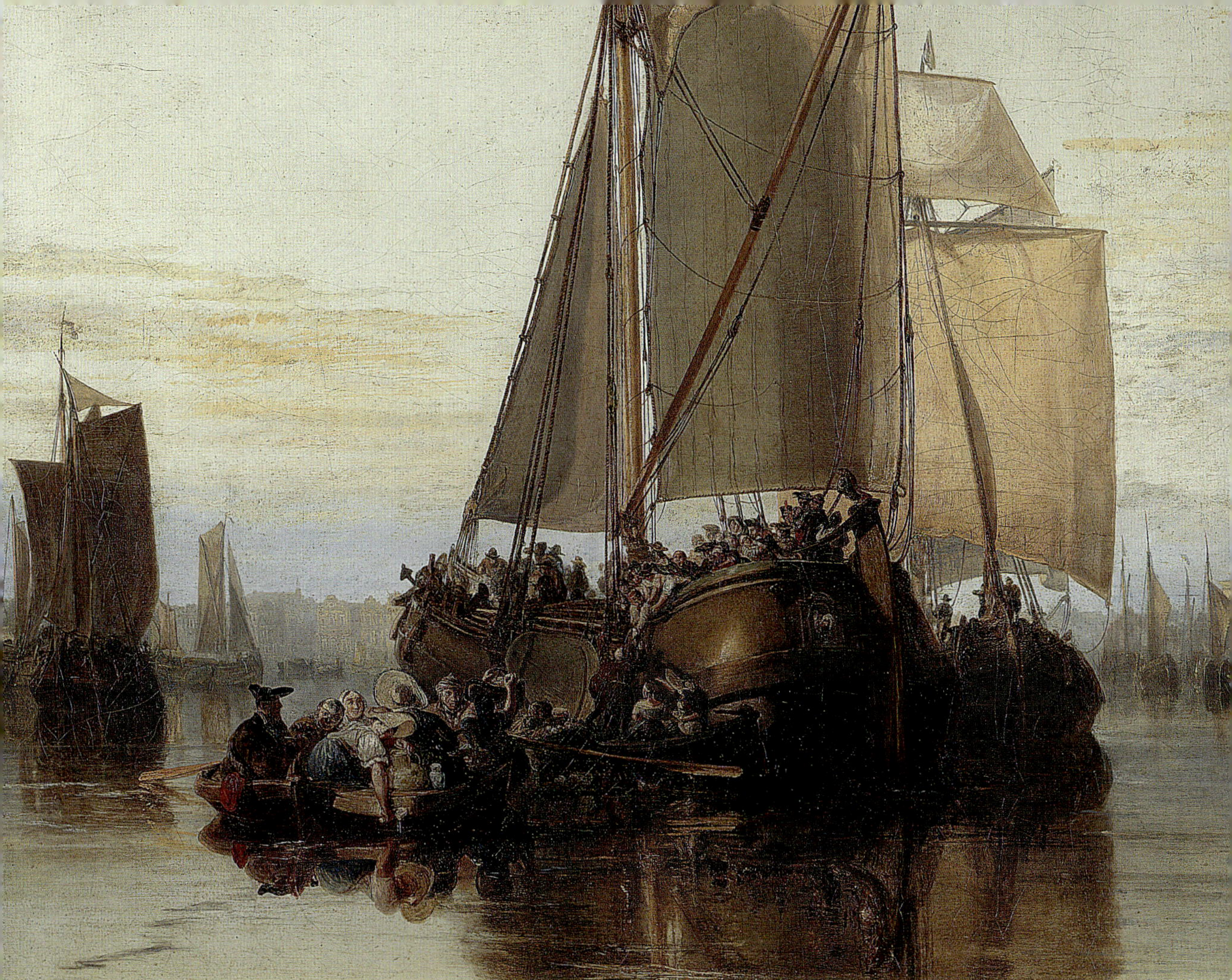

Detail of *Dort or Dordrecht*

paint and distinctive rendition of light was clearly strategic, however, constituting a radical statement of his autonomy.

Notes

1. Martin Butlin and Evelyn Joll, *The Paintings of J. M. W. Turner*, rev. edition (New Haven and London: Yale Univ. Press, 1984), 102–4, no. 134. See also Malcolm Cormack, "The Dort, Some Further Observations," *Turner Studies* 2, no. 2 (Winter 1983): 37–39.
2. British Institution for Promoting the Fine Arts in the United Kingdom, *Catalogue of pictures by Rubens, Rembrandt, Vandyke, and other artists of the Flemish and Dutch Schools*, exh. cat. (London: British Institution, 1815), 17, no. 67.
3. For Beaumont's critique of Callcott and Turner, see Sam Smiles, "'Splashers', 'Scrawlers' and 'Plasterers': British Landscape Painting and the Language of Criticism, 1800–40," *Turner Studies* 10, no. 1 (Summer 1990): 5–11.
4. David Cordingly, *Connoisseur* (October 1973): 99–101. For Callcott and Turner, see David Blayney Brown, *Augustus Wall Callcott*, exh. cat. (London: Tate Gallery, 1981), 78–79.
5. Kathryn Cave, ed., *The Diary of Joseph Farington*, 16 vols. and index (New Haven and London: Yale Univ. Press, 1978–84), 15:5190–1 (April 5, 1818). The present location of the *Mouth of the Tyne* is unknown.
6. Butlin and Joll, *The Paintings of J. M. W. Turner*, 101–2, 104–5, nos. 136, 138.
7. Butlin and Joll, *The Paintings of J. M. W. Turner*, 140–43, nos. 231–32. See also Susan Grace Galassi, Ian Warrell, Gillian Forrester, Joanna Sheers Seidenstein, Rebecca Hellen, and Eloise Owens, *Turner's Modern and Ancient Ports: Passages through Time* (New Haven and London: Yale Univ. Press, 2017).
8. John Gage, *J. M. W. Turner: 'A Wonderful Range of Mind'* (New Haven and London: Yale Univ. Press, 1987), 132–33. Cave, *The Diary of Joseph Farington*, 15:5191 (April 29, 1818).

John Constable RA (British, 1776–1837)
Stratford Mill, or *The Young Waltonians*, 1819–20

Oil on canvas, 51½ x 72½ in. (130.8 x 184.2 cm). Signed, lower right: "John Constable. R. A. | London." YALE CENTER FOR BRITISH ART, PAUL MELLON FUND, B1983.18

Mark Hallett

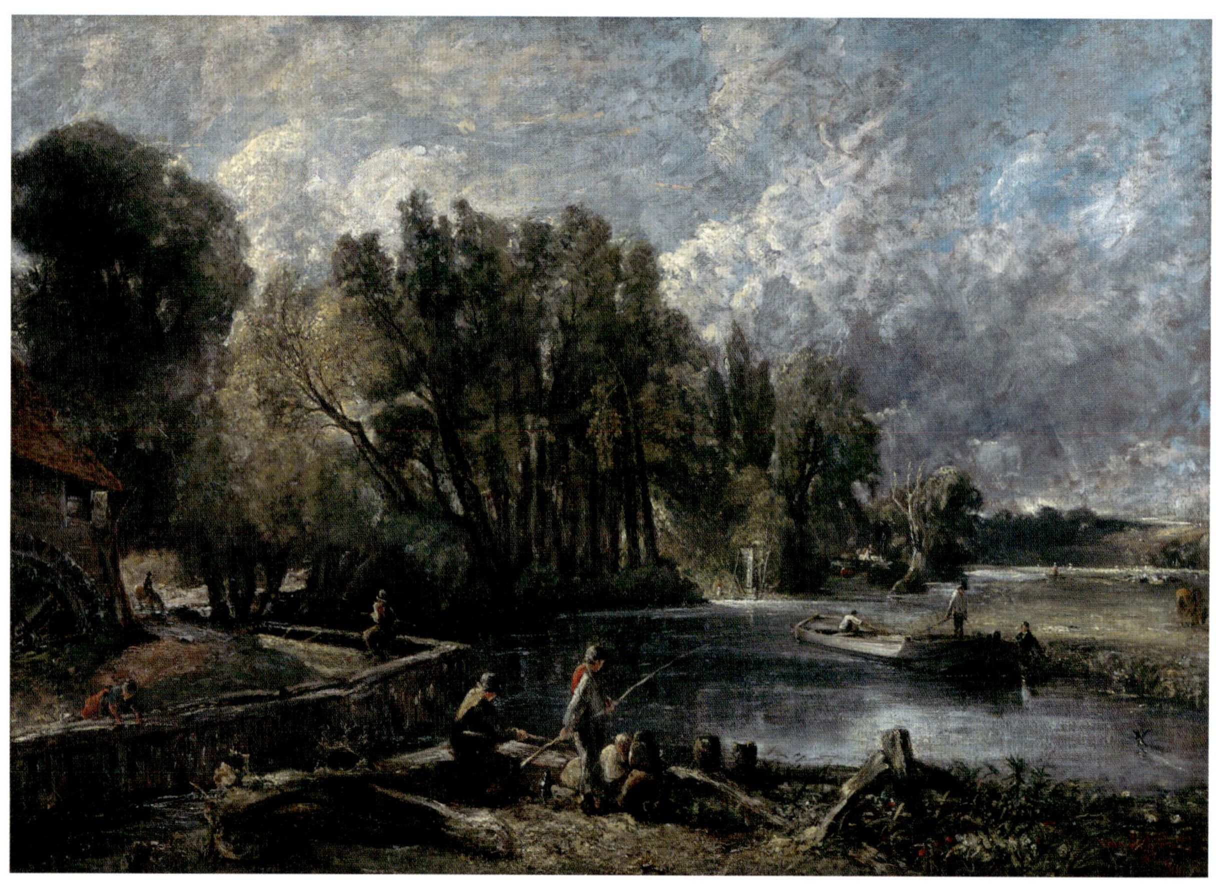

On October 26, 1821, the clergyman John Fisher wrote to his great friend, the artist John Constable, describing a recent fishing trip: "I was the other day fishing in the New Forest in a fine, deep, broad river, with mills, roaring backwaters, withy beds &c. I thought often of you during the day. I caught two pike, was up to the middle in watery meadows, and was as happy as when I was a 'careless boy.'"[1] Constable responded enthusiastically to the letter, projecting himself directly into the pictured scene: "How much I can imagine myself with you on your fishing excursion in the New Forest."[2] Prompted by Fisher's evocation of the sights, sounds, and experiences he had enjoyed on his expedition, Constable goes on to list the things that he, too, loved about rivers: "the sound of water escaping from Mill dams . . . Willows, Old rotten Banks, slimy posts, & brickwork."[3] And responding to his friend's allusion to the pleasures of his "careless" boyhood, Constable conjures up similar scenes in describing the joys of his own youth: "I associate my 'careless boyhood' to all that lies on the banks of the *Stour*."[4]

This exchange has become famous in the literature on the painter; however, little attention has been granted to the fact that it is built upon the report of a fishing expedition, or that the activity recalled and imagined by both men—angling—plays a significant pictorial role within a good number of Constable's Stour Valley paintings. This is particularly true of the six-foot sketch of *Stratford Mill*, painted two or so years before the correspondence noted above. Two male youths are shown fishing in the foreground, accompanied by a pair of crouching children. Nearby, another young man fishes in solitude, and a girl leans over the riverbank with a crude fishing rod in her hand.

Such figures are often considered as nothing more than pictorial staffage in discussions of Constable's paintings, intended to quietly animate the landscape and provide a sense of scale. In this instance, however, they were central to Constable's preoccupations from the very start. The Yale canvas is part of a sequence of preparatory studies that

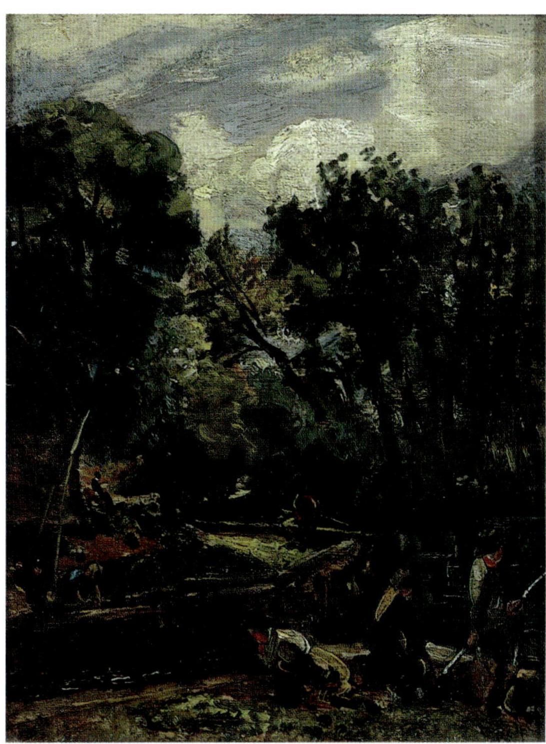

Fig. 43. John Constable, *Anglers at Stratford Mill*, 1811, oil on panel, 73⅝ x 57½ in. (187 x 146 cm). The Hart Collection

begins with a speedily executed outdoor oil sketch, dated August 17, 1811 (fig. 43). This is dominated by no less than six figures who are involved in some way or another with angling. And though Constable reduces the number of anglers in his later, horizontally expanded adaptations of the scene, he did so with an eye to distillation rather than dilution. This is carried through to the final version of the painting, exhibited at the Royal Academy of Arts in 1820, with the simple title of *Landscape* (fig. 44).

Why did Constable give so much attention to angling in his depictions of Stratford Mill? An answer is suggested if we turn to that English literary classic, Izaak Walton's *The Compleat Angler; or, The Contemplative Man's Recreation*, which was first published in 1653 and went through numerous editions—often illustrated—throughout the eighteenth and early-nineteenth centuries. Walton's text conjures up an ideal of angling, and of the

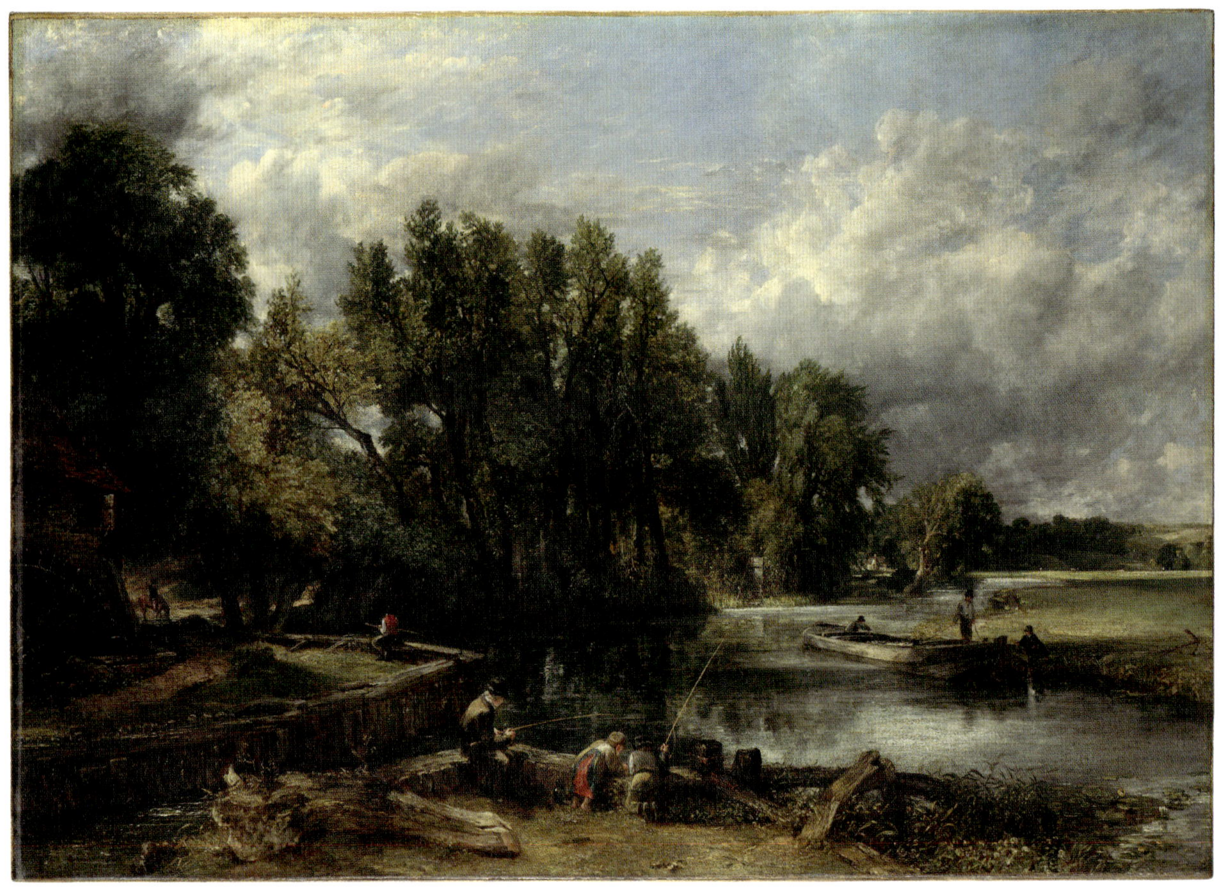

Fig. 44. John Constable, *Stratford Mill*, exhibited 1820, oil on canvas, 50 x 72 in. (127 x 182.9 cm). National Gallery, London

companionable, modest, learned, and religious-minded gentlemanly angler, that chimes beautifully with Fisher and Constable's own sense of masculine companionship, and with their mutual evocation of the pleasures of the riverside.

The Compleat Angler is structured around a friendly dialogue between a genteel fisherman, Piscator, and his companion, Venator, who had hitherto privileged the pleasures of falconry but who is gradually persuaded, as they walk, fish, and talk together, of the merits and virtues of angling.[5] Angling, Piscator argues, offers an exemplary gentlemanly activity because it fuses action—the physical, artful, and technically challenging activity of fishing itself—with, as the book's subtitle suggests, contemplation. And in relation to the latter virtue, Piscator argues that "the very sitting by the river's side, is not only the quietest and fittest place for contemplation, but will invite the anglers to it."[6] Over the pages of *The Compleat Angler*, this form of contemplation is revealed as twofold: it encompasses, firstly, a highly tuned attentiveness to the physical and atmospheric details of the landscape through which the angler walks, and in which he so often pauses to sit; and, secondly, a form of meditation that dwells upon the recognition of God's role as the bountiful creator of Nature.

Walton's vision of angling is one that corresponds rather closely to Constable's own attitudes toward landscape painting, which he similarly saw as a quiet, learned art that fused a technically challenging, physical form of activity with, at times, extended forms of outdoor contemplation, during which he, too, would pore over all the details of a river and its surroundings, and interpret the features of the countryside in religious terms. In *Stratford Mill*, and in a host of other paintings, that parallel must have made it feel natural for him to introduce the figures of anglers in the pictorial foreground. There, they can be understood as analogs, or even surrogates, for the figure of the painter. More importantly, perhaps, they help encourage the viewer to look at the painted landscape in a particular way: like these anglers, like the fishermen described by Walton, and like Constable himself, whenever he sat down to sketch on the banks of the Stour, we are invited, in turn, to contemplate the expanse of water that flows through the center of the picture; to cast our eyes across the surrounding countryside, appreciating even its most modest beauties; and, finally, to see in such features as a bank of trees, or some submerged water lilies, or the glimpse of a distant plowman, the creative hand of a Christian deity.

Of course, Constable substitutes a group of youthful anglers for the kind of adult protagonists found in *The Compleat Angler* and in the artist's exchange of letters with his friend. In doing so, he can be seen to yoke the ideal of angling articulated so famously by Walton, and maintained in Fisher's report of his New Forest expedition, to that nostalgic notion of "careless boyhood" that the latter shared with the artist in their correspondence. For Constable—now a man in his forties, working in a London studio far from that riverside setting—the scene he pictured in *Stratford Mill* was a remembered environment as much as an observed one, and one that he especially associated with the period of his own youth, during which he had spent so much time "on the banks of the Stour"; Constable's young anglers, we can suggest, serve to encapsulate his own fantasy-laden memories of a riverbank childhood. For other viewers, including ourselves, these same figures, unburdened by the cares and anxieties of adult life and happily absorbed in their modest pastime, help reinforce and confirm the pictured scene's character as a landscape of relaxation and ease in which, not far from the scattered group of anglers, a working barge is brought to rest and, on the left of the picture, a horse stops to sip some water. Yes, this array of young anglers embody the virtues and possibilities associated with both fishing and painting; but they also help align the pictured landscape with an escapist, preadult realm of freedom, tranquility, and play.

Another pictorial variation on *Stratford Mill* provides us with a fitting conclusion. In 1840, just three years after Constable's death, David Lucas published a mezzotint after the final, exhibited version of the picture. Lucas declared that the print was "Dedicated to Every Lover of Angling." Furthermore, he called it *The Young Waltonians*.[7] Given the parallels between Constable's practice and the forms of riverside art celebrated in Walton's *The Compleat Angler*, and given the artist's focus on the pleasures and pastimes of youth in his pictures of Stratford Mill, this seems to have been an especially inspired and apt choice of title.

Notes

1. R. B. Beckett, ed., *John Constable's Correspondence*, vol. 6 (of 6): *The Fishers* (Ipswich: Suffolk Records Society, 1962–68), 6:76.
2. Beckett, *John Constable's Correspondence*, 6:77.
3. Beckett, *John Constable's Correspondence*, 6:77.
4. Beckett, *John Constable's Correspondence*, 6:78.
5. Izaak Walton, *The Compleat Angler; or, The Contemplative Man's Recreation* (London: 1653).
6. Walton, *The Compleat Angler*, 16–17.
7. Andrew Shirley, *The Published Mezzotints of David Lucas after John Constable, R.A, a Catalogue and Historical Account* (Oxford: The Clarendon Press, 1930), 201, no. 38.

William Darton (British, 1781–1854)
The Noble Game of the Elephant and Castle, or Travelling in Asia (London: William Darton, 1822)

Game board: hand-colored engraving on linen, 20 x 16 in. (51 x 41 cm), opened

YALE CENTER FOR BRITISH ART, PAUL MELLON COLLECTION, GV.1199.N6

Romita Ray

Looking up at the pediment above the portico of East India House (the East India Company's headquarters on Leadenhall Street in London), a pedestrian in the early 1800s might have easily spotted an elephant's head a few feet away from Britannia's snarling lion. A conspicuous celebration of Company commerce in India, the imposing sculptural ensemble ensured that global mercantilism was simultaneously recognized as patriotic service. Meanwhile, on the north side of the Strand, Chunee, a live elephant imported from Bengal in 1809, was the star attraction at the Exeter Change, his stage debut in 1811 at Covent Garden in the pantomime *Harlequin and Padmanaba, or the Golden Fish* making him London's most popular exotic animal.[1] What then do we make of an elephant in a box?

In 1822 William Darton, map seller and purveyor of children's toys and games in Holborn Hill, published *The Noble Game of the Elephant and Castle, or Travelling in Asia*, a board game covering the broad sweep of Asia from Russia to China and Turkey to Japan.[2] A hand-colored engraving of an elephant adorned with a "castle" perched on its back and a *mahout* sitting astride its neck constitutes its principal image. Sprawled across the linen on which the game is printed, the elephant features twenty-five numbered vignettes fitted into its body and folds down to a small rectangle that, together with a pocket-size guidebook, slips into a storage box or case, also decorated with the image of an elephant (fig. 45).[3] Be it through the elephant motif, the portable case, or the counters called

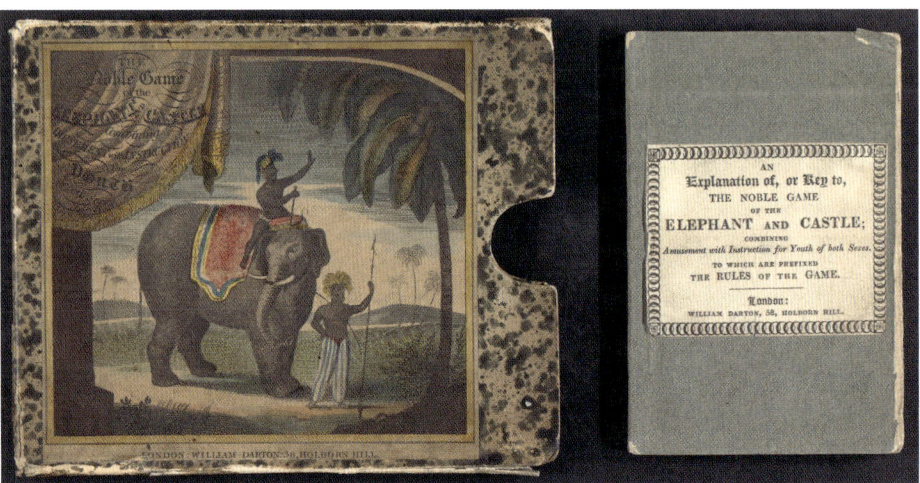

Fig. 45. William Darton, storage case and guidebook from *The Noble Game of the Elephant and Castle, or Travelling in Asia* (London: William Darton, 1822); case: 14 x 7 in. (35.6 x 17.8 cm), booklet: 11 x 17 in. (27.9 x 43.2 cm). Yale Center for British Art, Paul Mellon Collection

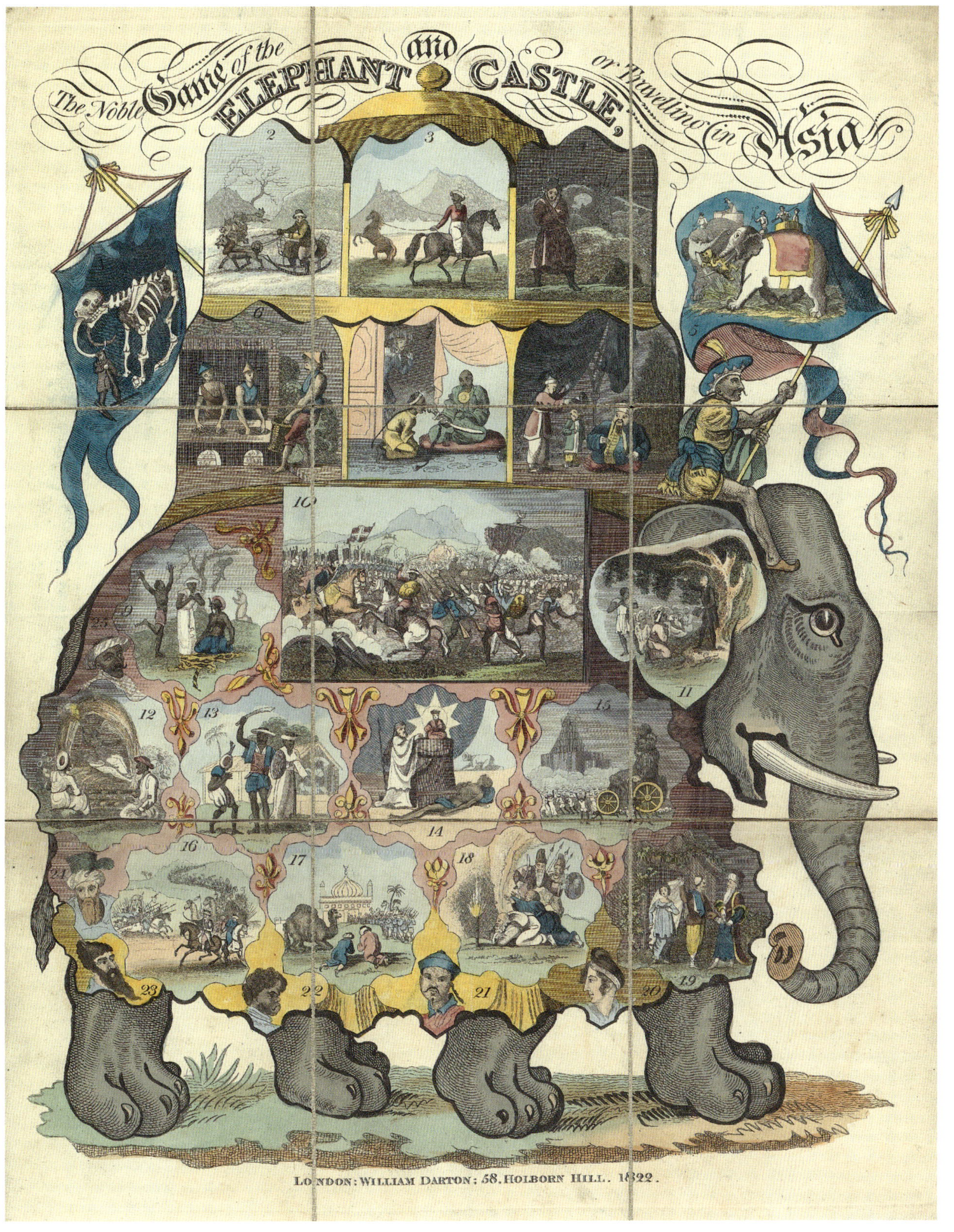

The Noble Game of the ELEPHANT and CASTLE, or Travelling in Asia
LONDON: WILLIAM DARTON; 58, HOLBORN HILL. 1822.

"Travellers" that players moved across the board, the intertwined ideas of travel and mobility were fundamental to the visual and tactile pleasures of playing *The Noble Game*. Enhancing these dual pleasures was the guidebook that players consulted in between moves to learn about the people and places depicted in the vignettes that they landed on after spinning a teetotum (fig. 46). Materially, too, the game resembles a map, a portable artifact in which key geographic information is organized and codified; it was even carried in the manner of eighteenth- and nineteenth-century maps that were tucked away in similar flat cases.[4]

Quite simply, *The Noble Game* transforms players into travelers. It also turns geographical exploration into an instructional lesson in history, religion, culture, "morality and genealogy,"[5] a didactic strategy found in several other contemporary geographical games and books for children that promoted powerful messages about morality and patriotism through graphic entertainment.[6] Published at a timely moment when Britain's expanding empire in the Indian subcontinent was shaping "new geographies of the exotic" and new histories for Britons, the game invited players to imagine distant places, peoples, customs, and traditions, but always with Britain as the main focal point.[7] In Darton's own words, the player might admire "the treasures of the East" as the "eye's great feast," but that "of the heart must be at home."[8] With Britain's strong foothold in India and a steady influx of Indian raw materials like cotton harnessed for the Industrial Revolution, not surprisingly, the game focused mainly on India, by then widely recognized as Britain's most prized colony. Indeed, the very motif of the elephant—whose image peppered countless drawings, prints, paintings, books, journals, and maps linked to India—instantly oriented the player eastward.

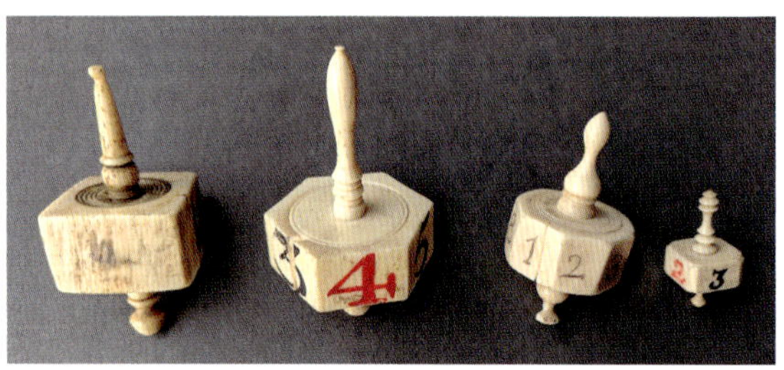

Fig. 46. Teetotums, 19th century, bone. Left two, Yale Center for British Art, Paul Mellon Fund; right two, Yale Center for British Art, Gift of Ellen and Arthur Liman (Yale JD 1957)

Yet Darton's game is fundamentally geared toward self-reflection and patriotic duty. With its strong moralizing tone, it accentuates the relationship between imperial ambition and Christian identity, while simultaneously paying homage to Darton's Quaker roots. Nowhere is this more apparent than on the elephant's ear, where a Christian missionary is shown preaching to a group of brown-skinned "natives." Indeed, the tame elephant itself mirrors the taming of the Indian "native." Seen another way, the castle-bearing elephant may have had a visual precedent closer to home in medieval Alexander romances that featured images of soldiers ensconced in wooden towers strapped to the backs of elephants—fanciful references to Alexander the Great's legendary exploits in India. It may also hark back to medieval bestiaries in which elephants were depicted frequently with castles, "flowery" ears, trumpet-like trunks, and paws (note the elephant's feline feet in *The Noble Game*),[9] their anthropomorphized descriptions paving the way for nineteenth-century characterizations of the creature as "the most intellectual animal in the creation after man."[10]

If Darton's elephant gratified the taste for the exotic, it certainly made its presence "felt" in the bone and ivory of its counters and teetotum. With the animal's corporeality incorporated into the very experience of playing the game, geographical knowledge was rendered tactile, while luxury goods like ivory were made more accessible to young consumers. Distillations like these demonstrate the desire to compress an ever-expanding corpus of information about Britain's Asian encounters on a manageable scale, thus laying the foundation for making knowledge more portable, visible, and graspable—a modernizing impulse

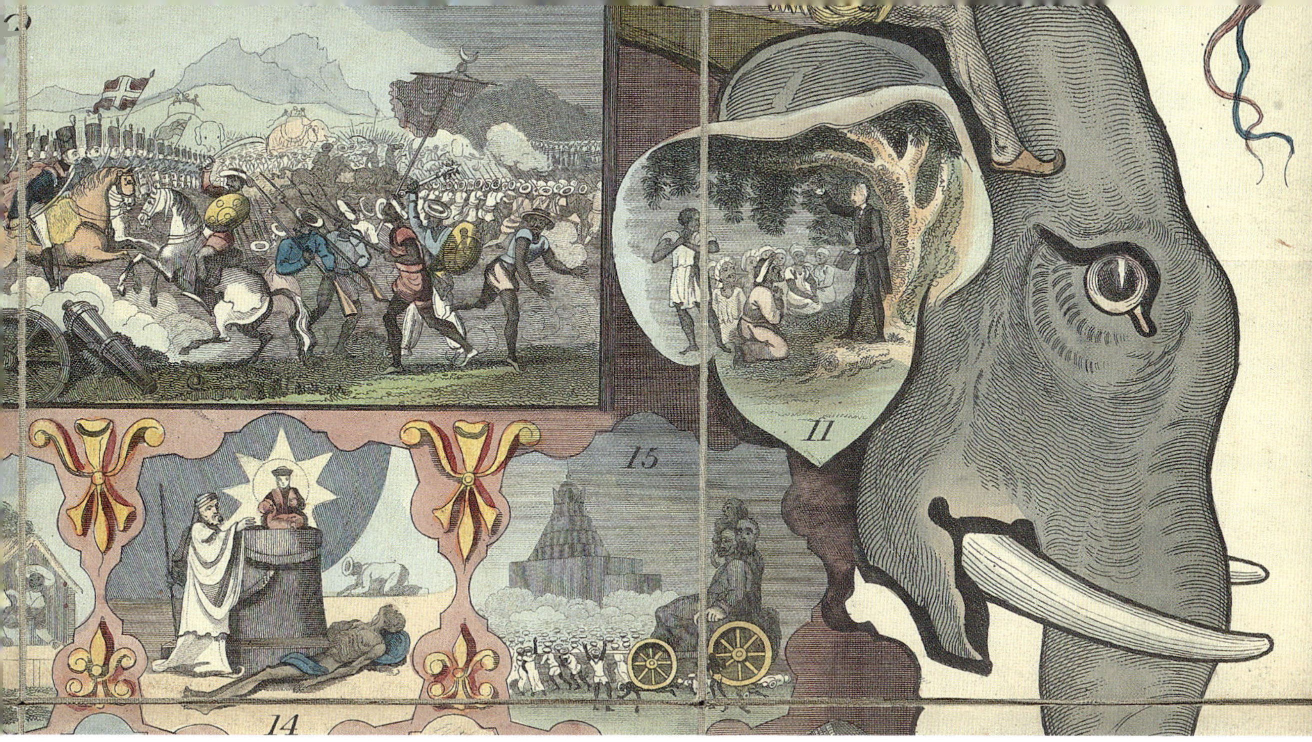

Detail of *The Noble Game*

that we see carried forward today by mobile phones, tablets, and video games.

Notes

I thank Elisabeth Fairman and Francis Lapka (Yale Center for British Art) and Hannah Fleming (Victoria & Albert Museum of Childhood) for their help at various stages of writing this essay.

1. Richard D. Altick, *The Shows of London* (Cambridge, MA: Harvard Univ. Press, 1978), 310–16; Caroline Grigson, *Menagerie: The History of Exotic Animals in England* (Oxford: Oxford Univ. Press, 2016), 190–92; Sujit Sivasundaram, "Trading Knowledge: The East India Company's Elephants in India and Britain," *Historical Journal* 48, no. 1 (March 2005): 55–60.

2. Darton's father, also named William Darton (1755–1819), was an engraver, stationer, and printer who set up a print publishing firm that became known mainly for its children's publications. In 1787 the senior Darton established his publishing house in White Lion Alley, Birchin Lane, London, before moving the following year to 55 Gracechurch Street. In 1791 he formed a partnership with Joseph Harvey. While one of his sons, Samuel Darton (1785–1840), became a partner in his firm, his son William Darton, who published the *The Noble Game* discussed in this essay, established his own publishing firm in Holborn Hill in 1804. See Linda David, Children's Books Published by William Darton and His Sons: A Catalogue of an Exhibition at the Lilly Library, Indiana University, April–June 1992 (Bloomington: Indiana University, 1992), Lilly Library Publications Online, http://www.indiana.edu/~liblilly/etexts/darton/.

3. For a detailed analysis of Darton's game, see Romita Ray, *Under the Banyan Tree: Relocating the Picturesque in British India* (New Haven and London: Yale Univ. Press, 2013), 15, 235–59; Romita Ray, "The Beast in a Box: Playing with Empire in Early Nineteenth-Century Britain," *Visual Resources* 22, no. 1 (March 2006): 7–31.

4. Linda Hannas, *The English Jigsaw Puzzle, 1760–1890: With a Descriptive Check-list of Puzzles in the Museums of Great Britain and the Author's Collection* (London: Wayland, 1972), 212.

5. John Brewer, introduction, in *The Cottage of Content: or, Toys, Games, and Amusements of Nineteenth-Century England*, eds. John B. Thomas, Paula D. Matthews, and Deborah S. Berman (New Haven: Yale Center for British Art, 1977), iv. See also Rev. John Hartley, *Geography for Youth, Adapted to The Different Classes by Learners* (Dublin: Printed for J. Parry, 1813), 18–32.

6. Darton himself published a large number of children's books, which focused on building knowledge and character. See David, Children's Books. For an overview of British geographical games, see Caroline Goodfellow, *A Collector's Guide to Games and Puzzles* (London: Apple Press, 1991), 20–27.

7. *The Noble Game* was published when Britain's global reach had extended, with varying degrees of success, to North America, the Caribbean islands, West Africa, New South Wales and Tasmania, and the Indian subcontinent. Miles Ogborn and Charles Withers, introduction, in *Georgian Geographies: Essays on Space, Place, and Landscape in the Eighteenth Century*, eds. Ogborn and Withers (Manchester: Manchester Univ. Press, 2004), 6–7.

8. William Darton, *An Explanation of, or Key to, The Noble Game of the Elephant and Castle; or, Travelling in Asia; During which the Sagacious Animal Introduces Us to Various and Instructive Scenes. To Which are Prefixed the Rules of the Game* (London: William Darton, 1822; printed by George Smallfield, Hackney), 81.

9. Pamela Gravestock, "Did Imaginary Animals Exist?" in *The Mark of the Beast: The Medieval Bestiary in Art, Life, and Literature*, ed. Debra Hassig (New York and London: Garland Publishing, 1999), 119.

10. *A Visit to the Tower Being, An Account of Several Birds, and Beasts* (York: Printed by J. Kendrew, Colliergate, 1820), 4.

Robert Smith (British, 1787–1873)
Inside the Main Entrance of the Purana Qila, Delhi, 1823

Oil on canvas, 30 1/16 x 42 in. (76.4 x 106.7 cm). Signed and dated, lower left: "RS 1823."

YALE CENTER FOR BRITISH ART, PAUL MELLON COLLECTION, B1976.7.73

Morna O'Neill

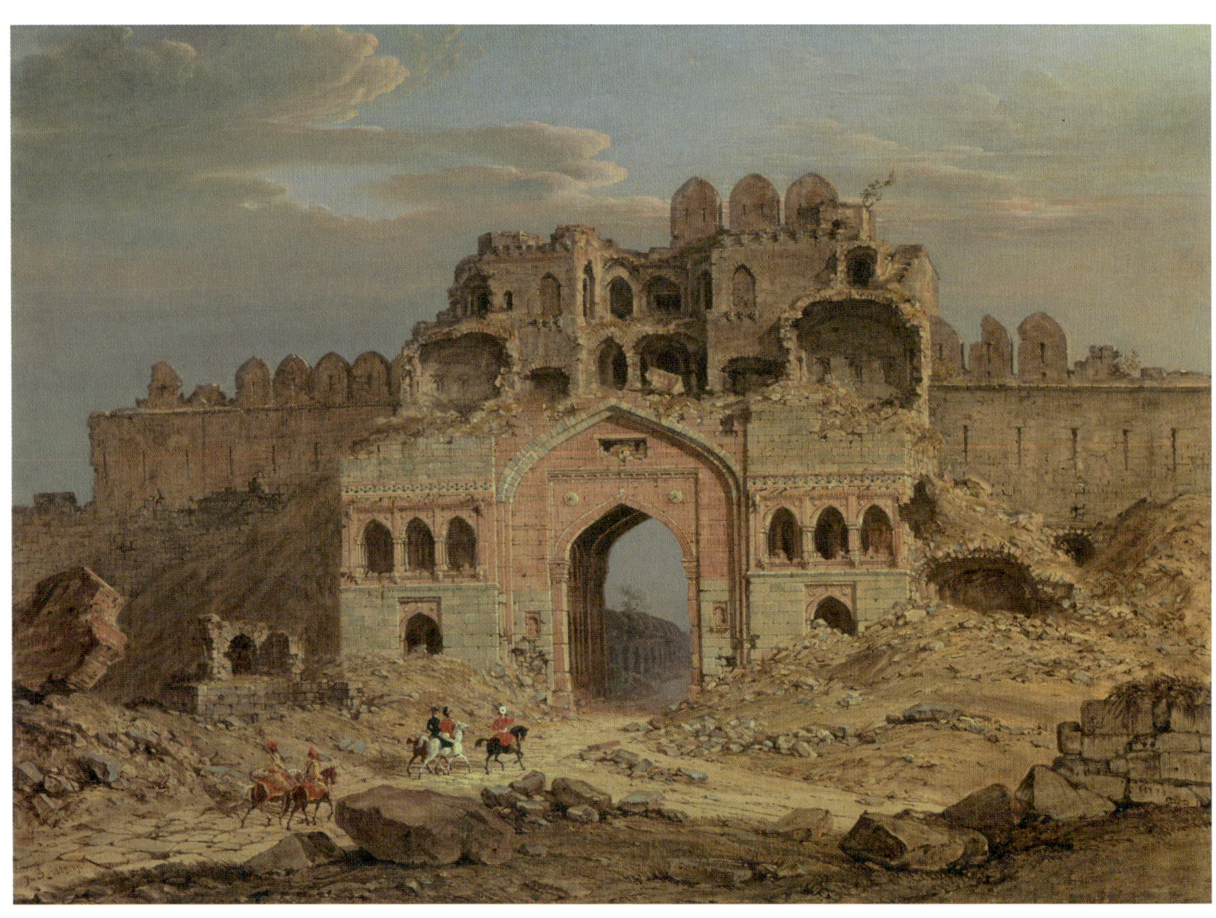

Writing from late eighteenth-century London, the politician William Pitt the Elder, first Earl of Chatham, marveled that "the riches of Asia have been poured in upon us."[1] Tea, spices, fabrics, and other luxury goods from the Indian subcontinent transformed everyday life in Britain. Yet these goods were not so much "poured in" as "sought after." They were the products of an aggressive and dynamic colonial endeavor spearheaded by the East India Company.

Founded in 1600, this powerful collective of London-based merchants competed with similar ventures launched by maritime rivals such as the Dutch and the Portuguese. The Company controlled every aspect of British involvement on the Indian subcontinent until 1813, often regardless of its cataclysmic effects on indigenous cultures and society. Although Parliament ended its commercial monopoly on all trade east of the southern tip of Africa in that year, the Company continued as the governing bureaucratic and military presence on the subcontinent until 1857. "The Company Raj," the name given to the period of British ascendancy in India under the auspices of the East India Company, endured from 1770 to 1830.[2] Although English traders and Indian kingdoms interacted for almost a century prior, in this period what began as a trading venture became a territorial empire. For politician and philosopher Edmund Burke, this shift constituted "a very great revolution in commerce as well as dominion."[3] Among the "riches of Asia" exported to Europe were paintings, drawings, and prints produced by the many British artists, draftsmen, surveyors, engineers, and amateurs who traveled to the Indian subcontinent in search of patronage and aesthetic inspiration.

The career of Colonel Robert Smith exemplifies the various roles and itinerant lifestyle of an East India Company employee. He served as an architect, archaeologist, painter, and military engineer during his lengthy career in India and elsewhere.[4] Trained as an engineer in the East India Company's Great Marlow Academy, Smith learned surveying, mapping, and draftsmanship. As a colonel in the Bengal Engineers, he used these skills in the service of military ventures, including the capture of Mauritius (1811) and the Nepal War (1816), as well as the building of infrastructure. He served as Superintending Engineer of the Company's Chinese holdings in Penang, and in 1821 he became Garrison Engineer at Delhi.

An ancient city, Delhi rose to importance as the capital of the Islamic sultanate of Northern India, the seat of the Mughal dynasty. Smith took an active interest in the local Mughal architecture, and he was put in charge of the city's ancient monuments, including the Purana Qila, whose name means "old fort." Begun in the sixteenth century under the Emperor Humayun, it was completed by his successor Sher Shah Sur. By the early nineteenth century, religious strife and insurrection weakened the lineage of the celebrated Mughal Empire, and the area came under the influence of the Company in 1804. The structure fulfilled the same defensive function for the Company militia in Delhi.

While the accurate rendering of topography was an important skill for a Company engineer, Smith's interest in drawing extended to a leisure activity, eventually earning him a reputation as an accomplished artist. In this painting, the hulking shell of the Purana Qila evokes both grandeur and decay. It is likely that he used a drawing device known as a camera obscura, a darkened "camera" or chamber with a lens that projects an image of the outside world inside the box, to accurately render the depth of the alcoves and the layers of brick. Near the center of the canvas, the artist depicts a number of figures: two Europeans, possibly an Indian guide, and two Indian soldiers, who are riding out of the fort's northern gate, signifying the continued life and shifting fortunes of the Mughal monument. As an immense fort structure whose walls encircled the city of Delhi, the Purana Qila housed the Kila Kona Masjid, or mosque, shown in another of Smith's painting (fig. 47). Here, the interplay between grandeur and decay continues. The imposing building seems to rest on shaky ground, with the tunnels beneath collapsing into

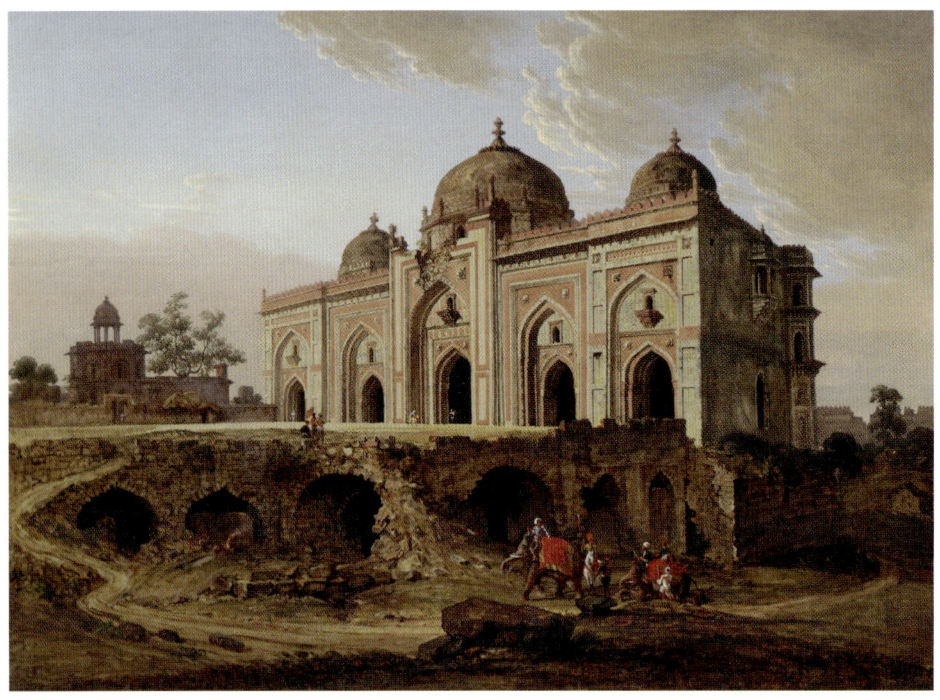

Fig. 47. Robert Smith, *The Kila Kona Masjid, Purana Qila, Delhi,* ca. 1823, oil on canvas, 29½ x 41¾ in. (74.9 x 106 cm). Yale Center for British Art, Paul Mellon Collection

rubble while some fragments of the delicate pink sandstone facade have fallen away or been overtaken by foliage. As art historian Romita Ray has noted, Smith's paintings present "history, time, and memory in flux."[5] In this painting, is the Purana Qila in the process of falling down or being rebuilt?

Although Smith was not a professional artist, his work was in dialogue with contemporary artistic practice. Company training did not include oil painting, and it is likely that Smith acquired this skill while on furlough in England in 1819.[6] The vistas, prospects, and monuments of this "new" Indian landscape attracted artists such as William Hodges and Thomas and William Daniell. Hodges toured the subcontinent under the patronage of Warren Hastings, the controversial head of the East India Company, from 1780 to 1783, while Thomas Daniell and his nephew William traveled in India from 1786 to 1793. Through publications and exhibitions of their work in London, these artists raised British awareness of Indian natural history and architectural history. They experienced the subcontinent, however, as artists trained in the tradition of European landscape painting and supported by the resources and infrastructure of the East India Company. The Daniells arrived in India, probably as part of a Company military expedition, and explored the Jami Masjid in Delhi, commissioned by Shah Jahan and completed in 1658. Painting in London more than twenty years later, Thomas Daniell places the monumental Eastern Gate in the middle distance (fig. 48). He presents the mosque as massive and solid, impervious to the flow of time suggested in Smith's paintings. In 1827, when Smith spearheaded the restoration of the Jami Masjid, colleagues praised his "exquisite judgement and taste."[7]

While paintings by Smith and others provide documents of place, they are also exercises in pictorial formulae. In Britain, landscape painting rose to prominence in this period of imperial expansion. The hallmarks of the picturesque style, such as the misty background, the middle distance holding the interest, the intricate foreground with the entire composition set within a frame of foliage, as well as the depiction of architectural ruins, define the Indian landscapes of Smith as well as professional artists such as William Hodges and

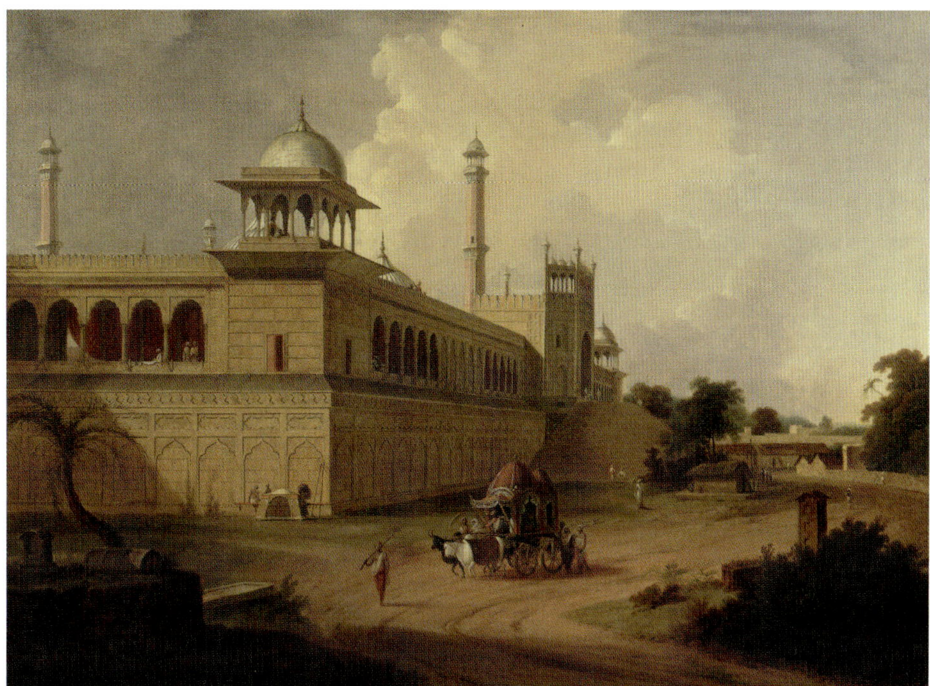

Fig. 48. Thomas Daniell, *Jami Masjid, Delhi*, 1811, oil on canvas, 40 x 54 in. (101.6 x 137.2 cm). Yale Center for British Art, Paul Mellon Collection

Thomas Daniell. Although the Company itself was no great patron of the arts, it provided the infrastructure to connect artists with patrons, both British and Indian, as well as to enable travel. In fact, artists traveling to India in this period had first to obtain permission from the Company. The art historian W. J. T. Mitchell has described landscape as "the 'dreamwork' of imperialism," expressing a subconscious desire for ownership or domination while still picturing "unresolved ambivalence and unsuppressed resistance."[8] Ruins were a central feature of the Western picturesque, meant to encourage the viewer to reflect upon the passage of time and the interplay between nature and culture. But Indian ruins as depicted by British landscape painters take on other cultural meanings, as a concern with decay would justify British stewardship of Indian monuments in the decades to follow; in a similar fashion, the Company used this rationale—decay in the form of the perceived weakness and mismanagement of Indian rulers—to justify their administrative and military control of India.

Notes

1. As quoted in C. A. Hagerman, *Britain's Imperial Muse: The Classics, Imperialism, and the Indian Empire, 1784–1914* (London: Palgrave, 2013), 115.
2. Antony Wild, *The East India Company: Trade and Conquest from 1600* (New York: HarperCollins, 1999).
3. Edmund Burke, "Ninth Report from the Select Committee (of the House of Commons) appointed to take into consideration the state of the administration of Justice in the Provinces of Bengal, Bahar, and Orissa (25 June 1783)," in *The Works of Edmund Burke*, 9 vols. (Boston: Charles C. Little and James Brown, 1839), 6:36.
4. See Mildred Archer, "An Artist Engineer—Colonel Robert Smith in India (1805–1830)," *Connoisseur* (February 1972): 79–88; Diane James, "A Fairy Palace in Devon: Redcliffe Towers, built by Colonel Robert Smith (1787–1873), Bengal Engineers," *East India Company at Home* (July 2014): 1–25, http://blogs.ucl.ac.uk/eicah/colonel-robert-smith-and-redcliffe-towers-case-study/; John McAleer, *Picturing India: People, Places and the World of the East India Company* (Seattle: Univ. of Washington Press, 2017), 112–15.
5. Romita Ray, *Under the Banyan Tree: Relocating the Picturesque in British India* (New Haven and London: Yale Univ. Press, 2013), 211.
6. See Archer, "An Artist Engineer," 81.
7. E. Archer, *Tours in Upper India*, 2 vols. (London: Richard Bentley, 1833), 1:107.
8. W. J. T. Mitchell, "Imperial Landscape," in *Landscape and Power*, ed. W. J. T. Mitchell (Chicago: Univ. of Chicago Press, 1994), 10.

John Scarlett Davis (British, 1804–1845)
The Interior of the British Institution Gallery, 1829

Oil on canvas, 44½ x 56 in. (113 x 142.2 cm). Signed and dated, lower right: "J. Scarlett Davis | 1829." YALE CENTER FOR BRITISH ART, PAUL MELLON COLLECTION, B1981.25.212

Catherine Roach

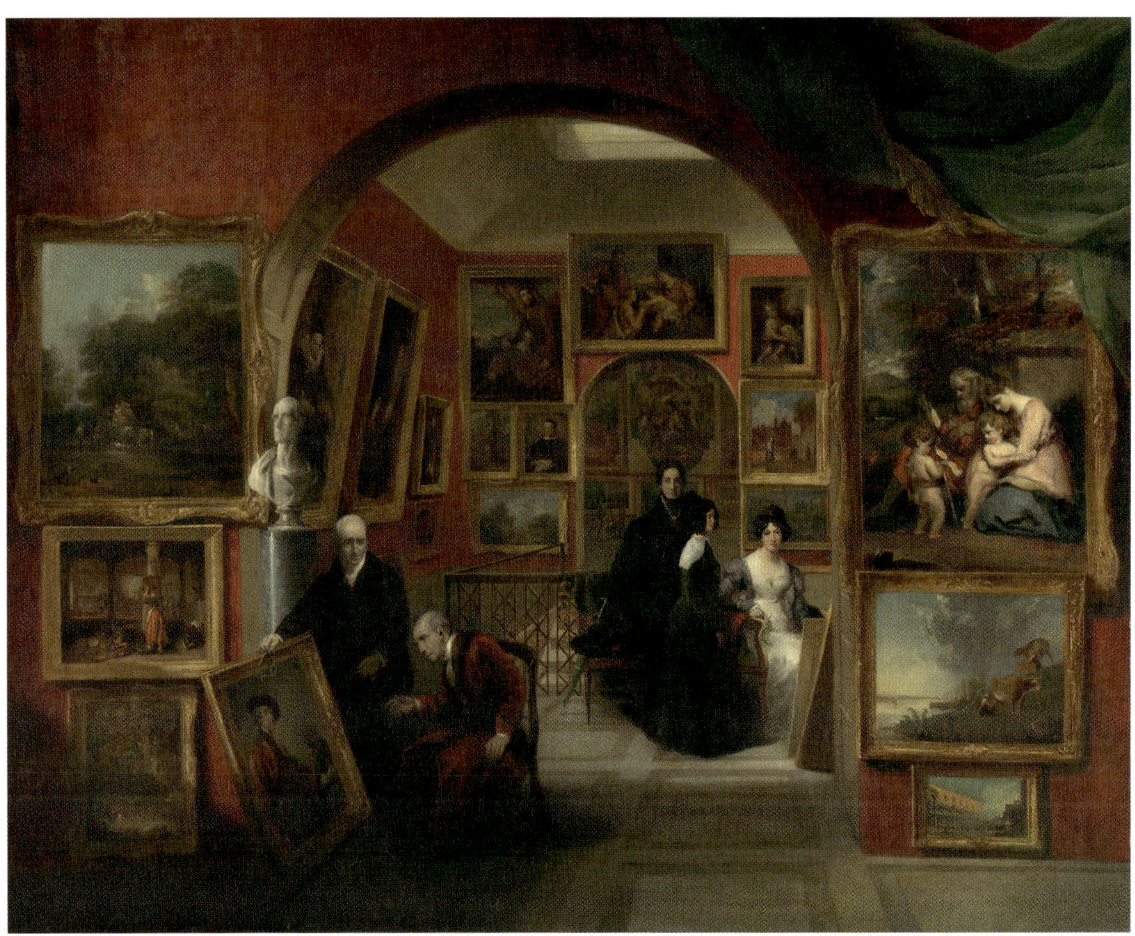

The galleries seen here, hung floor to ceiling with pictures, belonged to an innovative London arts organization, the British Institution for Promoting the Fine Arts in the United Kingdom.[1] In his depiction of this space, the painter John Scarlett Davis took considerable liberties. Drawing on the tradition of the Netherlandish gallery picture, he created a fantasia inspired by an exhibition in 1829.[2] Indeed, of all the known images of the Institution, this picture is the least

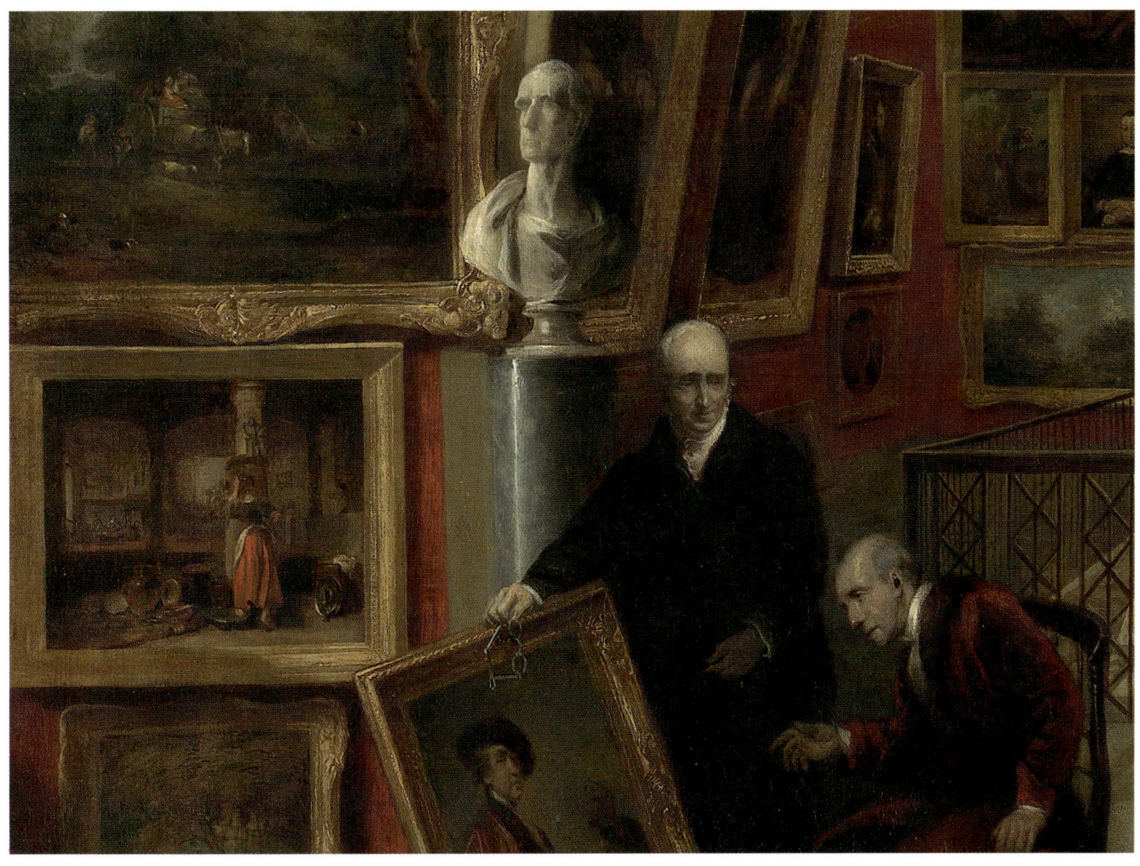

Detail of *The Interior of the British Institution Gallery*

reliable as a document because the artist was seeking not to record but to persuade.[3] The pictures on the walls and the people shown viewing them all contribute to a story about British art and its relationship to the world.

When the Institution was founded by a group of wealthy patrons in 1805, Britain had been at war with France for over a decade in the latest iteration of a worldwide, century-long contest over imperial expansion.[4] The current war was fought first against the French revolutionary government and later against the newly proclaimed Emperor Napoleon. Seeking legitimacy for his new regime, Napoleon invested heavily in the arts, augmenting the collections of the Louvre with spoils from his conquests. No comparable museum existed in London. Moreover, despite the development of a vibrant exhibition culture in the previous century, British artistic production was still widely considered to be behind that of the Continent. The founders of the Institution sought to ensure that their nation would be able to compete culturally as well as militarily. To that end, they urged native artists to emulate past art in pursuit of future excellence.

The committee of Directors that ran the Institution sponsored a wide array of activities. They purchased artworks on behalf of the nation, commissioned new paintings, campaigned for the foundation of a national gallery, and held annual sale exhibitions of contemporary art. They also created novel educational opportunities, including a painting school that, unlike the Royal Academy of Arts, was open to female students. In 1813 the Directors initiated another groundbreaking program, annual loan exhibitions of the art of the past.[5] The first of these events, dedicated to Sir Joshua Reynolds, was a landmark in the history of exhibitions: it marked the first time that an arts organization staged a posthumous retrospective, a format still widely used by museums today. But the significance of these displays goes beyond that of any one show. At a time when most European collections were increasingly arranged chronologically and by national school, the Directors employed an earlier installation style that juxtaposed objects from a range of times and places. Far from being retrograde, this approach allowed the Directors to advance a novel thesis: that British art had a place in the international canon.

Scarlett Davis's imaginative recreation of an exhibition expressed this thesis by drawing visual parallels between British and Continental objects. The Directors had recently purchased two sterling examples of eighteenth-century British art as gifts

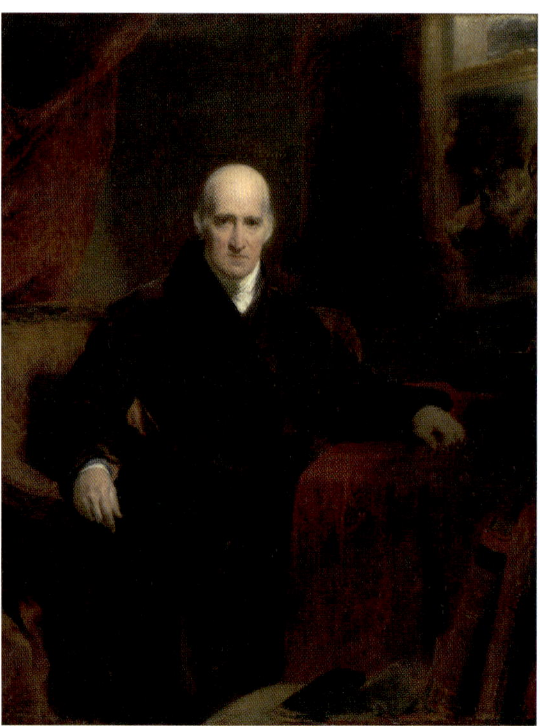

Fig. 49. Sir Thomas Lawrence, *Benjamin West, P.R.A.*, 1810, oil on panel, 60½ x 47½ in. (153.7 x 120.7 cm). Yale Center for British Art, Paul Mellon Collection

to the new National Gallery. Scarlett Davis depicts these works, Thomas Gainsborough's *Market Cart* and Reynolds's *Holy Family*, hanging to either side of the archway, in harmony with works attributed to Titian, Murillo, and Cuyp.[6] Reynolds himself is pictured at left, where his *Self-Portrait as a Doctor of Laws* is examined by two of his fellow painters, James Northcote, who had studied with him, and Benjamin West, who succeeded him as President of the Royal Academy. Reynolds's self-portrait was not actually shown at the Institution in 1829. Similarly, we know that it is impossible for Benjamin West to have attended the exhibition, because he died nine years earlier. His likeness, like all of those in the painting, was closely copied from a preexisting portrait (fig. 49).[7] Yet Scarlett Davis depicts West as alive and well and examining a picture that was not there, in order to suggest an orderly succession among generations of British artists.

The painting thus constructs a visual history of British art. At the same time, it is also a family portrait. The portrait bust looming above the artists is Edward Hodges Baily's likeness of the Bristol merchant Richard Hart Davis (no known relation to the painter) (fig. 50).[8] The man and woman seen at right are Hart Davis's daughter and her husband, Louisa and John Scandrett Harford. Hart Davis used the fortune he had gained in the West Indies trade to build an impressive collection of Old Masters and contemporary art. In 1810 he became a Hereditary Governor of the Institution; although less influential than a Directorship, this position allowed him to vote at annual membership meetings. By 1819, however, Hart Davis was bankrupted by a failed speculation in government funds, and his art collection was transferred to a business partner in payment of his debts. But he retained his membership in the Institution, and with it, the status of a patron of the arts. By including him in a celebration of the national school, *The Interior of the British Institution Gallery* commemorates Hart Davis's role as a benefactor, rather than as a debtor.

Hart Davis's presence in this image raises larger questions about Britain's relationship to the wider world in this historical moment. Scarlett Davis's painting expresses British cultural aspirations. But the realm in which those aspirations are carried out is resolutely European. No hint or whisper suggests the sources outside Europe that funded the purchase of the artworks depicted and, likely, Scarlett Davis's picture itself. Yet the wealth of the Hart Davis and Harford families, like so much of the wealth that supported the Institution, was generated through empire. The Harford fortune derived from importing tobacco and exporting metalwares, including goods bartered for human beings in the slave trade.[9] John Scandrett Harford repudiated the origins of his inheritance and advocated for abolition of this trade.[10] Not so with Harford's father-in-law. Hart Davis profited directly from the labor of enslaved people through commerce with sugar-producing islands in the West Indies. After the abolition of the British slave trade, he used his position in Parliament to advocate against measures designed to compel more humane treatment of the enslaved.[11] The British Institution was a nationalist project enabled by the profits of empire. This image, created as an affirmation of native art, is also an unintentional monument to the human costs of British artistic achievement.

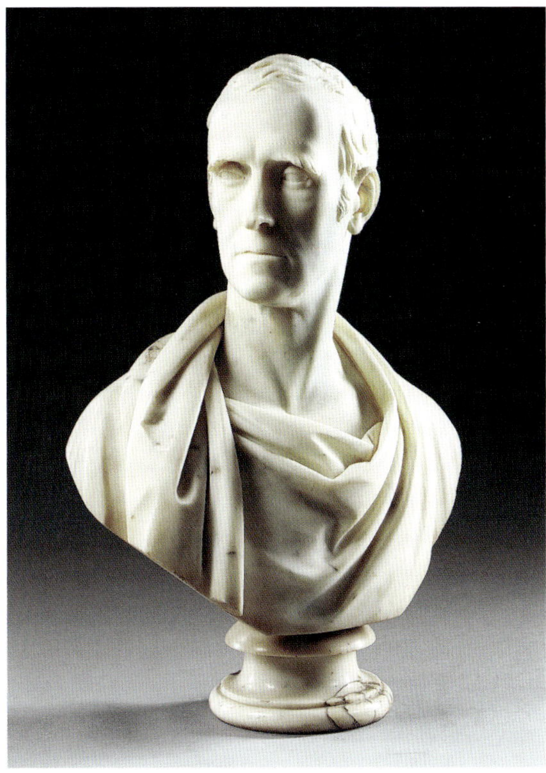

Fig. 50. Edward Hodges Baily, *Richard Hart Davis*, 1823, marble, h. 27.2 in. (69 cm). Private collection, France

Notes

1. For an extended consideration of this painting, see Catherine Roach, *Pictures-within-Pictures in Nineteenth-Century Britain* (London: Routledge, 2016), 24–63. This essay also draws on research for a forthcoming book on the British Institution, supported by a National Endowment for the Humanities Fellowship at the Huntington Library. Any views, findings, conclusions, or recommendations expressed in this essay do not necessarily reflect those of the National Endowment for the Humanities.
2. Catherine Roach, "Images as Evidence? Morse and the Genre of Gallery Painting," in *Samuel F. B. Morse's Gallery of the Louvre and the Art of Invention*, ed. Peter John Brownlee (New Haven and London: Yale Univ. Press, 2014), 46–59.
3. Catherine Roach, "Rehanging Reynolds at the British Institution: Methods for Reconstructing Ephemeral Displays," *British Art Studies* 4 (Autumn 2016), https://doi.org/10.17658/issn.2058-5462/issue-04/croach/p21.
4. On the Institution, see Peter Fullerton, "Patronage and Pedagogy: The British Institution in the Early Nineteenth Century," *Art History* 5 (March 1982): 59–72; Ann Pullan, "Public Goods or Private Interests? The British Institution in the Early Nineteenth Century," in *Art in Bourgeois Society, 1790–1850*, eds. Andrew Hemingway and William Vaughan (Cambridge: Cambridge Univ. Press, 1998), 27–44; Nicholas Tromans, "Museum or Market? The British Institution," in *Governing Cultures: Art Institutions in Victorian London*, ed. Paul Barlow and Colin Trodd (Aldershot, UK: Ashgate, 2000), 44–55.
5. Francis Haskell, *The Ephemeral Museum: Old Master Paintings and the Rise of the Art Exhibition* (New Haven and London: Yale Univ. Press, 2000), 46–81.
6. Now at the National Gallery, London, and Tate Britain, respectively. See Roach, *Pictures-within-Pictures*, 29–34.
7. Peter Funnell, "John Scarlett Davis: *The Interior of the British Institution Gallery*," Painting in Focus pamphlet (New Haven: Yale Center for British Art, 1984); Roach, *Pictures-within-Pictures*, 48–51.
8. Roach, *Pictures-within-Pictures*, 38–47.
9. Peter Wakelin, "Harford Family (per. c. 1700–1866), Merchants, Brass Manufacturers, and Bankers," *Oxford Dictionary of National Biography*, http://www.oxforddnb.com/view/10.1093/ref:odnb/9780198614128.001.0001/odnb-9780198614128-e-47495; Stephanie Barczewski, *Country Houses and the British Empire, 1700–1930* (Manchester: Manchester Univ. Press, 2014), 27.
10. Alice Harford, *Annals of the Harford Family* (London: Westminster Press, 1909), 75.
11. Lawrence Taylor and R.G. Thorne, "Davis, Richard Hart (1766–1842)," http://www.historyofparliamentonline.org/volume/1790-1820/member/davis-richard-hart-1766-1842.

William Henry Fox Talbot (British, 1800–1877)
The Pencil of Nature, 1844–46, part 4
(London: Longman, Brown, Green & Longmans, 1845)

Printed book: 9⅝ x 12 in. (24.3 x 30.5 cm), closed

YALE CENTER FOR BRITISH ART, PAUL MELLON FUND. TR144.T35 1844+ OVERSIZE

Chitra Ramalingam

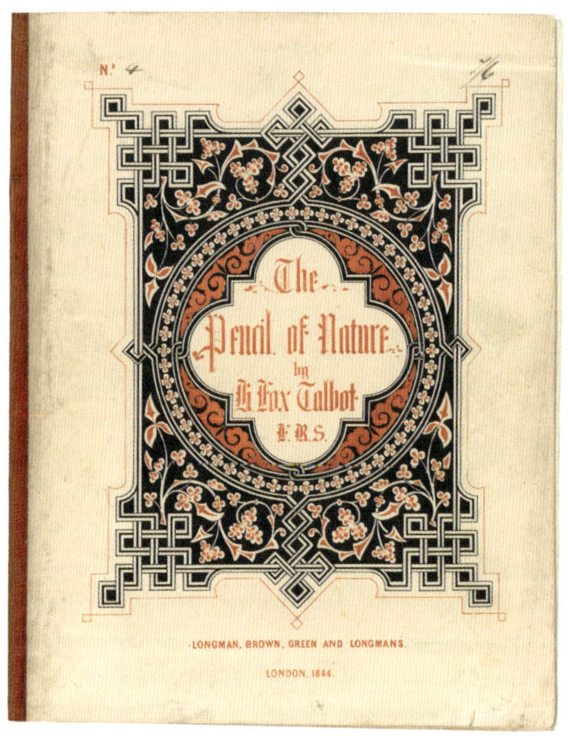

William Henry Fox Talbot's *The Pencil of Nature* has been recognized for decades as one of the most significant works in the history of photography.[1] Published in six installments (called fascicles) between 1844 and 1846, it was an early experiment in the illustration of printed text with photographs. Its twenty-four salted paper prints were commissioned by Talbot to be printed from his own negatives at a photographic printing workshop in Reading, financed by him and run by his former assistant, Nicolaas Henneman. They include what are now some of the most iconic images of early photography, such as *The Open Door*, *The Haystack*, and *Articles of Glass* (fig. 51). Each hand-mounted print was accompanied by a brief text by Talbot himself, describing or responding to it, printed in letterpress. As a novel composite of printed text and photographic image, *The Pencil of Nature* proposed, with extraordinary eloquence and ingenuity, a wide array of archival, scientific, and aesthetic possibilities for what the new medium could already do, and what it might eventually become in the future.

Decades of scholarship on *Pencil* have left us with a rich understanding of the iconographic and representational possibilities for photography, sometimes in contradiction with each other, that Talbot envisioned and articulated in its pages. It has been studied as a self-portrait of a man of possessions, and an evocation of the aesthetics of landed gentility;[2] an extended allegory of labor, skill, and image-making;[3] an exploration of the role of chance in photography;[4] and an expression of Romantic literary historicism.[5] Other influential interpretations abound. It has been variously an emblem of positivism, empiricism, Romanticism, idealism, postmodernism, gentlemanly amateurism, industrial capitalism, genius and authorship, mechanization and automatism, painterly composition, and brute indexicality. It is such a shape-shifting work—the text so rich and suggestive and

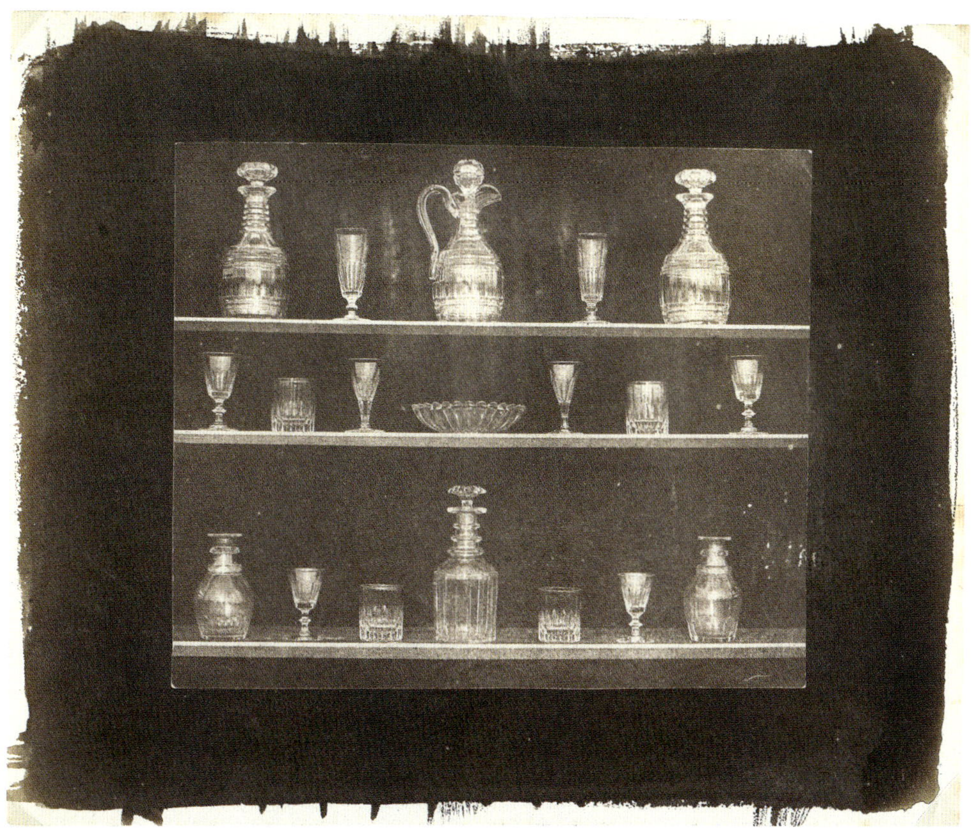

Fig. 51. William Henry Fox Talbot, *Articles of Glass*, ca. 1843, salted paper print from paper negative, 5 x 6 in. (12.7 x 15.2 cm). Yale Center for British Art, Paul Mellon Fund

yet so maddeningly contradictory, the photographic works so miscellaneous and so inventive in their creation of new photographic genres—that it has lent itself flexibly to the service of many intellectual agendas. What more could there possibly be to say about it?

One limitation of this insightful and varied body of scholarship is that it continues to consider *Pencil* as a singular, stable work of art.[6] Yet anyone who has ever had the privilege of encountering an original copy—such as the partial one (fascicles 1–4) at the Yale Center for British Art—has been forced to confront the disorienting realization that *The Pencil of Nature* does not look at all the way art historians have continually told us it does (see fig. 52). Many of its prints have faded nearly beyond recognition. The rest show varying levels of discoloration and image degradation, from ever-present edge fading to foxing to enigmatic chemical splotches. As Talbot scholar Larry Schaaf has put it bluntly, the surviving photographs published in *Pencil*, when considered collectively across all the known copies in dozens of institutions and private collections, "form a miserable lot."[7] There is no "perfect" original copy of *Pencil* anywhere, and no copy is identical to any other.[8] When taught in history of art courses and cited and analyzed in scholarly publications, more often than not it is represented by reproducing a print made from one of the negatives used for *Pencil*, which then survives as a loose print, never having been bound into a copy in the first place (such as figure 51). The stunning facsimile edition of *Pencil* published in 1989, alongside the increased availability of digital images of the finest existing loose prints from *Pencil* negatives in major museums, has raised the visibility and accessibility

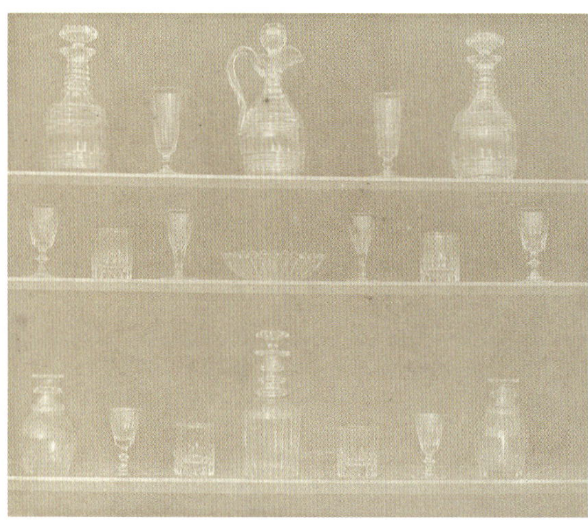

Fig. 52. William Henry Fox Talbot, "Articles of Glass," plate 4 from *The Pencil of Nature*, part 1 (London: Longman, Brown, Green & Longmans, 1844), salted paper print from paper negative, 5¾ x 5¼ in. (15 x 13 cm). Yale Center for British Art, Paul Mellon Fund

of an "idealized" version of *The Pencil of Nature* that seems never to have existed.[9] This has unintentionally engendered an entire generation of art-historical teaching and scholarship on *Pencil* that has been severed from the material peculiarities and perplexing obscurities of its original copies—even as this same work has continually inscribed *Pencil* as a masterwork of the early medium and a touchstone for photographic aesthetics that remains relevant today.

What if instead of ignoring the physical attributes of its prints, their varied appearance, and their differing degradation over time, we treated those as essential aspects of the work that influenced the way they were viewed and interpreted historically? How might our perception of *The Pencil of Nature* change if we stop considering it to be a singular set of twenty-four stable images and instead begin to explore the materiality, multiplicity, and temporality of the many instantiations of the work scattered around the world? We might then restore to *Pencil* its material history and character as an affective object for its historical viewers (who were, incidentally, few and elite). We now understand that a photograph's material form—paper, chemical composition, surface effects, retouching, mounts, adhesives, inscriptions, folds, and other marks of making and use—is absolutely central to its function as a socially salient object, and is as much a part of its meaning as the iconographic content of the image it presents.[10]

We might also reframe *Pencil* as a spatiotemporal cultural object, making sense of what has happened to its many instantiations during its passage through culture. It was produced and issued over time, such that every individual fascicle is composed of prints made over the course of months, from negatives themselves made across a period of years, and then was finally purchased or acquired by owners at different times and assembled with other fascicles into a complete "set," which then had different trajectories. Bringing *Pencil* into dialogue with recent approaches from the historical and literary analysis of serial publications, we might then read the complex temporality of *Pencil*'s making and its consumption against other part books and serially issued compilations of prints, situating it against the instability of serial literature in both time and space.[11] Coming to terms with the unruly variation and differential degradation of the individual prints in *Pencil*, we might begin to absorb that decay was an essential element of the science and the aesthetics of the early photographic surface, ever present in the photographic press, and certainly a constant theme of writings about *Pencil* in its own historical moment. An account of *Pencil* and its production that takes this seriously might then recast a seemingly stable object as the product of an ongoing and dynamic engagement with its materials and environment.[12]

We might end up approaching *Pencil* as an evolving experimental record, in material form, of photography's development.[13] Talbot's goal in his publication was for Henneman, who ran the Reading workshop, to produce multiple, identical copies of each print for each copy of the publication, but they encountered many problems as production was scaled up. As he proceeded,

Henneman gradually simplified Talbot's recommended process for making prints, which he found too time-consuming and resource-intensive to keep up with Talbot's production demands: the paper Talbot originally selected for the prints ceased manufacture and had to be replaced; the chemicals purchased from suppliers in London were unstandardized; variable levels of industrial pollutants in the water supply in Reading changed from day to day; the unreliable English summer sun made uniform exposures impossible; fuel shortages limited the temperature of the water used for washing prints; and the binder's adhesives used to mount the prints to each page interacted with the prints in unexpected ways.[14] Each and every mounted print was truly an uncontrolled chemical experiment. It is unsurprising, then, that the material and aesthetic qualities of the prints varied so much across the many prints and copies of *Pencil*, with variations in hue and tone and surface effects, as well as the problem of fading, which plagued the majority of prints within a few years of production. Each print thus remains as a record, physical and chemical, of how Talbot and Henneman adapted, adjusted, and reformulated their procedures in their attempt to demonstrate that photographs could be uniformly mass-produced.

Conceiving of *Pencil* as a fragmented, multiply authored, temporally extended, spatially distributed photographic work would grapple with essential aspects of its material form and its history. We would then understand it as a composite of extremely variable material objects with different histories of production, circulation, and use—and as an evolving record of chemical experimentation. A newly grounded material history of *The Pencil of Nature* might point toward a more integrated history of photography in which works like *Pencil* are not only part of the history of art but also of the history of science.[15]

Notes

1. William Henry Fox Talbot, *The Pencil of Nature* (London: Longman, Brown, Green, & Longmans, 1844–46).
2. Carol Armstrong, *Scenes in a Library: Reading the Photograph in the Book, 1843–1875* (Cambridge, MA: MIT Press, 1998).
3. Steve Edwards, *The Making of English Photography: Allegories* (University Park, PA: Pennsylvania State Univ. Press, 2006), chap. 1.
4. Robin Kelsey, *Photography and the Art of Chance* (Cambridge, MA: Harvard Univ. Press, 2015), chap. 1.
5. Vered Maimon, "Displaced 'Origins': William Henry Fox Talbot's *The Pencil of Nature*," *History of Photography* 32, no. 4 (December 2008): 314–25.
6. The most important exception is the extensive scholarly essay accompanying the facsimile edition: Larry J. Schaaf, "Introductory Remarks," in *The Pencil of Nature: Anniversary Facsimile* (New York: Hans P. Kraus Jr., 1989). Carol Armstrong has insightfully discussed Talbot's own stated concerns about the variability of prints in Armstrong, *Scenes in a Library*, 123–24, 160–65.
7. Schaaf, "Introductory Remarks," 38.
8. All known copies of *Pencil* are documented in Larry J. Schaaf, "Third Census of H. Fox Talbot's *The Pencil of Nature*," *History of Photography* 36, no. 1 (February 2012): 99–120, https://doi.org/10.1080/03087298.2012.632561.
9. Larry J. Schaaf, *The Pencil of Nature: Anniversary Facsimile* (New York: Hans P. Kraus Jr., 1989).
10. See Elizabeth Edwards and Janice Hart, eds., *Photographs Objects Histories: On the Materiality of Images* (London: Routledge, 2004); Geoffrey Batchen, *Forget Me Not: Photography & Remembrance* (New York: Princeton Architectural Press, 2006).
11. See James Mussell, *Science, Time and Space in the Late Nineteenth-Century Periodical Press: Movable Types* (Aldershot, UK: Ashgate, 2007).
12. See Tim Ingold, "Materials against Materiality," *Archaeological Dialogues* 14, no. 1 (June 2007): 1–16; Tim Ingold, *Lines: A Brief History* (London: Routledge, 2007); Matthew C. Hunter, "Joshua Reynolds's 'Nice Chymistry': Action and Accident in the 1770s," *Art Bulletin* 97, no. 1 (January 2015): 58–76.
13. Such an analysis would integrate *Pencil* into the broader disciplinary project of rethinking Talbot's archive of documents and photographs as material traces of the knowledge economy of nineteenth-century science and scholarship. See Mirjam Brusius, Katrina Dean, and Chitra Ramalingam, eds., *William Henry Fox Talbot: Beyond Photography*, Studies in British Art, vol. 23 (New Haven: Yale Center for British Art, 2013).
14. These details of the making of *Pencil* are richly documented in Schaaf, "Introductory Remarks."
15. Pamela Smith, "The History of Science as a Cultural History of the Material World," in *Cultural Histories of the Material World*, ed. Peter N. Miller (Ann Arbor: Univ. of Michigan Press; New York: Bard Graduate Center, 2013), 210–25.

George Chinnery (British, 1774–1852)
A View of Victoria, Hong Kong Island, 1846

Graphite and pen and brown ink on two joined pieces of medium, smooth, beige wove paper, 10 x 15 in. (25.4 x 38.1 cm). YALE CENTER FOR BRITISH ART, PAUL MELLON COLLECTION, B1975.4.1064

Alicia Weisberg-Roberts

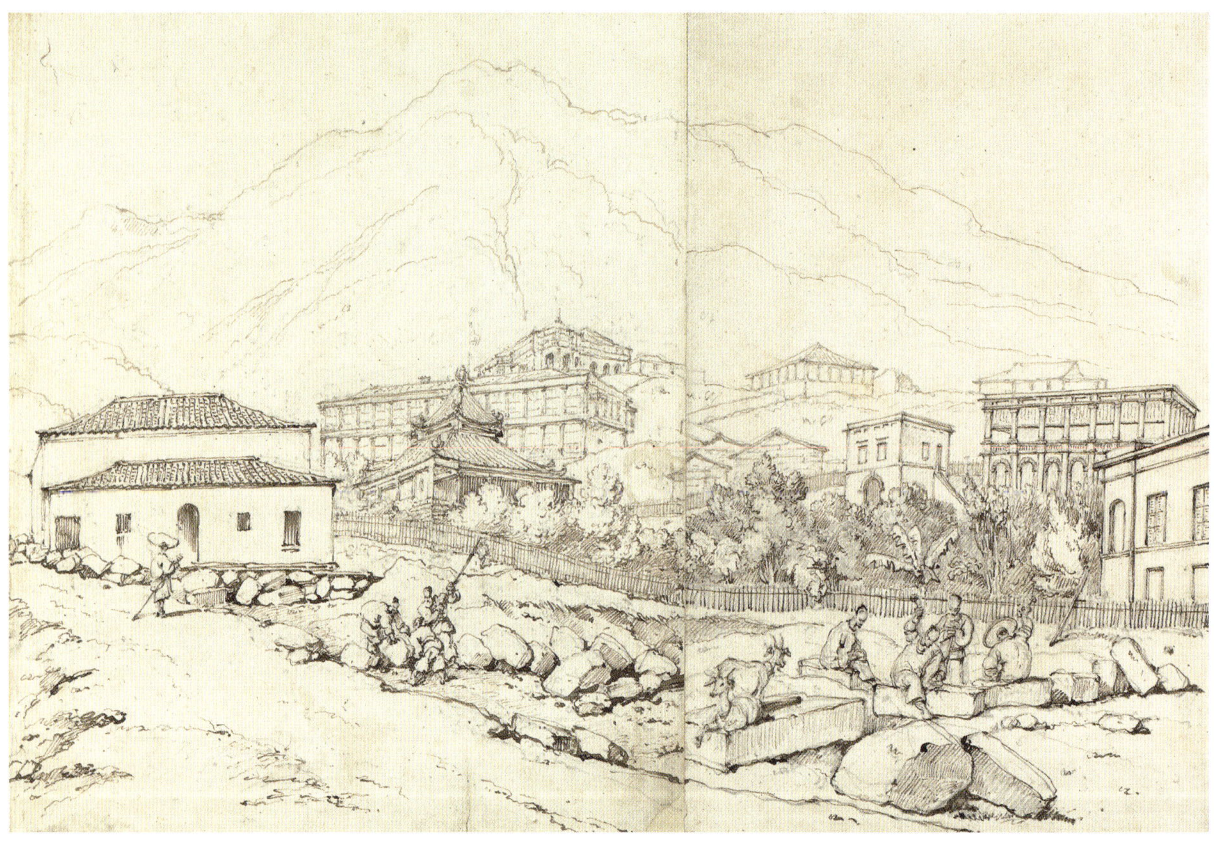

George Chinnery was born in London and trained at the Royal Academy Schools before moving in 1796 to Dublin, where he pursued a career as a portraitist. In 1802, with the permission of the East India Company, he sailed for Madras (Chennai) moving on over the next two decades to Kolkata and Dhaka.[1] During his time in India, Chinnery produced portraits of British residents, but landscapes and images of Indian life became a significant part of his oeuvre. These lively sketches form a counterpoint to his conventional portrait practice; if Chinnery's paintings pleased by ensconcing his sitters within a familiar frame, his drawings and oil sketches drew his viewers' imaginations outward, blending elements of the exotic and the picturesque with close observation. His work would continue along these dual paths when he sailed to the South China Coast in 1825.

Chinnery would spend the rest of his life in the Portuguese colony of Macau, occasionally traveling to Canton (Guangzhou), and making a single visit to Hong Kong in 1846. The *View of Victoria, Hong Kong Island* at the Yale Center for British Art was executed during Chinnery's sojourn in the British colony, which had been established less than five years previously. According to his own account, Chinnery produced fifteen views of Hong Kong, "large and full of detail," which he was able to show to a patron in 1848.[2] It is not clear whether these fifteen drawings correspond with any of his currently known depictions of Hong Kong. However, the attested drawings reveal the multiple preparatory stages typical of the academic training that underpinned Chinnery's commercial practice. He sketched daily, worked up compositions from various studies, kept a stock of fair copies on hand, and produced collections of sketches, as well as finished compositions in a variety of media, to order. The medium—graphite, traced and modeled with ink—and the degree of finish of *View of Victoria, Hong Kong Island* are consistent with a number of other landscape studies that Chinnery produced of Macau and Hong Kong.

The Center's view shows one of the first plots to be developed in the city of Victoria, as the British settlement on Hong Kong Island was then known, just to the south and uphill from the central waterfront (fig. 53). Chinnery populates the foreground of his drawing with casual groups of Chinese masons, dressing stones in the recently laid-out Wyndham Street, conveying a sense of the young settlement as a site under construction. Above the laborers, as the slope rises toward Victoria Peak, we can see some of the founding institutions of Hong Kong in their earliest forms. The first Magistracy building (1841–46) occupies the topographical high ground; this was Hong Kong's first law court and prison, as well as the headquarters of its first police force from 1844. The Magistracy was built under the auspices of William Caine, the first Chief Magistrate. In the middle

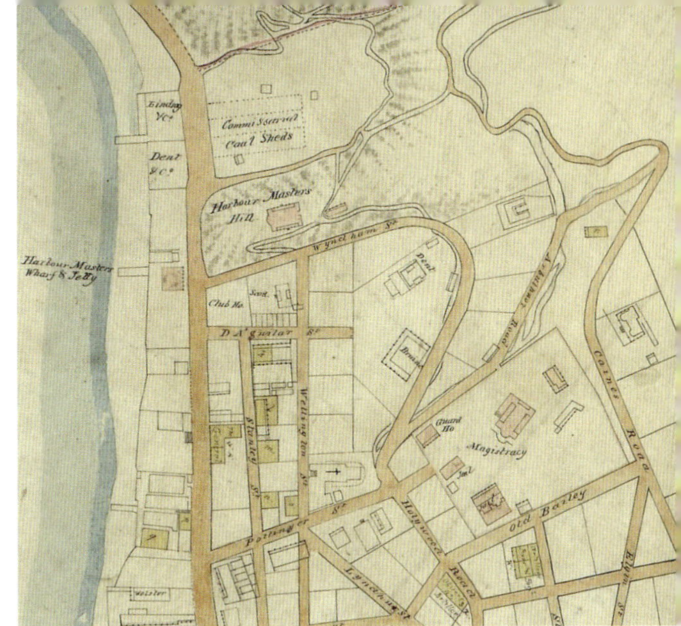

Fig. 53. "Plan of Victoria, Hong Kong, Copied from the Surveyor General's Dept" (detail), 1845. The National Archives, Kew

ground, slightly to the left of center, we can identify the building with the pagoda-like roof as the first permanent Western dwelling in Hong Kong, completed for Caine in September 1841.[3] Caine sold the house and its surrounding lot to Dent & Co., one of the most prominent merchant firms involved in the Canton trade.[4] In Macau, Lancelot and Wilkinson Dent had been among Chinnery's patrons, and Wilkinson Dent seems to have acted as Chinnery's host in Hong Kong.[5]

In addition to a prominent godown (i.e., warehouse) situated on the shoreline, just to the northeast of the site shown in Chinnery's drawing, Dent & Co. also had the use of the flat-roofed building with an arched colonnade surmounted by a loggia, seen on the right. This building was utilized as a company dwelling house but owned and occupied by Charles Joseph Braine, a merchant with the firm and an amateur botanist who corresponded regularly with the Royal Horticultural Society.[6] From about 1845 the garden surrounding both this house and Dent's Bungalow, shown in Chinnery's drawing bounded by a low fence running along Wyndham Street, came to be called Green Bank and was cultivated under Braine's supervision.[7]

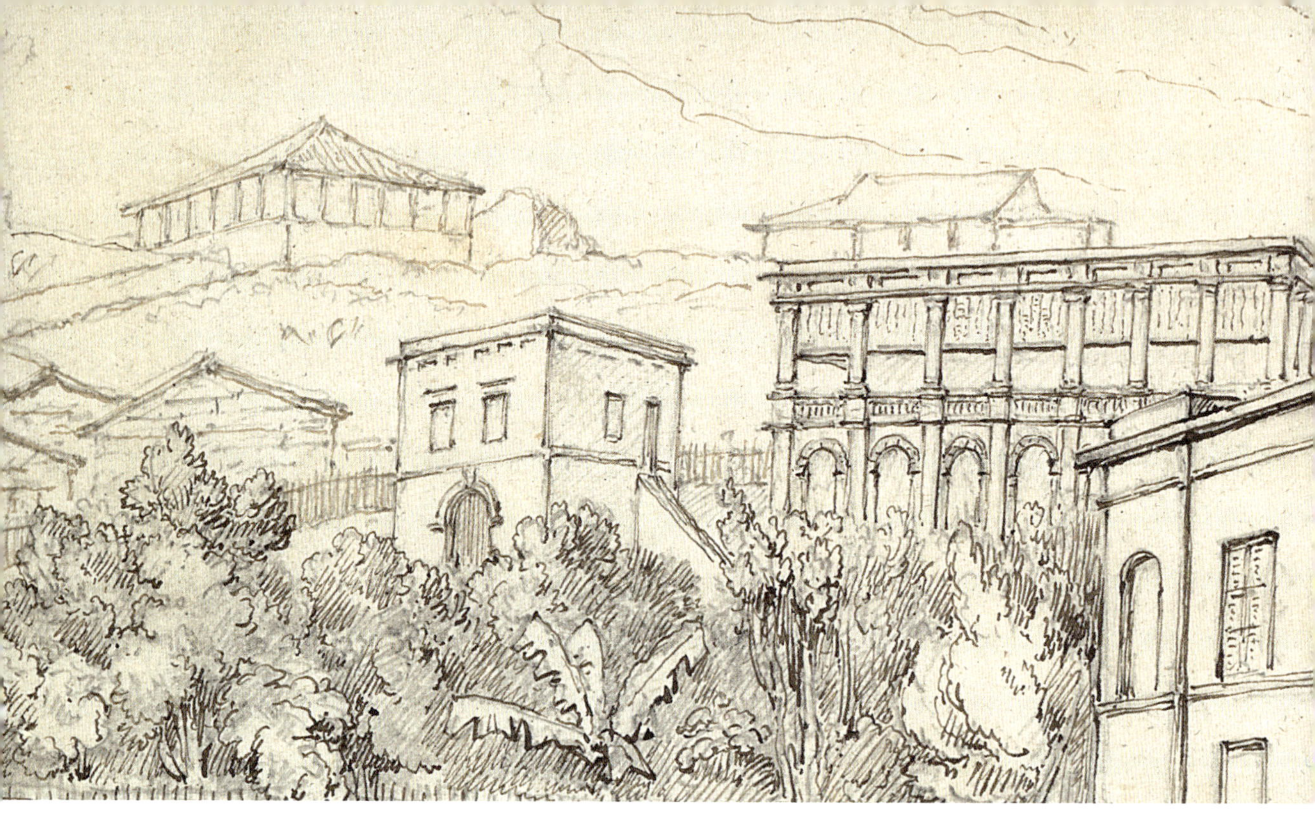

Detail of *A View of Victoria*

In 1845 another private trader, Thomas Chay Beale, joined Dent & Co., at which point the botanist and plant hunter Robert Fortune assisted in transplanting the movable plants from his father Thomas Beale's famous and botanically significant garden at Macau to Green Bank.[8] This was facilitated by an advantageous relationship between Fortune and Dent & Co.; he used Beale's garden at Shanghai and Braine's garden in Hong Kong as depositories for the plants he prospected in China and shipped back to England.[9]

Fortune included an extensive description of Green Bank in 1848 in his *Journey to the Tea Countries of China* (1852).[10] He emphasized the speed with which Green Bank had developed into one of Victoria's "greatest ornaments."[11] In Fortune's text this is in no small part due to the novel, beautiful, and economically useful plant species that had been cultivated in the garden and whose propagation he advocated in Hong Kong and abroad: the Chinese banyan (*Ficus nitida* Thumb.); the Chinese gooseberry (*Averrhoa carambola* L.), now better known as the kiwi fruit; numerous orchids; and painted bamboo (*Bambusa vulgaris* Schrad. ex J. C. Wendl. 'Vittata'), "of a fine yellow colour and beautifully striped with green, as if done by hand of a first-rate artist," which Fortune himself had sent to the Royal Horticultural Society in 1844.[12] Fortune's description corresponds with both Chinnery's drawing and a detailed plan from 1850 (fig. 54). Braine commissioned this bird's-eye view of Green Bank to support an offer to sell the property to the Hong Kong government as a combined botanical garden and governor's house.[13] The sale was rejected, and in 1861 Green Bank and Dent's Bungalow were demolished to make way for housing for the emergent Hong Kong Chinese gentry.[14] In the same year funding was finally approved to create a public botanical garden on a site closer to the colony's principal government buildings, rather than nestled among commercial plots.[15] Of Green Bank, the only echo that remains is the name of the modern road that traces the path that once led through the garden, Lan Kwai Fong (蘭桂坊), "Orchid Osmanthus Lane."

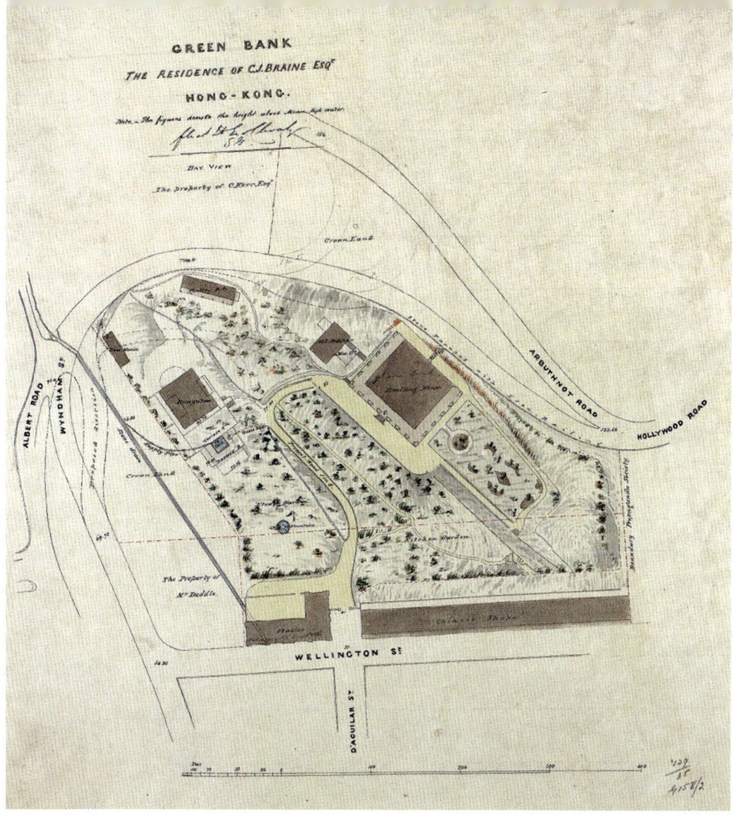

Fig. 54. "A plan of 'Green Bank', a residence at Hong Kong, the property of C J Braine," 1850. The National Archives, Kew

Notes

I would like to thank Dr. Peter Cunich, Dr. Alexandra Cook, Jonathan Wattis, and Nicole Fung for their assistance with this first entry.

1. Patrick Conner, *George Chinnery, 1774–1852: Artist of India and the China Coast* (Woodbridge, UK: Antique Collectors' Club, 1993), 51.

2. George Chinnery to Captain D'Aguilar, February 20, 1848; Hong Kong and Shanghai Banking Corporation.

3. William D. Bernard, *Narrative of the Voyages and Services of the Nemesis, from 1840 to 1843; and of the Combined Naval and Military Operations in China: Comprising a Complete Account of the Colony of Hong Kong, and Remarks on the Character and Habits of the Chinese*, 2 vols. (London: Colburn, 1844), 2:83.

4. Christopher A. Cowell, *Form Follows Fever: Malaria and the Making of Hong Kong, 1841–1848* (M. Phil. thesis, Univ. of Hong Kong, 2009), 111.

5. Conner, *George Chinnery*, 251–52, 302, nn. 11, 12; Edward H. Cree, *Naval Surgeon: The Voyages of Dr. Edward H. Cree, Royal Navy, as Related in His Private Journals, 1837–1856* (New York: Dutton, 1981), 178.

6. Emil V. Bretschneider, *History of European Botanical Discoveries in China*, 2 vols. (London: Sampson Low, Marston, 1898), 1:383–84; George Bentham, *Flora Hongkongensis: A Description of the Flowering Plants and Ferns of the Island of Hong Kong* (London: Lovell Reeve, 1861), 459–60; Berthold Seemann, *The Botany of the Voyage of H.M.S. Herald, under the Command of Captain Henry Kellett, R.N., C.B., during the Years 1845–51* (London: Lovell Reeve, 1852), 427.

7. James Legge, "The Colony of Hong Kong—From a lecture by the Rev. James Legge, D.D., L.L.D., on reminiscences of a long residence in the East, delivered in the City Hall, November 5, 1872," *China Review* 3 (1874): 164.

8. R. F. (Robert Fortune), "Notes of a traveller—No. III," *Gardener's Chronicle* (March 31, 1849): 196–97.

9. Alistair Watt, *Robert Fortune: A Plant Hunter in the Orient* (Richmond: Kew Publishing, 2017), 73, 103–5.

10. Robert Fortune, *A Journey to the Tea Countries of China; Including Sung-Lo and the Bohea Hills; with a Short Notice of the East India Company's Tea Plantations in the Himalaya Mountains* (London: John Murray, 1852), 5–9.

11. Fortune, *A Journey to the Tea Countries of China*, 6.

12. Fortune, *A Journey to the Tea Countries of China*, 8; Watt, *Robert Fortune*, 105.

13. D. A. Griffiths and S. P. Lau, "The Hong Kong Botanical Gardens, a Historical Overview," *Journal of the Royal Asiatic Society Hong Kong Branch*, 26 (1986): 57–58.

14. Carl T. Smith and Christopher Munn, *Chinese Christians: Elites, Middlemen, and the Church in Hong Kong* (Hong Kong: Hong Kong Univ. Press, 2005), 121–22.

15. Griffiths and Lau, "The Hong Kong Botanical Gardens," 60.

Unknown artist, Agra School (Indian, nineteenth century)
Taj Mahal (a pair of miniatures), 1857

Watercolor on ivory, each 2 x 2½ x ¼ in. (5.1 x 6.4 x .6 cm). Inscribed on the verso in black ink: "W.R.M. | Tag Magal | 1857," and "W.R.M. | Tag Magal | Agra | 1857."

YALE CENTER FOR BRITISH ART, GIFT OF ROSEMARIE HAAG BLETTER AND MARTIN FILLER IN MEMORY OF PAUL MELLON, YALE COLLEGE, CLASS OF 1929, B2015.23.2, B2015.23.3

Fred Bohrer

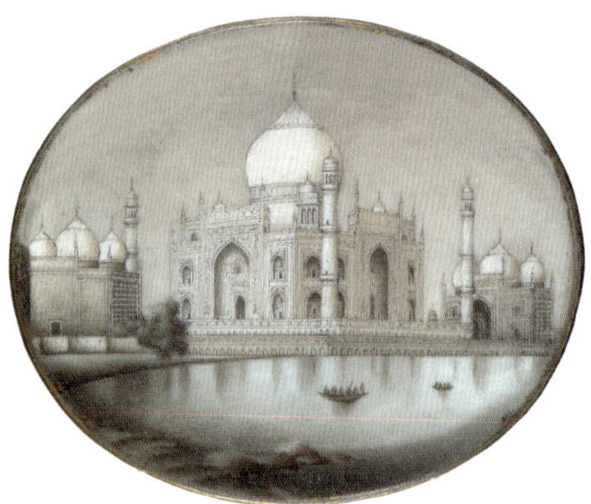

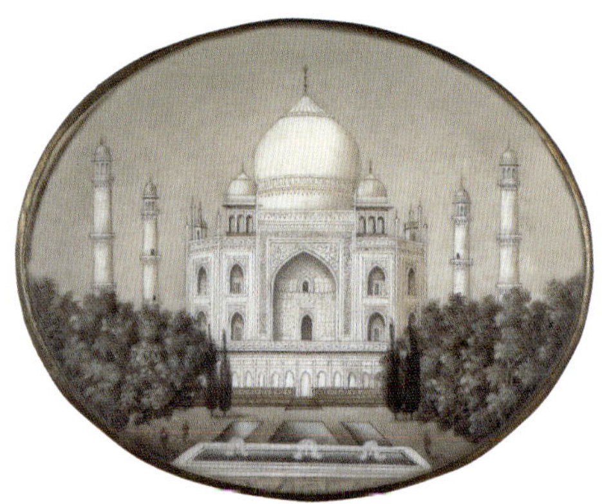

Real and unreal are two in one: New Haven
Before and after one arrives or, say,
Bergamo on a postcard, Rome after dark,
Sweden described, Salzburg with shaded eyes
Or Paris in conversation at a café

—Wallace Stevens,
"An Ordinary Evening in New Haven"[1]

By definition, a souvenir is a memory object: a tangible artifact suffused with association, acquired within a larger process of experience and desire. In his poem, Wallace Stevens sought to summon, perhaps even to celebrate, the virtual infinitude of ways places exist in our consciousness, through seeing, telling, and remembering, whether imagined or actual. On an ordinary day in an art museum in New Haven, one shares space with many such objects that focus the multifarious memories of place. While we may never be able to completely recount the chain of experiences and associations around them, when looked at closely they can tell much about the very processes, makers, viewers, and contexts involved.

A pair of mid-nineteenth-century palm-sized miniatures in watercolor painted on ivory portray two views of the Taj Mahal, the remarkable

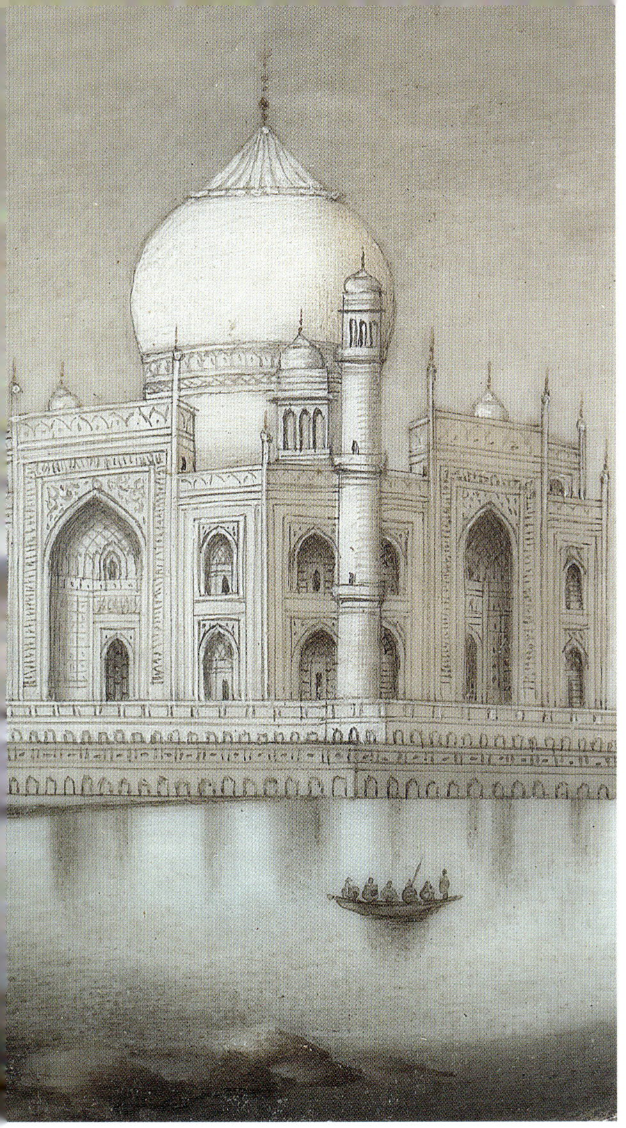

Detail of *Taj Mahal* at left on facing page

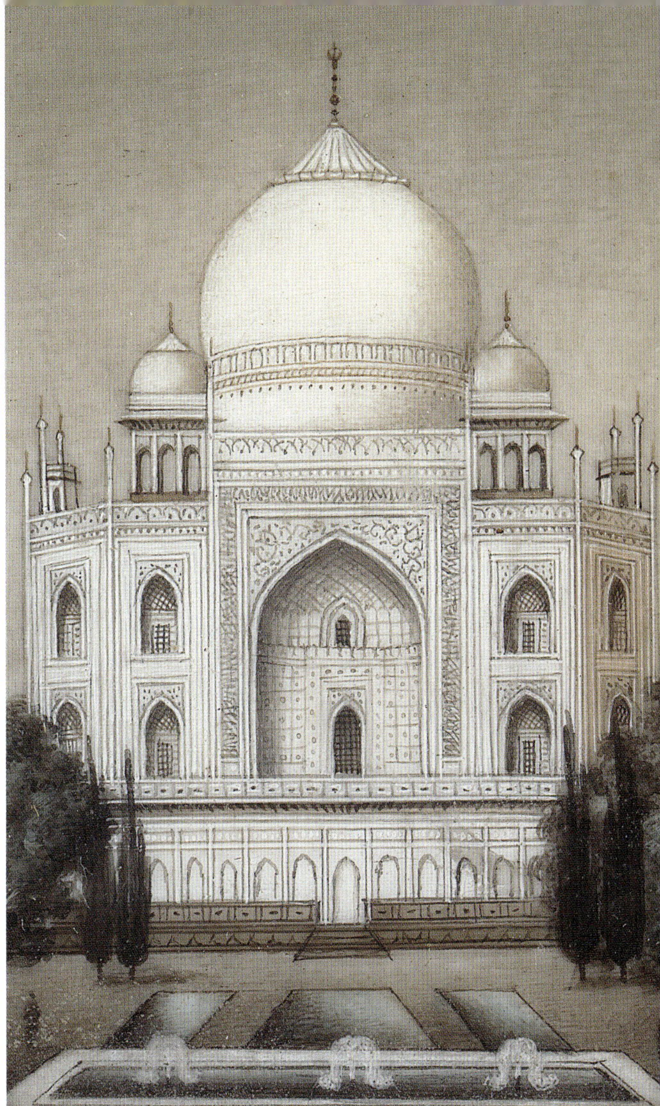

Detail of *Taj Mahal* at right on facing page

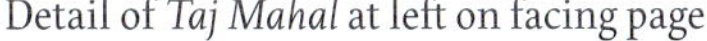

funerary monument to the Mughal Empress Mahal Mumtaz built by her husband Emperor Shah Jahan. Then as now, the Taj Mahal was among the most prominent monuments of the Indian subcontinent and almost surely its greatest attraction for Western tourists. These particular paintings are attributed to an unknown artist of the Agra School, which specialized in producing images of local scenes for tourists, notably the Taj Mahal.

Like much of what is attributed to the Agra School, the scenes are minutely detailed through a filigree of exquisitely thin lines representing complex shapes and elaborate decorations. Color is largely muted and shadowing almost nonexistent. The viewpoints correspond to the two principal approaches to the Taj. One depicts the approach from across the Yamuna River, the main building viewed on a picturesque diagonal that highlights the interplay of forms. Two small craft on the river are lined with people. However, the Taj's small pier built for river landings is not shown, and the slight rocky promontory at bottom hardly looks like an adequate dock. Both the boats and the promontory are Western-inspired devices to suggest scale and depth to the image, documentary details.

The other miniature depicts the Taj Mahal frontally, placing it at the image's very center. It is flanked by towers, in what remains the principal approach to the building complex. Again, the artist takes pains to present the building in depth, but now rather than omitting a feature one is invented. When entering by land, the viewer sees the Taj Mahal in the distance. In front of it is the vast garden complex that was as striking as the building itself. The miniature clearly registers the gardens in the thick foliage that stands at the edges of the building platform, filling up the lower edges of the visual field. But at the center of the lower part of the image, objects are depicted with no precise correspondence to the Taj Mahal's (extraordinarily well-documented) setting. One sees a rectangular fountain with three founts, in an orientation parallel to the Taj. Behind it are what appear to be three parallel pools of still water, running perpendicular to the building.

By contrast, the view recorded in a photographic album in the Center's collection, compiled in the later 1880s by Sir John Edge, a leading magistrate in British India, clearly shows this portion of the monument. The center allée of the garden was actually a single water channel lined with founts that ran perpendicular to the building, all the way from the front gate to the building itself (fig. 55). It was broken only by a small parallel wall, over the water channel, halfway toward the building.

Much like the subtraction in the other image, the addition in this miniature of features in the Taj Mahal garden makes it easier to portray a Western depth perspective. Moreover, the resulting image is more easily traversable for the viewer, both side to side and top to bottom. Ultimately, though, the artist's decision about how to portray the monument has much to do with his anticipation of what will sell to his audience, so that appealing to Western viewing habits is perhaps even more important than presenting an "authentic" view. On this, the artist's judgment was perfect. Each of these miniatures has an almost identical inscription, surely made by their Western purchaser. They read "W.R.M. / Tag Magal / 1857." (The inscription on the frontal view also states "Agra.") Just as the monument itself is visually adjusted, so its very name is also subtly remade to fit Western conventions.

In all, these two modest artifacts exemplify what is "lost in translation" or, perhaps more exactly, refigured in cultural circulation as a Hindu artist makes an image of an Islamic monument for a Christian tourist. Most strikingly, the particular moment of these objects highlights the complex tensions between cultures on which such circulation depended. In May of 1857, the very year the objects were purchased, Indian citizens rose up in their first concerted war of independence against the British: the Sepoy Rebellion. It was led by Indian soldiers (called "sepoys") at strategic sites throughout Northern and Central India. The rebellion lasted over a year and led ultimately to India being even more controlled by the British, now under direct rule of Queen Victoria: the period of the Raj. Thus the modest and seemingly innocent miniatures, depicting a monument bathed in timeless romance, are part of a time of conflict between groups and even organized violence. They are two sides of the same coin.

The photographer Samuel Bourne, the most commercially successful British photographer in India, commented on the process of finding the Indian image that satisfied the Western viewer. About visiting the Taj Mahal, he complained, with the condescension that is a hallmark of the British attitude of the period, that "the authorities of Agra permit the road to the incomparable Taj to remain almost as incomparable for dreariness and squalor." Upon arriving at the site, the touristic viewer is accosted by "some grey-beard" wanting to earn a few rupees by giving a tour. While the visitor "probably listens impatiently . . . he would do well to follow the old guide's advice" and climb the steps above the gateway to the Taj. There, lifted literally above the crowd, "No subsequent view of the Taj he may obtain will eclipse that. Many a traveler from many an European country, besides the

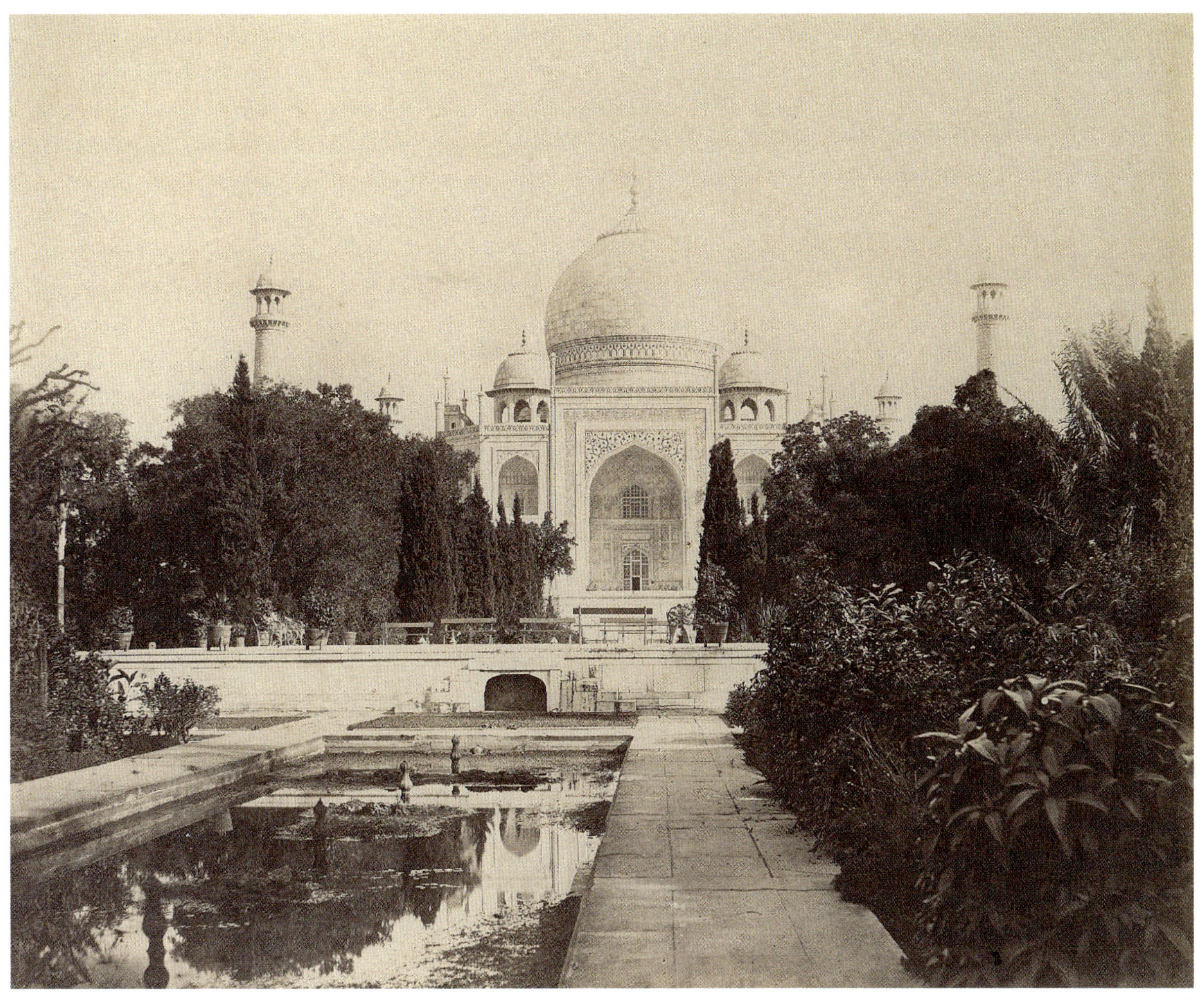

Fig. 55. Sir John Edge, "Taj Mahal," from Photograph Album of Sir John Edge in Allahabad, India, ca. 1888–94. Yale Center for British Art, Paul Mellon Fund

Prince of Wales, has confessed that then and there for the first time has the India of his imagination and romance been realized to the full."[2]

It is just that approach, floating high above the masses, with no clear space for the viewer to stand, which is proffered by these two tiny watercolor images, for this same audience. Here, though, in a way free of the ostensible objectivity of photography (as Bourne could only dream), the imagined India extends even beyond what is available to see at its actual site. In Bourne's own term, these miniatures thus work to "realize" the Taj Mahal, and perhaps even the India, of British desire at least as much as they portray the actual monument.

Notes

1. Wallace Stevens, "An Ordinary Evening in New Haven," *The Auroras of Autumn* (New York: Alfred A. Knopf, 1950).

2. *Bourne and Shepherd's Royal Photographic Album of Scenes and Personages Connected with the Progress of H.R.H. The Prince of Wales through Bengal, the Northwest Provinces, The Punjab and Nepal* (Calcutta: Bourne & Shepherd, 1876), 29–30.

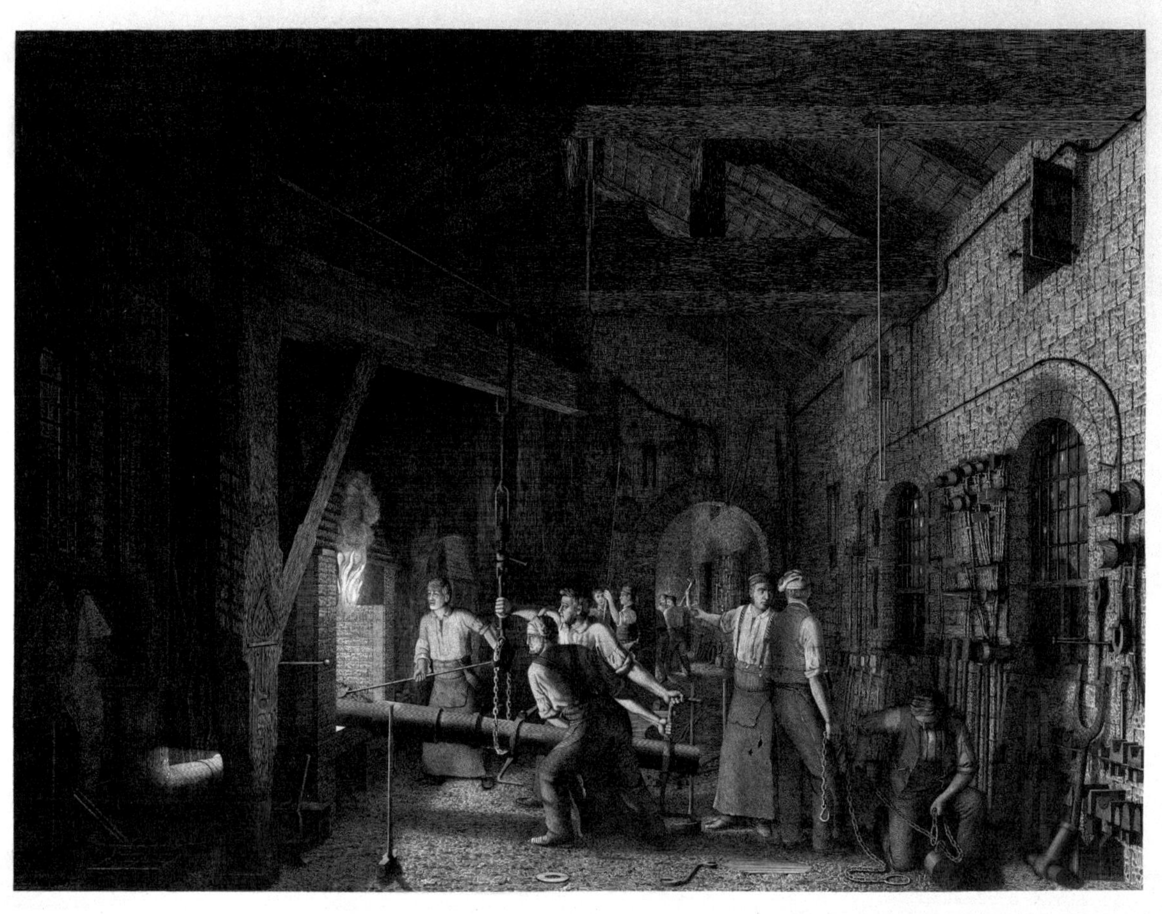

THE FORGE.

Painted and Engraved by James Sharples

Published by James Sharples 44 Audley Lane Blackburn

James Sharples (British, 1825–1893)
The Forge, 1859, late impression, undated, ca. 1870

Engraving on paper, 17.9 x 20.9 in. (45.5 x 53 cm). YALE CENTER FOR BRITISH ART. PRESENTED BY TIM BARRINGER IN HONOR OF AMY MEYERS, 2019

Tim Barringer

Among representations of labor in Victorian England, *The Forge* stands as an exception, for here an image of manual work is crafted by one of its protagonists. James Sharples was an industrial blacksmith at the firm of Yates & Co. in Blackburn, Lancashire, who became a self-taught artist.[1] His autodidactic journey merited inclusion in Samuel Smiles's bestselling publication *Self-Help* (1860).[2] Contemporaries were quick to note the parallels with Quentin Massys, the early Netherlandish painter, whose life began as a "rough Cyclopean smith," who, through an epiphanic transformation, became an artist noted, like Sharples, for precision in the representation of detail.[3] Although Sharples's surviving oeuvre is small, and he never made a living as a professional artist, remaining a blacksmith through most of his working life, his contribution to Victorian visual culture is significant.

Sharples's engraving was based on a large oil painting he himself had made. According to news reports at the time, this work "took the evenings of nearly three years in its execution; and when finished, he got a steel plate and spent the evenings of about five more years engraving it."[4] The steel plate that Sharples "got," now in the Victoria and Albert Museum, is thicker and heavier than commercially produced plates and was probably adapted from spare industrial materials. Contemporary accounts make clear that Sharples also fashioned his own engraving tools.

Skilled labor stands, both compositionally and conceptually, at the center of the image. The smiths in the foreground are heating the main shaft for a stationary steam engine, which will be hammered into the precise form required while white-hot from the forge, a process underway in a different shop in the background. Most of the figures are dressed in the smith's leather apron, a potent emblem of their occupational identity. That of the gesturing figure in the right foreground, the most experienced, carries the signs of long and hard usage: jagged holes in its smooth surface are carefully delineated.

Far from presenting a detached view of working men in general, or a documentary snapshot of a labor process, *The Forge* is deeply engaged, locked into the particularities of period and locality. It lays out for inspection groups of male manual workers as disciplined, skilled, and responsible individuals. Twelve men—four groups of three—are engaged in different aspects of forging iron. In the foreground, three are in physical action by the furnace; nearest to the flames is the smith (Sharples's own trade) "busily engaged in building the fire round the end of the shaft."[5] Two men lean heavily onto the suspended metal shaft, pushing it farther into the fire; their muscles are taut with the strain, their faces rapt in concentration. This, as Sharples himself wrote, "demands the exercise of great skill, tact and judgment, and often during its progress the suspense and anxiety is so great when a certain object *must* be attained whilst the iron is welding hot, that the success of the undertaking seems almost a question of life and death to the men who are responsible."[6] The "great skill, tact and judgement" described here are, of course, Sharples's own: *The Forge* is a self-portrait, a passionate essay in self-fashioning.

Yet it also signals a proud insistence on the self-regulation of skilled labor, for there is no overseer or forge owner to be seen. Sharples joined the Amalgamated Society of Engineers on its foundation in 1851, providing the union with a complex emblem.[7] The main initial aim of the Society was the protection of independent craft autonomy—preventing unskilled, low-paid laborers from taking work away from skilled craftsmen—but a cartel of employers broke the union's resolve in a bitter lockout in 1851. *The Forge* may thus be seen as a fantasy of self-governance in the workplace, rooted in precise observation but formulated in the service of an ideal and unrepresentative of the harsh facts of industrial organization in the 1850s.

When Sharples circulated it to major figures in the art world in 1859, with a printed text explaining its origins, the print garnered some celebrity. Though Sharples stood entirely outside the conventional art world, and never exhibited his work publicly, this direct method of approach proved successful. John Ruskin, the leading critic of the day, ordered ten copies.[8] A letter to Sharples reported that Ruskin "spoke highly of it and of the perseverance displayed in it,"[9] and he showed the print to his drawing class at the Working Men's College, who "had three cheers for you."[10] In 1872 Ruskin recalled *The Forge* as "a plate which, in manipulation, no professional engraver would be ashamed of." Sharples, Ruskin continued, "engraved his blast-furnace and the casting of a beam of a steam engine. This, to him, was the power of God,—it was his life. No greater earnestness was ever given by man to promulgate a Gospel."[11] Yet this prompted from the aging critic a dark reflection, displaying his increasingly skeptical view of industrialization: "The blast-furnace *is not* the power of God; and the life of the strong spirit was as much consumed in the flames of it, as ever driven slave's [*sic*] by the burden and heat of the day."[12]

Sharples took a very different view. While a brief attempt to become a professional artist failed, and he remained a working blacksmith until ill health forced him into retirement, he became committed to the Co-Operative Movement, among whose principles were that "true workmen should be fellow workers" and that "justice, not selfishness, must govern exchanges." Sharples's last, unfinished work, a drawing for a *Co-Operative Emblem*, offers a radical solution to the labor question, a utopian vision of working-class solidarity in which artistic enterprise and manual work could take place in a world structured by cooperation rather than competition.[13] It envisions an ideal that remains elusive today.

Notes

Provenance: The artist by descent to Marian Sharples, the artist's granddaughter; acquired from her by Tim Barringer, 1993.

1. For a full account, see Tim Barringer, *Men at Work: Art and Labour in Victorian Britain* (New Haven and London: Yale Univ. Press, 2005), 133–85.
2. Samuel Smiles, *Self-Help; with Illustrations of Character and Conduct*, second edition (London: John Murray, 1860), 132–38.
3. See Larry Silver, *The Paintings of Quinten Massys* (Oxford: Phaidon, 1984), 1; 25, n. 1.
4. "Announcement: The Forge," Sharples Family Papers, People's History Museum, Manchester. The oil painting *The Forge* is on permanent loan to Blackburn Museum and Art Gallery.
5. Joseph Baron, *James Sharples: Blacksmith and Artist* (London: Jarrold, 1893), 24.
6. James Sharples, "A letter written to a correspondent in 1881," quoted in Baron, *James Sharples*, 22.
7. Blackburn Museum and Art Gallery.
8. Baron, *James Sharples*, 8; George Allen states that Ruskin "ordered 10 copies of the engraving when first he saw it, and has them now to give away &c." George Allen to John Baddeley, April 1860, transcribed in John Baddeley to James Sharples, May 1, 1860. Sharples Family Papers, People's History Museum, Manchester.
9. Allen to Baddeley, Sharples Family Papers.
10. Baron, *James Sharples*, 8.
11. John Ruskin, *Ariadne Florentina*, in *The Works of John Ruskin*, eds. E. T. Cook and Alexander Wedderburn, Library Edition, 39 vols. (London: George Allen, 1908), 22:456.
12. Ruskin, *Ariadne Florentina*, 22:456.
13. James Sharples, *Co-Operative Emblem*, pencil on thick paper, Blackburn Museum and Art Gallery.

Right: detail of *The Forge*

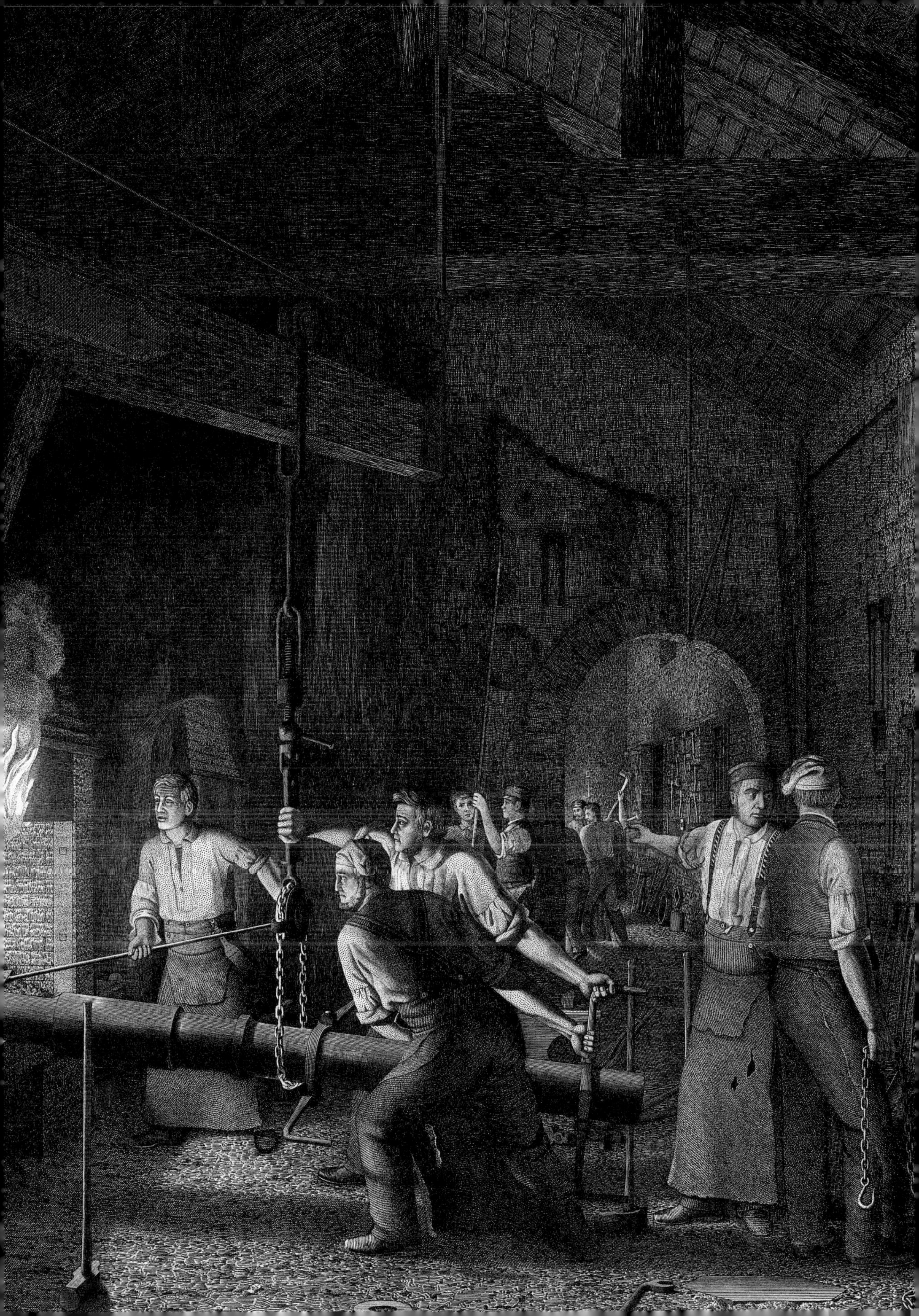

Edward Lear (British, 1812–1888)
Kinchinjunga, or Kangchenjunga, from Darjeeling, 1879

Oil on canvas, 47⅛ x 72 in. (119.7 x 182.9 cm). Signed and dated in monogram, lower left: "EL 1879." YALE CENTER FOR BRITISH ART, GIFT OF DONALD C. GALLUP, YALE BA 1934, PHD 1939, B1997.7.3

Robert McCracken Peck

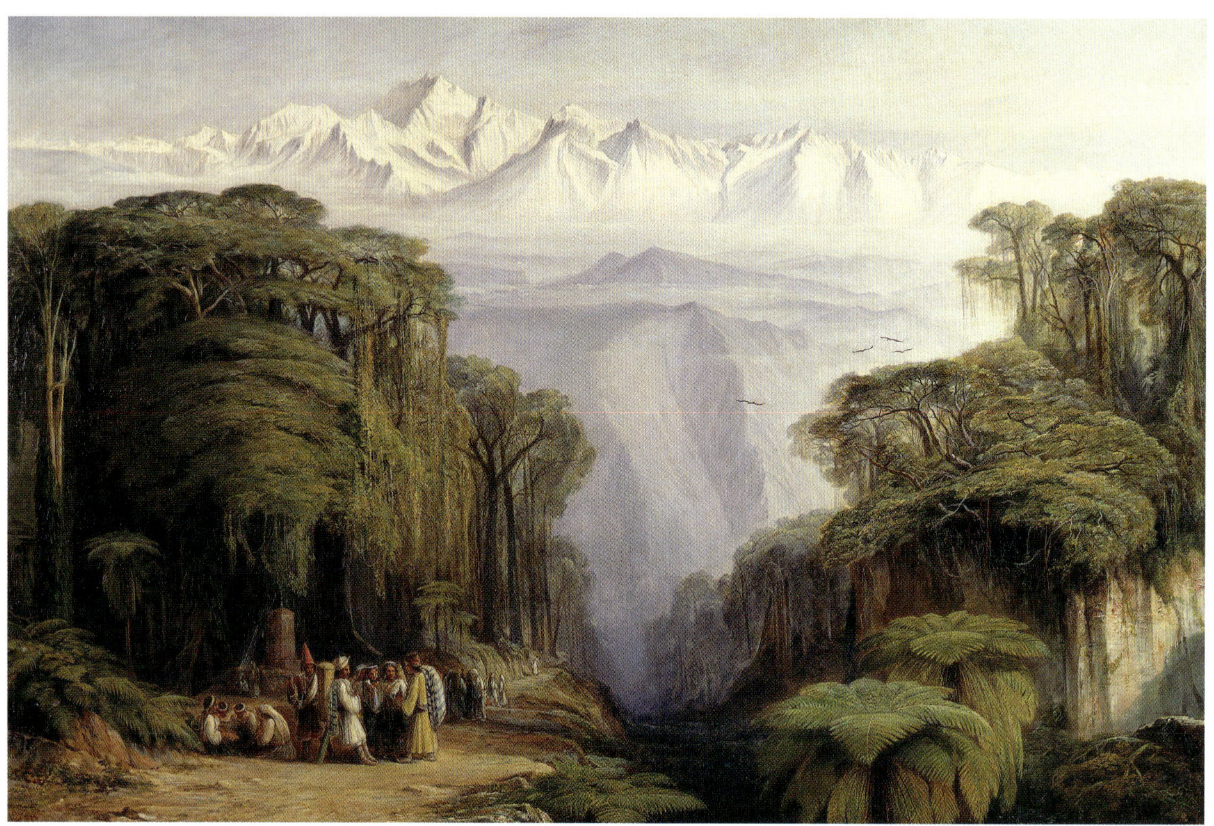

Although the name of Edward Lear is more often associated with whimsical limericks and charming, childlike cartoons than with serious paintings, the much-beloved nonsense poet was a prodigious painter whose artistic reputation has experienced a resurgence of popularity in the last half century. The thousands of delicate watercolors of landscapes in Italy, throughout the Mediterranean, in parts of the Middle East, and in India that Lear created during his long and productive career helped him record his extensive travels and pay for his modest lifestyle, but they fell out of favor after his death and remained so during much of the twentieth century. His large oil paintings,

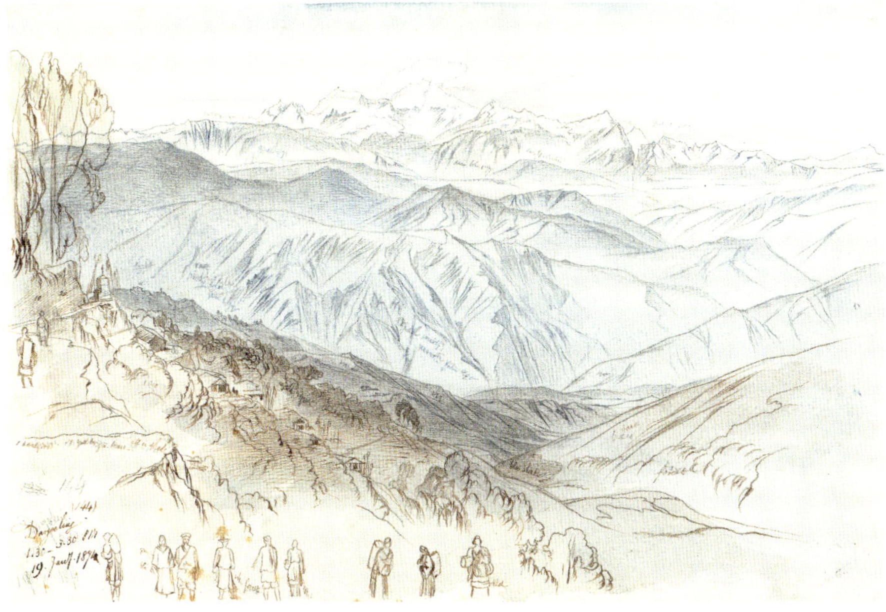

Fig. 56. Edward Lear, *[Kangchenjunga from] Darjeeling, 1.30–3.30 PM, 19 January 1874. (144)*, sepia and blue ink wash over graphite on white paper. Harvard University, Cambridge, Houghton Library

far fewer in number than his watercolors, also suffered a long period of neglect.[1]

It was during this low point in Lear's popularity that the components of what are today the two largest institutional collections of his works were assembled. William Osgood Field and Philip Hoffer collected thousands of Lear's paintings, all of which eventually ended up at Harvard's Houghton Library (figs. 56 and 57). Donald Gallup, a literary historian at Yale, formed a somewhat smaller but equally important Lear collection that he gave to the Yale Center for British Art in 1997. Among the three hundred fifty items in his collection was a massive oil of Kangchenjunga, created from field paintings made in northern India during Lear's last and most distant painting trip (1873–74). Purchased by Osgood Field from the second Earl of Northbrook, it was acquired by Gallup in 1951.[2] It was arguably one of the artist's proudest achievements.

The youngest son in a large, middle-class family, Edward Lear was raised from the age of four by his oldest sister, Ann (1791–1861).[3] It was she who was responsible not only for his education but also his early instruction in painting.[4] Lear began his artistic career by coloring decorative prints, screens, and fans "for bread and cheese" and painting "morbid disease drawings for hospitals and certain doctors of physic."[5] As he reached his late teens and early twenties, he found enough other patrons to allow him to shift his time and attention from these unpalatable subjects to more appealing ones, including the birds, mammals, and other wildlife that was then being collected and displayed at the newly founded Zoological Society of London. Beginning in the late 1820s, he learned how to make lithographs of his wildlife watercolors for use in his own publications and those of others. Lear's self-published monograph on parrots, *Illustrations of the Family of Psittacidae, or Parrots* (1830–32), while unsuccessful for him financially, won wide praise in scientific circles and led to other illustrations of birds commissioned by many of the leading naturalists of the day.[6]

After a decade of working on the details of feathers, fur, and vertebrate anatomy, Lear grew weary of the exacting demands of scientific illustration and began to experiment with landscape drawing and painting. Although he could have

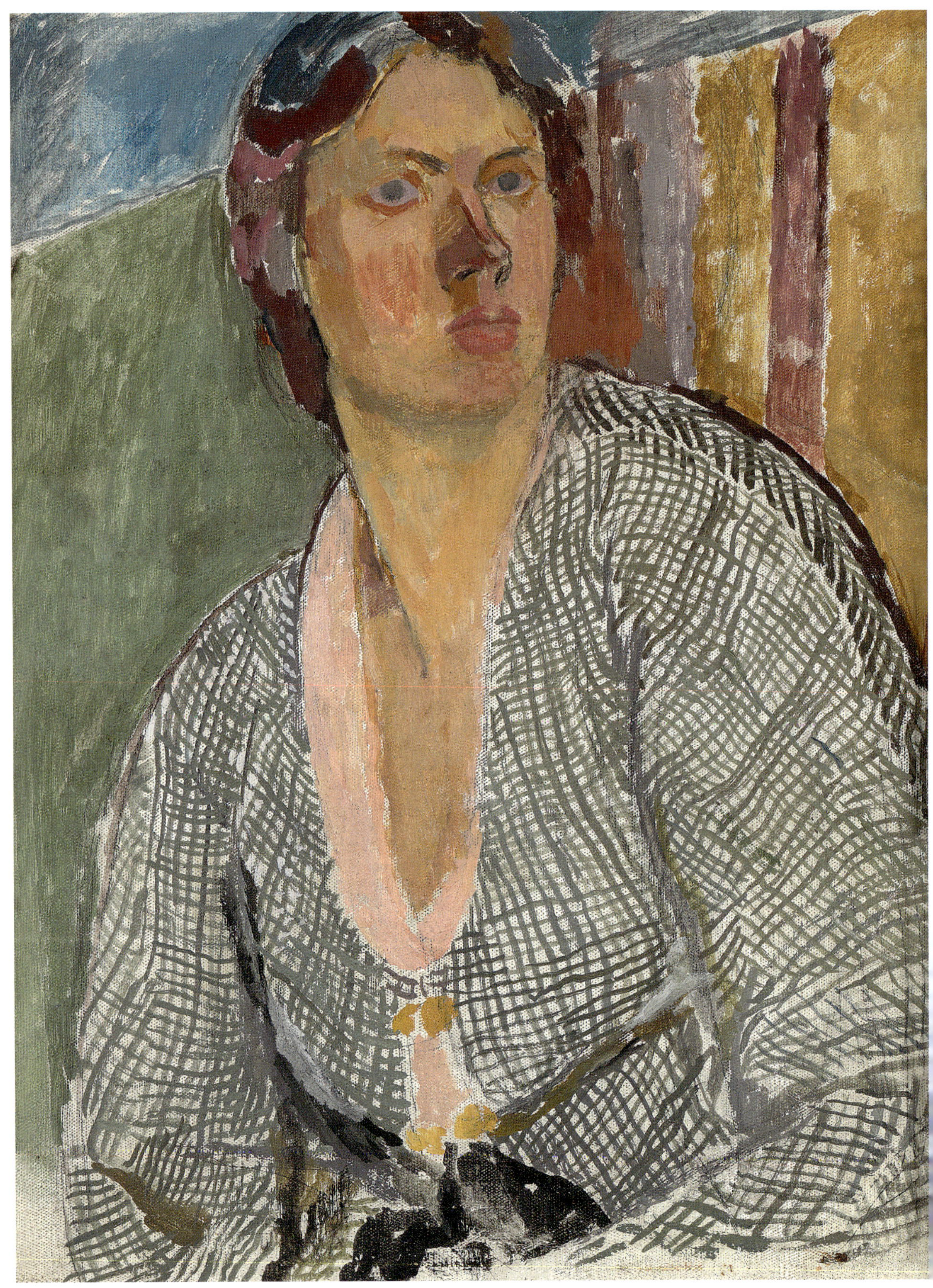

Vanessa Bell (British, 1879–1961)
Self-Portrait, ca. 1915

Oil on canvas laid on panel, 25⅛ x 18$^{1}/_{16}$ in. (63.8 x 45.9 cm)

YALE CENTER FOR BRITISH ART, PAUL MELLON FUND, B1982.16.2

Gillian Beer

Self-portraits combine opposed experiences: the passivity of the sitter and the action of the painter. Our body and face are among the things we know from inside, at the level of muscle and flesh and bone, but we see them from outside far less often than do others. We do not see them continuously in the flow of movement and regard that, nonchalantly, others possess as they look in our direction. David Garnett, in his later memoir, evokes an aspect of Vanessa Bell's appearance that no painter could render:

> What was she like? A tall woman who stooped and swayed while she walked and moved erratically, swiftly for a few steps and then slower.[1]

Ordinarily painters, like other people, walk about more or less oblivious to the body and face they carry with them, though occasionally caught short by reflections. In the predominant relationship of the self-portrait, there is thus something even forensic: but, though the painter must examine, the subject submit, here painter and subject are the same person, at least until the painting is achieved. That is to say, the artist works, as well as looks; the hatching on a garment may preoccupy equally with the interpretation of a face. Self-examination is inevitable, self-protection may follow, but the busyness of making will assuage any too-intense contemplation of self. The self-portrait can be a declaration of intent, even a manifesto. Convenience or poverty may be part of the mix. But it is inevitably a process of making, like any other artwork. It captures physical bulk at a period in time and resolves it into brushstrokes and lines that mimic bodily presence, and last beyond it. At that point of completion, the art object sheds the mass of the personal that went into its making.

Vanessa Bell's self-portrait of 1915 avoids the viewer in a way that runs counter to many artists' concentration on the outward gaze and on reciprocity. Her bulk is the first thing that strikes the eye, occupying much of the canvas and set against green and yellowish stripes with a suggestion of outdoor foliage and sky behind her. Her stance is forceful, declarative, her body and head moving in different directions, the neck powerful and elongated by the deep neckline of her dress. Her gaze penetrates beyond the viewer but suggests also an inward stare fixed on nothing. Her hands are excluded from the canvas. We are not shown the activity of the painter. This is not a painting offering acquaintance or spectacle. The viewer is invited, so far as any invitation is issued, to observe and muse. The subject remains reserved. She has her own concerns. Duncan Grant's portrait of Bell, *Vanessa Bell Painting*, also from 1915, again includes a kind of concealment (fig. 59).[2] It shows her from the rear, engrossed in painting a still life of kitchen implements, a humdrum assemblage here shaped into a vortex and propped over a bookcase in a manner that is both casual and controlling. Her painting hand is barely indicated, but a strong sweep of paint controlled by that hand interrupts the

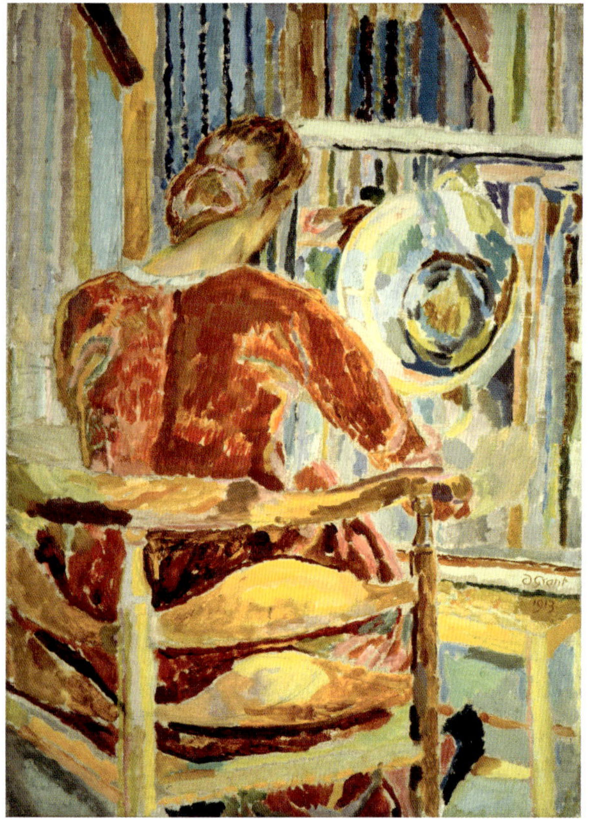

Fig. 59. Duncan Grant, *Vanessa Bell Painting*, 1915, oil on canvas, 30 x 22 in. (76.2 x 55.9 cm). National Galleries Scotland, Edinburgh

straight lines that run vertically behind. Another of Grant's images, *Vanessa Bell at Her Easel*, 1914, now in the collection of the Yale Center for British Art, again shows her from behind, in painterly concentration as she works on a portrait, not that time of herself but of another woman whose face we glimpse over the artist's shoulder in a contrapuntal motion (fig. 60).[3]

When Bell painted her own image in 1915, she was thirty-six and the mother of two boys. In 1912 she had seen the paintings by Matisse in Roger Fry's *Second Post-Impressionist Exhibition* and was deeply affected by them. Matisse's emphasis on simplification of form became crucial in her artistic practice. Her own weathered and used body is given massive presence by simplification in the self-portrait. She relished too the tints of flesh and the pressures of fabric. Her hatched black and white dress, perhaps gingham, is softened by a pink collar that frames the brown of her chest. It billows through the foreground of the picture. The shape of the figure in this painting seems to prefigure Virginia Woolf's character Isa, the principal focus for experience in Woolf's last (and much later) novel, *Between the Acts*, who thinks of herself as shaped like a bolster.[4]

At this earlier time, about 1915, Woolf, Bell's younger sister, was suffering a period of madness, and the power of her career as a writer was yet to emerge fully. When it did, one signal triumph was *To the Lighthouse*.[5] That novel poises two women side by side as opposites: Mrs. Ramsay is mother of the tribe, holding family and friends together; Lily Briscoe is the single woman, an artist, devoted to her own work whatever may become of it. The book throngs with people, each preoccupied with needs and joys and resentments. Structurally, its family sections are set on either side of the 1914–18 war: in the course of the work, the picture of Mrs. Ramsay and James, who are at the start sitting for Lily, becomes transformed. By the book's end, which is also the picture's completion, individual representation gives way to abstraction. Line, color, triangle, and mass compose the work. The step is empty. Mrs. Ramsay is dead; James is no longer a little boy; Lily's life is outwardly unchanged. The generations have shifted. The old world has been shed but continues to haunt the present.

This marvelously rich novel is ordered on a simple underlying contrast of possibilities presented for women: motherhood or art. Woolf may have needed that contrast for her own psychic reasons. Bell, who was both artist and mother, is thus absented from the economy of Woolf's novel. There is no room for such a figure there. Bell's biographer Frances Spalding indicates that Bell thought of herself predominantly as an artist and was content for her children to be looked after by others, sometimes for weeks at a time.[6] But the children were also essential to her life, and to her life as an artist. The encompassing figure who dominates the canvas in the self-portrait includes

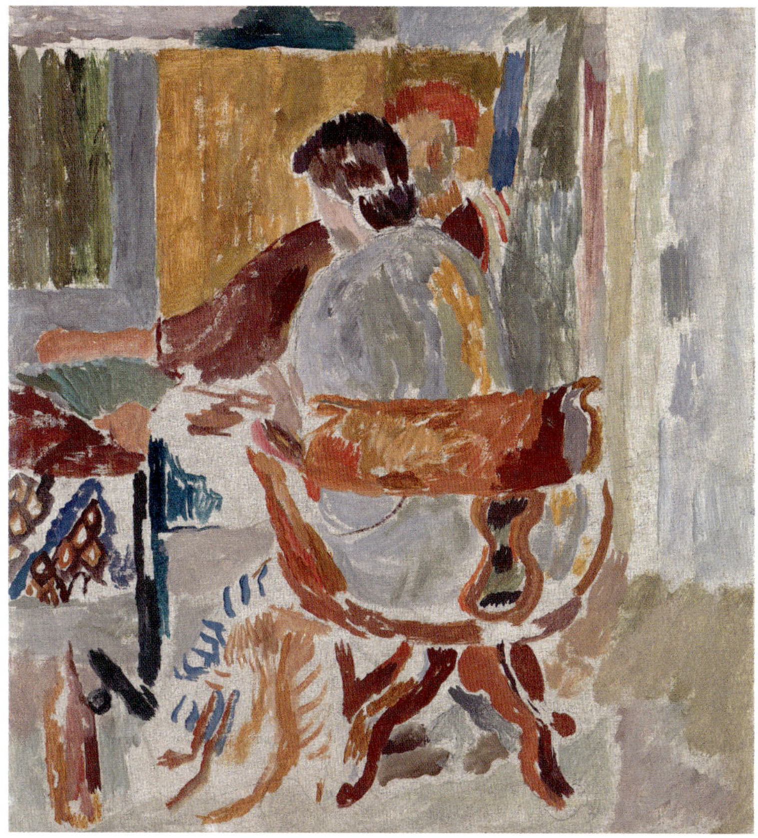

Fig. 60. Duncan Grant, *Vanessa Bell at Her Easel*, 1914, oil on canvas, 19 x 18 in. (48.3 x 45.7 cm). Yale Center for British Art, Gift of the Libra Foundation, from the family of Nicholas and Susan Pritzker

that largesse, and that severity. The three images, the self-portrait and the reversed images by Duncan Grant, together indicate the power of her presence, at once occluded and absorbed. The self-portrait also lets that presence go, content to mute the person in the contours of the canvas.

Notes

1. Quoted in Frances Spalding, *Vanessa Bell: Portrait of the Bloomsbury Artist* (London: George Weidenfeld and Nicholson, 1983), 136. See her note on p. 371: "David Garnett, unpublished essay on Vanessa Bell originally intended for inclusion in his *Great Friends* (1978)."
2. Duncan Grant, *Vanessa Bell Painting*, National Galleries Scotland, GMA900, Estate of Duncan Grant, DACS 2018. The commentary from the National Gallery of Scotland states that this "still life of kitchen utensils . . . was executed in a boat-house on the Sussex coast in the early summer of 1915 (the date inscribed on the canvas, 1913, is incorrect)."
3. Yale Center for British Art, Gift of the Libra Foundation, from the family of Nicholas and Susan Pritzker, B2012.30.25; see Samuel Shaw, "'Characters in Search of an Author': Single-Figure Studies in the Pritzker Collection," in *Modernism and Memory: Rhoda Pritzker and the Art of Collecting*, eds. Ian Collins and Eleanor Hughes (New Haven and London: Yale Univ. Press, 2016), 93–125, fig. 69. The YCBA also holds another portrait of Bell by Grant, this time gazing into the air: *At Eleanor: Vanessa Bell*, 1915, oil on canvas, 29 15/16 x 21 7/8 in. (76 x 55.6 cm), B1982.16.1.
4. Virginia Woolf, *Between the Acts* (London: Hogarth Press, 1941).
5. Virginia Woolf, *To the Lighthouse* (London: Hogarth Press, 1927).
6. Spalding, *Vanessa Bell*, 140.

Constance Stuart Larrabee (British, 1914–2000)
Ezenzeleni School for the Blind, 1948, printed 1983

Gelatin silver print on moderately thick, semigloss photographic paper, 20 x 16 in. (50.8 x 40.6 cm). Inscribed in black ink on the verso, lower left: "Constance Stuart Larrabee | 94 Ezenzeleni School for Blind 1948"; signed in black ink on the verso, lower left: "Constance Stuart Larrabee | 1948." YALE CENTER FOR BRITISH ART, PAUL MELLON FUND, B1996.6.80

Glenn Adamson

A half-finished basket tips toward us, its maker sitting behind on a low step. He is barefoot. The knees of his overalls are torn open from long use, suggesting that he kneels habitually while working. His fingers, resting on the wicker's still-forming edge, are configured in the expert gesture of a practiced craftsman. Perhaps he has only stopped weaving momentarily, for the photo. The next strand he will integrate stretches out to the left, beyond the frame, while the basket's vertical stakes thrust upward like a clutch of javelins or the sharpened pickets of a fence. The basket maker looks through them, fixing us with a guarded stare. Or rather, he does not: for as the photo's caption reveals, he is blind.[1]

Success has many authors, and that certainly applies to this remarkable image. The picture was shot by Constance Stuart Larrabee (1914–2000), an English-born, German-trained photographer who spent the most significant portion of her career in South Africa. One of that country's pioneering modernists, she is celebrated today for the exacting formalism of her compositions—black-and-white, uncropped, and square, taken with a Rolleiflex reflex camera. Many of her prints came into the collection of the Yale Center for British Art following a 1995 exhibition of her work.[2] The photo of the basket maker is one of these, and it has many of the characteristics that distinguish her work. Larrabee often used incidental architecture to powerfully frame her subjects, as she does here with the heavy door, held ajar. Formally too, the picture has all the hallmarks of her style: "smooth surfaces, clear design, sharp tonal contrasts, uncluttered composition, textural veracity and the elimination of extraneous detail," in the words of art historian Brenda Danilowitz.[3]

There was another author who contributed to the making of this photograph, too: Alan Paton, whose book *Cry, The Beloved Country*—arguably the best-known of all South African novels—was published in 1948 (see fig. 61). Immediately following its publication, Larrabee was sent on assignment to take Paton's portrait. Later, in an interview with the Center's curator Scott Wilcox, she recalled that she and Paton "shared attitudes, and ideas, compassion . . . he took me into the territory where his book begins, and I took more photographs with him—of him, and of those places."[4] The images were retroactive book illustrations, of a kind.

This picture was one of them. It was taken at the Ezenzeleni Blind Institute, the setting for the novel's thirteenth chapter. The protagonist, Steven Kumalo, has come to Johannesburg from his rural home in search of his son. He is guided by a fellow priest, Msimangu, who serves as the Virgil to his Dante, leading him through the baffling thickets of the metropole and acting as a wise counselor in his time of need. The two arrive at Ezenzeleni at a moment of crisis: Kumalo has just learned that his

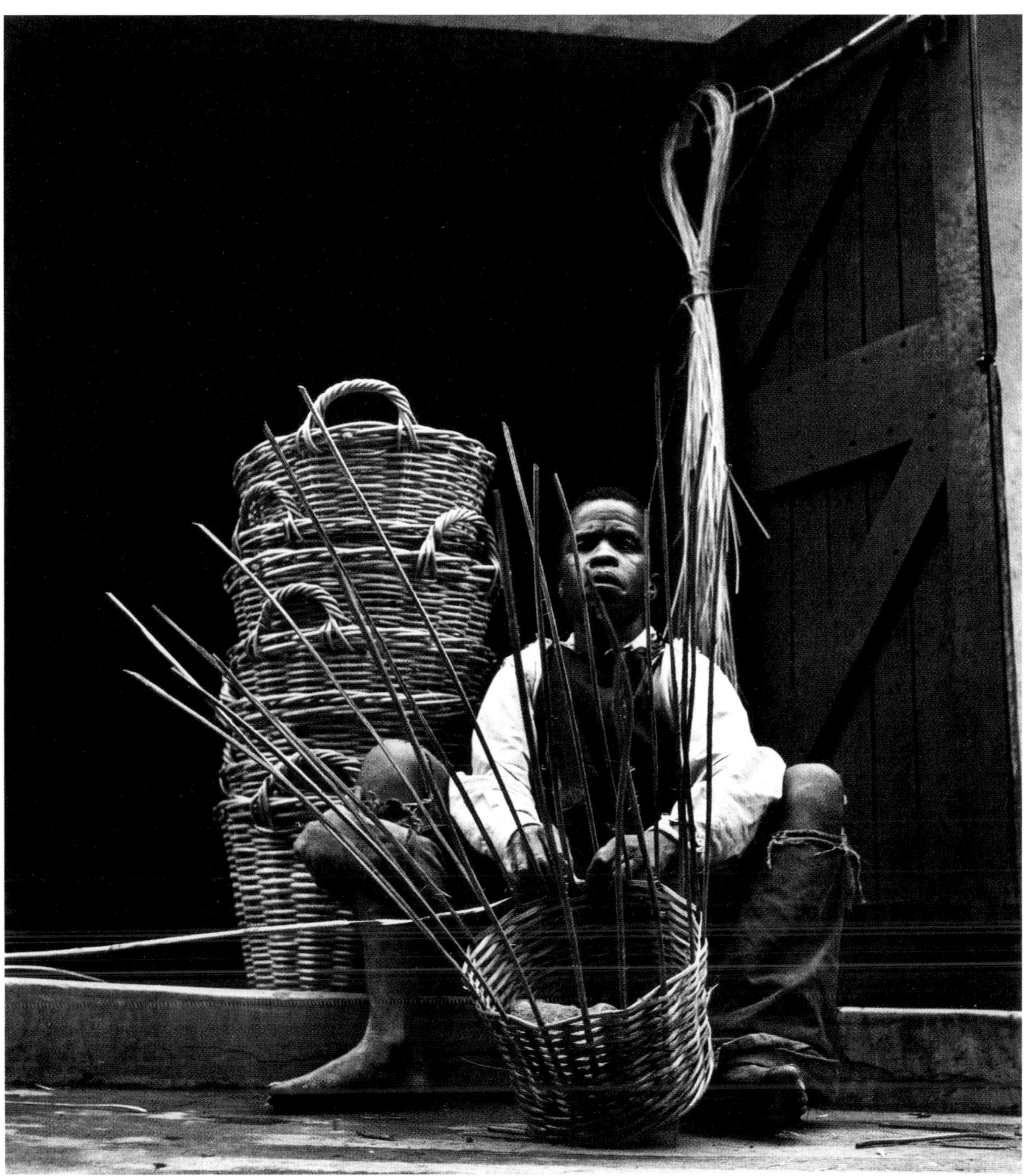

son has killed a white man. The Blind Institute affords a moment for reflection, and wonder:

> It was a wonderful place, this Ezenzeleni. For here the blind, that dragged out their days in a world they could not see, here they had eyes given to them. Here they made things that he for all his sight could never make. Baskets stout and strong, in osiers of different colours, and these osiers ran through one another by some magic that he did not understand, coming together in patterns, the red with the red, the

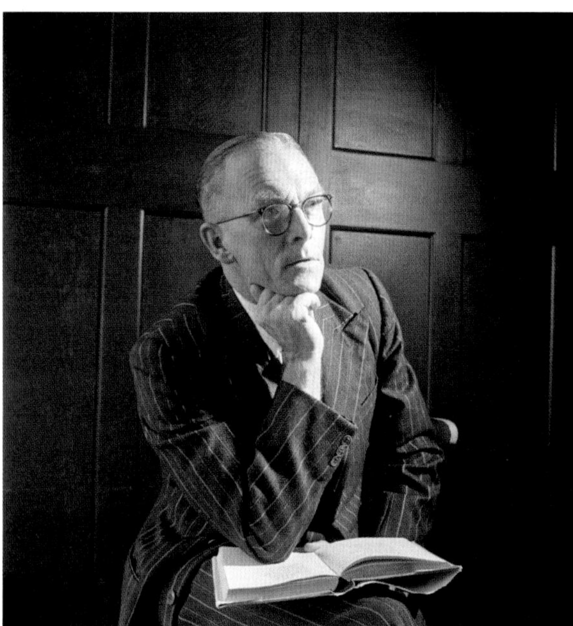

Fig. 61. Constance Stuart Larrabee, *Alan Paton Reading*, 1949, photograph. Smithsonian Institution, National Museum of African Art, Washington, DC, Eliot Elisofon Photographic Archives

> blue with the blue, under the seeing and sightless hands. He talked with the people, and the blind eyes glowed with something that could only have been fire in the soul.[5]

This last perception of Kumalo's, or rather of Paton's, alludes to the intense religiosity of the place. Ezenzeleni was founded in Roodepoort in 1939 by Arthur and Florence Blaxall, a British missionary couple. Like other liberally minded whites in South Africa at the time, they sought to uplift the least fortunate among the black population. It was a paternalistic project, to be sure, but it also positioned them directly in opposition to the racist legal system of apartheid, which was established when the National Party assumed power. As it happens, that decisive political shift also occurred in 1948. It is one of the poignant aspects of the book, and the photographs it inspired, that they preserve the very last moment when South Africa could have been otherwise.

If we were to further expand the authorship of the photograph, then, the Blaxalls might be accorded a place. Certainly, their good works were widely known and deeply influential. Desmond Tutu spent a formative few years at Ezenzeleni when he was young (his mother worked at the Institute as a cook), and it was there that he met the activist bishop Trevor Huddleston, whom he embraced as a role model.[6] The author Es'kia Mphahlele also worked at the Institute as a teacher, and wrote his first stories there.[7] And Helen Keller visited Ezenzeleni in 1951, as part of a charity tour of South Africa. Speaking to the residents, she extolled "these fine rooms where you can be trained and given means of employment."[8] This was a stark contrast to the plight of the many other afflicted South Africans, who "sit staring into the dark with nothing but the dark staring back at them. They live long, long days, and life is made up of days."[9]

Keller's words return us to the matter of looking—and looking back. For there is, of course, another author in this photo: the basket maker himself. He has given shape to the unfinished work in front of him, and to the seven-high stack of baskets at his side, whose consistent size, bold gestural handles, and neatness all testify to his skill. Beyond this, as is so often true in portraiture, the picture itself is a cocreation between Larrabee and this anonymous man. It is most unusual, in her "ethnic photographs" (as she called them), to witness such a profound sense of confrontation. Instead they tend to communicate, through their coolly controlled formalism, "the notion of an idealised and essential Africa," as Danilowitz has argued.[10] There is no hint of disquiet, either, in Paton's literary handling of Ezenzeleni, nor the Blaxalls' sense of spiritual purpose, nor Keller's laudatory commentary. All of them spoke of the Blind Institute as a place of placid benevolence.

That is ruptured, here, by the visually weaponized basket, sharp points brandished toward us, and the basket maker's gaze, which indeed seems to glow with "fire in the soul," but surely not of an exclusively religious origin. What set him apart

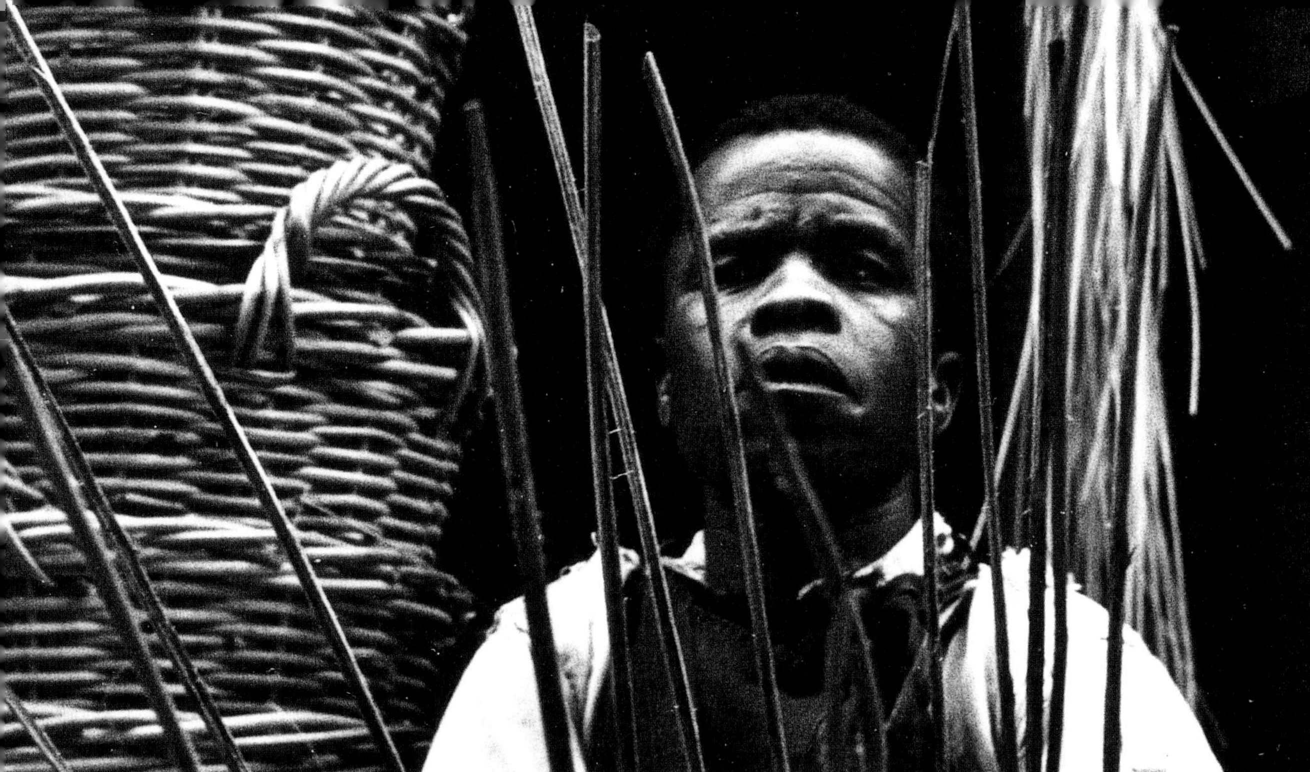

Detail of *Ezenzeleni School*

from the other authors of this photo that depicts him, apart from his anonymity, was of course his race. Nor did this play any less a role in his life because he could not see the color of his own skin. At about this time, Frantz Fanon wrote in *Black Skin, White Masks* (1952) that to experience one's own racial identity is to experience a "crushing objecthood," fixed by the observation of others as "a chemical solution is fixed by a dye."[11] Yet it is the basket maker, as much as the photographer, whose agency is felt in this extraordinary photograph. He never saw it, of course. But it is his presence, and his craftsmanship, that literally make the picture—an image in which blackness, the pride of craft, the desire to empathize, and the specter of unbridgeable difference are all entwined.

In his interview with Larrabee, Wilcox asked her to account for the "sense of inevitable rightness," of truth and power, that radiates from so many of her photographs. "A lot of it," she said, "is eye contact."[12]

Notes

1. My thanks to Edward S. Cooke, Jr., for the helpful observations incorporated in this passage.
2. *Constance Stuart Larrabee: Time Exposure* (New Haven: Yale Center for British Art, 1995).
3. Brenda Danilowitz, "Constance Stuart Larrabee's Photographs of the Ndundza Ndebele: Performing and History Beyond the Modernist Frame," in *Between Union and Liberation: Women Artists in South Africa, 1910–1994*, ed. Marion I. Arnold (Aldershot, UK: Ashgate, 2005), 71.
4. Larrabee interviewed by Scott Wilcox, in *Constance Stuart Larrabee: Time Exposure*, 21–22. Another photograph related to *Cry, The Beloved Country*—depicting a minister and his wife walking along a dirt track—is illustrated here, as is a later portrait of Paton, from 1988.
5. Alan Paton, *Cry, The Beloved Country* (1948) (New York: Scribner, 1987), 121. Osier is a species of willow.
6. Steven Gish, *Desmond Tutu: A Biography* (Westport, CT: Greenwood Press, 2004), 6.
7. Rob Gaylard, "'A Man Is a Man Because of Other Men': The 'Lesane' Stories of Es'kia Mphahlele," *English in Africa* 22, no. 1 (May 1995): 73.
8. Helen Keller, speech to the blind at Ezenzeleni and Kutlwanong, May 12, 1951. Helen Keller Archive, American Foundation for the Blind.
9. Helen Keller, speech to Arthur Blaxall and friends in South Africa advocating for the African blind, date unrecorded, probably March 1951. Helen Keller Archive, American Foundation for the Blind.
10. Danilowitz, "Constance Stuart Larrabee's Photographs of the Ndundza Ndebele," 72.
11. Frantz Fanon, *Black Skin, White Masks* (1952), trans. Charles Lam Markmann (London: Pluto Press, 1986), 81.
12. Larrabee interviewed by Scott Wilcox, 14–15.

Dame (Jocelyn) Barbara Hepworth (British, 1903–1975)
Biolith, 1948–49

Blue limestone (Ancaster stone) on marble plinth, overall: 61½ x 30¼ x 19 in. (156.2 x 76.8 x 48.3 cm). YALE CENTER FOR BRITISH ART, GIFT OF VIRGINIA VOGEL MATTERN IN MEMORY OF HER HUSBAND, W. GRAY MATTERN, YALE BA 1946, B2004.3

Sarah Victoria Turner

Geology fascinated the sculptor Barbara Hepworth. From an early age, she was alive to the ways in which the shape of the landscape had been fashioned by millennia of movements beneath the surface of the world. Giving her memories three-dimensional form, she described the sensation of driving through West Yorkshire with her father as a child and being struck by "the sensation of moving physically over the contours of fullness and concavities, through hollows and over peaks—feeling, touching, through mind and hand and eye."[1] Later on in her career, after she had moved from London to the Cornish seaside town of St Ives, where she lived from 1939 until her death in 1975, her sense of the earth's rhythms was sharpened further, as was her appreciation of the "fragility and obstinacy of human tenure of land and sea."[2] Walking along the beach, Hepworth noticed that the "incoming and receding tides made strange and wonderful calligraphy on the pale granite sand that sparkled with feldspar and mica. The rich mineral deposits of Cornwall were apparent on the very surface of things; geology and prehistory—a thousand facts induced a thousand fantasies of form and purpose, structure and life which had gone into the making of what I saw and what I was."[3] The layering of sediments, the turbulence of tectonics, the collision of masses, the flow and recession of vast oceans and lakes leaving behind deposits that created a myriad of patterns and colors provided a rich "prehistory" in the stones that Hepworth often employed as a sculptor with a preference for carving her materials. Scanning a list of her works reads like a geologist's field guide to the British Isles: Hopton Wood stone from Derbyshire; Corsehill stone extracted in southern Scotland; Cumberland stone; blue limestone from Ireland; and blue Ancaster stone, only quarried in one place in England since the Roman period, the Ancaster Glebe quarry in Lincolnshire.

Ancaster is the stone from which Hepworth chose to carve *Biolith*—a Middle Jurassic oolitic limestone that was also the source of building material for great English country houses, such as the Elizabethan Wollaton Hall in Nottinghamshire and Mentmore Towers in Buckinghamshire, commissioned by the Rothschild family in the nineteenth century. The "ooids" (from the ancient Greek word for egg), spherical grains that pepper this sedimentary rock, form the flow and speckle of the natural grain across this semiabstract sculpture. This stone's shimmer gives off chronological clues, evidence of a warm tropical sea that once bathed huge swaths of what we now call England. For Hepworth, these marks and patterns were not just incidental or decorative but an integral part of the look, feel, and potential meanings of her sculpture. The title she gave to the work underscores the importance of geology for her sculptural imagination. Bioliths, or biolites as they are sometimes known, are sedimentary rocks formed by the remains of living organisms. This fossilization did not conjure notions of death or decay for Hepworth; on the contrary, these little oval pits contained

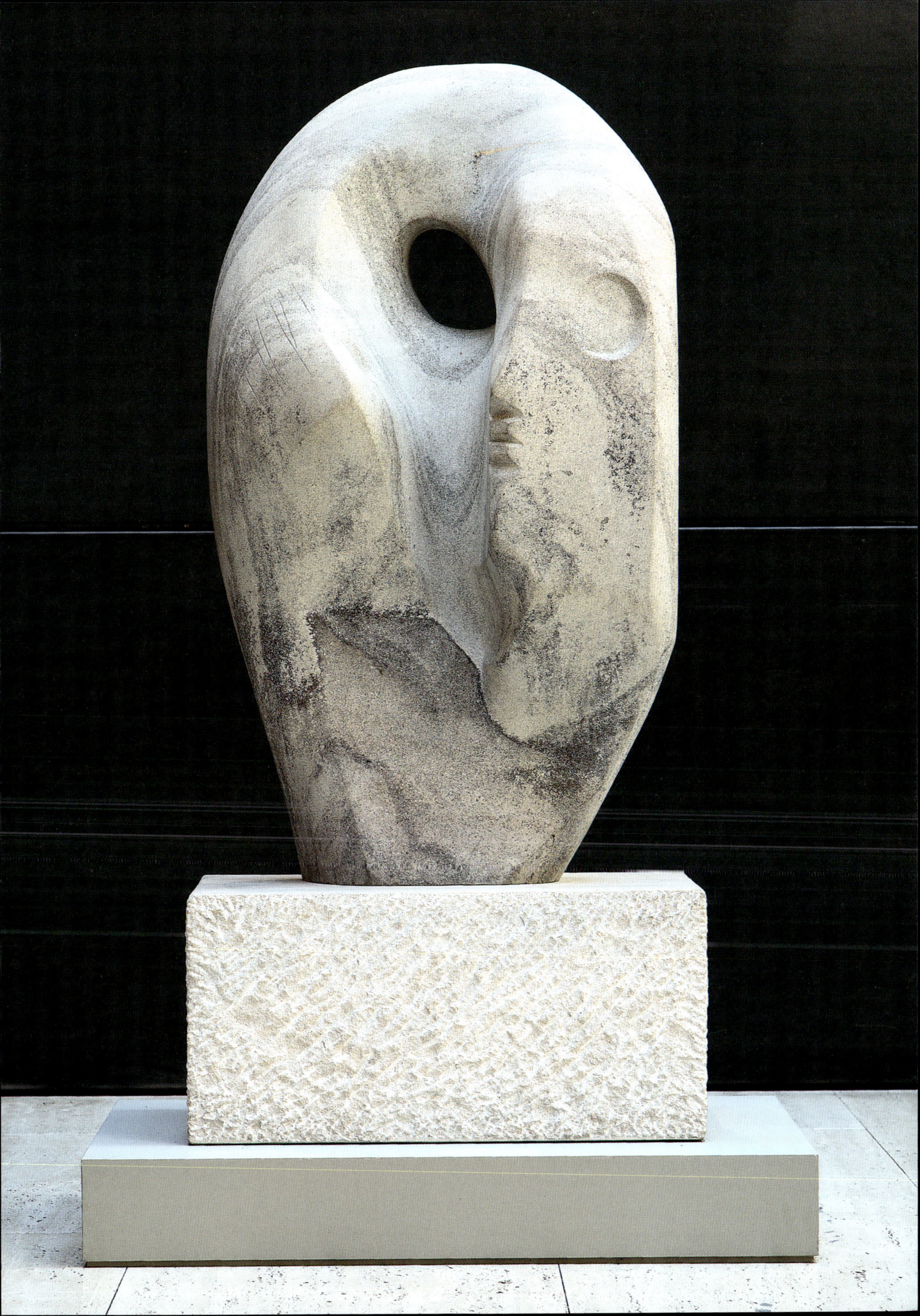

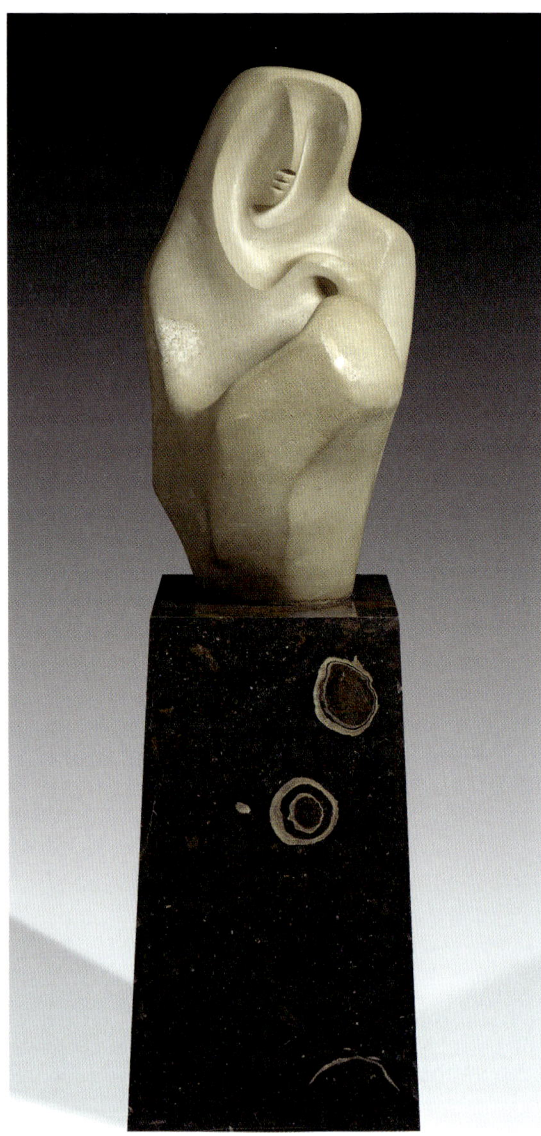

Fig. 62. Dame Barbara Hepworth, *Eocene*, 1949, Portland stone. St Albans Girls' School, St Albans, Hertfordshire, UK

the energy of past life, which, as the carver, she then released through her sculpture. With her chisel and mallet, Hepworth revealed these ancient layers, bringing them to the "surface of things," giving them a modern life. The titles of other sculptures from this period speak of Hepworth's geological research. In the same year she finished *Biolith*, she carved *Eocene* (fig. 62), a work whose title directly references the geological period lasting from 56 to 33.9 million years ago.

Of this group of works made in the difficult years after World War II (many of the essentials of daily life were still rationed), David Lewis, her secretary at the time, wrote: "Their lithic forms are synonymous with the most ancient of man's symbols, the monolith, lonely and foreboding, a form which she has . . . absorbed from the cromlechs and the stone circles and granite obelisks of the Cornish landscape of Penwith."[4] The influence of the ancient stones that occupy the lonely hills of Cornwall can be seen in the shape of many of Hepworth's sculptures carved in the late 1940s with their upright, blocky shapes. Again, Hepworth animated this ancientness, giving it modern form; here cutting, shaping, and inscribing this block of Ancaster stone with her own particular style. Contained within *Biolith*, there are the smooth edges, the perfect circle that forms the dish of an eye for the outline of a face, which has been knocked into the stone with a disciplined economy. There is also the trace of a hand on the other side of the stone block to the face, giving the viewer the sense of bodily envelopment and caress.

Biolith is both abstract and figurative, refusing to be only one or the other—it is "deliberately double rather than . . . weakly ambiguous," as Penelope Curtis has observed of this work.[5] The presence of two figures emerging from the stone is detectable, and Hepworth noted in 1952 that she was interested during this period in the "idea of two or more figures as a unity, blended into one carved and rhythmic form."[6] The overall shape of *Biolith* resembles a misshapen egg, perhaps in reference to its oolitic origins, or it might be interpreted as the enveloping shape of a conch shell, picked up on one of Hepworth's beach walks. From one side, it looks more like an ear, and it is perhaps not too fanciful to make links between *Biolith* and the drawings Hepworth made in the same year she began that work, especially *Fenestration of the Ear (The Hammer)* (fig. 63), when she observed this surgery in hospitals in Exeter and London at the dawn of the National Health Service. The fenestration operation (which was performed until

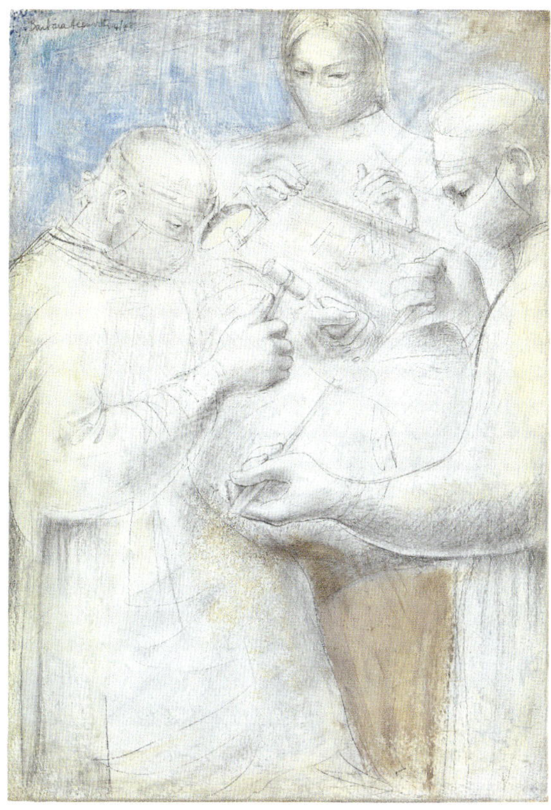

Fig. 63. Dame Barbara Hepworth, *Fenestration of the Ear (The Hammer)*, 1948, oil and pencil on board, 15⅛ x 10⅝ in. (38.4 x 27 cm). Tate Britain, London

the early 1950s) involved the making of a new window (fenestra) in the inner ear.[7]

Biolith was made at a pivotal moment in Hepworth's career. In 1949 she moved into her Trewyn studio (now the Barbara Hepworth Museum and Sculpture Garden, St Ives). She exhibited *Biolith* in February 1950 at the Lefevre Gallery in London, along with thirteen other carvings, all of which had been made in the previous two years.[8] A few months later, *Biolith* traveled to Italy for the 25th Venice Biennale, where Hepworth shared the British Pavilion with the painters John Constable (1776–1837) and Matthew Smith (1879–1959). The British Council's archives contain a letter from Hepworth with a drawing of how *Biolith* should be moved into place using a sling, with the words of warning: "Please do not let grease or dirty rope-marks or handmarks get on to it. Otherwise the patina will be ruined."[9] The detail of display, the quality of that surface of the Ancaster stone which she had labored so long over, was crucially important to Hepworth. Having such a prominent international stage for a retrospective exhibition of her sculpture from 1927 to 1949 (as well as eleven abstract drawings, eleven hospital drawings, and fifteen drawings of the human figure) was highly significant for Hepworth at this moment in her career.[10] *Biolith* now stands in the entrance court of the Yale Center for British Art. It was gifted to the Center in 2004 by Virginia Vogel Mattern in memory of her husband, W. Gray Mattern. Here, exhibited in New Haven, the cool, patterned stone of the sculpture seems almost to flow again, a wave of welcome rising up from the gray travertine floor of Louis Kahn's building.

Notes

1. Barbara Hepworth, *Barbara Hepworth: A Pictorial Autobiography* (London: Tate Publishing, 1985), 9.
2. David Lewis, "Barbara Hepworth: A Memoir," in *Barbara Hepworth: Centenary*, ed. Chris Stephens (London: Tate Publishing, 2003), 9.
3. Hepworth, *Barbara Hepworth: A Pictorial Autobiography*, 55.
4. David Lewis, "The Sculpture of Barbara Hepworth," *Eidos* 2 (September–October 1950): 30.
5. Penelope Curtis, "Barbara Hepworth's *Biolith*, 1948–49," *Burlington Magazine* 148, no. 12 (December 2006): 841.
6. Hepworth, "Rhythm and Space," in *Barbara Hepworth: Carvings and Drawings*, with an introduction by Herbert Read (London: Lund Humphries, 1952), section 5, unpaginated.
7. Matthew Gale and Chris Stephens, *Barbara Hepworth: Works in the Tate Gallery Collection and the Barbara Hepworth Museum St Ives* (London: Tate Gallery Publishing, 1999), 112.
8. *New Sculpture and Drawings by Barbara Hepworth* (London: Lefevre Gallery, 1950).
9. Letter from Barbara Hepworth, March 1, 1950; Venice Biennale: correspondence about the loan of sculptures and pictures by Barbara Hepworth, Record of the British Council, The National Archives, Kew (BW 2/420).
10. Henry Meyric Hughes, "The Promotion and Reception of British Sculpture Abroad, 1948–1960: Herbert Read, Henry Moore, Barbara Hepworth, and the 'Young British Sculptors,'" *British Art Studies* 3, https://doi.org/10.17658/issn.2058-5462/issue-03/hmhughes.

Bruce Davidson (American, b. 1933)
Wales, 1965

Gelatin silver print on moderately thick, semigloss photographic paper, 8 ¼ x 12 ½ in. (21 x 31.8 cm). Signed on the verso in graphite, at center: "Bruce Davidson."

YALE CENTER FOR BRITISH ART, GIFT OF HENRY S. HACKER, YALE BA 1965, B2009.13.10

Bruce Davidson, in conversation with Scott Wilcox
August 31, 2018

SW: Your first serious stint photographing in Britain came in the autumn of 1960 as an assignment from *Queen* magazine. Your next visit came in 1965, when you traveled to Wales. What took you to Wales?

BD: I was aware of Robert Frank having photographed South Wales, and I wanted to see what it was like for myself. I was in the military in Paris in the 1950s, working in a photo lab. My sergeant was Welsh, and I asked him one day where was the place he'd send his worst enemy. He said Cwmcarn, Wales. So I went to Cwmcarn on a three-day pass; I just had to see it. I was only there for a couple hours, looking around, just watching and observing the light, but I knew that at some point after my military service, I would have to come back. When in 1965 a job from *Holiday* magazine took me back to Britain, I decided to go back. The Welsh Magnum photographer Philip Jones Griffiths gave me the name of the poet Horace Charles Jones, who had been a miner. He showed me around. We went to Cwmcarn and to Ebbw Vale and to other places I can't pronounce.

SW: What was the intended purpose of your photographs of the Welsh miners and their communities?

BD: I didn't know. I just took photographs for a few days until I felt I couldn't be there anymore. It was a very sad place. The mines were closing. The pit ponies were becoming wild. Those pit ponies were important to me. And there was something about the blackness of coal. When you come out of the mines, you're covered in black. The combination of coal dust and perspiration on the skin had an eerie quality. You would never get that black coal dust off.

SW: You were an outsider, trying to make meaningful photographs of these people living really hard lives. How did you approach them?

BD: The miners were angry and closed off. But they knew and respected Horace Jones, who was close to ninety when I met him. After Horace arranged for the miners to come up out of the pit and pose for me, then I became more comfortable, and I think they did too.

SW: What camera were you using?

BD: For much of it, it was a Leica with a wide-angle lens. But I also had a four-by-five Sinar view camera for photographing groups, and that came into play too. For the photograph of the boys on the rope swing, it was probably the Leica with a 28 mm lens. I was interested in the way the landscape looked.

SW: How do you see the Welsh photographs of 1965 relating to your various photographic projects in the United States in the years immediately before and after?

BD: After my book *Brooklyn Gang*, I had received a Guggenheim Fellowship in 1961 to photograph youth in America. Someone told me that a group of college students were taking a bus south to protest segregation, the Freedom Riders. So I hopped on too. I got a sense of the pain and the danger in the South. I realized that my Guggenheim Fellowship would not be about youth in America but about youth putting themselves in danger for a cause. I got a taste of reality that I wasn't expecting. It was for me a moment of truth. As photographers, we can observe, and we can change things. I saw the camera not as a means of making beautiful pictures but as a way to change people's thinking. Between 1961 and 1965 I had grown and come to understand the meaning of the civil rights movement. When you get to the East 100th Street photographs, beginning in 1966, it was about community, and—about showing people's homes. The photographs not only had an artistic quality but also played a positive useful role in effecting change.

SW: The Welsh pictures form a bridge between those earlier civil rights photographs and the East 100th Street photographs?

BD: Possibly. Photographing is always a learning experience for me. Going into a place, I'm not sure why I'm there and just what I'm doing. As I begin to take the photographs, I feel my way in. But one project flows into another, and a project builds on the one before.

SW: When did the Welsh photographs first appear in print or in exhibition?

BD: There was an exhibition of some of my photographs at the Museum of Modern Art in 1966, which included a small group of the Wales photographs, including this one of the boys with the rope swing. It was then published in a book of my photographs in 1978, and it has appeared in various exhibitions and books since then.

SW: How did the picture of the boy in the balaclava with the rope swing behind him come to be?

BD: It was just a moment. I walked into the scene and saw them swinging, and the tension of the image seemed to work for me. I was drawn to the tension between the rope and the boys. They were free, and the freedom was important to me. I could very easily be the boy on the rope.

SW: But the boy in the balaclava is clearly interested in you.

BD: He's looking at me, but I was really just an invisible man. And then I moved on.

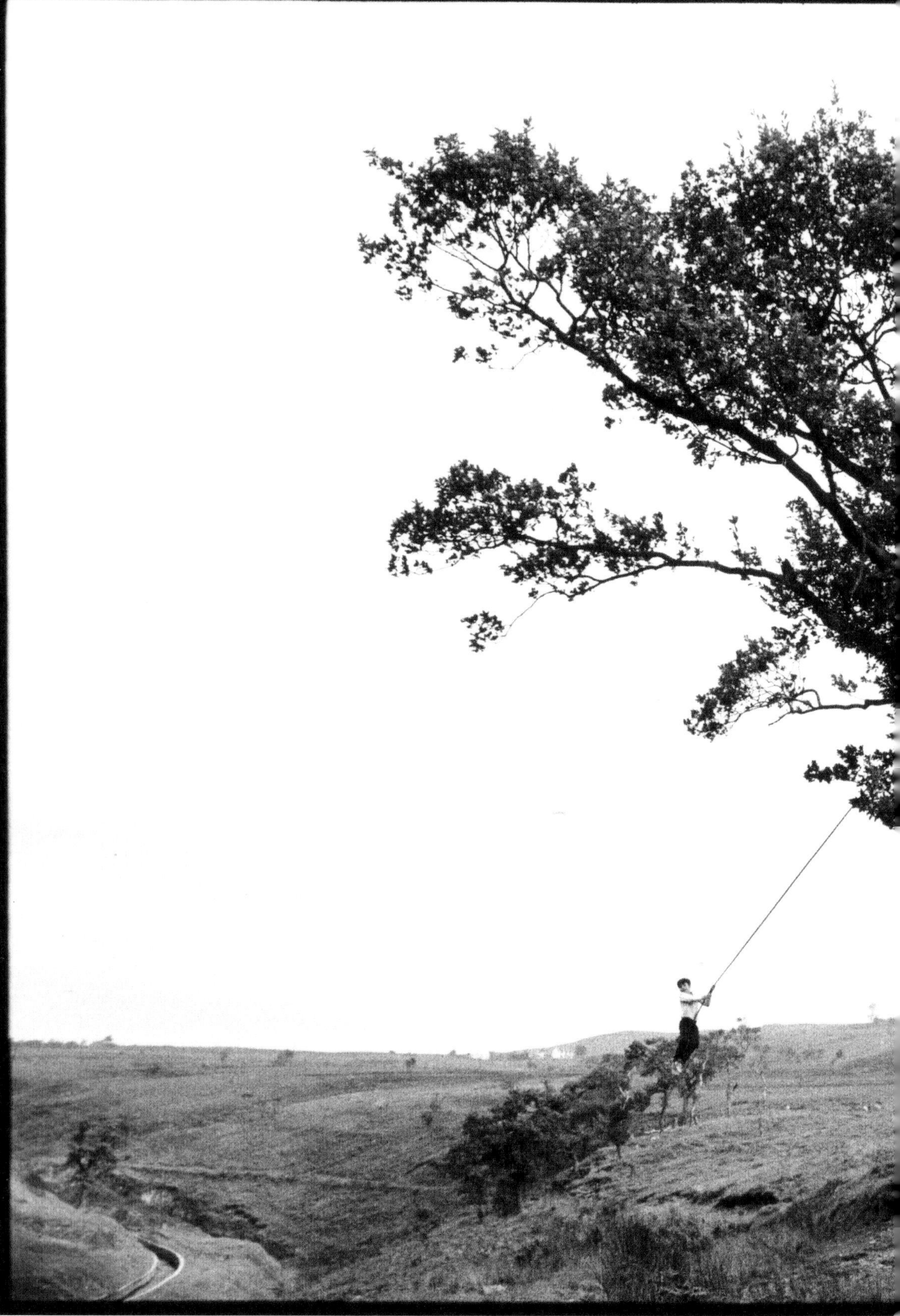

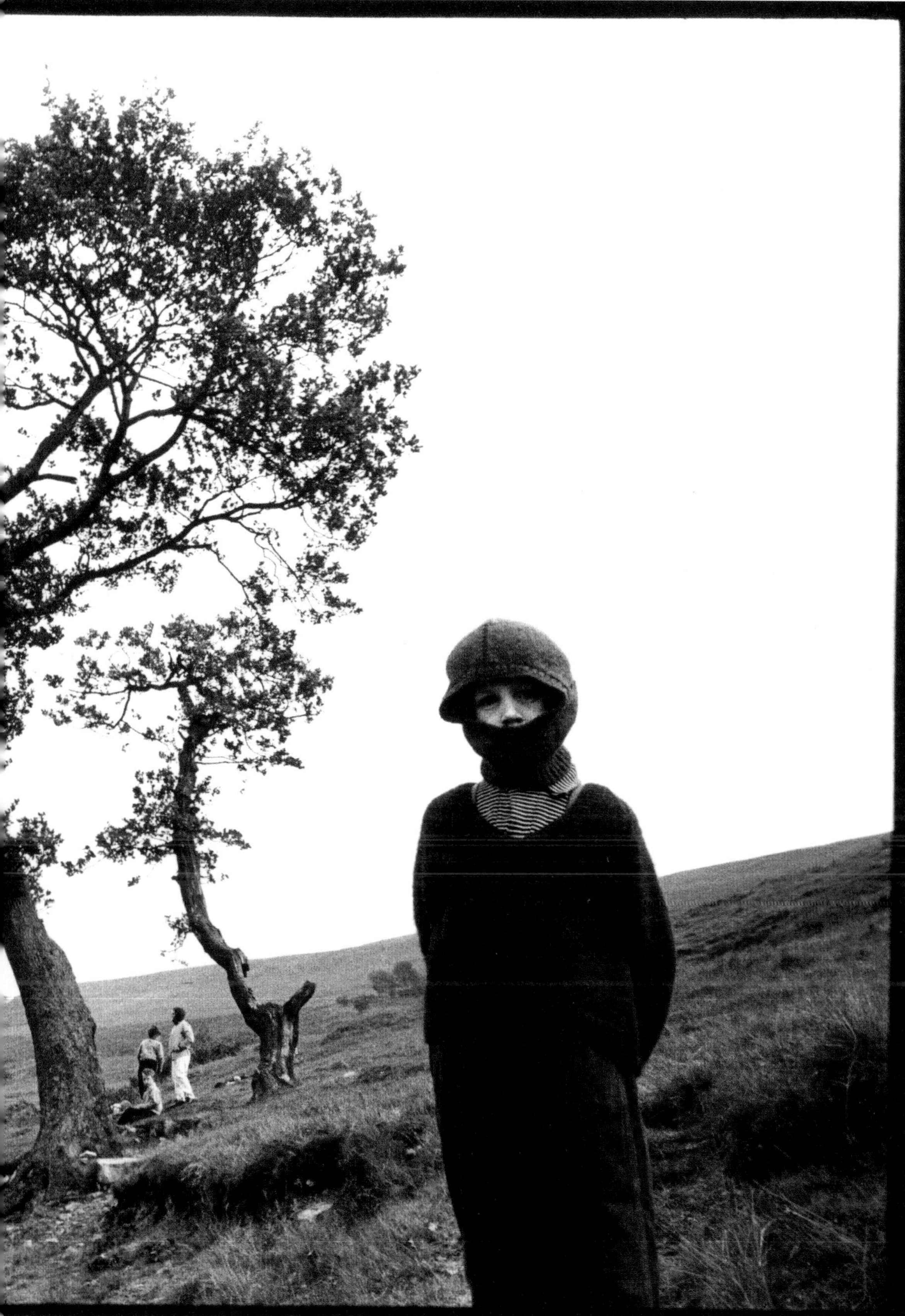

Rebecca Salter (British, b. 1955)
K37, 1996

Mixed media on canvas, 72 x 96 in. (182.9 x 243.8 cm). YALE CENTER FOR BRITISH ART, FRIENDS OF BRITISH ART FUND AND GIFT OF JULES DAVID PROWN, MAH 1971, IN MEMORY OF LOUIS I. KAHN, B2011.8

Jules David Prown

Rebecca Salter's *K37* is a large two-part composition. A vertical line divides the two parts with the optical illusion of the dark side recessed and the light side advancing (the right side does project slightly forward). As one moves closer, what at first had seemed a flat gray plane on the left becomes a rich but subtle pattern of emerging and receding shapes, texture, and value (light and dark). We see a maelstrom of activity—a variety of lights and darks, faint squares and rectangles. On the right, there is a sweeping curve, and echoes of the dark realm emerge, disappear, and reemerge, some with more persistence than others. The brushed arc on the left speaks to its shadowy counterpart, and there is slight darkness in the upper right and lower right. If the painting were folded, the right side might seem almost an impression of the left. Forms and colors emerge and recede calmly throughout the entire painting.

Complexity becomes evident as you move closer. Brushwork is at times discontinuous. In the darkness on the left, the large bulging and increasingly light form rushes like a bullet to the right on the verge of penetrating a darker framing parenthesis, which is lighter near the center at the tip of the approaching missile.

The right-side parenthesis offers resistance, but its similar lightness in the middle allows it possibly to be penetrated by the force from the left. The subtle, multiple pale colors on the right—to my eye greenish in the sweeping parenthesis, elsewhere soft peach, rose, or lavender—contrast with the play of light and dark on the left. Six horizontal strips of canvas on the right side are quite evident, but six vertical columns are almost entirely obscured by surface work. These evanescent bands and columns come and go. The surface is alive with movement. A quilt-like pattern of squares emerges, apparently six by six but difficult to pin down because edge lines do not consistently engage.

On the left side, where the surface is more textured, six rows are also evident, but perhaps only five columns. Various square or rectangular shapes configure themselves, again evanescent. Interstices where patches engage each other also seem at times offset, yielding different sizes, all obscured by brushstrokes that sometimes continue over the joins and lines and sometimes not—that sometimes suggest continuity, but on close examination turn out to be discontinuous.

From left to right, the surface of the painting becomes smoother. On the right side, a darker horizontal rectangle with a barely visible central seam sits in the center, greenish from a distance but up close resolving into various tints. No comparable rectangle appears on the left. The rectangle seems surmounted by a lighter form, twice as large, making a larger uneven vertical rectangle. A vague penumbra of light surrounds the geometry of the rectangle, which, along with the actual structure of the horizontal bands and vertical columns of pieces of canvas, contrasts with the overall softness. The effect does not agitate or excite the viewer, but quite the opposite. Once one enters this realm visually, it is boundless as the paint surface continues around the outer edges of the stretcher. One's imagination roams free. The exquisite balance of ambiguous forms, textures, values, and colors transports the viewer into a meditative state that leads to wherever the inner self wants to go.

When I first saw the painting, I was struck by the way in which it resonated with the Center's architecture (fig. 64) beyond echoing its bipartite organization around two courtyards, with the arrangement of the patches resembling the bay system of the galleries and the forward projection of the right side similar to the projection of the Center over the street-level shops. Both the painting and the building invite contemplation. More importantly, the painting seems to embody some basic philosophical convictions of the architect, Louis I. Kahn. There is, of course, no necessary correlation between what an artist intends and what a viewer perceives. Moreover, any Kahn influence on Salter seems unlikely since at the time she produced it she was not familiar with Kahn or his writings, and had not visited the Center prior to her stay at the Albers Foundation in Bethany,

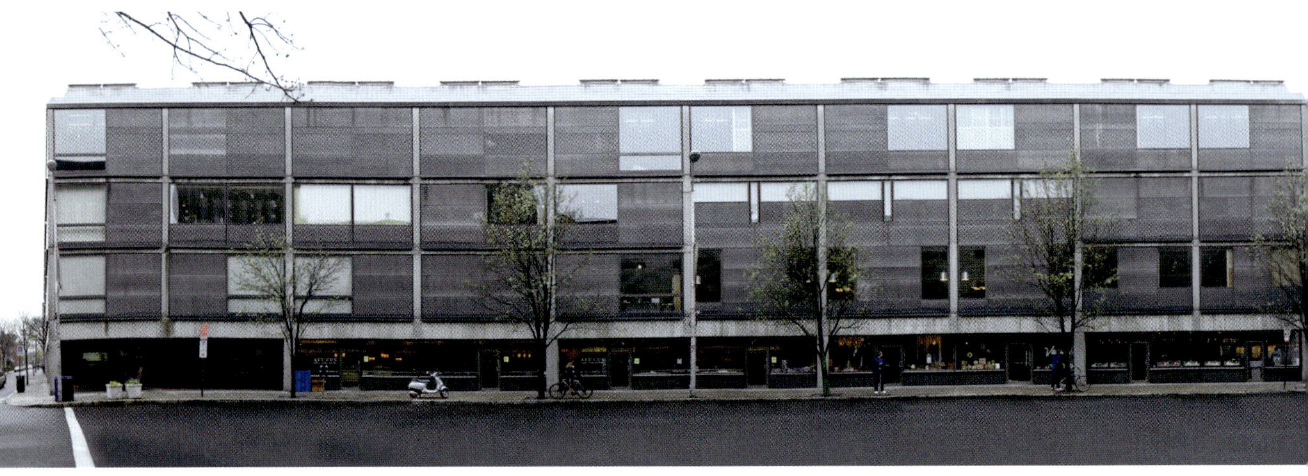

Fig. 64. Exterior of Yale Center for British Art

Connecticut, in 2003, seven years after the painting was made. Yet *K37* seems an abstract expression of Kahn's thinking about the role of architecture in shaping the resources of the natural world to meet and satisfy human needs and desires.

Any commonality between Kahn's Yale Center for British Art and Salter's painting is further complicated by the fact that their actual working philosophies and procedures are quite different, even opposed. Kahn strove for simplicity, getting to the essence of things, trying, he said time and again, to get back not to the number one but to the number zero. His reductionism aimed for clarity and transparency. The facade of the Center, Kahn's last building, articulates important aspects of his philosophy. Honesty is paramount. The structure is exposed, telling how the building was built (columns narrow, beams thicken and disappear, depending on the work they do). The materials are natural (concrete, steel, glass, brick, bluestone), each used in a manner true to its nature. Glass is transparent; it admits light. Steel is opaque; it excludes light and bends to enclose the glass in a single sheer plane. Sometimes Kahn referred to the glass and the steel panels respectively as windows and opaque windows. Light—not light.

The interior rooms also tell you how they are made. Visible columns, beams, ducts, and light tracks announce their function. There are no hung ceilings. Nothing is hidden. The materials of the building remain pristine, no paint, no dyes, no cosmeticizing: glass, concrete, steel, brick, slate, travertine, linen, wool, oak, aluminum—all used as they are.

Salter, in contrast to Kahn's insistence on clarity, is comfortable with ambiguity. Her work is complex, built up over time through working and reworking, front and back. She frequently uses multiple media in a single work, inextricable combinations of painting, drawing, print making, and collage that seem to yield unpredictable results, perhaps even to the artist herself, among whose gifts is knowing when to stop. She is a consummate craftsman, and her work emerges from the complexity of its making, the interaction of her mind, hand, and a multiplicity of tools. Kahn, too, was concerned with craftsmanship and detail, but expressed in the simplest and clearest way possible.

Despite these differences, I would like to suggest that seen through the lens of Kahn's philosophy, Salter's *K37* unconsciously represents the complex dialogue between the darkness that Kahn called Silence and its counterpart Light (fig. 65).

The dark left side is Silence, what Kahn also called The Treasury of the Shadows or The Sanctuary of Art. In the Platonic realm of Silence

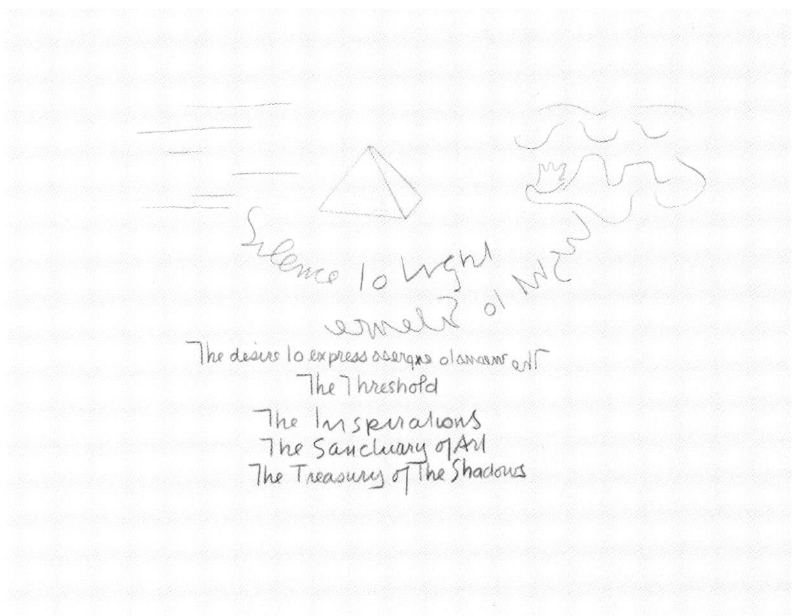

Fig. 65. Louis I. Kahn, *Silence and Light*, ca. 1969, sketchbook drawing. The University of Pennsylvania and the Pennsylvania Historical and Museum Commission

reside essential Ideas and Forms. One of Kahn's favorite epigrammatic sayings was "What *is* has always been, what *was* has always been.[1] The task of the architect is to seek, find, and bring the appropriate essential forms across a threshold from Silence into Light, into what he called Presence, in ways that obey the laws of nature, creating in response to human desire that which nature itself cannot do. Nature cannot make a building.

K37 is suggestive, not a definitive statement. Various speculative interpretations of the binary composition of *K37* can be pursued: war and peace, male and female, etc. I have speculated that out of the chaos on the left emerges a calm resolution on the right—chaos resolves into regularity. More particularly, I read the bullet-like form as rushing from the left toward the weakest part of the bracketing parentheses and a target, the small rectangle, a geometric core in the center of the right side. Is it a target or a resolution? If a target, will it be obliterated or absorbed, assimilated?

I have specifically suggested a Kahnian interpretation of the picture as a representation of Silence and Light, with implicit movement from Silence to Light, Idea to Presence. In this reading, the left side, Silence, The Sanctuary of Art, is the repository of all potential, where all that is—or can be—was. The right side across the threshold is the realm of Light, where man, the human, can give Presence to Idea. At the center is an emerging rectangle. Geometry is a product of the human mind, and the rectangles represent mind. Kahn believed that material was spent light. An architect or an artist, through a desire to express, moves from Silence to Light to material form. Kahn himself offered an allegory in which there are two brothers, one of whom has a desire to express. The other brother, loving him, sacrifices himself to create an instrument of expression by moving into Light, condensing into material, and becoming a violin. Or perhaps the Yale Center for British Art.

Notes

1. Jules David Prown and Karen E. Denavit, eds., *Louis I. Kahn in Conversation: Interviews with John W. Cook and Heinrich Klotz, 1969–70* (New Haven and London: Yale Univ. Press, 2014), 33.

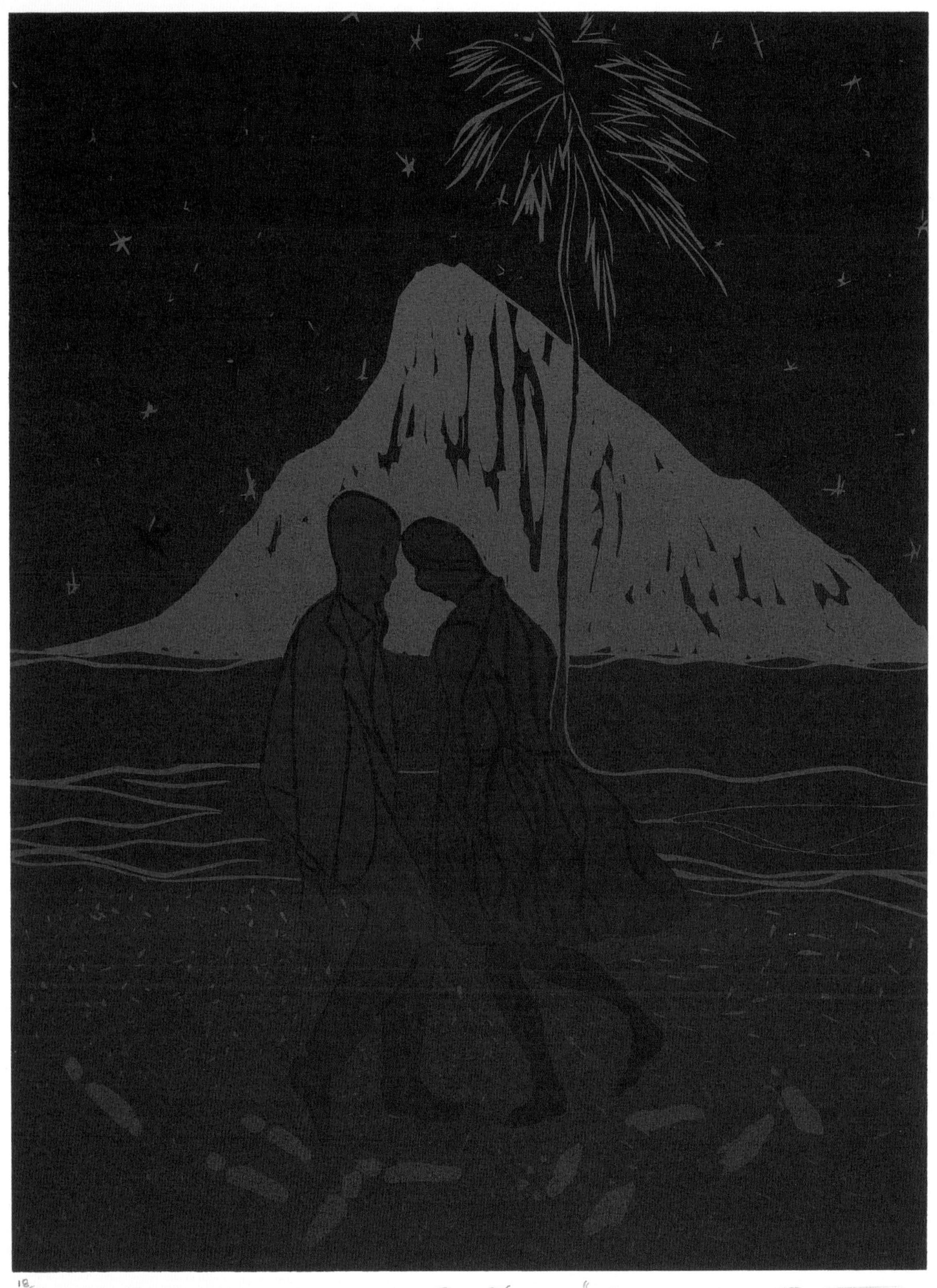
18/50
"After The Dance"
2006

Sonia Boyce (British, b. 1962), Isaac Julien (British, b. 1960), Glenn Ligon (American, b. 1960), Hew Locke (British, b. 1959), Chris Ofili (British, b. 1968), and Carrie Mae Weems (American, b. 1953)
Rivington Place Portfolio (six prints), 2006–7

Inkjet prints on paper, each 30 x 20 in. (76.2 x 50.8 cm) or 20 x 30 in. (50.8 x 76.2 cm), depending on orientation. YALE CENTER FOR BRITISH ART, FRIENDS OF BRITISH ART FUND, B2008.10.1–8

Courtney J. Martin

In many ways, *Rivington Place Portfolio* (2006–7) was the end product of a nearly thirty-year discussion about the concept of identity in British art. Artists, art historians, critics, and other cultural workers developed a free-form conversation in which the collision of art and sociopolitical concerns came to bear not only on artists but also on the ways in which art was shown. Aesthetic dialogue among artists like Rasheed Araeen and Lubaina Himid joined academic and institutional debate, participated in by critical theorists like Stuart Hall or curators like Sandy Nairne, in feeding a chain of dialogue that found its way into state-sanctioned venues, most significantly Arts Council England. In 1994 the Institute of International Visual Arts (Iniva) was founded with the goal of supporting projects "concerned with an interrogation not of blackness, black Britishness, or cultural diversity in the United Kingdom, but of what *Britishness* is and how it has evolved."[1] Following the turn of the millennium, this idea had grown in proportion to encompass exhibitions, publications, research, and symposia; it thus needed a larger space to house both its program and its expansive ideals. The *Portfolio* was produced to support the building of the titular Rivington Place, an art and cultural center in east central London.

After 2000 the founding director of Iniva, Gilane Tawadros, began talks with the Arts Council; Iniva trustees, including Hall, the founding chairperson of the board; various international foundations; and one of the organizations that shared its building, a photography agency called Autograph ABP, to discuss a new building for the institution. Its ambitious exhibitions had long outgrown the small, limited space that it occupied on the narrow lane, Rivington Place, and the fact that the gallery's exhibitions were being shown in other venues in Britain and elsewhere only created a further sense of disproportion between its building's footprint and its renown in the world.

Alongside the development of the organization were other factors that affected its presence internationally. The founding of Iniva was contemporary with the shift in the art market that positioned London as a center, largely due to the prominence of a group of British artists, the so-called young British artists (YBAs) who had begun to bring attention not only to their own practices but also to the city as an incubator for artists. The center of

Fig. 66. Chris Ofili, *After the Dance*, 2006, screen print, 30 x 20 in. (76.2 x 50.8 cm). Yale Center for British Art, Friends of British Art Fund

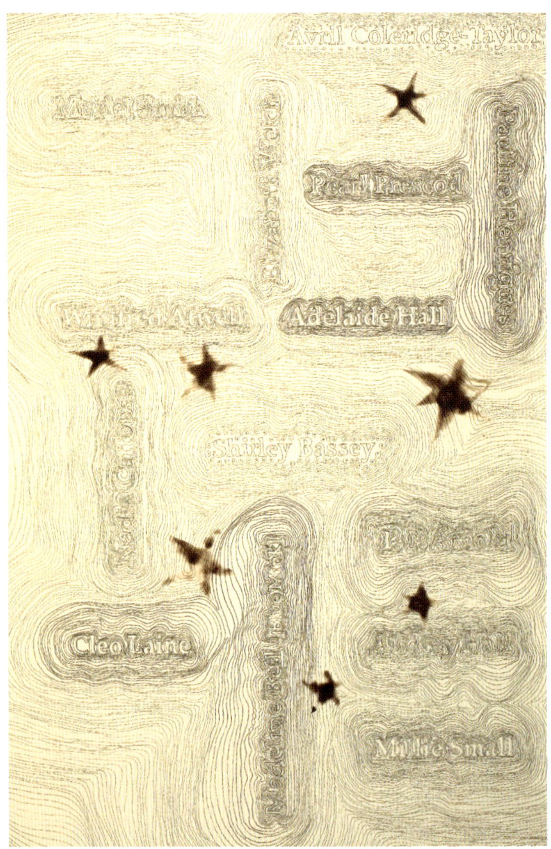

Fig. 67. Sonia Boyce, *1930s to 1960s*, 2007, hard- and soft-ground etching with spitbite aquatint, 30 x 20 in. (76.2 x 50.8 cm). Yale Center for British Art, Friends of British Art Fund

YBA London was the East End, a formerly economically depressed area of the city, known historically for its industrialization and acceptance of immigrant groups from as early as the sixteenth century.

Rivington Place was the first new purpose-built public art gallery to be erected in London since 1968, the year that the Hayward Gallery opened. The brutalist Hayward was the last of the new arts and culture venues of the Southbank Centre, which began in 1951 with the Festival of Britain, a key constituent in rebuilding the city's infrastructure and morale following World War II. Like the Southbank Centre, Rivington Place proposed itself as a champion of London's resilience. To that end, the selection of Royal College of Art (RCA)-trained architect David Adjaye spoke to the import of the building in the East End. Adjaye was the son of Ghanaian diplomats and had attended the RCA with artists who would define British art internationally in the 1990s and 2000s, such as Chris Ofili (fig. 66). His keen understanding of the building as a site that "has been re-colonised" became the theoretical underpinning of both the structure and the art that it would house.[2]

The final budget for the building was £8 million, funded in large part by the public/private partnership of Arts Council England and Barclays. The *Portfolio* provided essential revenue and demonstrated the support of the artists who donated their work to it. The relationship between the building and the *Portfolio* is an explicit one. The *Portfolio* was in service to the building and the building, once completed, would be in service to the art that would be shown in it. Published by the Brodsky Center (then at Rutgers University, now at the Pennsylvania Academy of Fine Arts, Philadelphia) in an edition of fifty, the *Portfolio* entered the Yale Center for British Art in 2007 when some of the prints were shown in *Art and Emancipation in Jamaica: Isaac Mendes Belisario and His Worlds* (September 27–December 30, 2007). It was accessioned in 2008.

Of the six artists contained in the *Portfolio*—Sonia Boyce, Isaac Julien, Glenn Ligon, Hew Locke, Chris Ofili, and Carrie Mae Weems—two are American and four are British. The inclusion of American artists Ligon and Weems reinforced Iniva and Autograph ABP's call for an international outlook. Of the four British artists, all had participated in exhibitions or programs at Invia, and Julien had served as a member of the institution's board. All had previously worked with print, though none had done so exclusively.

For the *Portfolio*, Boyce contributed hard- and soft-ground etching with spitbite aquatint titled *1930s to 1960s*, which was a continuation of her *Devotional* series (fig. 67). First shown at the National Portrait Gallery in 2007, *Devotional* is an immersive hand-drawn installation for which Boyce drew the names of 180 black female singers culled from a group of women in Liverpool. The large-scale drawing features each singer's name in a clear typography, thickly outlined to reveal voluminous negative space that she used to define the area between the name and the script contours she drew around each name. In the etching, 14 of the 180 names appear. The singers span pop to classical music genres and the early to late twentieth century, each drawing attesting to the embodied presence of black women as public, cultural figures.

Like Boyce's contribution, Locke's *The Prize* (fig. 68) relates to another body of work, in which he amassed large amounts of metal and plastic elements (some found, others fabricated) into an assemblage of heraldry reminiscent of the arms and trophies of British imperialism. He collaged plastic items (beads, decorative flowers, toy guns, dolls, etc.) with digital prints with silkscreen on board. Unlike the others in Locke's series, this print is at a relief of up to five inches.

Julien's two digital prints in the portfolio, collectively titled *Untitled (Déjà-Vu No.2, Baltimore Series)*, are production stills from his film *Baltimore* (2003). Shot in 16 mm on location in Baltimore's National Great Blacks in Wax Museum, George Peabody Library, and Walters Art Museum, the film uses the style of Blaxploitation as a form of institutional critique of both the predominately black city of Baltimore and the ways in which it has been depicted on film, or what Julien calls its *cinematization*. Three wax figures depict Baltimoreans: civic leader Beatrice F. Gaddy, gospel singer Pauline Wells Lewis, and Congressman Kweisi Mfume, with the last figure positioned at the Walters admiring Leandro Bassano's *Allegory of the Element Earth* (ca. 1580). Further referencing Renaissance materiality, the stills were printed on paper with a gold-leaf border.

After the Dance (2006), Ofili's screen print of a young couple, head to head in the foreground of a seascape and mountain view, quotes from Malick Sidibé's 1963 photograph of a couple dancing at a Malian Christmas party, *Nuit de Noël*. The image of the mountain may also depict Trinidad's Andean northern range, where the artist lived and worked at the time of the *Portfolio*'s completion. Both references demonstrate Ofili's long-term interest in broadening the concept of internationalism to look across multiple locations at various times in much the same way that Rivington Place proposed at its opening in October 2007.

Notes

1. Gilane Tawadros, "A Case of Mistaken Identity," in *Shades of Black: Assembling Black Arts in 1980s Britain*, eds. David A. Bailey et al. (Durham, NC: Duke Univ. Press, 2005), 125; emphasis added.
2. Peter Allison, ed., *David Adjaye: Making Public Buildings* (London: Whitechapel Gallery, 2006), 48.

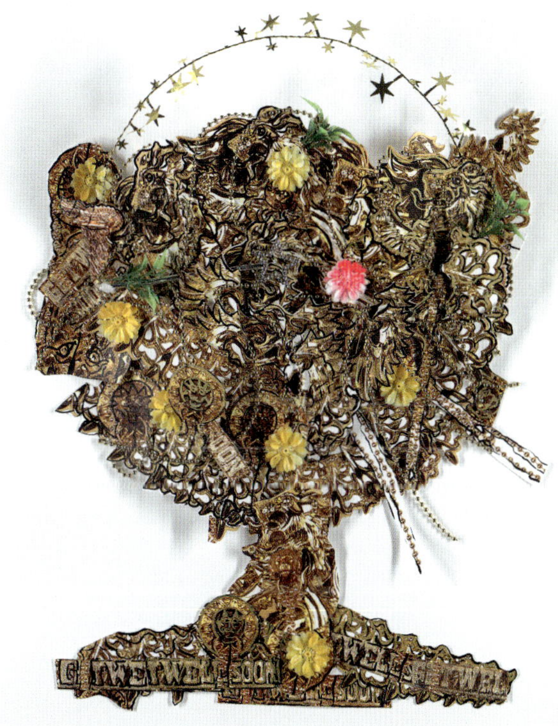

Fig. 68. Hew Locke, *The Prize*, 2007, digital inkjet prints with silkscreen, collaged into a 3D structure, with plastic beads and flowers on moderately thick, smooth, white wove paper, mounted on white board, 30 x 20 x 5 in. (76.2 x 50.8 x 12.7 cm). Yale Center for British Art, Friends of British Art Fund

Yinka Shonibare MBE (RA) (British, b. 1962)
Mrs Pinckney and the Emancipated Birds of South Carolina, 2017

Fiberglass mannequin, Dutch wax-printed cotton textile, birdcage, birds, leather, and globe, overall (hand to hand and without platform): 97 x 51 x 27 in. (246 x 130 x 69 cm)

YALE CENTER FOR BRITISH ART, ACQUIRED WITH FUNDS FROM THE BEQUEST OF DANIEL S. KALK, THE DIRECTOR'S DISCRETIONARY FUND, AND THE FRIENDS OF BRITISH ART FUND, B2017.17

Yinka Shonibare MBE (RA), in conversation with Martina Droth
November 30, 2018

MD: This work was commissioned by the Center for the exhibition *Enlightened Princesses: Caroline, Augusta, Charlotte, and the Shaping of the Modern World*, which examined the role of women in shaping court culture. You made your piece in response to a specific historical figure featured in that exhibition—Mrs. Eliza Pinckney, a slave holder who ran an indigo plantation in South Carolina. What was it about Mrs. Pinckney's story that drew your attention and made you feel interested to make a work?

YS: I thought Mrs. Pinckney was fascinating. Her particular history was that she had slaves who brought a skill from Africa, which was the making of indigo. They introduced this skill to the United States. That gave those people agency. They helped Mrs. Pinckney grow those plants and were able to create a viable industry through their skills. They were enterprising, and joined in her enterprise, in that endeavor. They were not entirely passive. They were Africans who introduced a skill, an enterprise, into America. That indication of agency interests me.

Mrs. Pinckney was a British subject, and the slaves were subjected to her, as it were. Those were important hierarchies, as were the hierarchies of class. I was fascinated that Mrs. Pinckney met Princess Augusta[1]—a direct meeting between her and the Princess would have been unusual—and that they also exchanged letters. One of the things they talked about in the letters was breastfeeding their babies. Mrs. Pinckney told the Princess about the Black wet nurses—the Princess was surprised that this didn't affect the skin color of the babies. We read something like this today through our present-day attitudes, and we have different ideas about what is a politically correct way of speaking of people. I am fascinated by this shift in morals—between then and now. It is difficult to have a twenty-first-century lens on something from so long ago.

MD: Your work does make a twenty-first-century response. You named the work after Mrs. Pinckney, a relatively obscure figure in history. What made you want to hold onto her name?

YS: The piece is about power relations. It is about Mrs. Pinckney's encounter with Princess Augusta.[2] The Princess is the dominant one in the relationship. She already has all the power. My instinct is always to champion the underdog. The piece acknowledges someone who might otherwise disappear in history. I felt I needed to make a lyrical and poetic response to that meeting, with symbolic metaphors. I wanted to register the indigo, the dress, and the history of that in relation to African culture. I wanted to turn the gift of birds, which Mrs. Pinckney gave to the Princess, into a metaphor for emancipation. That's why she has a cage for a head, and the birds are emancipated.

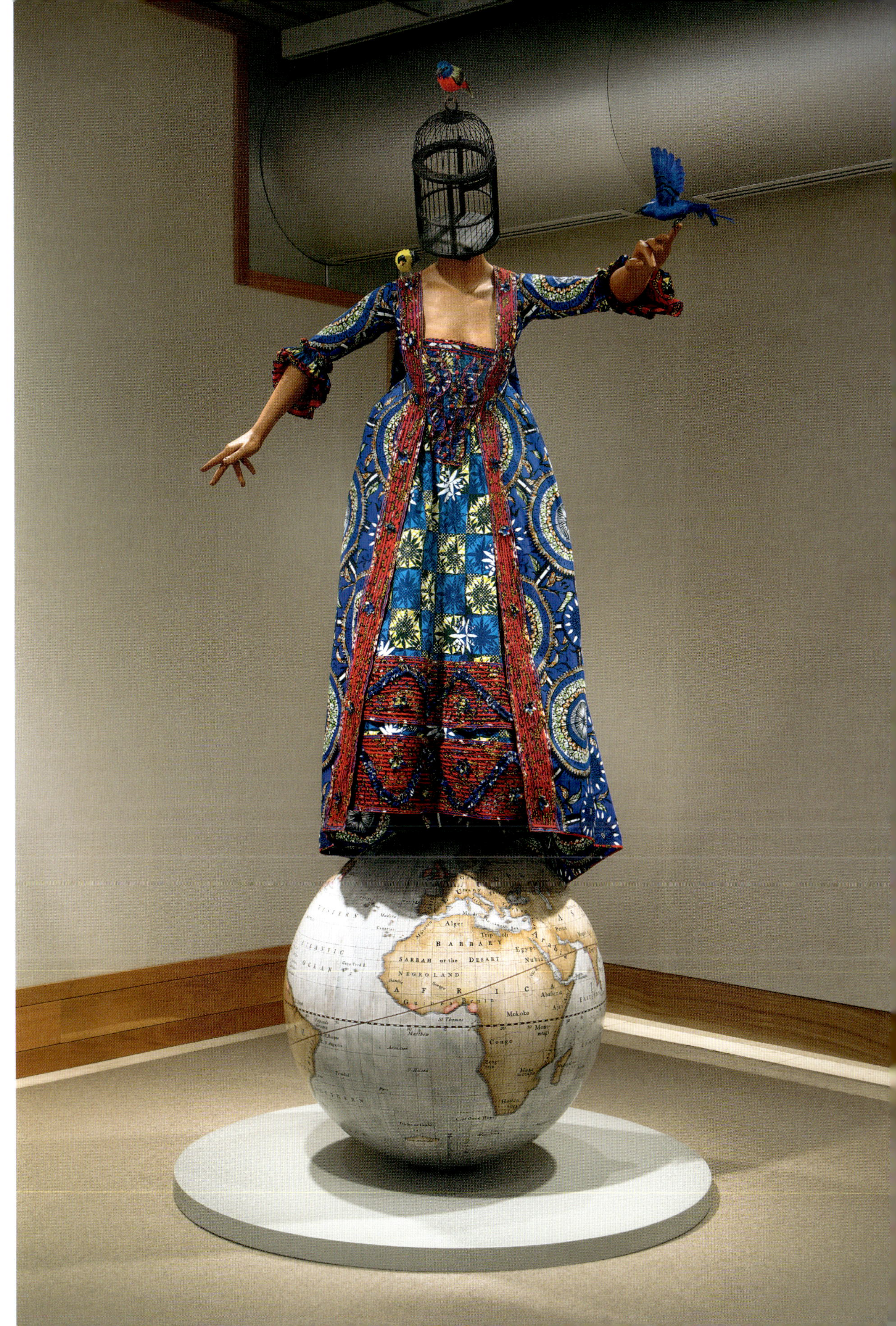
Alger
Trip oli
BARBARY
Egypt
SARRAH or the DESART
Nubia
NEGROLAND
AFRICA
Guinea Benin
Mokoko
St Thomas
Congo
OCEAN

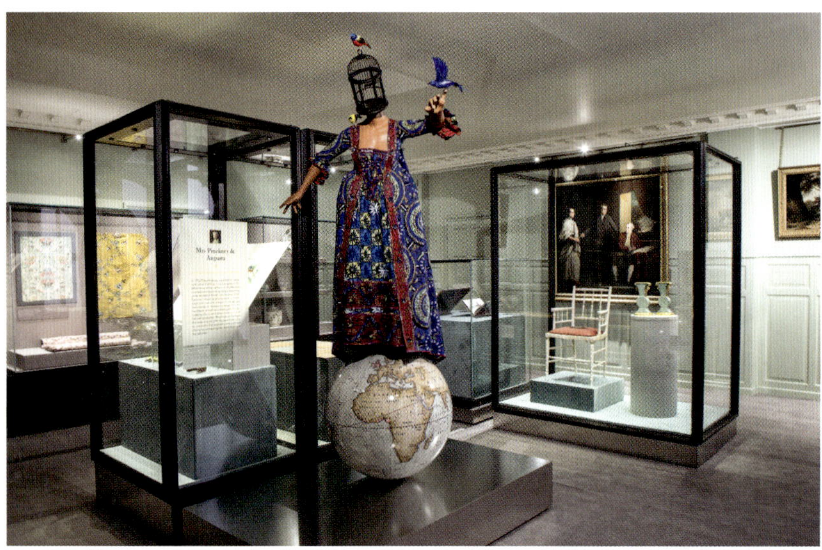

Fig. 69. Installation image of *Mrs Pinckney* at Kensington Palace

MD: This piece ended up being shown in Kensington Palace (fig. 69). How did you feel about this?

YS: It was the perfect place for my work. I am a bit of a rebel, but at the same time I love the establishment. It is a real paradox. The piece ending up in the Palace embodies that paradox. Maybe it comes from a strict upbringing from a Victorian father, who was royalist—I rebelled against him, while absorbing some of his values.

MD: When your work goes out into the world—into exhibitions, collections—how do you feel about the way it is interpreted? Is there something you wish museums would say about your work?

YS: I don't like to close down the poetic possibilities of a work of art. I would like people to bring their own readings to the work. The work starts from the various things we discussed here—but that can be open-ended, which is why I give it a poetic and lyrical title. The emancipated birds of South Carolina could be about a wide range of things. For example, it could be about feminism—the notion of emancipation, juxtaposed with a figure of a woman, could result in a feminist reading—or one could make a postcolonial reading. I would like museums to be more open, allowing audiences to engage in their own ways with works of art, and to encourage a conversation around a number of themes. In this work, you could talk about the history of Victorian fashion, about slavery, about notions of nationality, identity politics, feminism, the politics of color, surrealism and Dada. There are also the different approaches to art making—why is it not painting, why is it a mannequin, and what is the history of using mannequins in art, for example. Those are the kinds of layered conversations that involve art history and politics that I would like to see happen. Museums have a tendency to be more didactic. Curators have that kind of an education—they feel they ought to explain things.

MD: You just mentioned surrealism and Dada. The mannequin and birdcage bring to mind surrealist and Dada tropes (Marcel Duchamp, Man Ray, Max Ernst, André Masson). Is that something that interests you? Did you set out to make those references?

YS: Some of it is more of a coincidence, but the references to art history are there. The surrealist aspect is not a coincidence. Like the sewing machine and umbrella (per Dalí), my work is

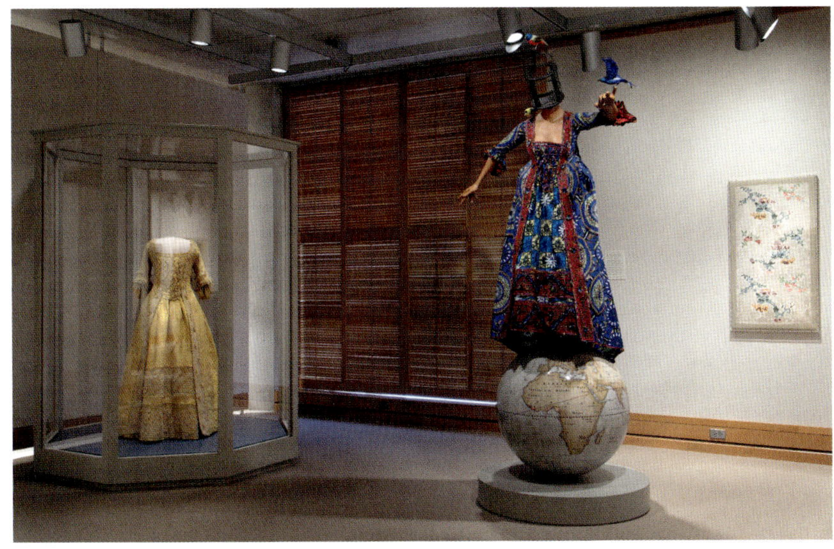

Fig. 70. Installation image of *Mrs Pinckney* at Yale Center for British Art

eclectic. My career started in the 1980s, at the height of postmodern discourse, the height of deconstruction, French continental theory. Deconstructing is second nature to me, and that is what I do in my work. The question has always been about the non-Eurocentric voice. That's what I came into, and it was quite normal to take a different approach. I deliberately clash the things that are not supposed to clash, and that comes out of the surrealist manifesto. I am a contrarian, as all artists are. It's about getting out of the box and getting more freedom. If I want to use fabric in my sculpture, I should be able to do so. My work has always been anti-sculpture sculpture.

MD: Our collections are particularly strong on paintings of the long eighteenth-century, especially portraiture and landscape. Where there are representations of people of color, it is mostly as figures of slaves. There are very few positive images. Your work effectively makes an intervention (fig. 70). How do you feel about where your work ends up?

YS: "People of color" is such an American term. I think it's a silly phrase. Ethnic origin might be more appropriate. There is a suggestion that white people have no color. There is a conversation going on within American universities right now about the decolonization of public spaces, what we do with statues, and also about the representation of ethnic minorities within those institutions. There are increasing numbers of ethnic minority students in these institutions, and they want to see something that represents them more positively—any kind of representation that speaks to their perspective rather than the Eurocentric curriculum they encounter. It's a process of education, having works like this in your collection. This is also happening in the feminist movement. This is an important time for challenges to pedagogy.

Notes

1. Augusta of Saxe-Gotha (1719–1772) became Princess of Wales in 1736 when she married Frederick, Prince of Wales. She was one of only four Princesses of Wales who never became Queen Consort.
2. Mrs. Pinckney met Princess Augusta in 1753. See *Enlightened Princesses: Caroline, Augusta, Charlotte, and the Shaping of the Modern World* (New Haven and London: Yale Univ. Press, 2017), 530–31, fig. 31.03.

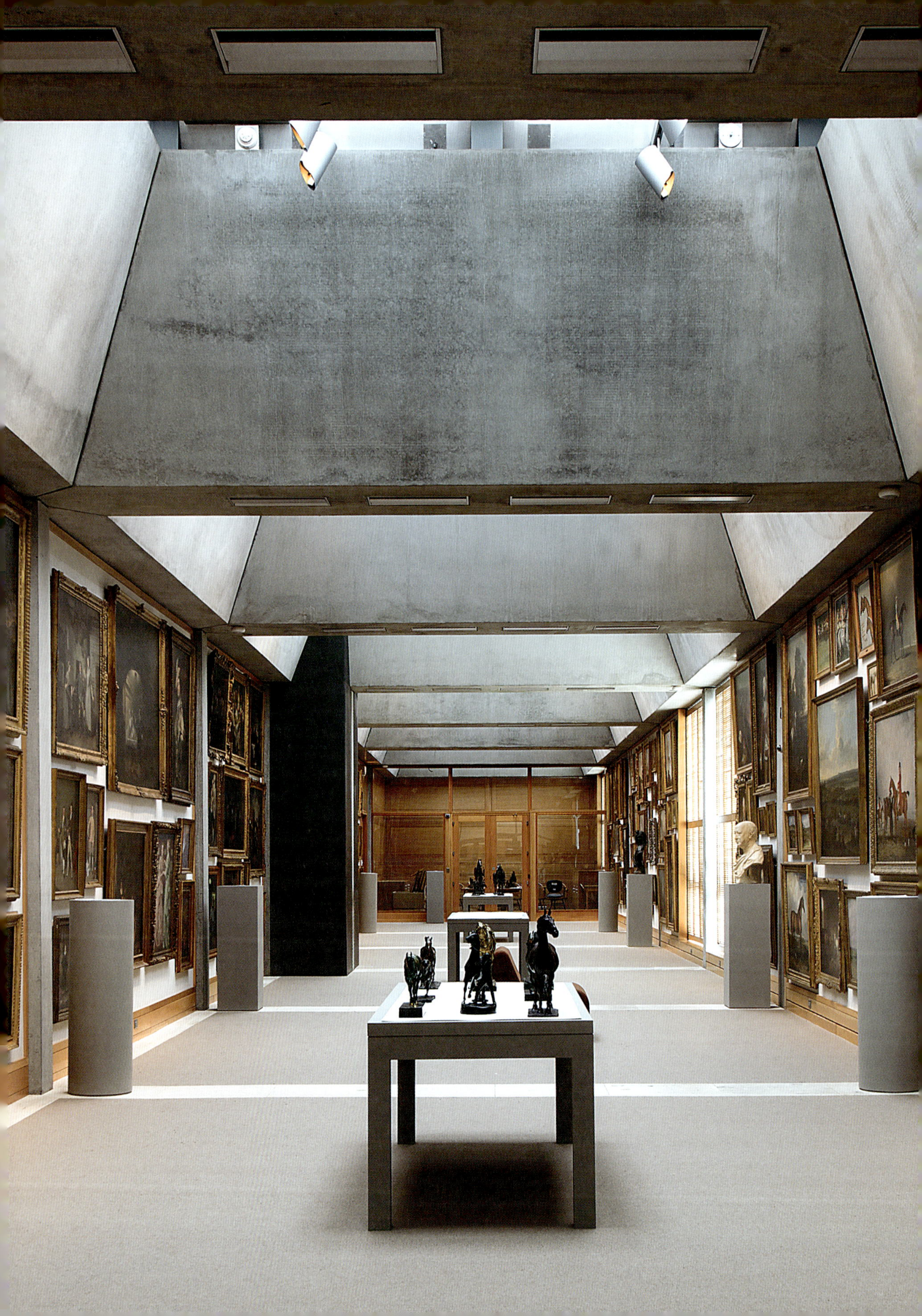

EPILOGUE

John Baskett

On a warm summer day in 1963, Paul Mellon invited me to lunch at the Metropolitan Club in Washington. I had, for the previous two years, been helping him organize the collection of British paintings and drawings that he had begun to form with the advice of Basil Taylor, the English art historian. Paul Mellon told me at our luncheon he had decided that, in a few years' time, he would place his growing collection, including his books and manuscripts, into the public domain and he wanted to discuss where it should go; the three possibilities being the National Gallery of Art, or to a large house behind the British Embassy that Paul Mellon owned (like the Phillips Collection), or to his alma mater, Yale University.

He settled on Yale, partly at the persuasion of Andrew Carnduff Ritchie, then Director of the Yale University Art Gallery, but instead of incorporating his collection of British art into the Art Gallery's holdings as Ritchie had hoped, he decided to commission a separate museum to house it. He made it clear, however, that he did not wish the collection to become just a teaching instrument but that it should be there also for the sheer enjoyment of visitors. I have therefore had the privilege, over the past fifty-five years, of being able to watch the gestation and development of the Yale Center for British Art from its beginning as an inspired thought in Paul Mellon's head to its present flourishing state.

Jules Prown, the first director, from 1969 helped to oversee the choice of architect and the construction of Louis Kahn's building; Ted Pillsbury organized the opening in 1977, and then Duncan Robinson took over in 1981. Paul Mellon had complete confidence in all three, but it was during Duncan's long tenure as director that the Center's focus was really established. When Duncan left in 1995 to take up the directorship of the Fitzwilliam Museum at Cambridge, Paul Mellon, who by then was near the end of his life, was concerned that the Center, into which he had invested so much of himself, might be about to lose the purpose he had intended for it.

I was present, with Duncan Robinson, when Amy was interviewed by Paul Mellon's executors shortly before her appointment. It was a testing moment, as they bore in mind the anxieties of Paul Mellon's last days, and I was very impressed by her quiet diplomatic responses. We all adjourned afterward to the Red Fox Tavern in Middleburg for lunch. I was delighted when I was told later that Amy was to become director. She took up the post in July 2002 following the interim directorship of Cecie Clement.

I need not expand here on what a wonderful job Amy has made of her role. My only regret is that she never was able to meet Paul Mellon and that he did not live on to witness all that she has accomplished. One only needs to look at the Center's periodic calendars to see what a hive of activity it has become. The acquisitions, exhibitions, publications, lectures, public program, and a multitude of other activities all speak of a thriving institution, and a happy one.

On a personal note, I would like to add how much I have appreciated Amy's generosity during my retirement for keeping me in touch with the Center's activities and sometimes allowing me to have a little input. She has become a treasured friend, and I hope she feels some satisfaction, as she steps down from her directorship, in seeing the Center, to which she has dedicated herself so fully and for which she has worked so hard, in such excellent and healthy condition.

ACKNOWLEDGMENTS

Britain in the World would not have come to fruition without the unhesitating support of the staff of the Yale Center for British Art, the Paul Mellon Centre—especially Mark Hallett and Sarah Turner—and the Provost's Office at Yale University. We sincerely thank all the contributors to the publication, whose work illuminates the rich diversity of the Center's collection, with special thanks to Hilton Als for his poetic dedication and to John Baskett for his thoughtful epilogue.

It has been an enormous pleasure to work again with Miko McGinty and her design team, Rita Jules and Claire Bidwell. Their graphic interpretations of our vision over the last decade has never failed to be well conceived, provocative, accessible, and beautiful, as their elegant design of this publication shows. We are grateful to John Ewing for copyediting and to Livia Tenzer for proofreading; it was a pleasure to work with both again. We would also like to thank the team at Yale University Press, especially Mark Eastment and Clare Davis, for their assistance with the book's planning and production.

Special thanks are owed to the Center's Imaging Department, headed by Melissa Fournier, and to her team, Maria Singer, Anna Bozzuto, Robert Hixon, Richard Caspole, and Bernie Staggers. They have provided invaluable assistance, remaining cheerful and focused in the face of our most daunting deadlines. We are deeply grateful to the Center's Head Conservator of Works on Paper, Soyeon Choi, for carrying out the treatment of *A Young Daughter of the Picts*, enabling the inclusion of a photograph of the beautifully restored drawing for the first time in this publication.

We also thank the Center's Finance Department, headed by Rebecca Sender, and her dedicated team, including John Champlin, Catherine Esposito, and Marsha Dobson, for their level-headed support of this publication's goals. We furthermore extend gratitude to our Communications and Marketing team, April Swieconek and Ronnie Rysz, and to Beth Miller, Deputy Director of Advancement and External Affairs, whose invaluable knowledge of the Center's audiences have helped to make this book more impactful.

Last but certainly not least, we owe an immeasurable debt to the Exhibitions and Publications team at the Center, Deborah Cannarella, Shaunee Cole, and Belene Day, for their unflagging resourcefulness and efficiency as they helped to bring the various pieces of this project together.

Martina Droth
Nathan Flis
Michael Hatt

CONTRIBUTORS' BIOGRAPHIES

GLENN ADAMSON
Senior Scholar, Yale Center for British Art

HILTON ALS
Pulitzer Prize–winning author, staff writer and theater critic for *The New Yorker*, and Associate Professor of Writing, Columbia University

MARK ARONSON
Chief Conservator, Yale Center for British Art, and Chair of the Conservation Laboratory at the Institute for the Preservation of Cultural Heritage, Yale University

MALCOLM BAKER
Distinguished Professor of the History of Art, University of California, Riverside

TIM BARRINGER
Paul Mellon Professor of the History of Art, Yale University

JOHN BASKETT
Paul Mellon's longtime friend and art advisor

GILLIAN BEER
Emeritus Professor of English, University of Cambridge; President of Clare Hall 1994–2001

FRED BOHRER
Professor of Art History, Hood College

EDWARD S. COOKE, JR.
Charles F. Montgomery Professor in the History of Art and Professor of American Studies, Yale University

JESSICA DAVID
Senior Conservator of Paintings, Yale Center for British Art

BRUCE DAVIDSON
Photographer, Member of Magnum Agency since 1958

MARTINA DROTH
Deputy Director of Research, Exhibitions and Publications, and Curator of Sculpture, Yale Center for British Art

ELISABETH R. FAIRMAN
Chief Curator of Rare Books and Manuscripts, Yale Center for British Art

NATHAN FLIS
Head of Exhibitions and Publications, and Assistant Curator of Seventeenth-Century Paintings, Yale Center for British Art

LISA L. FORD
Senior Manager of Special Projects for the Director, Yale Center for British Art

GILLIAN FORRESTER
Former Senior Curator of Prints and Drawings at the Yale Center for British Art

MARK HALLETT
Director of Studies, Paul Mellon Centre for Studies in British Art, London

MATTHEW HARGRAVES
Chief Curator of Art Collections, Yale Center for British Art

MICHAEL HATT
Professor in the History of Art Department, University of Warwick

ELEANOR HUGHES
Deputy Director for Art and Program, The Walters Art Museum, Baltimore

MARK LAIRD
Associate Professor at the John H. Daniels Faculty of Architecture, Landscape, and Design, University of Toronto

CYRA LEVENSON
Deputy Director and Head of Public and Academic Engagement, The Cleveland Museum of Art

JULIA MARCIARI-ALEXANDER
Andrea B. and John H. Laporte Director, The Walters Art Museum, Baltimore

JOANNA MARSCHNER
Senior Curator, Historic Royal Palaces, London

COURTNEY J. MARTIN
Deputy Director and Chief Curator, Dia Art Foundation

HENRIETTA McBURNEY
Independent art historian and art curator; former Deputy Curator, Royal Library, Windsor Castle

ALEXANDER NEMEROV
Department Chair and Carl and Marilynn Thoma Provostial Professor in the Arts and Humanities, Department of Art and Art History, Stanford University

THERESE O'MALLEY
Associate Dean, Center of Advanced Study in the Visual Arts, National Gallery of Art, Washington, DC

MORNA O'NEILL
Associate Professor, Eighteenth and Nineteenth Century European Art, Wake Forest University

ROBERT McCRACKEN PECK
Curator of Art and Artifacts and Senior Fellow at The Academy of Natural Sciences of Philadelphia, Drexel University

MARTIN POSTLE
Deputy Director for Grants and Publications, Paul Mellon Centre for Studies in British Art, London

JULES DAVID PROWN
Paul Mellon Professor Emeritus of the History of Art, and Senior Research Fellow, Yale Center for British Art

CHITRA RAMALINGAM
Associate Curator of Photography, and Acting Head of Prints and Drawings, Yale Center for British Art

ROMITA RAY
Associate Professor of Art History and Department Chair, Department of Art and Music Histories, Syracuse University

CATHERINE ROACH
Associate Professor, Department of Art History, Virginia Commonwealth University

JOSEPH ROACH
Sterling Professor Emeritus of Theater and Professor Emeritus of English, Yale University

HOLLY SHAFFER
Assistant Professor of History of Art and Architecture, Brown University

SAMUEL SHAW
Teaching Fellow in the History of Nineteenth-Century Art, Department of Art History and Film, University of Leicester

YINKA SHONIBARE MBE (RA)
Conceptual artist

PAMELA H. SMITH
Seth Low Professor of History, Department of History, and Director of the Center for Science and Society, Columbia University

EDWARD TOWN
Head of Collections Information and Access, and Assistant Curator of Early Modern Art, Yale Center for British Art

JENNIFER TUCKER
Associate Professor, History Department, Wesleyan University

SARAH VICTORIA TURNER
Deputy Director for Research, Paul Mellon Centre for Studies in British Art, London

ALICIA WEISBERG-ROBERTS
Honorary Assistant Professor, Department of Fine Arts, University of Hong Kong

SCOTT WILCOX
Deputy Director for Collections, Yale Center for British Art

JANE WILDGOOSE
Artist and Keeper of the Wildgoose Memorial Library, London

Published by

Yale Center for British Art
P.O. Box 208280, New Haven, CT 06520-8280
britishart.yale.edu

and

The Paul Mellon Centre for Studies in British Art
16 Bedford Square
London WC1B3JA
www.paul-mellon-centre.ac.uk

Distributed by
Yale University Press
P.O. Box 209040, New Haven, CT 06520-9040
47 Bedford Square, London WC1B 3DP
yalebooks.com / yalebooks.co.uk

ISBN 978-0-300-24747-3
Names: Yale Center for British Art, author. | Meyers, Amy R. W., honouree. | Droth, Martina, editor. | Flis, Nathan, editor. | Hatt, Michael, 1960- editor.
Title: Britain in the world : highlights from the Yale Center for British Art in honor of Amy Meyers / edited by Martina Droth, Nathan Flis and Michael Hatt.
Description. New Haven : Yale Center for British Art, 2019. | Includes bibliographical references.
Identifiers: LCCN 2019008308 | ISBN 9780300247473 (pbk.)
Subjects: LCSH: Art, British–Catalogs. | Art–Connecticut–New Haven–Catalogs. | Yale Center for British Art–Catalogs.
Classification: LCC N6761.Y33 2019 | DDC 709.41–dc23 LC record available at https://lccn.loc.gov/2019008308

Volume edited by Martina Droth, Nathan Flis, and Michael Hatt

Designed and produced by Miko McGinty, Rita Jules, and Claire Bidwell
Copyedited by John Ewing
Proofread by Livia Tenzer
Set in Edita by Tina Henderson

Printed in Italy by Printer Trento s.r.l.

Cover: George Stubbs, *Zebra* (detail), exhibited 1763, oil on canvas. Yale Center for British Art, Paul Mellon Collection

Frontispiece: Jacques Le Moyne de Morgues, *A Young Daughter of the Picts*, ca. 1585, watercolor and gouache, touched with gold on parchment, 10 ¼ x 7 ⅜ in. (26 x 18.7 cm). Yale Center for British Art, Paul Mellon Collection

P. 6: Sir Joshua Reynolds RA, *Mrs. Abington as Miss Prue in "Love for Love" by William Congreve* (detail), 1771–73, oil on canvas, 30 ¼ x 25 ⅛ in. (76.8 x 63.8 cm). Yale Center for British Art, Paul Mellon Collection

P. 10–11: Mark Catesby, "An Thymelaea foliis obtusis; Anseri Bassano &c: The Great Booby," plate 86 from *The Natural History of Carolina, Florida and the Bahama Islands* (London: 1731–43), vol. 1, second edition (London: C. Marsh, 1754), 1754, etching and engraving with original hand coloring on medium, moderately textured, cream laid paper, 14 ⅜ x 20 ½ in. (36.5 x 52.1 cm). Yale Center for British Art, Gift of John D. Viener, Yale AB 1961

P. 172: View of the Long Gallery at the Yale Center for British Art, 2018

PHOTOGRAPHY CREDITS

Every effort has been made to credit the photographers and sources of all illustrations in this volume; if there are any errors or omissions, please contact Yale University Press so that corrections can be made in any subsequent editions.

Unless otherwise mentioned, all images from the Yale Center for British Art's collection have been photographed by Richard Caspole.

Alamy Stock Photo/The History Collection: fig. 42; Barbara Hepworth © Bowness: page 153; Barbara Hepworth © Bowness/Photograph: Matthew Hollow: fig. 62; Barbara Hepworth © Bowness/© Tate, London: fig. 63; Beinecke Rare Book & Manuscript Library, Yale University: figs. 24, 36; Beinecke Rare Book & Manuscript Library, Yale University, The James Marshall and Marie-Louise Osborn Collection: fig. 16; Courtesy the artist and James Cohan Gallery, New York, Co-commissioned by Yale Center of British Art and Historic Royal Palaces, Kensington Palace: page 169, fig. 70; Courtesy the artist and James Cohan Gallery, New York, Co-commissioned by Yale Center of British Art and Historic Royal Palaces, Kensington Palace/Photograph: Historic Royal Palaces: fig. 69; Courtesy of the artist and Victoria Miro: fig. 66; © Bruce Davidson/Magnum Photos: pages 158, 159; © Estate of the Artist: page 144; © Estate of Duncan Grant. All rights reserved, DACS 2019: fig. 60; © Estate of Duncan Grant. All rights reserved, DACS 2018/National Galleries Scotland: fig. 59; Harvard University, Houghton Library: figs. 56, 57; © Hew Locke. All rights reserved, DACS 2019: fig. 68; © Historic England/Bridgeman Images: fig. 26; © Historic Royal Palaces/SWNS: fig. 69; Image Courtesy of Sotheby's London: fig. 50; Lewis Walpole Library, Yale University: figs. 22, 39; Library of Congress, Lessing J. Rosenwald Collection: fig. 3; © National Gallery, London/Art Resource, NY: fig. 44; National Gallery of Art, Andrew W. Mellon Collection, Washington, DC: fig. 41; © National Museum of African Art, Smithsonian Institution, Eliot Elisofon Photographic Archives: page 149, fig. 61; National Museum of Wales, Cardiff: figs. 6, 58; Photo © Peter Nahum at The Leicester Galleries, London/Bridgeman Images: fig. 25; Photo by John Hammond: fig. 17; © Sonia Boyce. All rights reserved, DACS 2019: fig. 67; © Rebecca Salter: page 160; © The British Library Board: fig. 40; The Hart Collection: fig. 43; The Historic New Orleans Collection: fig. 31; The Library Company of Philadelphia: fig. 35; The Metropolitan Museum of Art, New York: fig. 33; The National Archives, Kew: figs. 53, 54; The Royal Collection Trust / © Her Majesty Queen Elizabeth II 2019: figs. 7, 11, 18, 20; © The Royal Society: fig. 21; The Society of Antiquaries, London: fig. 5; The University of Pennsylvania and the Pennsylvania Historical and Museum Commission: fig. 65; University of North Carolina at Chapel Hill, Louis Round Wilson Special Collections Library: fig. 4; Victoria Art Gallery, Bath and North East Somerset Council/Bridgeman Images: fig. 12; Yale Center for British Art: page 172, figs. 34, 64; Yale Center for British Art, Gift of Donald C. Gallup, Yale BA 1934, PhD 1939: page 140; Yale Center for British Art, Gift of Ellen and Arthur Liman (Yale JD 1957): fig. 46; Yale Center for British Art, Gift of John D. Viener, Yale AB 1961: pages 10, 11, 40; Yale Center for British Art, Gift of Paul Mellon in memory of the British art historian Basil Taylor (1922–1975): page 36; Yale Center for British Art, Gift of Rosemarie Haag Bletter and Martin Filler in memory of Paul Mellon, Yale College, Class of 1929: page 132; Yale Center for British Art, Paul Mellon Collection: pages 2, 6, 17, 20, 25, 29, 32, 44, 49, 52, 56, 65, 68, 72, 76, 80, 81, 84, 89, 92, 96, 104, 113, 116, 120, 128, 140, figs. 1, 2, 19, 27, 28, 29, 30, 32, 37, 38, 45, 47, 48, 49; Yale Center for British Art, Paul Mellon Collection/X-ray by Eric Stegmaier: figs. 13, 14; Yale Center for British Art, Paul Mellon Fund: pages 29, 102, 103, 108, 124, figs. 46, 51, 52, 55; Yale Center for British Art, Paul Mellon Fund, in Honor of Jane and Richard C. Levin, President of Yale University (1993-2013): page 61, fig. 23; Yale Center for British Art, Presented by Tim Barringer in honor of Amy Meyers, 2019: page 137.